THE
EXTERNAL EVIDENCE
FOR INTERPOLATION
IN
HOMER

THE
EXTERNAL EVIDENCE
FOR INTERPOLATION
IN
HOMER

BY
GEORGE MELVILLE BOLLING

OXFORD
AT THE CLARENDON PRESS

Oxford University Press, Ely House, London W. 1

GLASGOW NEW YORK TORONTO MELBOURNE WELLINGTON
CAPE TOWN SALISBURY IBADAN NAIROBI LUSAKA ADDIS ABABA
BOMBAY CALCUTTA MADRAS KARACHI LAHORE DACCA
KUALA LUMPUR HONG KONG TOKYO

FIRST PUBLISHED 1925
REPRINTED LITHOGRAPHICALLY IN GREAT BRITAIN
FROM CORRECTED SHEETS OF THE FIRST EDITION
AT THE UNIVERSITY PRESS, OXFORD
BY VIVIAN RIDLER
PRINTER TO THE UNIVERSITY
1968

IRENAE

CONIVGI OPTIMAE CARISSIMAE

D. D. D.

PREFACE

THIS book has grown out of my own experience of
a need. I desired to study the Homeric language
with a view to determine what variations—if any—
exist in different parts of the poems. For that
purpose it seemed important to ascertain just which
lines have a *prima facie* claim to pass as Homeric.
The question, as I soon realized, could be answered
for no single line without the evidence for all. I
have endeavoured to gather it with completeness,
and now place it at the disposal of others. Its
collection has caused me to view the tradition of the
poems in a new light, but whether it will have a
similar effect upon others must be left to the future
to determine. This seems to me, however, the
portion of the Homeric problem in which the hope
for some approximation to unity of opinion may be
entertained most reasonably, and I have therefore
striven to isolate it as rigorously as possible from all
other questions.

The work was closed in 1923, when the final
drafting was begun : I have made no effort to regard
the very considerable literature that has since
appeared. An unforeseen visit to England has
enabled me, however, to add the testimony of a
number of vulgate papyri, and to answer some
questions about readings of Ptolemaic papyri that

I should otherwise have been forced to leave open. In this I have had the assistance of Mr. H. Idris Bell, Mr. E. Lobel, and Dr. A. S. Hunt. All three have most generously placed at my disposal their extensive knowledge of papyri publications, and their wonderfully developed keenness and accuracy of vision. I have profited much by their kindness, and wish to express to them my deep appreciation of it.

My gratitude is also due, and is most gladly given, to those members of the staff of the Clarendon Press who have worked with so much scholarship and technical mastery of their complicated art to make the external form of my book all that I could desire it to be.

Finally I wish to thank publicly my sister, Mrs. Robert Malcolm Littlejohn, for the generous assistance that has relieved me of the financial anxieties and burdens that the publication of this work would otherwise have entailed.

G. M. B.

OXFORD, *August* 1925.

CONTENTS

WORKS CITED BY ABBREVIATED TITLES, OR BY THE NAMES OF THEIR AUTHORS.

The list does not include Texts of Homer cited by the names of their editors.

ALLEN, T. W. The Homeric Catalogue of Ships. Oxford 1921.

ALY, W. Volksmaerchen, Sage und Novelle bei Herodot und seinen Zeit-genossen. Goettingen 1921.

AMONEIT, H. de Plutarchi studiis Homericis. Regimonti 1887.

BECHTEL, FR. Lexilogus zu Homer. Halle 1914.
Die Vocalcontraction bei Homer. Halle 1908.

BEKKER, I. Homerische Blaetter. Bonn 1863, 1872.

BELZNER, E. Homerische Probleme. Leipzig 1911, 1912.

BENICKEN, H. K. Studien und Forschungen auf dem Gebiete der homerischen Gedichte. Innsbruck 1883.

BERGER, J. de Iliadis et Odysseae partibus recentioribus, sive de arte indu-cendi et concludendi sermonis Homerica. Marpurgi Cattorum 1908.

BETHE, E. Homer : Dichtung und Sage. Berlin 1914, 1922.

BIDDER, H. de Strabonis studiis Homericis. Gedani 1889.

BLASS, FR. Die Interpolationen in der Odyssee. Halle 1904.

BOISACQ, E. Dictionnaire étymologique de la langue grecque. Paris 1923.

BRUGMANN, K. Griechische Grammatik ; 4te Aufl. bearb. von A. Thumb. Muenchen 1913.

CAUER, P. Grundfragen der Homerkritik ; 3te Aufl. Leipzig 1921-3.

DEBRUNNER, A. Griechische Wortbildungslehre. Heidelberg 1917.

DRERUP, E. Das fuenfte Buch der Ilias. Paderborn 1913.
Homerische Poetik. Wuerzburg 1921.

DUENTZER, H. de Zenodoti studiis Homericis. Gottingae 1848.
Aristarch. Das erste, achte und neunte Buch der Ilias kritisch eroertert. Paderborn 1862.
Homerische Abhandlungen. Leipzig 1872.
Die homerischen Fragen. Leipzig 1874.

ERHARDT, L. Die Entstehung der homerischen Gedichte. Leipzig 1894.

EVANS, Sir A. The Palace of Minos. i. London 1921.

FINSLER, G. Homer. 2te Aufl. Leipzig 1913, 1918.

FRAENKEL, H.   Die homerischen Gleichnisse.   Goettingen 1921.

FRIEDLAENDER, L.   Die homerische Kritik von Wolf bis Grote.   Berlin 1853.

FRIEDLAENDER, U.   de Zoilo aliisque Homeri obtrectatoribus.   Regimonti 1895.

HENNINGS, P. D. Ch.   Homers Odyssee.   Berlin 1903.

HERMANN, E.   Silbenbildung im griech. und in den andern idg. Sprachen. Goettingen 1923.

HOFFMANN, C. A. J.   Quaestiones Homericae.   Clausthaliae 1842, 1848.

HOPPIN, J. C.   A handbook of Attic red-figured vases.   Cambridge 1919.

JEBB, R. C.   Homer : an introduction to the Iliad and the Odyssey.   7th ed. Boston (undated).

LACHMANN, K.   Betrachtungen ueber Homers Ilias ; mit Zusaetzen von Moriz Haupt.   3te Aufl.   Berlin 1874.

LA ROCHE, J.   Homerische Studien.   Wien 1861.
Die homerische Textkritik im Alterthum.   Leipzig 1866.
Homerische Untersuchungen.   Leipzig 1869, 1893.

LEAF, W.   Troy, a study in Homeric geography.   London 1912.

VAN LEEUWEN, J.   Enchiridium Dictionis Epicae.   ed. alt.   Lugduni 1918.

LEHRS, K.   de Aristarchi studiis Homericis.   ed. tertia.   Lipsiae 1892.

LENTZ, E.   de versibus apud Homerum perperam iteratis.   Bartenstein 1881.

LOERCHER, A.   Wie, Wo, Wann ist die Ilias entstanden.   Halle 1920.

LUDWICH, A.   Aristarchs homerische Textkritik.   Leipzig 1884-5.
Die aeltesten Odyssee-fragmente.   Homerica vi.   Regimontii 1894.
Ueber Homercitate aus der Zeit von Aristarch bis Didymos.   Koenigsberg 1897.
Die Homervulgata als voralexandrinisch erwiesen.   Leipzig 1898.

MEISTER, K.   Die homerische Kunstsprache.   Leipzig 1921.

MUELDER, D.   Die Ilias und ihre Quellen.   Berlin 1910.

MUELLER, F.   Die antiken Odyssee-illustrationen.   Berlin 1913.

MURRAY, G.   The Rise of the Greek Epic.   2nd ed.   Oxford 1911.

VON NAEGELSBACH, C. FR.   Homerische Theologie.   Nuernberg 1884.

NIESE, B.   Die Entwickelung der homerischen Poesie.   Berlin 1882.

NUTZHORN, F.   Die Entstehungsweise der homerischen Gedichte.   Leipzig 1869.

ROBERT, C.   Studien zur Ilias.   Berlin 1901.
Oidipus, Geschichte eines poetischen Stoffs im griechischen Altertum. Berlin 1915.

ROEMER, A.   Ueber die Homerrecension des Zenodot (Abh. d. k. bayer. Akad. d. Wiss., i. Cl., xvii. Bd., 641-722).   Muenchen 1885.
Homerische Studien (*ibid.*, xxii. Bd., 389-452).   Muenchen 1902.   Repeated in part in Homerische Aufsaetze (65-142).   Berlin 1914.
Aristarchs Athetesen in der Homerkritik.   Leipzig 1912.

ROTHE, C. Die Ilias als Dichtung. Paderborn 1910.
Die Odyssee als Dichtung. Paderborn 1914.

SCHULZE, W. Quaestiones Epicae. Gueterslohae 1892.

SCHWARTZ, E. Adversaria. Gottingae 1908.

SEECK, O. Die Quellen der Odyssee. Berlin 1887.

SHEWAN, A. The Lay of Dolon. London 1911.

STUERMER, F. Die Rhapsodien der Odyssee. Wuerzburg 1921. (= Drerup, Homerische Poetik, vol. iii.)

THUMB, A. Handbuch der griechischen Dialekte. Heidelberg 1909.

WACKERNAGEL, J. Sprachliche Untersuchungen zu Homer. Goettingen 1916.

WECKLEIN, N. Textkritische Studien zur Odyssee (SB. d. k. bayer. Ak. d. Wiss., Philos.-philol. u. hist. Kl. 1915, 7 Abh.). Muenchen 1915.
Ueber Zusaetze und Auslassung von Versen im Homerischen Texte (*ibid.* 1918, 7 Abh.). Muenchen 1918.
Ueber Zenodot und Aristarch (*ibid.* 1919, 7 Abh.). Muenchen 1919.

VON WILAMOWITZ-MOELLENDORFF, U. Homerische Untersuchungen (= Philologische Untersuchungen vii). Berlin 1884.
Die Ilias und Homer. Berlin 1916.

WOLF, FR. A. Prolegomena ad Homerum. ed. sec. Berolini 1876.
Vorlesungen ueber die vier ersten Gesaenge von Homers Ilias. Bern 1830–1.

INTRODUCTION

THE tendency for science to begin with answers to ultimate questions is natural enough and easily comprehensible. The Ionian philosophers with their search for the ἀρχή, Bopp with his wish to fathom the mystery of the origin of inflexions, and Schliemann with the trench that should lay bare King Priam's Troy, are familiar examples; but in each case it has proved necessary *reculer pour mieux sauter*. Homeric criticism has its parallelism to offer: the early analyses started from the primeval poems—the *Ur-Ilias* and the *Ur-Odyssee*—and only recently have we realized that it is better to begin from the nearer end, and remove the accretions stratum by stratum, as in the excavation of a buried temple. The change is to be welcomed—only in my opinion it has not gone far enough.

We assume too easily that the object of our study—the poems themselves—is defined for us with sufficient precision. Yet the *Odyssey* of Wolf is not the *Odyssey* of Aristarchus, nor is the *Iliad* of Aristarchus the *Iliad* of Pisistratus. Our first effort must be to recover with all possible exactness the form of the poems as they existed at the beginning of our tradition. Until that is accomplished we are carrying an unnecessary risk of error[1] in all our discussions of the genesis of the poems; we are like archaeologists who

---

[1] The size of this risk cannot be predicted in advance. Loercher 6 assumes that it is negligible, but his own analysis starts with Λ 543—an interpolation.

would discuss the style and authorship of a vase-painting before cleansing it.

The question with which I shall deal is, however, not so sweeping. To reconstruct the Pisistratean text is at present too ambitious an undertaking, but I think that we may at least begin to answer the question of the lines that it contained. That is first and foremost a problem of *recensio*—to determine what are for it the best attested lines. My attention shall therefore be confined normally to variants a line or more in length, and I ask that this restriction be borne in mind even when it is not reiterated.

PART I

AFTER ARISTARCHUS

In the recension of the Homeric poems the first problem that confronts us is the treatment to be accorded to verses for which our MSS., ranging from the tenth to the sixteenth or seventeenth century, give conflicting testimony. Early editors — Dacier, Stephanus, Barnes, for instance—were inclined to favour the weakly attested verses that they knew, just as they welcomed also the additional verses they could glean from scholia and quotations. Wolf was more critical (cf. *Proll.* 26 f., 259 n. 45, 261 n. 46, 265 n. 50), but he was already under the pressure of tradition, and, besides, he had vastly over-estimated (p. 265) the age of these interpolations. His best course would have been to follow the *Venetus* A ; but he did not bring himself that far and printed 15,693 verses in the *Iliad*, 12,110 in the *Odyssey*. These are in reality eclectic combinations, but time has made them sacrosanct in the eyes of many. For instance, Drerup—cf. *AJP* 42 (1921). 87— regards this, no more, no less, as Homer ; while Shewan, *The Lay of Dolon*, p. 17, demands *proof*, meaning thereby demonstrative certainty, before it may be changed. The Oxford edition varies from the Wolfian vulgate only in that it adds the weakly attested σ 111ᵃ and omits some lines, Θ 548, 550-2, I 458-61, Λ 543, that are found in no MS., retaining, however, Σ 604/5, ο 295, of which the same is true.[1] Its junior editor, T. W. Allen, *The Homeric Catalogue of Ships*, p. 56, now sees that B 558 falls in 'with the other lines preserved in a minority of Homeric MSS., of which we do not hesitate to say that they are additions' ; but when it comes to the printing of the text he continues to follow Wolf. Leaf and

---

[1] φ 276 is on a slightly different footing, as Chalcondylas is likely to have found it in some MS.

Ludwich are more independent,[1] but neither goes far enough. Ludwich sees the worthlessness of lines so badly attested as Θ 224-6, 466-8, Π 614-15, but, as he says (*HV* 29 f.), time has given such lines a charmed life. Few have the courage to attack them—compromises seem preferable.

Less tenderness in dealing with these squatter claims is to be expected of scholars who are not hampered by the responsibilities of an editor. Of recent writers Blass (*Die Interpolationen in der Odyssee*, 1904), Wecklein (*Über Zusätze und Auslassung von Versen im Homerischen Texte*, 1918), Wilamowitz (*Die Ilias und Homer*, 1916), may be taken as representing the best use that has been made of τεκμήρια of this sort. Their conclusions are frequently correct, but their treatment is not such as to give to the MSS. their full evidential value. The fundamental trouble is that the origin of these MS. variants was not then understood. In consequence mere accidents of copying[2] are at times pressed into service, while significant variations are passed in silence or explained away. The result is to leave an impression of eclecticism.

Without attempting an exhaustive criticism I may give a few illustrations. Wecklein (p. 29) regards *I* 44 as a useless addition, and notes that Aristarchus athetized it. But he does not—as he fancies—strengthen his case when he refers to its omission by T. In the first place we can make no correlation between omissions in our MSS. and the atheteses of Aristarchus. The only other exact coincidences[3] are *B* 143 om. i. t. add. i. m. J ; *Δ* 117 om. Z^p ; Θ 284 om. X^{b1}, add. X^{b2} i. m.; 557-8 om. H^b (haplogr. αἰθήρ, αἰθήρ). Five examples in five different MSS., three corrected and one clearly a mechanical blunder—the thing must be purely accidental. Secondly, we must note that the scribe of T seems rather prone to skip with

---

[1] Leaf's edition is in this respect the better. He misses, to be sure, B 558, H 368 f., N 316, 749, Ψ 804—to cite only passages he might have been expected to detect—and his distinction between lines omitted and lines bracketed is valueless ; but he has the great merit of touching no line except vulgate interpolations. Ludwich, for instance, puts on a par with them many others ; while his distinction between lines omitted and those in small type is positively confusing.

[2] I may cite here R. G. Kent, *The Textual Criticism of Inscriptions*, valuable for questions of method, but published in a place (*Jour. Am. Oriental Soc.* 40 (1920). 289 ff.) not likely to come under the notice of classicists.

[3] For approximate correspondence, cf. B 130-3, Δ 149, K 51-2, M 363, Π 97-100, X 199-201, 329, 393, Ω 556.

or without temptations to haplography; cf. B 320, $\varDelta$ 87, 441, H 221, I 67, 267-9, 397, K 474, $\varLambda$ 107, 615, M 47, N 645, $\varXi$ 489, P 316, $\varPhi$ 525, 548-50, $\varOmega$ 430, 528, 789. Sometimes he corrects himself, sometimes later hands correct him. In none of these omissions is T supported by other MSS. except at K 474, M 47, $\varPhi$ 525, where the temptations to haplography are great, and the support given extremely slight. Finally in this passage (I 44) the first hand of T itself adds the line in the margin. The behaviour of T must be regarded then as a medieval blunder destitute of all significance in the question of whether Wecklein and Aristarchus are right or wrong. This carries implicitly my opinion of Wecklein's treatment of $\varDelta$ 441 (pp. 27 f.) and M 47 (p. 30); that of I 269 ᴧ 127 (p. 29) is even worse. Here the first hand of T has by haplography ($\H{a}\rho o\nu\tau o$, $\H{a}\rho o\nu\tau o$) omitted lines 267-9 as is stated by Leaf and Ludwich. La Roche, too, makes the same statement, except that he does not distinguish between the hands. According to Leaf a second hand has added the missing lines. Ludwich notes separately '269 om. T', which at the best can mean only that this line was not supplied by the corrector. This leads Wecklein to a criticism of the parallel passage. If U^b has, as he states, transposed lines 126-7, the confusion comes merely from haplography ($o\H{v}\ \kappa\epsilon\nu$, $o\H{v}\delta\acute{\epsilon}\ \kappa\epsilon\nu$); but according to Ludwich the MS. itself agrees with all others, and it is a second hand who has been thus confused—a matter of still less importance. Wecklein (p. 21) urges against θ 545 its omission by the first hand of F. The following line is omitted by the same hand, but must be retained; its omission is ascribed therefore to haplography ($\dot{a}\nu\tau\acute{\iota}$, $\dot{a}\nu\acute{\epsilon}\rho\iota$). But haplography ($\tau\acute{\epsilon}\tau\upsilon\kappa\tau a\iota$, $\tau\acute{\epsilon}\tau\upsilon\kappa\tau a\iota$) is the obvious cause for the omission of both lines. The omission of ι 31-2 by D is also merely haplography ($\lambda\iota\lambda a\iota o\mu\acute{\epsilon}\nu\eta\ \pi\acute{o}\sigma\iota\nu\ \epsilon\hat{\iota}\nu a\iota$, $\lambda\iota\lambda a\iota o\mu\acute{\epsilon}\nu\eta\ \pi\acute{o}\sigma\iota\nu\ \epsilon\hat{\iota}\nu a\iota$)—D being one of the two MSS. with line 30 in the text. After what has been said above we must argue: if Aristarchus athetized ι 34-6, the omission of 35-6 by a single MS. can be nothing but accident. The conclusion is confirmed by the obvious temptation ($\tau o\kappa\acute{\eta}\omega\nu$, $\tau o\kappa\acute{\eta}\omega\nu$) to haplography.

For Blass, note that he accepts the evidence against λ 60, and attempts to explain away the stronger evidence against the same line, as λ 92. In doing so he puts forward the improbable theory [1] that

---

[1] Cf. also Kirchhoff at ψ 127-8.

the omissions at line 60 were due to some (unrecorded) athetesis, and that the scribes extended the condemnation to the next recurrence of the line. The omission of ξ 515–17 is also ascribed to some unrecorded and erroneous athetesis. Hypotheses of that sort must be ruled out, until it can be shown that at least in one case such omissions are found in connexion with a passage, the athetesis of which is recorded. The MS. evidence is also set aside at γ 19 ; while at δ 432, κ 569, μ 6, σ 131 there is no discussion of the considerable fluctuations in the MSS.

Examples of the last fault are plentiful in the work of Wilamowitz ; for instance, E 42, 57, 901, M 219, N 255, 316, Ξ 70, 269, O 481, Π 381, 614–15, P 585. One cannot criticize his preferences for lines attested in no MS. (B 848ᵃ [p. 85], I 119ᵃ(?) 458–61 [p. 66 n. 2]), without bearing in mind that he is attempting not a recension of the vulgate, but a reconstruction of the poetry at a much earlier stage. Is may then be said that he has permitted the *recensio* to be entangled with the *emendatio*, or that he has not kept separate two different stages in the *recensio* problem. The latter can be seen elsewhere, for instance, p. 60 n., K 191, 497, 531, 'haben in der Überlieferung keinen festen Stand', a lumping together of interpolations of different ages. This is not as harmless as it may seem ; it opens the door for impossible explanations of the MS. variants. A few MSS. contain B 168 = 17 ; they are supposed (p. 263 n.)[1] to have preserved a Zenodotean line that is unattested as the reading of his text. Comparison of the similar interpolations in our MSS. will show, however, that we have no right to look beyond B 17 for the source of this interpolation. Wilamowitz believes that K 240, ὣς ἔφατ', ἔδδεισεν δὲ περὶ ξανθῷ Μενελάῳ, which was not in the text of Zenodotus, is genuine. He then remarks (p. 61 n. 2): 'Einige junge Handschriften haben den Menelaos aus der Liste der Bewerber um den Auftrag beseitigt: das ist ganz konsequent, wenn 240 fehlt.' Here is the supposition of a connexion between a medieval blunder and the text of Zenodotus, similar to the attempts of Wecklein and of Blass noted above, and open to the same objections. The omission of 230 by QᶜZ is obviously nothing but haplography

---

[1] I cannot pause to criticize the surprising procedure here attributed to the Aristarcheans.

($\mathring{\eta}\theta\epsilon\lambda\acute{\epsilon}\tau\eta\nu$, $\mathring{\eta}\theta\epsilon\lambda\epsilon$, $\mathring{\eta}\theta\epsilon\lambda\epsilon$, $\mathring{\eta}\theta\epsilon\lambda\epsilon$); just as for ultimately the same reason O^{b}X place 228 after 230. The confusion is purely mechanical. The question was put in an entirely different light by the discovery of Homeric papyri, which have gradually been accumulating until now nearly 300 are known. Of this material neither Blass, nor Wecklein, nor Wilamowitz had complete command. It was first brought to bear in its entirety upon the criticism of the Homeric poems by myself in the following articles[1]: 'The Archetype of our *Iliad* and the Papyri', *AJP* 35 (1914). 125-48: 'The Latest Expansions of the *Iliad*', *ib.* 37 (1916). 1-30; 'The Latest Expansions of the *Odyssey*', *ib.* 452-8; 'Vulgate Homeric Papyri', *ib.* 42 (1921). 253-9; 'On the Interpolation of certain Homeric Formulas', *CP* 17 (1922). 213-21. Here I shall give merely an outline of the argument and of the results obtained.

A necessary preliminary step had been taken in 1906 by Grenfell and Hunt, *Hibeh Papyri*, pp. 68-75, in distinguishing between the Ptolemaic and the vulgate papyri. These scholars showed that a new text of Homer appeared in Egypt about 150 B.C.[2] and succeeded almost at once in monopolizing the market. Its most striking characteristic is that in contrast to the longer texts of the Ptolemaic period, it contains 'substantially' the same combination of lines that is found in the medieval MSS. Besides this it must be noted (cf. *AJP* 258) that the new text introduced, to the general public at least, a new peculiarity of form, the now familiar division of each poem into twenty-four books.

We can follow the transmission of this text with considerable detail. The papyri begin shortly before 100 B.C. and continue to about A.D. 700. They cover about 10,400 lines of the *Iliad*, 4,200 lines of the *Odyssey*; their testimony is available for every line of $B \, \Gamma \, M \, N \, \Xi \, O \, \chi \, \psi \, \omega$, and for almost every line of $A \, \varDelta \, \varLambda \, \varSigma \, \varOmega \, \phi$. The repetitions of the same passage I have not attempted to compute; but of the lines of interest here some will be found to be covered two or three times. On a par with the latest of these

---

[1] References to these will be made merely by periodical and page. For lists of the papyri, cf. *AJP* 13-18, 454-6; W. Schubart, *Einführung in die Papyruskunde*, pp. 478-80, and corrections thereto *AJP* 253 n.

[2] Cauer, *Grundfr.*[3] p. 42, criticizes the dating as 'wohl etwas allzu scharf'. I have never understood it as meant for anything but a round date.

papyri are two uncial MSS.: the *Ambrosianus Pictus* (Θ) of the fifth or sixth century, containing 800 lines scattered through all the books except $\Gamma \Sigma T \Upsilon$; and the *Syriac Palimpsest* (Σ) of the sixth or seventh century, containing 3,873 lines from M–Ω. The two following centuries are unrepresented, and then the *Codex Venetus* (A) opens the line of the complete MSS.

Throughout the whole of this period, from the earliest papyri to the latest MSS., there is likely to occur surface corruption—the unintended blunders that will appear in the copying of any extensive text. The great mass of them are easily recognizable (*AJP* 2–7, 22 f., 452 f., 457, 253 n., 256 f.). Others over which we might hesitate at first are detected by a closer observation of the habits of the tradition (cf. *AJP* 12 f., 20, 454, 457); and finally (cf. *AJP* 20, 457) a few cases must remain doubtful. Setting aside this surface corruption, we can see that the reason why the MSS. and the papyri contain only 'substantially' the same lines is that the vulgate text has been interpolated. In discussing a suggestion of Monro, Leaf wrote at E 487 : 'But there is no single case in Homer where the loss of a line can be assumed with reasonable probability; the tradition was wonderfully tenacious of all it had got, as well as acquisitive of new matter.' What he wrote in 1900 of the tradition as a whole can be shown for its later stages now with surprising clearness.

'Habent sua fata interpolationes.' There is nothing to suggest that the interpolations—or even the bulk of them—were the work of one man; we do not find a pure text and an interpolated text running side by side. On the contrary, each interpolation is a separate individuality, and how far it succeeds in making its way in the world is largely a matter of luck.[1] In general we should expect, and as a rule we do find, that the sooner an interpolation gets its start the farther it goes; and similarly the later any copy of the poems is, the more likely is it to harbour interpolations. But even to this there are exceptions—the whims of fortune.

The papyri contain practically no lines that do not reappear[2]

---

[1] Cf. Ludwich, *HV* 29 : 'Nicht einer jeden solchen Zuthat ist immer das gleiche Los zu Teil geworden. . . . Das ist Spiel des Zufalls, weiter nichts.'

[2] Here and in what follows I disregard of course surface corruption, except where attention is drawn to it specifically; thus ν 339[a] (PRyl. 53) is not treated.

well attested in the medieval MSS. The exceptions serve merely to emphasize the fact. POxy. 20 contains B 798ᵃ; PMorgan contains Λ 316ᵃ = 346ᵃ, Ξ 231ᵃ, O 409ᵃᵇ; the second hand of PMus. Br. 128 adds in the margin Ψ 757ᵃ⁻ᶜ. From the Syriac palimpsest can be cited Ξ 306ᵃᵇ, Φ 96ᵃ, X 10ᵃ. Of these only Λ 316ᵃ has MS. support, and that only in a few (T² Eᶜ Yᶜ *sine paraphr.* K²) of Ludwich's MSS. On the other hand, we have also papyrus evidence against these lines: B 798ᵃ, Λ 316ᵃ, 346ᵃ, Ξ 306ᵃᵇ, are each omitted in a papyrus; Ξ 231ᵃ, X 10ᵃ, in two; Ξ 231ᵃ, O 409ᵃᵇ, Ψ 757ᵃ⁻ᶜ are not found in Σ. Clearly these are nothing but interpolations; they are early in date, but stillborn. We can indicate their sources: Ξ 306ᵃᵇ, O 409ᵃᵇ, X 10ᵃ, and perhaps (but cf. below) Ψ 757ᵃ⁻ᶜ are thoughtless repetitions, hardly more than surface corruption; B 798ᵃ, Ξ 231ᵃ, have come from scholia, and Φ 96ᵃ seems to be of the same character.[1]

Some MSS.—different ones in different passages, sometimes more of them, sometimes less—contain lines that are either not in the papyri at all, or are found there under suspicious conditions. Examples of the latter sort are few, and it is convenient to begin with the other class.

The verses with least attestation from the MSS. are, generally speaking,[2] those that have not made their way into the Wolfian vulgate. Below I have listed some 33 such verses from the *Iliad* and 60 from the *Odyssey*.[3] Not one of these verses is found in $\Sigma\Theta$ or the papyri. How much direct evidence can be brought against any single line from Σ and the papyri [4] is purely a matter of luck— the luck of the excavators. There are four such witnesses against N 218ᵃ; three against Λ 463 (464)ᵃ, B 642ᵃ, N 266ᵃ, 808ᵃ; two against Λ 359ᵃ, M 424ᵃ, N 463 (464)ᵃ, 566ᵃ, 567ᵃ, P 145ᵃ, X 43ᵃ; one against Γ 86ᵃ, E 58ᵃᵇ, 836ᵃᵇ, Z 461ᵃ, Λ 485ᵃ, M 162ᵃ, Π 129ᵃ,

---

[1] Λ 316ᵃ = 346ᵃ (cf. H 234 (!), 385 (!), N 255, 266ᵃ, κ 456, 504, λ 60, 92, μ 153ᵃ, ω 121) suggests that vocative lines may have been interpolated to some extent at an early time. It would be helpful for school exegesis. Evidence in support of such an idea has not been forthcoming, as it has for the superfluous speech formulas.

[2] But compare, for instance, Λ 463 (464)ᵃ, Γ 86ᵃ, with Θ 183, Ο 481, Π 614-15.

[3] The list from the *Odyssey* has not been cleared like that of the *Iliad* (*AJP* 3-7) from surface corruption. Even so there is more of this rubbish in the *Odyssey*—regard being had for the length of each poem and the number of MSS. containing it.

[4] I have since had access to the original publication of Θ. It omits Ξ 420, X 10ᵃ, and testifies to no other of these lines. For Σ I have used Bekker, *Hom. Bl.* i. 114 ff.

288ᵃ, T 361ᵃ, Υ 3ᵃ, X 330°, Ψ 628ᵃ, θ 348ᵃ, ν 197ᵃ, 241ᵃ, 369ᵃ, ρ 233ᵃ, 603ᵃ, σ 111ᵃ, τ 558ᵃᵇ, ω 4ᵃ, 171ᵃ; and none against the others. But in weighing this evidence we must estimate it as a whole; these earlier witnesses have had the opportunity to be heard 51 times, and they have testified invariably against these lines. As a matter of *recensio* the case is clear: these differences within the MSS. have been caused not by the omission but by the interpolation of verses. The establishment of that fact is a matter of importance, for it is helpful in judging the cases that will follow.

There are printed in the Wolfian vulgate a number of lines better attested (as a rule) than these, but for which the testimony of the MSS. is by no means a unit. I have listed (*AJP* 8–12, 453) some 50 passages of this sort from the *Iliad*, and 65 from the *Odyssey*. These conflicts in the MS. testimony are undoubtedly significant; and our previous experience must lead us to expect that they are the result of interpolation. This expectation is confirmed by the papyri, though not with such complete unanimity. Σ and three papyri testify against N 255, Ξ 269; three papyri against B 168, 206, N 316; two papyri testify against A 265, B 558, Θ 183, O 481, Ω 693, χ 43, ψ 320, and also against Σ 200 f., 381, 427, o 113–19, if we accept for one reasonable inferences. Against Σ 200 f., 427, we have in addition the testimony of the Syriac palimpsest; it and single papyri testify against Π 381, Ψ 565, 864. Single papyri also give evidence against E 42, 57, H 368 f., N 731, 749, Ξ 70, Π 614 f., Ψ 804, Ω 790, β 407, γ 493, δ 399, κ 368–72, λ 604, ν 347 f., ξ 154 (515–17 may be inferred), ϕ 109, 276, ψ 48, 127 f., ω 121, 143. Σ testifies against Π 689 f., T 177, Υ 312, 447, Φ 480, 510, for which papyrus evidence has not yet come to light. To take the other side of the picture, X 121, χ 191, are each omitted by one papyrus but found in another; Ω 558 has been added in the margin of a papyrus by a second hand. PMorgan contains M 219; it and PSoc. It. 10 contain Λ 662. It must be noted that PMorgan gives other evidence that it is interpolated, and that the papyrus containing X 121 (POxy. 1818) is as late as the fifth or the sixth century. For the other passages we have as yet no evidence. Again the group must be considered as a whole: the evidence is against 49 passages, in favour of two, contradictory for three; or to put it differently, testimony has been given 80 times against these

lines, six times in their favour. The favouring evidence is thrice
contradicted, and four of the witnesses who give it are under
suspicion. I do not see that we have any right to hesitate. In a
recensio of the vulgate we must pronounce these lines interpolations, similar to those of the preceding group, but slightly more
successful, presumably therefore somewhat earlier. An attestation
of one of them in a papyrus is of value only in giving a *terminus
ante quem* for the interpolation.

There remain in the Wolfian vulgate a number of passages (listed
AJP 12 f., 453 f.) for which we must doubt whether the MS. fluctuations are significant or accidental. Here the *Iliad* and the
Odyssey begin to diverge, and it is necessary to treat each poem
separately, in applying the evidence of the papyri to them as a test.
Two papyri and Θ give testimony against Ξ 420; two papyri
testify against Θ 6, and one against P 219. There are two papyri
which do not contain Δ 196 f., but also a third in which these lines
are present; Σ 441 is not present in one papyrus, and its absence
from another may be inferred. It is found, however, in Σ, which
contains also X 363 that is absent from a papyrus. In PMorgan
O 562, 578 are misplaced—an indication that they stood in
the margin of the MS. from which this papyrus was copied.
The former is lacking in one papyrus, the latter is attested by
another. With a certain amount of hesitation for O 578, all these
must be pronounced interpolations. Four cases, Γ 78, 235, Θ 315,
Ξ 12, must remain doubtful (cf. *AJP* 20), while for a fifth, B 141,
found in three papyri, the MS. variation can be nothing but surface
corruption. For the *Odyssey* only my list II^b is strictly com-
parable : ten of the lines in it are found in papyri while but one
(ϕ 308) is omitted. List III was purposely made to include much
that was probably surface corruption. Of the lines in it 45 are
attested by papyri, and the absence of ϕ 219 f., ω 480 (but not 479)
cannot be stressed.

The interpolations of the last paragraph are more successful
than those previously discussed. We must now face the question :
May there not be still more successful interpolations—ones that
will have reached all our MSS. and may be expected to appear
more frequently in the papyri ? As such I have indicated a group
of superfluous formulas for introducing speeches (cf. *CP* 213–19) ;

also *Δ* 461, not found in PJandan 93 of the first century B.C., nor
in PMus. Br. 136 ; *Ψ* 626 not written by the first hand of PMus. Br.
128 (perhaps [1] of the first century B.C.), and known not to have
been in the edition of Aristarchus.   There are probably more
interpolations of this sort, and some may lurk in the list [2] given
AJP 23 ; but the risk of confusing them with mere surface corruption is too great, and so it seems necessary to stop at this point.
For the *Odyssey* we can merely say that *γ* 487, *ν* 396, *τ* 581, *φ* 65,
are omitted by single papyri ; but whether the omissions are
significant or accidental must remain uncertain.

I have not discussed the intrinsic merits and demerits of these
lines, and to some that may seem an omission. For none of the
lines I have designated as interpolations can it be maintained that
its omission produces an evident lacuna ; the one line that I
formerly regarded as an exception (*Σ* 381) having been explained
most convincingly by Cauer, *Grundfr.*[3] 49 f.; cf. also Wecklein,
ZAV 18.   In the establishment of the vulgate of the second
century B.C. that is all that is necessary.   Whether this vulgate or
the Wolfian vulgate is the ' better ' text is a question that belongs
—if it be raised at all—to a later stage of the inquiry.   Here two
questions must be discussed : the source of the vulgate, and the
source of the interpolations.

The vulgate when freed from these interpolations agrees in the
Iliad line for line with the edition of Aristarchus.   The Wolfian
vulgate contained on MS. authority lines which can be proved
(cf. *AJP* 25 ff.; Wecklein, *ZAV* 67–72) to have been absent from
the text of Aristarchus : B 168, 206, 558, *Δ* 196 f., E 901, N 255,
731, *Φ* 73, 480, *Ψ* 626, 804, *Ω* 558 ; two others of the sort, N 808[a],
T 39[a], have got into some MSS. ; one, *Ξ* 231[a], into the PMorgan.
All of these have been proved by the *recensio* to be interpolations ;
all except *Φ* 73, and it belongs to the group of speech formulas
that can be detected only by papyrus evidence which for *Φ* 73 is
still lacking.   All lines known from other sources as non-Aristarchean—for instance, I 458–61, *Σ* 604/5—are absent from the
vulgate, and it contains every line for which an Aristarchean

---

[1] But cf. Hunt, *JPh.* 26 (1899). 25.

[2] Transfer to it from the preceding page Λ 313, not attested by the second hand of
PMorgan.   The omission of B 794 by 1 *a*. POxy. 1086 is probably accidental.

reading or athetesis can be cited.[1]   That the exclusion of so many
interpolations on other grounds should touch no Aristarchean line,
but every one that is demonstrably non-Aristarchean, is a strong
corroboration of my argument.   From every other known edition
the vulgate can be shown to be different.   We must conclude then
that the vulgate starts as a popular text [2] based on the edition of
Aristarchus.

For the *Odyssey* the case stands somewhat different.   The
vulgate, to be sure, contains every line that can be shown to be
Aristarchean ; but the *recensio* has removed only some [3] (κ 315,
λ 604, τ 153, ψ 320), not all, of the non-Aristarchean lines.   Thus
δ 511, θ 142, κ 189, 243, λ 525, are known to be non-Aristarchean,
but there is no evidence from MSS. or papyri [4] against them.   The
explanation is to be found in the nature of our material.   Above
I have noted that we could not parallel from the *Odyssey* the two
earliest strata of interpolations found in the *Iliad*.   The reason is
that the papyri of the *Odyssey* are not extensive in the early
periods : before our era there is next to nothing, and only about
600 lines from the first two centuries.   The MSS. also seem to run
back to archetypes not earlier than the third century.   If there are
traces in them of an earlier text, with fewer interpolations, such
traces are so isolated that they cannot be distinguished from surface
corruptions.   The result is that while the *recensio* of the *Iliad* takes
us back to the beginning of the vulgate, the *recensio* of the *Odyssey*

---

[1] My suggestion (*AJP* 18, 21) that the first hand of PMus. Br. 128 did not write
Ψ 359–61 was of course a guess to account for the insertion of these lines by the second
hand after line 757 and for the stichometry of the papyrus.   It conflicted with the scholium δρόμους πληθυντικῶς ’Αρίσταρχος, but that comes to us (*AJP* 27) only through 5 A¹,
a suspected source.   The lines are now attested by POxy. 1818, which is, however,
of the fifth or sixth century, so that the occurrence in it of an interpolation so early as
this was assumed to be would not be surprising.   The whole matter must be left *sub
iudice*.

[2] Drerup, *Hom. Poet.* i. 87 and n. 2, assumes a plurality of such editions containing
the same lines.   That may prove necessary to account for the smaller variants, but
does not affect my problem.   The further assumption that the lines in them and in
Aristarchus were determined by some old text in the Alexandrian library, perhaps
even ‘ das attische Normalexemplar ’, is a desperate attempt to avoid the obvious conclusion.

[3] I have not included ε 157, for the proof of its being non-Aristarchean, though
accepted by Ludwich, and Wecklein *ZAV* 21, seems to me weak.

[4] λ 525 is contained in POxy. 780, perhaps of the second century ; the other
passages are not covered by papyri.

stops short of that point by some 400 years. Part of the interpolation it suffered during that period is revealed by these non-Aristarchean lines.[1]

Ludwich has collected the *Homercitate aus der Zeit von Aristarch bis Didymus* (Königsberg, 1897); from their nature little evidence is to be expected of them. All seem to use the vulgate, for the MSS. of Dionysius of Halicarnassus must bear the blame for the omission (pp. 29 f.) of I 71–3 and part of I 57–9. Attestation is given to B 674, Σ 597, 604/5, η 120 f., in the form adopted by Aristarchus and the vulgate in contrast to other authorities. Lines foreign to Aristarchus and the vulgate, B 206, λ 604, are at least not quoted, where their quotation might be expected. The same is true of I 498 (p. 30) and τ 110 (p. 15). Both may be interpolations as yet undetected. Neither can be connected with Aristarchus, and for neither have we as yet papyrus evidence. If they are interpolated the Aristarchus text agreed (cf. below) at these points with that of Plato.

A study of the interpolations as a whole soon reveals certain common characteristics. The bulk of them are single lines, occasionally distichs. In the *Iliad* three lines (Θ 224–6, 466–8, Ψ 359–61 (?)) are the maximum; in the *Odyssey* we find not only examples of this (ζ 313–15, ξ 515–17), but also interpolations of five (κ 315, 315^{a-d}, 368–72, 475–9), and even seven (o 113–19) lines. With few exceptions—Γ 235 (?), N 731, 808^a, Υ 3^a, Φ 96^a, 124 (as expanded), Ψ 359–61 (?), 804, α 329^a, δ 432, 598^a, θ 62^a, λ 622^{ab}, μ 133^a, ν 241^a, ρ 233^a, υ 83^a, ϕ 109, ψ 320—the interpolations are $\sigma\tau i\chi o\iota$ $\delta\iota\phi o\rho o\acute{\upsilon}$-$\mu\epsilon\nu o\iota$: cf. for their sources the *marginalia* of the following list. In the *Iliad* they never come from the *Odyssey*; in the *Odyssey* only rarely—β 4^a, 191, 429, δ 228^a, ϵ 91, σ 131 (?), χ 43—from the *Iliad*. Both poems draw to a slight extent upon Hesiod—A 265, Υ 223^a, β 107^a = κ 470 = τ 153 = ω 143, λ 604; but more frequently, B 558, N 255, 731, 808^a, Ξ 231^a, T 39^a, α 93^{ab}, 329^a, κ 315, upon editions other than that of Aristarchus. One line (Θ 183) is found also in a Ptolemaic text; while anecdotes prove to be the source of K 159^a, α 329^a, and ultimately (cf. *AJP* 29 f.) of B 558.

---

[1] To them could perhaps be added γ 427–9, if Ludwich, *Homerica*, vi, p. 5 (Königsberg, 1894), has supplied correctly the papyrus commentary ὅτι Τ(ίμαρχος ?) οὐκ (ἔγραφεν). The matter is too uncertain to discuss. Other possible cases will be found in Part IV.

Part of this material has evidently reached the MSS. from the scholia : for the lines from ancient editions that is clear, and in one other case (cf. *AJP* 18 f.) we happen to be in a position to prove it. To the same channel we may ascribe the Ptolemaic line (Θ 183) and those taken from Hesiod. That others—especially some of those that are not repetitions—come in the same fashion we may feel sure, though we are not able to designate them.

The remainder—and they constitute the bulk of all the inter-polations—are the work of the copyists. Some are merely uncon-scious glidings into familiar combinations ; others show a feeble effort to improve the text—to fill out a construction, complete an idea, or show just who is meant or addressed. Scholars have been too prone to make the copyists in their own image and likeness— to imagine them as bent on preserving the text with devoted scrupulosity, or endeavouring to purge it of interpolations. In reality [1] a copyist, in so far as he is not a machine, desires simply to get as good a poem as he can—its goodness judged by his own purposes and taste. The shortness of these interpolations, their lack of originality, the way each poem draws its interpolations from itself, are all testimonials to the limited powers of the copyists of this period. Their achievements have, to be sure, won some enthusiastic admirers in modern times—that is a matter of taste. But in the *recensio* of the Homeric poems—my only present con-cern—we must deny them all value. The interpolated lines that have come down through the scholia from pre-Aristarchean times are thus left alone to testify about the Homeric text. As witnesses they stand on a par with the plus verses of the scholia and the Ptolemaic papyri. How much or how little that may mean will be discussed in the following part of my work.

[1] John Meier, *Werden u. Leben des Volksepos* (Halle, 1909), n. 76, ' Jeder Kopist ändert das Original wie es der Rezitator auch tut '. He is speaking of a period when the epos has greater life—but that difference is only a matter of degree. The epos is as tenacious of life as Hans Andersen's eels : not even printing (witness σ 111ᵃ) can bury it.

CONSPECTUS OF VULGATE INTERPOLATIONS

The following list includes the lines interpolated in the vulgate with the following exceptions: (*a*) The most obvious cases of surface corruption, and those of the *Iliad* cited *AJP* 3–7; (*b*) the lines inserted in the Wolfian text merely from quotations; (*c*) the lines of the *Odyssey* which the *recensio* could not reach. The commentary gives the evidence from ΣΘ, and the papyri known to me [1] with completeness, silence meaning that no evidence is available. Readings of MSS. are cited only occasionally. The presence of the line in this list, its presence or absence from the Wolfian text, the attitude taken to it by other scholars, indicate the general nature of the evidence to be expected from the MSS.; further details must be sought in the critical editions.[2] Finally I have presented completely—silence indicating agreement with the Wolfian text—the opinions of the following scholars: for the *Iliad* Bekker[1] (1843), La Roche (1873), Nauck (1877), Christ (1884), Leaf (1900), Ludwich (1902), van Leeuwen (1912); for the *Odyssey*, Bekker[1] (1843), La Roche (1867), Nauck (1874), Ludwich (1889), Merry (1899), Blass, *Die Interpolationen* (1904), van Leeuwen (et Mendes da Costa) (1921).

A 265 Θησέα τ' Αἰγεΐδην, ἐπιείκελον ἀθανάτοισι = Hes. *Scut.* 182
463 (464)[a] σπλάγχνα δ' ἄρ' ἀμπείραντες ὑπείρεχον Ἡφαίστοιο
= B 426

B 168 καρπαλίμως δ' ἵκανε θοὰς ἐπὶ νῆας Ἀχαιῶν. = B 17
206 σκῆπτρόν τ' ἠδὲ θέμιστας ἵνα σφίσι βασιλεύῃ ∾ I 99
558 στῆσε δ' ἄγων ἵν' Ἀθηναίων ἵσταντο φάλαγγες from legend

A: 265 om. 3 *p*. PRyl. 43, 3 *p*. POxy. 537; afferunt Dio Chrys. lvii. 1, Paus. x. 29. 10; om. Bekker, Nauck, Ludwich, van Leeuwen, damn. La Roche, Christ, Leaf. 463 (464)[a] om. 1/2 *p*. PBerol. 6869, 3 *p*. PGr.-Fg. 106, 5 *p*. PSoc. It. 113.

B: 168 om. Aristarchus (cf. Nicanor ⟪A), 3 *p*. PSoc. It. 137, 4/5 *p*. PMus. Br. 126, 5 *p*. PBodl. a. 1, Ludwich van Leeuwen, damn. La Roche, Leaf. 206 om. Aristarchus (Aristonicus ⟪A B 192, cf. Wecklein, *ZAV*, p. 68), 2 *a*. PTebt. 4, 4/5 *p*. PMus. Br. 126, 5 *p*. PBodl. a. 1 (?); hab. Dio Chrys. i. 11; om. Bekker, Nauck, Ludwich, van Leeuwen, damn. La Roche, Christ, Leaf. 558 om. Aristarchus (Aristonicus ⟪A Γ 230), 2 *p*. PTebt. 265, 5 *p*. PBodl. a. 1; neque Aristotelem (cf. *AJP* 29) neque Dieuchidam (cf. Ludwich, *AHT* ii. 399 sq.) hunc vm. novisse demonstrari potest. Hermippus (ap. Plut. *Sol.*, c. 10) et Apollodorus (ap. Strab. ix. 394) famam afferunt Atheniensibus et Megariensibus de Salamine disputantibus ab oratore Atheniensi interpolatum esse. Ut haec interpolatio per verba sola fieri intelligatur plane necesse est. In Iliadis textu primum invenitur apud *τινάς* ab Aristonico allatos;

[1] Those cited in my articles- and POxy. 1815–20. Inferred readings are enclosed in parentheses.
[2] For the *Iliad* a collection has been made *AJP* 8-13.

642ᵃ καὶ Τυδεὺς ἐν Θήβαις, ὅτ' ἀπώλετο λαὸς Ἀχαιῶν cf. Z 223
798ᵃ ἔνθα ἴδον πλείστους Φρύγας ἀνέρας αἰολοπώλους = Γ 185

Γ 78 (?) μέσσου δουρὸς ἑλών· τοὶ δ' ἱδρύνθησαν ἅπαντες = Η 56
86ᵃ ὄφρ' εἴπω τά με θυμὸς ἐνὶ στήθεσσι κελεύει = Η 349 etc.
235 (?) οὕς κεν ἐὺ γνοίην καί τ' οὔνομα μυθησαίμην
319 ὧδε δέ τις εἴπεσκεν Ἀχαιῶν τε Τρώων τε formulaic
389 τῇ μιν ἐεισαμένη προσεφώνεε δῐ' Ἀφροδίτη formulaic

Δ 196 f. ὅν τις ὀιστεύσας ἔβαλεν, τόξων ἐὺ εἰδώς, = Δ 206
Τρώων ἢ Λυκίων, τῷ μὲν κλέος, ἄμμι δὲ πένθος = Δ 207
369 καί μιν φωνήσας ἔπεα πτερόεντα προσηύδα formulaic
461 αἰχμὴ χαλκείη· τὸν δὲ σκότος ὄσσε κάλυψεν = Ζ 11

Ε 42 δούπησεν δὲ πεσών, ἀράβησε δὲ τεύχε' ἐπ' αὐτῷ = Δ 504
57 ὤμων μεσσηγύς, διὰ δὲ στήθεσφιν ἔλασσεν = Ε 41
58ᵃᵇ αἰόλα παμφανόωντα παρέτρεσσαν δέ οἱ ἵπποι = Ε 295
ὠκύποδες· τοῦ δ' αὖθι λύθη ψυχή τε μένος τε = Ε 296
377ᵃ Αἰνείαν, ὅν ὑπ' Ἀγχίσῃ τέκον βουκολέοντι ∽ Β 820, Ε 313
468ᵃ εὔχεται ἐκγεγάμεν, μήτηρ δέ οἵ ἐστ' Ἀφροδίτη = Ε 248
836ᵃᵇ ὡς ἄρα καρπαλίμως ἰήσατο θοῦρον Ἄρηα = Ε 904
τὸν δ' Ἥβη λοῦσε, χαρίεντα δὲ εἵματα ἕσσε = Ε 905
901 ἠκέσατ'· οὐ μὲν γάρ τι καταθνητός γ' ἐτέτυκτο = Ε 402

Ζ 461ᵃ ἥρωες Δαναοί, πάντες θεράποντες Ἄρηος ∽ Β 256 + Θ 79

Quintilianus (v. 11. 40) etiam eum non in omni editione inveniri testatur; om. Bekker, damn. La Roche, Christ, Ludwich.   642ᵃ om. 2p. PFay. 309, 2p. PTebt. 265, 5p. PBodl. a. 1.   798ᵃ hab. 2p. POxy. 20; om. 5p. PBodl. a. 1, Ω.

Γ: 78 om. AG¹; hab. 4/5p. PMus. Br. 126, Ω, cf. AJP 20.   86ᵃ om. 4/5 p. PMus. Br. 126.   235 om. i. t. 4/5p. PMus. Br. 126, Dᵇ¹ add. i. m. m. 2 ; hab. Ω; damn. Payne Knight.   319 om. 4/5p. PBerol. 263 ; hab. 3p. PMus. Br. 136, 4/5p. PMus. Br. 126, Ω; cf. CP 213 ff.   389 om. 2/3p. PTebt. 427, 3p. POxy. 542; hab. 4/5p. PMus. Br 126, Ω ; cf. CP 213 ff., Wecklein, ZAV 69 f.

Δ: 196-7 om. Aristarchus (Aristonicus ap. ϛ A, cf. AJP 138, 26), 2p. PCairo G. & H. p. 56, 3p. POxy. 544, SYᵇD¹Nᵃ¹ ; vm. 197 solum om. J ; hab. 3p. PBerol. 7119(?), Ω et i. m. D²Nᵃ²; vss. 195-7, om. van Leeuwen, damn. Ludwich.   369 om. 3p. POxy. 753 et A¹; hab. 3p. PMus. Br. 136 et A²Ω; cf. CP 213 ff., Wecklein, ZAV 69. 461 om. 1 a. PJandan 93, 3p. PMus. Br. 136 ; hab. Ω.

Ε: 42 om. 3p. POxy. 223, van Leeuwen, damn. La Roche, Nauck, Leaf, Ludwich. 57 om. 3p. POxy. 223, van Leeuwen, damn. La Roche, Nauck, Leaf, Ludwich. 58ᵃᵇ om. 3p. POxy. 223.   836ᵃᵇ om. 2p. PChicag. 6.   901 om. Aristarchus, qui habet (ϛ T) in 900 πάσσεν, Nauck, Ludwich, van Leeuwen, damn. La Roche, Christ, Leaf.

Ζ: 461ᵃ om. 2/3p. POxy. 445.

H 150 (151)ᵃ ἀντίβιον μαχέσασθαι ἐν αἰνῇ δηιοτῆτι = H 40, 51

234(?) Αἴαν διογενές, Τελαμώνιε, κοίρανε λαῶν = I 644, $Λ$ 465

368 f. κέκλυτέ μευ, Τρῶες καὶ Δάρδανοι ἠδ' ἐπίκουροι = H 348

ὄφρ' εἴπω, τά με θυμὸς ἐνὶ στήθεσσι κελεύει = H 349

380 δόρπον ἔπειθ' εἵλοντο κατὰ στρατὸν ἐν τελέεσσιν ∽ $Λ$ 730

385(?) Ἀτρείδη τε καὶ ἄλλοι ἀριστῆες Παναχαιῶν = H 327

$Θ$ 6 ὄφρ' εἴπω τά με θυμὸς ἐνὶ στήθεσσι κελεύει = H 349

123 ὠκύποδες· τοῦ δ' αὖθι λύθη ψυχή τε μένος τε = E 296, $Θ$ 315

183 Ἀργείους παρὰ νηυσίν, ἀτυζομένους ὑπὸ καπνοῦ cf. I 243

224 ff. ἠμὲν ἐπ' Αἴαντος κλισίας Τελαμωνιάδαο = $Λ$ 7

ἠδ' ἐπ' Ἀχιλλῆος, τοί ῥ' ἔσχατα νῆας ἐίσας = $Λ$ 8

εἴρυσαν ἠνορέῃ πίσυνοι καὶ κάρτεϊ χειρῶν = $Λ$ 9

277 πάντας ἐπασσυτέρους πέλασε χθονὶ πουλυβοτείρῃ = M 194

315(?) ὠκύποδες· τοῦ δ' αὖθι λύθη ψυχή τε μένος τε = E 296,

$Θ$ 123

383 Ἥρη, πρέσβα θεά, θυγάτηρ μεγάλοιο Κρόνοιο = E 721

410 βῆ δὲ κατ' Ἰδαίων ὀρέων ἐς μακρὸν Ὄλυμπον = O 79

458(?) πλησίαι αἵ γ' ἤσθην, κακὰ δὲ Τρώεσσι μεδέσθην = $Δ$ 21

465ᵃ ἀνδρὸς ἑνὸς ῥιπῇ, ὁ δὲ μαίνεται οὐκέτ' ἀνεκτῶς = $Θ$ 355

466 ff. ἀλλ' ἤτοι πολέμου μὲν ἀφεξόμεθ', εἰ σὺ κελεύεις· = $Θ$ 35

βουλὴν δ' Ἀργείοις ὑποθησόμεθ', ἥ τις ὀνήσει = $Θ$ 36

ὡς μὴ πάντες ὄλωνται ὀδυσσαμένοιο τεοῖο = $Θ$ 37

I 224ᵃ καί μιν φωνήσας ἔπεα πτερόεντα προσηύδα formulaic

627ᵃ εἰπέμεν Ἀτρείδης, Ἀγαμέμνονι καὶ Μενελάῳ = H 373

K 159ᵃ μή τίς τοι [καθ]εύδοντι μεταφρένῳ ἐν δόρυ πήξῃ from
anecdote ∽ $Θ$ 95

191 καί σφεας φωνήσας ἔπεα πτερόεντα προσηύδα formulaic

H: 368-9 om. 5 *p*. PSoc. It. 114, van Leeuwen, damn. La Roche, Nauck, Ludwich. 380 om. Bekker, damn. La Roche, Nauck, Leaf, Ludwich.

Θ : 6 om. 2 *p*. PGoodspeed 7, 2/3 *p*. PMus. Br. 736, van Leeuwen, damn. La Roche, Leaf, Ludwich.   123 damn. Leaf, Ludwich.   183 om. 2 *p*. PFay. 210, 2/3 *p*. PMus. Br. 736, Bekker, van Leeuwen, damn. La Roche, Nauck, Leaf, Ludwich. 224-6 om. Bekker, van Leeuwen, damn. La Roche, Nauck, Christ, Leaf, Ludwich. 277 om. Bekker, Nauck, van Leeuwen, damn. La Roche, Christ, Leaf, Ludwich. 315 om. i. t. AGK ; hab. 3/4 *p*. PBerol. 7499, Ω, et i. m. AG³K², cf. *AJP* 20. 383 om. van Leeuwen, damn. Ludwich.   410 om. van Leeuwen, damn. Leaf, Ludwich.   466-8 om. Bekker, Nauck, van Leeuwen, damn. La Roche, Leaf, Ludwich.

K : 159ᵃ add. Eustathius e ioco Diogenis Cyn. ap. Diog. La. vi. 53.   191 om. Bekker, Nauck, van Leeuwen, damn. La Roche, Christ, Leaf, Ludwich.

531 νῆας ἔπι γλαφυράς· τῇ γὰρ φίλον ἔπλετο θυμῷ = Λ 520

Λ 316ᵃ, 346ᵃ διογενὲς Λαερτιάδη, πολυμήχαν' 'Οδυσσεῦ = Β 173
485ᵃ χάλκεον, ἑπταβόειον, ὅ οἱ Τυχίος κάμε τεύχων = Η 220
662 βέβληται δὲ καὶ Εὐρύπυλος κατὰ μηρὸν ὀιστῷ = Π 27

Μ 162ᵃ χερσὶ καταπρηνέσσ', ὀλοφυρόμενος δὲ προσηύδα ∽ Ο 114
219 αἰετὸς ὑψιπέτης ἐπ' ἀριστερὰ λαὸν ἐέργων = Μ 201
424ᵃ βάλλον ἀμυνόμενοι χαλκήρεσιν ἐγχείῃσιν = Μ 155 + Σ 534

Ν 46 Αἴαντε πρώτω προσέφη, μεμαῶτε καὶ αὐτώ = Π 555
218ᵃ τῷ μιν ἐεισάμενος προσέφη κρείων ἐνοσίχθων
v. l. ἔπεα πτερόεντα προσηύδα formulaic
255, 266ᵃ 'Ιδομενεῦ, Κρητῶν βουληφόρε χαλκοχιτώνων ∽ Ν 219
316 "Εκτορα Πριαμίδην, εἰ καὶ μάλα καρτερός ἐστιν = Ξ 375 +
Ε 410
463 (464)ᵃ αἰχμητήν τ' ἔμεναι καὶ θαρσαλέον πολεμιστήν =
Ε 602
480 τοὺς ὅ γ' ἐποτρύνων ἔπεα πτερόεντα προσηύδα formulaic
566ᵃ πάντοσε παπταίνων, μή τις χρόα καλὸν ἐπαύρῃ = Ν 649
567ᵃ ἐκλίνθη δ' ἑτέρωσε κάρη, ἐπὶ δ' ἀσπὶς ἐάφθη = Ν 543
731 ἄλλῳ δ' ὀρχηστύν, ἑτέρῳ κίθαριν καὶ ἀοιδήν Zen. of Mallos
749 αὐτίκα δ' ἐξ ὀχέων σὺν τεύχεσιν ἆλτο χαμᾶζε = Μ 81

531 om. Bekker, et cum 530 van Leeuwen, damn. La Roche, Nauck, Leaf, Ludwich, cf. Wecklein, ZAV 4.

Λ : 316ᵃ hab. 3/4p. PMorgan T²EᶜYᵉ, sine paraphr. K² (non ap. Ʂ T invenitur ut Wecklein, ZAV 14) ; om. 5/6p. PBerol. 262 (?), T¹Ω. 346ᵃ hab. 3/4p. PMorgan ; om. 5/6p. PBerol. 262 (?), Ω. 485ᵃ om. 3/4p. PMorgan. 662 hab. 3/4p. PMorgan, 4p. PSoc. It. 10 ; om. Bekker, Nauck, van Leeuwen, damn. La Roche, Leaf, Ludwich.

Μ : 162ᵃ om. 3/4p. PMorgan. 219 hab. 3/4p. PMorgan ; om. Nauck, van Leeuwen, damn. La Roche, Leaf, Ludwich. 424ᵃ om. 3/4p. PMorgan et Σ.

Ν : 46 om. 1p. PMus. Br. 732 et F²¹ ; hab. 1 a. PParis, 3/4p. PMorgan et Ω ; cf. CP 213 sqq. 218ᵃ om. 1 a. PBerol. 46, 1p. PMus. Br. 732, 3/4p. PMorgan, Σ. 255 om. Aristarchus (cf. Ʂ T ad 254), 1 a. PBerol. 46, 1p. PMus. Br. 732, 3/4p. PMorgan, Σ, Bekker, Leaf, Ludwich, van Leeuwen, damn. La Roche, Nauck. 266ᵃ om. 1 a. PBerol. 46, 1p. PMus. Br. 732, 3/4p. PMorgan. 316 om. 1p. PMus. Br. 732, 2/3p. POxy. 769, 3/4p. PMorgan ; damn. La Roche, Christ, Ludwich. 463 (464)ᵃ om. 1p. PMus. Br. 732, 3/4p. PMorgan. 480 om. 1p. PMus. Br. 732, ἐν πολλοῖς οὐ φέρεται Ʂ T ; hab. 3/4p. PMorgan, Σ et Ω ; damn. Ludwich, cf. CP 213 sqq., Wecklein, ZAV 31, 70. 566ᵃ, 567ᵃ om. 1p. PMus. Br. 732, 3/4p. PMorgan. 731 om. Aristarchus (cf. Ʂ T), 3/4p. PMorgan [Plut.] vita Hom. ii. 156 ; hab. Zenodotus Mallotes, Plut. de nobil. c. 21, 983ᵇ, Lucian, de Salt. c. 23, Clem. Alex. Strom. iv. 21. 135 (625) ; om. Bekker, Ludwich, van Leeuwen, damn. La Roche, Nauck, Christ, Leaf. 749 om. 3/4p. PMorgan, van Leeuwen, damn. La Roche, Nauck, Ludwich.

808ᵃ λίην γάρ σφιν πᾶσιν ἐκέκριτο θάρσεϊ πολλῷ Zenodotus

Ξ 12 (?) εἵλετο δ' ἄλκιμον ἔγχος, ἀκαχμένον ὀξέι χαλκῷ = Κ 135
70 νωνύμνους ἀπολέσθαι ἀπ' Ἄργεος ἐνθάδ' Ἀχαιούς = Μ 70
231ᵃ ἐρχομένῳ μετὰ φῦλα βροτῶν ἐπ' ἀπείρονα γαῖαν = τινές
269 Πασιθέην, ἧς αἰὲν ἱμείρεαι ἥματα πάντα ∽ Ξ 276
420 καὶ κόρυς, ἀμφὶ δέ οἱ βράχε τεύχεα ποικίλα χαλκῷ = Ν 544
+ Μ 396

Ο 409ᵃᵇ οὔτε ποτ' αἰχμηταὶ Δαναοὶ Λυκίους ἐδύναντο = Μ 419
τείχεος ἂψ ὤσασθαι, ἐπεὶ τὰ πρῶτα πέλασθεν = Μ 420
481 ἵππουριν· δεινὸν δὲ λόφος καθύπερθεν ἔνευεν = Γ 337
562 ἀλλήλους τ' αἰδεῖσθε κατὰ κρατερὰς ὑσμίνας = Ε 530
578 (?) δούπησεν δὲ πεσών, τὸν δὲ σκότος ὄσσε κάλυψεν = Π 325
v. l. ἀράβησε δὲ τεύχε' ἐπ' αὐτῷ = Δ 504

Π 129ᵃ Μυρμιδόνων, ἥν πού τι φόως Δαναοῖσι γένηαι ∽ Π 39
288ᵃ Ἀξιοῦ, οὗ κάλλιστον ὕδωρ ἐπικίδναται αἶαν = Β 850 ∽
Φ [158]
381 ἄμβροτοι, οὓς Πηλῆϊ θεοὶ δόσαν ἀγλαὰ δῶρα = Π 867
614 f. αἰχμὴ δ' Αἰνείαο κραδαινομένη κατὰ γαίης = Ν 504
ᾤχετ', ἐπεί ῥ' ἅλιον στιβαρῆς ἀπὸ χειρὸς ὄρουσεν = Ν 505
689 f. ὅς τε καὶ ἄλκιμον ἄνδρα φοβεῖ καὶ ἀφείλετο νίκην = Ρ 177
ῥηιδίως, ὅτε δ' αὐτὸς ἐποτρύνῃσι μάχεσθαι ∽ Ρ 178

Ρ 74 (?) καί μιν φωνήσας ἔπεα πτερόεντα προσηύδα formulaic
145ᵃ οἷος σὺν γαμβροῖσι κασιγνήτοισί τε σοῖσιν = Ε 474

808ᵃ om. Aristarchus (cf. 5 T), 3/4 p. PMorgan, 4 p. PSoc. It. 10, Σ; hab. Zenodotus (sed cf. infra, p. 141 f.).
Ξ: 12 om. 3/4 p. PMorgan; hab. Σ; cf. AJP 20.　　70 om. 3/4 p. PMorgan, Ludwich, van Leeuwen, damn. La Roche, Leaf.　　231ᵃ om. Aristarchus (cf. 5 T), 1 p. PMus. Br. 732, 2 p. POxy. 551, Σ et Ω; hab. τινές ap. 5 T, 3/4 p. PMorgan. 269 om. 1 p. PMus. Br. 732, 2 p. POxy. 551, 3/4 p. PMorgan, Σ, Bekker, Nauck, Leaf, Ludwich, van Leeuwen, damn. La Roche, Christ.　　420 om. 1 p. PMus. Br. 732, 3/4 p. PMorgan, Θ, van Leeuwen, damn. Ludwich.
Ο: 409ᵃᵇ hab. 3/4 p. PMorgan; om. Σ et Ω.　　481 om. 3/4 p. PMorgan, 5 p. PBerol. 230, Bekker, Nauck, Leaf, Ludwich, van Leeuwen, damn. La Roche, Christ. 562 om. 5 p. PBerol. 230; hab. sed post 530, 3 4 p. PMorgan; om. van Leeuwen. 578 hab. sed post 570, 3/4 p. PMorgan, in loco suo 5 p. PBerol. 230.
Π: 129ᵃ, 288ᵃ om. 3/4 p. PMorgan.　　381 om. 3/4 p. PMorgan (cf. AJP 19), Σ, Bekker, Nauck, Ludwich, van Leeuwen, damn. La Roche, Leaf.　　614 sq. om. 1/2 p. PGr.-Eg. 110, Bekker, Nauck, Leaf, Ludwich, et cum 613 van Leeuwen, damn. La Roche, Christ.　　689 sq. om. Σ, Bekker, Nauck, van Leeuwen, damn. La Roche, Christ, Leaf, Ludwich.
Ρ: 74 cf. CP 217 n. 1, Wecklein, ZAV 31.　　145ᵇ om. PRainer 533, 5 p. PBerol. 230.

219 τοὺς ὅ γ᾽ ἐποτρύνων ἔπεα πτερόεντα προσηύδα formulaic
326 τῷ μιν ἐεισάμενος προσέφη Διὸς υἱὸς Ἀπόλλων formulaic
455 δύῃ τ᾽ ἠέλιος καὶ ἐπὶ κνέφας ἱερὸν ἔλθῃ = Λ 194
585 τῷ μιν ἐεισάμενος προσέφη ἑκάεργος Ἀπόλλων formulaic
683ᵃ θεσπέσιον γάρ σφιν φόβον ἔμβαλε Φοῖβος Ἀπόλλων =
P 118

Σ 200 f. Τρῶες, ἀναπνεύσωσι δ᾽ ἀρήιοι υἷες Ἀχαιῶν = Λ 800, Π 42
τειρόμενοι· ὀλίγη δέ τ᾽ ἀνάπνευσις πολέμοιο = Λ 801, Π 43
381 τόφρα οἱ ἐγγύθεν ἦλθε θεά, Θέτις ἀργυρόπεζα = Σ 16 + 127
427 εἰ δύναμαι τελέσαι γε καὶ εἰ τετελεσμένον ἐστί = Ξ 196
441 οἴκαδε νοστήσαντα, δόμον Πηλήιον εἴσω = Σ 60

Τ 39ᵃ ἦ μὲν ἄρ᾽ ὣς ἔρξασ᾽ ἀπέβη Θέτις ἀργυρόπεζα cf. E 133,
σ 197
177 ἦ θέμις ἐστίν, ἄναξ, ἤτ᾽ ἀνδρῶν ἤτε γυναικῶν = I 276
361ᵃ ἐκ νηῶν ἐχέοντο· βοὴ δ᾽ ἄσβεστος ὀρώρει = Π 267

Υ 3ᵃ Ἕκτορι θωρήσσοντο μετὰ πρώτοισιν ἐόντι
135 ἡμέας τοὺς ἄλλους, ἐπεὶ ἦ πολὺ φέρτεροί εἰμεν ∽ Θ 211
223 (224)ᵃ ἐν μαλακῷ λειμῶνι καὶ ἄνθεσιν εἰαρινοῖσιν = Hes.
Th. 279
312 Πηλείδῃ Ἀχιλῆι δαμήμεναι, ἐσθλὸν ἐόντα ∽ X 176
316 f. (?) μηδ᾽ ὁπότ᾽ ἂν Τροίη μαλερῷ πυρὶ πᾶσα δάηται = Φ 375
δαιομένη, δαίωσι δ᾽ ἀρήιοι υἷες Ἀχαιῶν ∽ Φ 376
447 ἀλλ᾽ ὅτε δὴ τὸ τέταρτον ἐπέσσυτο δαίμονι ἶσος = Π 705

219 om. 5 p. PBerol. 230, cf. CP 216 f., Wecklein, ZAV 31, 70.   326 om. 3/4 p.
PBerol. 9783 ; hab. Ω, cf. CP 213 sqq.   585 om. Bekker, Nauck, van Leeuwen,
damn. La Roche, Leaf, Ludwich, cf. CP 213 sqq., Wecklein, ZAV 31, 57, 70.
Σ¹ : 200 sq. om. 1 a. PMus. Br. 107 (3/4 p. PMus. Br. 127, cf. AJP 141), Σ ; damn.
Ludwich, 201 solum damn. Christ.   381 om. 1 a. PMus. Br. 107 (3/4 p. PMus. Br.
127), cf. Cauer, Grundfr³. 49 sq., Wecklein, ZAV 18.   427 om. 1 a. PMus. Br. 107
(3/4 p. PMus. Br. 127), Σ ; damn. Ludwich.   441 om. 1 a. PMus. Br. 107 (3/4 p. PMus.
Br. 127), G, ἔν τισιν οὐ κεῖται ϛ A¹ ; hab. ΣΩ.
T : 39ᵃ om. Aristarchus ; hab. τινές ap. ϛ T.   177 om. Σ, Nauck, Ludwich, van
Leeuwen, damn. La Roche, Leaf.   361ᵃ om. Σ.
Υ : 3ᵃ om. Σ.   135 hab. Σ ; om. Bekker, Nauck, damn. La Roche, Christ, Leaf,
Ludwich, cf. Wecklein, ZAV 32.   312 om. Σ, Bekker, Nauck, Leaf, Ludwich, van
Leeuwen, damn. La Roche.   316 sq. om. Σ, add. i. m. Σ² ('one or more lines' Leaf),
hab. Ω, damn. Nauck, cf. Wecklein, ZAV 32.   447 om. Σ, ἐν ἄλλοις ὁ στίχος οὗτος
οὐ κεῖται ϛ Aʳ; om. Nauck, damn. Leaf, Ludwich.

¹ I accepted (AJP 253 n.) too quickly the assertion of Müller that a second
hand in PMus. Br. 107 has added 200 f., 427, 441. I was dependent on Ludwich,
but have now verified his statement in the papyrus.

Φ 73 καί μιν φωνήσας ἔπεα πτερόεντα προσηύδα formulaic
  96ᵃ ᾧ σὺ μάλιστα χολώε᾽ ἐνὶ φρεσίν, οἶδα καὶ αὐτός
  124 ἐνθεμένη λεχέεσσι γοήσεται [ἢ τὸ πάρος περ
       γείνατο κοῦρον ἐόντα   ] ἀλλὰ Σκάμανδρος
  158 Ἀξίου, ὃς κάλλιστον ὕδωρ ἐπὶ γαῖαν ἵησιν ∽ B 850, Π 288ᵃ
  434 ὣς φάτο, μείδησεν δὲ θεά, λευκώλενος Ἥρη = A 595
  480 νείκεσεν ἰοχέαιραν ὀνειδείοις ἐπέεσσιν ∽ B 277
  510 μαψιδίως ὡς εἴ τι κακὸν ῥέζουσαν ἐνωπῇ = E 374

X 10ᵃ Ἰλίου ἐξαλαπάξαι ἐυκτίμενον πτολίεθρον = Δ 33
  121 κτῆσιν ὅσην πτολίεθρον ἐπήρατον ἐντὸς ἐέργει ∽ Σ 512
  316 χρύσεαι, ἃς Ἥφαιστος ἵει λόφον ἀμφὶ θαμειάς = T 383
  330ᵃ καί μιν ἀμειβόμενος ἔπεα πτερόεντα προσηύδα formulaic
  363 ὃν πότμον γοόωσα, λιποῦσ᾽ ἀνδροτῆτα καὶ ἥβην = Π 857

Ψ 359 ff. τηλόθεν ἐν λείῳ πεδίῳ· παρὰ δὲ σκοπὸν εἶσεν = 757ᵃ⁻ᶜ
       ἀντίθεον Φοίνικα, ὁπάονα πατρὸς ἑοῖο
       ὡς μεμνέῳτο δρόμους καὶ ἀληθείην ἀποείποι
  565 Εὐμήλῳ δ᾽ ἐν χερσὶ τίθει· ὁ δὲ δέξατο χαίρων ∽ Ψ 624, 797
  626 ναὶ δὴ ταῦτά γε πάντα, τέκος, κατὰ μοῖραν ἔειπες ∽ K 169
  628ᵃ οἷαί περ πάρος ἔσκον ἐνὶ γναμπτοῖσι μέλεσσιν ∽ Λ 669
  804 ἀλλήλων προπάροιθεν ὁμίλου πειρηθῆναι
  864 ἀρνῶν πρωτογόνων ῥέξειν κλειτὴν ἑκατόμβην = Ψ 873

Φ: 73 om. Aristarchus (cf. Didymus ap. ς AT), hab. ΣΩ ; om. Bekker, damn.
Nauck, Ludwich, cf. *CP* 213 sqq., Wecklein, *ZAV* 69.   96ᵃ hab. Σ ; om. Ω.   124 ἤ
... ἐόν(τα) hab. M ; om. ΣΩ ; La Roche supplevit (ἐόν)τα καὶ ἔτρεφεν.   158 om. Σ ; hab.
ς B, sed affertur ex Eudoxo B 850; om. Bekker, Nauck, van Leeuwen, damn. La
Roche, Christ, Leaf, Ludwich.   434 damn. La Roche, Nauck, Leaf, Ludwich, cf.
CP 216.   480 om. Aristarchus (cf. Aristonicus ap. ς ATG), Σ, Bekker, Leaf,
Ludwich, damn. La Roche, cf. *CP* 216, Wecklein, *ZAV* 68 sq.   510 om. Σ, Bekker,
Nauck, Leaf, Ludwich, van Leeuwen, damn. La Roche.

X: 10ᵃ hab. Σ; om. 2*p*. POxy. 559, 3 *p*. PSoc. It. 139.   121 om. 2/3*p*. POxy.
558 ; hab. 5/6*p*. POxy. 1818 ; om. Bekker, Nauck, Ludwich, van Leeuwen, damn. La
Roche, Leaf.   316 hab. Σ ; om. van Leeuwen, damn. Christ, Leaf, Ludwich, cf.
Wecklein, *ZAV* 32.   330ᵃ om. Σ.   363 om. 1/2*p*. PFay. 211 ; hab. Σ, cf. Wecklein, *ZAV* 33.

Ψ : 359 sqq. om. (?) 1 *a*. PMus. Br. 128, add. post 757 m. 2, cf. supra p. 13 n. 1, hab.
5/6*p*. POxy. 1818 et Ω ; Duentzer reiecisse dicitur.   565 om. 1 *a*. (sed cf. Hunt,
JPh. 26 [1899] 25) PMus. Br. 128, Σ, Bekker, Nauck, Ludwich, van Leeuwen, damn.
La Roche, Leaf.   626 om. Aristarchus (cf. Aristonicus ap. ς A ad 627), i. t. 1 *a*.
PMus. Br. 128, add. i.m. m. 2; hab. Ω ; damn. Ludwich, cf. Wecklein, *ZAV* 71.
628ᵃ om. 1 *a*. PMus. Br. 128.   757ᵃ⁻ᶜ om. ΣΩ, add. 1 *a*. PMus. Br. 128 i. m. m. 2.
804 om. Aristarchus (cf. Nicanor in 802-6 ap. ς Λ), 1 *a*. PMus. Br. 128 ; damn. La
Roche, Ludwich, cf. Wecklein, *ZAV* 71 f.   864 om. 1 *a*. PMus. Br. 128, Σ ;
damn. Ludwich.

Ω 558 αὐτόν τε ζώειν καὶ ὁρᾶν φάος ἠελίοιο ∽ Σ 61
693 Ξάνθου δινήεντος ὃν ἀθάνατος τέκετο Ζεύς = Ξ 434, Φ 2
790 αὐτὰρ ἐπεί ῥ' ἤγερθεν ὁμηγερέες τ' ἐγένοντο ∽ Α 57
α 93ᵃᵇ κεῖθεν δ' ἐς Κρήτην τε παρ' Ἰδομενῆα ἄνακτα = α 285 Zen.
      ὃς γὰρ δεύτατος ἦλθεν Ἀχαιῶν χαλκοχιτώνων = α 286
148 κοῦροι δὲ κρητῆρας ἐπεστέψαντο ποτοῖο = γ 339, φ 271
148 (147)ᵃ νώμησαν δ' ἄρα πᾶσιν ἐπαρξάμενοι δεπάεσσιν =
                                                γ 340, φ 272
285ᵃ κεῖθεν δ' ἐς Κρήτην τε παρ' Ἰδομενῆα ἄνακτα = α 285 Zen.
329ᵃ ἐξ ποσὶν ἐμβεβαυῖα τριδάκτυλος ἐξεφαάνθη Jest of emperor
                                                Julian
β 4ᵃ ἀμφὶ δ' ἄρ' ὤμοισιν βάλετο ξίφος ἀργυρόηλον = Β 45
107ᵃ μηνῶν φθινόντων, περὶ δ' ἤματα πόλλ' ἐτελέσθη = κ [470],
                                τ [153], ω [143], Hes. Th. 59
191 πρῆξαι δ' ἔμπης οὔ τι δυνήσεται εἵνεκα τῶνδε ∽ Α 562
407 αὐτὰρ ἐπεί ῥ' ἐπὶ νῆα κατήλυθον ἠδὲ θάλασσαν = δ 428 (573)
                                θ 50, λ (1), μ 391, ν 70
429 ἡ δ' ἔθεεν κατὰ κῦμα διαπρήσσουσα κέλευθον = Α 483
γ 19 λίσσεσθαι δέ μιν αὐτόν, ὅπως νημερτέα εἴπῃ ∽ γ 327
78 ἠδ' ἵνα μιν κλέος ἐσθλὸν ἐν ἀνθρώποισιν ἔχῃσιν = α 95
416ᵃ αὐτὰρ ἐπεί ῥ' ἤγερθεν ὁμηγερέες τ' ἐγένοντο = β 9, θ 24, ω 421
487 δύσετό τ' ἠέλιος σκιόωντό τε πᾶσαι ἀγυιαί = β 388 etc.
493 ἐκ δ' ἔλασαν προθύροιο καὶ αἰθούσης ἐριδούπου ο 146, 191
δ 57 f. δαιτρὸς δὲ κρειῶν πίνακας παρέθηκεν ἀείρας = α 141
      παντοίων, παρὰ δέ σφι τίθει χρύσεια κύπελλα = α 142

Ω : 558 om. Aristarchus (cf. Didymus ap. ς AT), i. t. 2 p. PMus. Br. 114, add. i. m.
m. 2, οὐχ εὑρέθη ἐν τῷ παλαιῷ ς Aʳ ; vss. 556-8 om. Bekker, damn. Nauck ; vss. 556-7
damn. Ludwich omisso versu 558 quem damn. La Roche, Christ, Leaf, cf. Wecklein,
ZAV 33, 72.   693 om. 1 a. PMus. Br. 128, 2 p. PMus. Br. 114, Bekker, Ludwich,
van Leeuwen, damn. La Roche, Nauck, Leaf.   790 om. 2 p. PMus. Br. 114, Bekker,
Ludwich, damn. La Roche, Nauck, Leaf.

α : 93ᵃᵇ, 285ᵃ om. Aristarchus, hab. codd. singuli ex v. l. Zenodoti (cf. Aristonicus
in γ 313) male intellecta.   148 om. van Leeuwen, damn. Ludwich, Blass.

β : 191 om. Bekker, Nauck, Ludwich, van Leeuwen, damn. La Roche, Merry, Blass,
cf. Wecklein, ZAV 21.   407 om. 2 p. POxy. 773 ; damn. Blass (p. 297).   429 cf.
Wecklein, ZAV 20 f.

γ : 19 om. (cum 20) van Leeuwen, damn. Ludwich.   78 om. Bekker, Nauck,
Ludwich, van Leeuwen, damn. La Roche, Merry, Blass.   487 om. 1 a. PMus. Br.
271 ; hab. Ω, damn. Blass.   493 om. 1 a. PMus. Br. 271, Bekker, Nauck, Ludwich,
damn. La Roche, Merry, Blass.

δ : 57 f. om. Bekker, van Leeuwen, damn. Nauck, Ludwich, Merry, Blass.

218ᵃ αὐτὰρ ἐπεὶ πόσιος καὶ ἐδητύος ἐξ ἔρον ἔντο = α 150 etc.

228ᵃ Αἰγυπτίη | ἢ τόσα φάρμακα ἤδη ὅσα τρέφει εὐρεῖα χθών =
Δ 741

273 (?) Ἀργείων Τρώεσσι φόνον καὶ κῆρα φέροντες = θ 513

399 τοὶ γὰρ ἐγώ τοι ταῦτα μάλ' ἀτρεκέως ἀγορεύσω = α 179,
ξ 192

432 καὶ τότε δὴ παρὰ θῖνα θαλάσσης εὐρυπόροιο

598ᵃ οὓς λέλοιπα μετὰ νηὸς παρὰ Νέστορι ⟨δίῳ⟩

783 πάντα κατὰ μοῖραν· ἀνά θ' ἱστία λευκὰ πέτασσαν = θ 54

796ᵃ καλῇ τε μεγάλῃ τε καὶ ἀγλαὰ ἔργ' εἰδυίη = ν 289, π 158

ε 91 ἀλλ' ἔπεο προτέρω, ἵνα τοι πὰρ ξείνια θείω = Σ 387

157 δάκρυσι καὶ στοναχῇσι καὶ ἄλγεσι θυμὸν ἐρέχθων = ε 83

204ᵃ = 157

ζ 209ᵃ ἀλλ' ἄγε οἱ δότε φᾶρος ἐυπλυνὲς ἠδὲ χιτῶνα ∽ θ 392

313 ff. εἴ κέν τοι κείνη γε φίλα φρονέῃσ' ἐνὶ θυμῷ = η 75
ἐλπωρή τοι ἔπειτα φίλους τ' ἰδέειν καὶ ἱκέσθαι = η 76
οἶκον ἐυκτίμενον καὶ σὴν ἐς πατρίδα γαῖαν ∽ η 77

η 177ᵃ αὐτὰρ ἐπεὶ δείπνησε καὶ ἤραρε θυμὸν ἐδωδῇ = ε 95, ξ 111

203ᵃ ἀργαλέος γάρ τ' ἐστὶ θεὸς βροτῷ ἀνδρὶ δαμῆναι = δ 397

221ᵃ καὶ δ' ἔτι κεν καὶ πλεῖον ἐγὼ κακὰ μυθησαίμην = η 213

θ 27 ὄφρ' εἴπω τά με θυμὸς ἐνὶ στήθεσσι κελεύει = η 187 etc.,
φ [276]

58 ἀγρομένων· πολλοὶ δ' ἄρ ἔσαν νέοι ἠδὲ παλαιοί ∽ θ 17 +
α 395

62ᵃ Δημόδοκον λιγύφωνον ἐόντα θεῖον ἀοιδόν

303 βῆ δ' ἴμεναι πρὸς δῶμα, φίλον τετιημένος ἦτορ = β 298

348ᵃ εἴ κεν Ἄρης οἴχοιτο χρέος καὶ δεσμὸν ἀλύξας = θ 353

501ᵃ ἢ κατὰ πετράων βαλέειν ἐρύσαντας ἐπ' ἄκρας ∽ θ 508

___

399 om. 3 p. POxy. 775 ; damn. Blass (p. 297).   783 om. Bekker, van Leeuwen, damn. La Roche, Nauck, Ludwich, Merry, Blass.

ε: 91 om. Bekker, Nauck, Ludwich, van Leeuwen, damn. La Roche, Merry, Blass. 157 om. Bekker, Nauck, van Leeuwen, damn. La Roche, Ludwich, Merry, Blass.

ζ: 313 sqq. om. Bekker, Nauck, Ludwich, van Leeuwen, damn. La Roche, Merry, Blass.

θ: 27 damn. Ludwich, Blass, cf. Wecklein, ZAV 21.   58 om. Bekker, Ludwich, van Leeuwen, damn. La Roche, Nauck, Merry, Blass (p. 102).   303 om. Bekker, Nauck, Ludwich, van Leeuwen, damn. La Roche. Merry, Blass.   348ᵃ om. 2 p. PBerol. 7805.

ι 30 ἐν σπέσσι γλαφυροῖσι, λιλαιομένη πόσιν εἶναι = α 15
412ᵃ τοῦ γὰρ δὴ παῖς ἐσσι, πατὴρ δὲ σὸς εὔχεται εἶναι ꭥ ι 519
489 ἐμβαλέειν κώπῃς, ἵν' ὑπ' ἐκ κακότητα φύγοιμεν = κ 129
531 υἱὸν Λαέρτεω, 'Ιθάκῃ ἔνι οἰκί' ἔχοντα = ι 505
547 (?) ἐκ δὲ καὶ αὐτοὶ βῆμεν ἐπὶ ῥηγμῖνι θαλάσσης = ι 150, μ [6]
κ 201 f. κλαῖον δὲ λιγέως, θαλερὸν κατὰ δάκρυ χέοντες = π 216 +
κ 409 etc.
ἀλλ' οὐ γάρ τις πρῆξις ἐγίνετο μυρομένοισιν = κ 568
225ᵃ ὅ σφιν ἐὺ φρονέων ἀγορήσατο καὶ μετέειπεν = β 160 etc.
232ᵃᵇ ἦ τοι ὀισάμενος ἦ καὶ θεὸς ὡς ἐκέλευεν = ι 339
233ᵃ = τεῦχε δέ οἱ κυκεῶ χρυσέῳ δέπα ὄφρα πίοιεν ꭥ κ 316
253 ξεστοῖσιν λάεσσι, περισκέπτῳ ἐνὶ χώρῳ = κ 211
265 καί μ' ὀλοφυρόμενος ἔπεα πτερόεντα προσηύδα = λ 616 ꭥ
κ 418
310ᵃ Κίρκης δ' ἔνδον ἄκουον ἀειδούσης ὀπὶ καλῇ = κ 221
315 καλοῦ δαιδαλέου· ὑπὸ δὲ θρῆνυς ποσὶν ἦεν = κ 367
315ᵃ⁻ᵈ χέρνιβα δ' ἀμφίπολος προχόῳ ἐπέχευε φέρουσα = κ 368
καλῇ χρυσείῃ, ὑπὲρ ἀργυρέοιο λέβητος. = κ 369
319ᵃ = σῖτον δ' αἰδοίη ταμίη παρέθηκε φέρουσα, = κ 371
319ᵇ = εἴδατα πόλλ' ἐπιθεῖσα χαριζομένη παρεόντων. = κ 372
368 ff. χέρνιβα δ' ἀμφίπολος προχόῳ ἐπέχευε φέρουσα = α 136–
40, δ 52–6, η 172–6, ο 135–8 [139], ρ 91–5
καλῇ χρυσείῃ, ὑπὲρ ἀργυρέοιο λέβητος
νίψασθαι· παρὰ δὲ ξεστὴν ἐτάνυσσε τράπεζαν.
σῖτον δ' αἰδοίη ταμίη παρέθηκε φέρουσα,
εἴδατα πόλλ' ἐπιθεῖσα χαριζομένη παρεόντων.
409ᵃ ἀσπάσιος δ' ἄρα τοῖσί γ' ἐφάνη κακότητος ἀλύξας cf. ε 397
430 καί σφεας φωνήσας ἔπεα πτερόεντα προσηύδα = δ 77 ꭥ
α 122 etc.

ι : 30 om. Nauck, Ludwich, van Leeuwen, damn. La Roche, Merry, et cum 31-2
Blass. 489 om. van Leeuwen, damn. Ludwich, Blass, cf. Wecklein, ZAV 22.
531 hab. P³P⁷ (Allen), non Macrobius v. 12. 6 (ubi addidit Jan., cf. Eyssenhardt) ;
om. Ω, Bekker, Nauck, Ludwich, van Leeuwen, damn. La Roche, Merry, Blass.
κ : 232ᵃᵇ ap. Kirchhoff, p. 218. 253 om. Bekker, Nauck, Ludwich, van Leeuwen,
damn. La Roche, Merry, Blass. 265 om. Bekker, Nauck, Ludwich, van Leeuwen,
damn. La Roche, Merry, Blass, cf. CP 221, Wecklein, ZAV 22. 315 om. Aristarchus
(cf. Didymus ap. s Q), Nauck, van Leeuwen, damn. Ludwich, Blass. 368 sqq.
om. 1/2 p. PFay. 157, Bekker, Nauck, et cum 367 van Leeuwen, damn. La Roche,
Ludwich, Merry, Blass. 430 ignor. s H ; om. Bekker, Nauck, damn. La Roche,
Ludwich, Merry, Blass, cf. CP 221.

456 διογενὲς Λαερτιάδη, πολυμήχαν' 'Οδυσσεῦ = ε 203 etc.

459ª βοῦς περιταμνομένους ἠδ' οἰῶν πώεα καλά = ω 112

470 μηνῶν φθινόντων, περὶ δ' ἤματα μακρὰ τελέσθη cf. at β 107ª

475 ff. ὣς ἔφαν, αὐτὰρ ἔμοιγ' ἐπεπείθετο θυμὸς ἀγήνωρ. ꙥ κ 406
etc.

ὣς τότε μὲν πρόπαν ἦμαρ ἐς ἠέλιον καταδύντα = ι 161 f.,
556 f., κ 183 f. etc.

ἥμεθα δαινύμενοι κρέα τ' ἄσπετα καὶ μέθυ ἡδύ·
ἦμος δ' ἠέλιος κατέδυ καὶ ἐπὶ κνέφας ἦλθεν, = ι 168, 558,
κ 185 etc.

οἱ μὲν κοιμήσαντο κατὰ μέγαρα σκιόεντα. = μ 32 + λ 334
etc.

482 καί μιν φωνήσας ἔπεα πτερόεντα προσηύδων = δ 550 etc.

502ª ζωὸς ἐών· χαλεπὸν δὲ τά γε ζωοῖσιν ὁρᾶσθαι = λ 156

504 διογενὲς Λαερτιάδη, πολυμήχαν' 'Οδυσσεῦ = κ [456] etc.

569 (?) ἀλλ' ὅτε δή ῥ' ἐπὶ νῆα θοὴν καὶ θῖνα θαλάσσης ꙥ δ 779 etc.

λ 60, 92 διογενὲς Λαερτιάδη, πολυμήχαν' 'Οδυσσεῦ = κ [456] etc.

178ªᵇ κτῆσιν ἐμὴν δμῶάς τε καὶ ὑψερεφὲς μέγα δῶμα = τ 526

εὐνήν τ' αἰδομένη πόσιος δήμοιό τε φήμην = τ 527

266ª ἢ δὴ καὶ Ζηνὸς (l. Διὸς) εὔχετ' ἐν ἀγκοίνῃσιν ἰαῦσαι
= λ 261

343 ὃς δὴ Φαιήκων ἀνδρῶν προγενέστερος ἦεν = η 156

343ª καὶ μύθοις ἐκέκαστο παλαιά τε πολλά τε εἰδώς = η 157

369ª πᾶσι, μάλιστα δ' ἐμοί· τοῦ γὰρ κράτος ἔστ' ἐνὶ δήμῳ
= λ 353 etc.

407 ὄρσας ἀργαλέων ἀνέμων ἀμέγαρτον ἀϋτμήν = λ 400

604 παῖδα Διὸς μεγάλοιο καὶ "Ηρης χρυσοπεδίλου = Hes.
Th. 952

456 om. Bekker, Nauck, Ludwich, van Leeuwen, damn. La Roche, Merry, Blass.
470 om. Bekker, Nauck, van Leeuwen, damn. La Roche, Ludwich, Merry, Blass.
475 sqq. om. Bekker, damn. La Roche, Ludwich, Merry, Blass, cf. Wecklein, ZAV
22 sq. 482 om. Bekker, van Leeuwen, damn. La Roche, Nauck, Ludwich, Merry,
Blass, cf. CP 221. 504 om. Ludwich, van Leeuwen, damn. La Roche, Blass.
λ : 60 om. (2p. POxy. 1819 : γ' = 303), Bekker, Nauck, van Leeuwen, damn. La
Roche, Ludwich, Merry, Blass. 92 om. (2p. POxy. 1819) Bekker, Nauck, Ludwich,
van Leeuwen, damn. La Roche, Merry. 343 om. Bekker, Nauck, van Leeuwen,
damn. La Roche, Ludwich, Merry, Blass. 407 om. Ludwich, van Leeuwen, damn.
La Roche, Blass. 604 om. Aristarchus (cf. ꙅ TV λ 385), 1/2p. PFay. 310,
Bekker, Nauck, et cum 602-3 van Leeuwen, damn. Ludwich, Merry, et cum 602-3
Blass. 622ªᵇ cf. Kirchhoff, p. 233.

622^{ab} Εὐρυσθεύς· τῷ γάρ ῥα πατὴρ ἐκέλευσε Κρονίων
πλείστους δεδμῆσθαι τηλεκλειτῶν ἀνθρώπων
638ª ἑξῆς δ' ἑζόμενοι πολιὴν ἅλα τύπτον ἐρετμοῖς = δ 580 etc.

μ 6 ἐκ δὲ καὶ αὐτοὶ βῆμεν ἐπὶ ῥηγμῖνι θαλάσσης = ι 150
[547?]
99ª⁻ᵈ ἡ δ' ὑποκυσαμένη Πελίην τέκε καὶ Νηλῆα, = λ 254
τὼ κρατερὼ θεράποντε Διὸς μεγάλοιο γενέσθην = λ 255
ἀμφοτέρω· Πελίης μὲν ἐν εὐρυχόρῳ Ἰαωλκῷ = λ 256
ναῖε πολύρρηνος, ὁ δ' ἄρ' ἐν Πύλῳ ἠμαθόεντι = λ 257
133ª αὐτοκασιγνήτη Θέτιδος λιπαροπλοκάμοιο = Hesiod?
140 f. νηΐ τε καὶ ἑτάροις· αὐτὸς δ' εἴ πέρ κεν ἀλύξῃς = λ 113
ὀψὲ κακῶς νεῖαι, ὀλέσας ἄπο πάντας ἑταίρους = λ 114
147 ἑξῆς δ' ἑζόμενοι πολιὴν ἅλα τύπτον ἐρετμοῖς = δ 580,
λ 638ª etc.
153ª κέκλυτέ μευ μύθων κακά περ πάσχοντες ἑταῖροι cf. on
κ 189, Part IV
240ᵃ ἤτοι ὅτ' ἐξεμέσειε, λέβης ὡς ἐν πυρὶ πολλῷ = μ 237
365ª ὤπτησάν τε περιφραδέως ἐρύσαντό τε πάντα = ξ 431

ν 197ª τήνδ' Ὀδυσεὺς γήθησεν ἰδὼν καὶ ἐναντίος ἦλθεν = ν 226
241ª καὶ μέν τοι ἴσασ' Ἰθάκην σχεδὸν ἠδ' ἀποτηλοῦ
339ª χωόμενος ὅτι οἱ υἱὸν φίλον ἐξαλάωσας = ν 343
347 f. ἀγχόθι δ' αὐτῆς ἄντρον ἐπήρατον, ἠεροειδές, = ν 103
ἱρὸν Νυμφάων, αἱ νηιάδες καλέονται = ν 104
369ª ὤπασαν οἴκαδ' ἰόντι διὰ μεγάθυμον Ἀθήνην = ν 121
396 ἀνδρῶν μνηστήρων, οἵ τοι βίοτον κατέδουσιν = ν 428, ο 32
ξ 154 ἔσσαι με χλαῖνάν τε χιτῶνά τε, εἵματα καλά ∽ ξ 396
369 f. τῷ κέν οἱ τύμβον μὲν ἐποίησαν Παναχαιοί = α 239
∽ ω 31
ἠδέ κε καὶ ᾧ παιδὶ μέγα κλέος ἤρατ' ὀπίσσω = α 240
ω 32

μ: 133ª desideravit Buttmann, cf. Wecklein, ZAV 23. 140 sq. om. van Leeuwen,
damn. La Roche, Ludwich, Blass. 147 om. Bekker, Nauck, Ludwich, van Leeuwen,
damn. La Roche, Merry, Blass.
ν: 197ª om. 3p. PRyl. 53. 241ª om. 3p. PRyl. 53, Ω; hab. G ap. Wecklein, ZAV
13. 339ª hab. 3p. PRyl. 53, om. Ω. 347 sq. om. 3p. PRyl. 53, Bekker,
Nauck, van Leeuwen, damn. La Roche, Merry, Blass. 369ª om. 3p.
PRyl. 53. 396 om. 3p. PRyl. 53; hab. Ω, excepto Neap. II F 4.
ξ: 154 om. 3p. PRyl. 53, Bekker, Nauck, Ludwich, damn. La Roche, Merry, Blass.
369 sq. om. (6/7p. PBerol. 7517, cf. AJP 255 n.) Ludwich, van Leeuwen, damn. Blass.

515 ff. αὐτὰρ ἐπὴν ἔλθῃσιν Ὀδυσσῆος φίλος υἱός, = ο 337
αὐτός τοι χλαῖνάν τε χιτῶνά τε εἵματα δώσει, ∾ ο 338
πέμψει δ' ὅππῃ σε κραδίη θυμός τε κελεύει = ο 339
ο 44 (45)ᵃ ἀγχοῦ δ' ἱστάμενος προσέφη Τηλέμαχος θεοειδής ∾ ο 9
+ ξ 173 etc.
63 Τηλέμαχος, φίλος υἱὸς Ὀδυσσῆος θείοιο = ο 554 etc.
113 ff. δώρων δ' ὅσσ' ἐν ἐμῷ οἴκῳ κειμήλια κεῖται, = δ 613
δώσω ὃ κάλλιστον καὶ τιμηέστατόν ἐστι, = δ 614
δώσω τοι κρητῆρα τετυγμένον· ἀργύρεος δὲ = δ 615
ἔστιν ἅπας, χρυσῷ δ' ἐπὶ χείλεα κεκράανται· = δ 616
ἔργον δ' Ἡφαίστοιο· πόρεν δέ ἑ Φαίδιμος ἥρως, = δ 617
Σιδονίων βασιλεύς, ὅθ' ἐὸς δόμος ἀμφεκάλυψε = δ 618
κεῖσ' ἐμὲ νοστήσαντα· τεῒν δ' ἐθέλω τόδ' ὀπάσσαι = δ 619
139 εἴδατα πόλλ' ἐπιθεῖσα, χαριζομένη παρεόντων = α 140 etc.
345 ἀνέρες, ὅν τιν' ἵκηται ἄλη καὶ πῆμα καὶ ἄλγος
π 24ᵃ λάθρῃ, ἐμεῦ ἀέκητι φίλου μετὰ πατρὸς ἀκουήν = ρ 43
256ᵃ ἀρκέσει ἠέ τιν' ἄλλον ἀμύντορα μερμηρίξω = π 261
317 αἵ τέ σ' ἀτιμάζουσι καὶ αἳ νηλίτιδές εἰσιν = τ 498 ∾ χ 418
412ᵃ αὐλῆς ἐκτὸς ἐών· οἱ δ' ἔνδοθι μῆτιν ὕφαινον = δ 678
ρ 3ᵃ εἵματα ἐσσάμενος, περὶ δὲ ξίφος ὀξὺ θέτ' ὤμῳ = β 3 etc.
49 εἰς ὑπερῷ' ἀναβᾶσα σὺν ἀμφιπόλοισι γυναιξίν = ψ 364 ∾
α 362 etc.
233ᵃ ἦλθεν ἐσσυμένως μεγάλην σοφίην ἀνιχνεύων
547 πᾶσι μάλ', οὐδέ κέ τις θάνατον καὶ κῆρας ἀλύξει = τ 558
565 τῶν ὕβρις τε βίη τε σιδήρεον οὐρανὸν ἵκει = ο 329
568ᵃ δμώων οἳ κατὰ δώματ' Ὀδυσσῆος θείοιο = ρ 402 etc.
577ᵃ ὕβριν ἀλυσκάζειν ἀνδρῶν ὑπερηνορεόντων ∾ ρ 581
603ᵃ αὐτὰρ ἐπεὶ δείπνησε καὶ ἤραρε θυμὸν ἐδωδῇ = ε 95,
η [177ᵃ], ξ 111

515 sqq. om. (3 p. PRyl. 53) Bekker, Nauck, Ludwich, van Leeuwen, damn. La
Roche, Merry.
ο : 63 om. Bekker, Nauck, Ludwich, van Leeuwen, damn. La Roche, Merry, Blass.
113–19 vss. ignotos auctori Glossarii Homerici a/p. PAmh. ii. 18, om. (3 p. PRyl. 53),
Leeuwen, damn. Ludwich, Blass.   139 om. Bekker, Nauck, Ludwich, van Leeuwen,
damn. La Roche, Blass.   345 damn. Ludwich.
π : 317 om. van Leeuwen, damn. Blass.
ρ : 3ᵃ ignotus 5 Q.   49 om. Bekker, Nauck, van Leeuwen, damn. La Roche,
Ludwich, Merry, Blass.   233ᵃ om. 4 p. PAc. B. Lettres 1905, p. 215.   547 damn.
Ludwich, Blass.   565 damn. Nauck, Ludwich, Blass.   603ᵃ vm. ignotum s BT
ad A 469, om. 3 p. POxy. 955.

σ 59 (?) αὐτὰρ ἐπεί ῥ' ὄμοσάν τε τελεύτησάν τε τὸν ὅρκον = μ 304,
ο 438
111ᵃ ὧδε δέ τις εἴπεσκε νέων ὑπερηνορεόντων = β 324 etc.
131 (?) πάντων, ὅσσα τε γαῖαν ἔπι πνείει τε καὶ ἔρπει = Ρ 447
184ᵃ μίσγεσθαι μνηστῆρσιν ὑπερφιάλοισιν ἀνάγκῃ ∽ ζ 136 +
ξ 27
393 ἦ ἀλύεις, ὅτι ῎Ιρον ἐνίκησας τὸν ἀλήτην = σ 333
413 Νίσου φαίδιμος υἱὸς Ἀρητιάδαο ἄνακτος = π 395
τ 77 τοίῳ, ὁποῖος ἔοι καὶ ὅτευ κεχρημένος ἔλθοι = ρ 421
153 μηνῶν φθινόντων, περὶ δ' ἤματα πόλλ' ἐτελέσθη cf. on
β 107ᵃ
291 f. ἀλλ' ἐμὲ πρὶν ἀπέπεμψε· τύχησε γὰρ ἐρχομένη νηῦς =
ξ 334
ἀνδρῶν Θεσπρωτῶν ἐς Δουλίχιον πολύπυρον = ξ 335
558ᵃᵇ μνηστήρων, οἳ δῶμα κατ' ἀντιθέου 'Οδυσῆος = υ 369
ἀνέρες ὑβρίζοντες ἀτάσθαλα μηχανόωνται ∽ υ 370
581 τοῦ ποτε μεμνήσεσθαι ὀίομαι ἔν περ ὀνείρῳ = φ 79
υ 83ᵃ ἤτοι μέν τε βροτῶν ἄλλος ᾧ πένθος ἱκάνει
145 (?) ἔγχος ἔχων· ἅμα τῷ γε κύνες πόδας ἀργοὶ ἕποντο = ρ 62
327ᵃ κτῆσιν πήματά τε· τόδε κέρδιον ἔπλετο θυμῷ cf. υ 304
φ 65 f. ἄντα παρειάων σχομένη λιπαρὰ κρήδεμνα = α 334 etc.
ἀμφίπολος δ' ἄρα οἱ κεδνὴ ἑκάτερθε παρέστη = α 335 etc.
109 οὔτ' αὐτῆς Ἰθάκης οὔτ' ἠπείροιο μελαίνης
219 f. οὐλήν, τήν ποτέ με σῦς ἤλασε λευκῷ ὀδόντι ∽ τ 393, ψ 74
Παρνησὸν δ' ἐλθόντα σὺν υἱάσιν Αὐτολύκοιο ∽ τ 394
276 ὄφρ' εἴπω τά με θυμὸς ἐνὶ στήθεσσι κελεύει = η 187 etc.
308 εἰς ῎Εχετον βασιλῆα, βροτῶν δηλήμονα πάντων = σ 85, 116
353ᵃ ὣς φάτο, ῥίγησεν δὲ περίφρων Πηνελόπεια ∽ ε 116, 171

σ: 59 hab. 3 p. POxy. 572, om. Bekker. 111ᵃ om. 6/7 p. POxy. 1820, add. Ludwich, Monro-Allen, cf. CP 221. 131 om. Plut., consol. ad Apollon. 104 d, damn. Nauck. 393, 413 om. Bekker, Nauck, Ludwich, van Leeuwen, damn. La Roche, Merry, Blass. τ: 153 om. Aristarchus (cf. ş H ad τ 130, Blass, p. 190, Wecklein, ZAV 20, et infra), Bekker, van Leeuwen, damn. Ludwich, Merry, Blass. 291-2 damn. Blass. 558ᵃᵇ om. 4/5 p. PBerol. 10568. 581 om. 4/5 p. PBerol. 10568; hab. Ω. φ : 65-6 om. 3 p. PRyl. 53; vm. 65 hab. Ω ; vm. 66 solum om. Bekker, Nauck, damn. La Roche, Ludwich, Merry, Blass. 109 om. 3 p. PRyl. 53, Bekker, Nauck, damn. La Roche, Ludwich, Merry, Blass. 219-20 om. 3 p. PRyl. 53, damn. Blass. 276 vm. a Demetr. Chalc. prob. in MS. aliquo repertum om. 3 p. PRyl. 53, Ω, Bekker, Nauck, Ludwich, van Leeuwen, damn. La Roche, Merry, Blass. 308, 353ᵃ om. 3 p. PRyl. 53.

χ 43   πάπτηνεν δὲ ἕκαστος ὅπῃ φύγοι αἰπὺν ὄλεθρον = Ξ 507,
                                                                    Π 283
   43ᵃ   ἔνθ' ἄλλοι μὲν πάντες ἀκὴν ἐγένοντο σιωπῇ cf. θ 234 etc.,
                                                                    β 82, δ 285
   191   υἱὸς Λαέρταο, πολύτλας δῖος Ὀδυσσεύς cf. θ 18 + ε 171 etc.

ψ 48   αἵματι καὶ λύθρῳ πεπαλαγμένον ὥς τε λέοντα = χ 402
   127 f. ἡμεῖς δὲ μεμαῶτες ἅμ' ἐψόμεθ', οὐδέ τί φημι = Ν 785
           ἀλκῆς δευήσεσθαι, ὅση δύναμίς γε πάρεστιν = Ν 786
   320   πάντας· Ὀδυσσεὺς δ' οἶος ὑπέκφυγε νηὶ μελαίνῃ

ω 4ᵃ   τὴν μετὰ χερσὶν ἔχων πέτετο κρατὺς Ἀργειφόντης = ε 49
   121   Ἀτρείδη κύδιστε, ἄναξ ἀνδρῶν Ἀγάμεμνον = λ 397
   143   μηνῶν φθινόντων περὶ δ' ἤματα πολλὰ τελέσθη cf. on
                                                                    β 107ᵃ
   171ᵃ   ἀντιθέου Ὀδυσῆος ὅ τ' οὐ δυνάμεσθα τανύσσαι = φ 254

χ : 43 om. 3 p. PRyl. 53, 3 p. POxy. 448, Bekker, Nauck, Ludwich, van Leeuwen,
damn. La Roche, Merry, Blass.   43ᵃ om. 3 p. PRyl. 53, 3 p. POxy. 448.   191 hab.
3 p. PRyl. 53 ; om. 3 p. POxy. 448, Ludwich, van Leeuwen, damn. La Roche, Blass.
ψ : 48, 127-8 om. 3 p. PRyl. 53, Bekker, Nauck, Ludwich, van Leeuwen, damn. La
Roche, Merry, Blass.   320 om. Aristarchus (cf. s QV ad 310-43), 2/3 p. POxy.
956, 3 p. PRyl. 53, Bekker, Nauck, Ludwich, van Leeuwen, damn. La Roche, Merry,
Blass.
ω : 4ᵃ om. 3 p. PRyl. 53.   121, 143 om. (2 p. PTebt. 432, cf. AJP 457) 3 p. PRyl.
53, Bekker, Nauck, Ludwich, van Leeuwen, damn. La Roche, Merry, Blass.   171ᵃ
om. 3 p. PRyl. 53.

PART II

BEFORE ARISTARCHUS

§ 1. The Problem.

THE work has now reached the point beyond which a complete and continuous *recensio* becomes impossible. All witnesses competent to testify to the poems as wholes have been heard, and their stories traced to a single source. With the version of the poems thus given we have nothing to compare but the *disiecta membra* of other traditions. The action to be taken in the face of this obstacle is judged differently by different scholars.

Bethe and Wilamowitz hold views otherwise diametrically opposed; but both agree that the gap between Aristarchus and 'Homer' must be leapt rather than bridged. Only Bethe starts with the assumption that between the tradition has been rigidly immobile, while Wilamowitz takes off from the hypothesis of its unlimited fluidity. Thus Bethe (*Homer*, i. 53) declares: 'Aber es werden nur Kleinigkeiten sein, die gegen Aristarch zu ändern sind. Im allgemeinen darf sein Text für identisch mit den beiden Mutter-handschriften der Ilias und Odyssee gelten.' If in virtue of these restrictions this meant no more than what Bethe (*Homer*, ii, p. viii) has since stated—'niemals, seit dem V. Jahrhundert sicherlich nicht, hat es einen Iliastext gegeben, in dem die Dolonie, nun gar Θ und I fehlten oder die Glaukosepisode an anderer Stelle stand, Patroklos' Bestattung den Schluss gebildet hätte oder das Gedicht noch bis Achills Tod weitergelaufen wäre und was von dergleichen Vermutungen mehr geäussert ist'—I could assent most unhesitatingly. Variations on that scale, or anything approaching it, are unattested.[1]

---

[1] s T at K 1 merely records an opinion of certain unnamed critics; its silence about the existence of MSS. lacking the *Doloneia* is practically an admission that there were none such. Roemer, developing a suggestion of La Roche (cf. Cauer, *Grundfr.*[3]

But I can neither believe that Bethe would class passages of ten or a dozen lines as *Kleinigkeiten*, nor that interpolations of that extent are not to be found in the edition of Aristarchus. Certainly Aristarchus himself—witness his atheteses—would have claimed no such perfection for his edition. I am, therefore, constrained to join Wecklein (*Z A V* 82 n.) in dissenting from Bethe's opinion.

For Wilamowitz (*Ilias*, 8 ff.), on the other hand, the Homeric text before Zenodotus was in a chaotic condition. There were, for instance, in the library of Alexandria MSS. of the *Odyssey* that ended with ψ 296, and contained therefore as a matter of course another version of the poem—one in which Laertes was dead, and the parts referring to him were missing. There must have been also equally divergent and contradictory versions of the *Iliad*; we should get an *überraschende Aufklärung*, could we but use them. From these variants the critics built what seemed to them a consistent poem.[1] Their skill deserves, to be sure, our gratitude; but in the process they threw overboard much that we would value most highly and judge to be genuine. Their construction is not binding upon us; we too have the right and the duty to choose between the variants as far as we know them.

No more than Bethe (*loc. cit.*) can I find for these speculations any solid foundation. On the contrary, what we know of the earlier texts points decidedly in a different direction—in that indicated by Leaf as already quoted : ' There is no single case in Homer where

117 and the literature there cited), endeavours to show from τῇ ἐχομένῃ (sc. ῥαψωδίᾳ) in ς A at I 709 that Λ followed upon I in the edition of Aristarchus. The result is endless difficulty : conflict with the use of K made by Aristarchus (cf. Bachmann, i. 18) ; with the Aristarchean method of citing by twenty-four books ; with the presence of K in our MSS.

The note of Aristonicus on Z 119 does on the surface attest the existence of MSS. in which the Glaukos episode stood elsewhere. But it is impossible to suggest for it any other suitable location in the *Iliad* ; so that a MS. containing it elsewhere must have undergone some mechanical dislocation. Aristonicus would not have mentioned such a triviality unless it were his copy of Zenodotus (cf. his notes on Γ 334 f., Δ 123) that was thus deformed. If that is so, the epitomator has effectually concealed it behind his τινές and his ἀλλαχόσε. It is also possible (cf. Leaf, i. 256) that his abbreviation has turned a mere expression of preference into a definite statement of fact.

[1] The ideas are those of Wolf, *Vorlesungen*, p. 17: ' Man denke sich, es seyen zwölf Exemplare aus verschiedenen Gegenden nach Alexandrien gekommen; nun kommen die Philologen, z. B. Zenodotus, vor diese Exemplare ; er blättert, sieht eine Menge Diversitäten, und entschliesst sich, daraus eklektisch das beste, was als Homerisch angesehen werden könnte, zu wählen.'

the loss of a line can be assumed with reasonable probability ; the tradition was wonderfully tenacious of all it had got, as well as acquisitive of new matter.'

My own proposal is to push out our bridge, even though we know that we have not the material to carry it to the other shore. In the end we too shall have to leap, but our leap will be shorter and from a firmer foothold. To drop metaphor, I would carry on with the *recensio* where and how we can. If it brings us at points to the text of an earlier period we shall be by that much the gainers. And more than that, we shall have secured a standard by which to gauge the interpolations that may be assumed on other grounds in the Aristarchean text.

§ 2. Our Material and its Source.

To compare with the text of Aristarchus as determined in Part I we have : (1) the variants reported in the scholia ; (2) early quotations of Homer, collected by Ludwich (*HV* 71-133) ; and (3) the readings of the Ptolemaic papyri and of a few belated survivors of that type of text.[1] The first question to arise is whether the texts known to us in these ways have all a common source.

As far back as 1841 this question was answered in the affirmative when Lachmann (p. 31) wrote : ' Die schriftliche überlieferung der homerischen gedichte im griechischen alterthum beruhte einzig auf der arbeit des Pisistratus und seiner gefährten.' Since then much has been written about Pisistratus, the Pisistratean legend, and its explosion. The controversy still continues, but from it there seem to me to emerge certain fixed facts : all variants known to us are of the kind that arise in a written, not an oral, tradition, and that tradition can have, on account of its small divergence, but a single fountain-head. Nutzhorn's discussion (pp. 6-15) is still worth reading, and Jebb's neat presentation (p. 92) of the argument may

---

[1] These Papyri contain more or less completely a text corresponding to the vulgate between the following limits : A 484–94, 1 *p*. PVitelli ; B 174-Γ 371, 3 *a*. PHibeh 19 ; Γ 347-E 803, 3 *a*. PHibeh 20 ; Θ 17-258, 3 *a*. PHibeh 21 + PHeidelberg 1261 ; Λ 502-37, 3/2 *a*. PDublin ; Λ 788-M 9, 2 *a*. PGenav 6 ; Π 484-9, 3 *a*. PRylands 49 ; Σ 596-608, 1 *a*. PBerol. 9774 ; Φ 302-Ψ 281, 3 *a*. PGrenf. ii. 4 + PHibeh i. 22 + PHeidelberg 1262-6 (this I shall cite as PGerhard) ; υ 41-68, 3 *a*. PHibeh 23. The publication of fragments of *a* and of δ-ε is promised—cf. Grenfell, *JHS* 39. (1919) 17— in the near future.

be quoted: ' There is no trace of larger discrepancies or dislocations. Such, however, could not have failed to exist if there had not been a common basis of tradition.' Bethe is but emphasizing what should need no emphasizing when he writes (*Homer*, ii, p. ix): ' Ich betone es wieder als unwiderlegliche und grundlegende Tatsache: alle Iliashandschriften gehen auf eine einzige zurück . . . Ebenso steht es mit der Odyssee.' For my purpose that is as much as is strictly needed. I shall add, however, my belief that this fountain-head of our tradition is an Athenian text not earlier than the sixth century.[1]

So far most scholars—Wilamowitz and Meister being the outstanding exceptions—are in substantial agreement; cf. Murray, *RGE*[2] 320–4; Finsler, *Homer*[2], i. 70 f.; Wackernagel, *SU* 1; Wecklein, *ZAV* 82; Drerup, i. 319; Cauer, *Grundfr.*[3] i. 99–135; Bethe, *Homer*, ii. 355–60. Divergence comes with the question of what that text may have been—recension, redaction, or original composition. That problem lies entirely beyond the scope of the present work; my only endeavour being to determine what lines are ' best attested ' for this source.

I regret the need of leaving this question open, for its solution would probably save the discussion of the question to which I must next turn—the possibility that in addition to the one main stream of tradition, there may have been minor confluents.

(1) We have already seen how a certain amount of pre-Aristarchean material seeped into the later vulgate; it seems natural therefore to assume that there may have been at Athens a similar carry-over from pre-Pisistratean times. In reality nothing of the sort is to be expected, because the conditions are essentially different. In the one case there was a whole body of literature about Homer, and the scholia to serve as a channel of communication; in the other case we have no warrant for assuming anything of the kind. To be sure, Wolf (*Vorlesungen*, p. 16) did conceive the margins of the Pisistratean edition as filled with variants. But on Bethe's theory of the origin of the poems the thing is impossible, and on any theory most unlikely; for the purpose of Pisistratus' edition was not historical, but artistic—to get for the Panathenaia as good a poem as possible.

---

[1] It is convenient to have for it a short designation, and I shall speak of it as the edition of Pisistratus; it was made in or about his day, and is the nucleus of fact that has led to the association of his name with the Homeric text.

(2) There is, indeed, one curious bit of evidence which seems to show a pre-Pisistratean text cropping out in the third century. Hipponax, fragm. 85. 3–4 (Bergk), runs as follows :

ἔννεφ᾽, ὅπως ψηφῖδι ⟨κακὸς⟩ κακὸν οἶτον ὄληται
βουλῇ δημοσίῃ παρὰ θῖν᾽ ἁλὸς ἀτρυγέτοιο.

Parody of Homer is evident, and we may notice that the phrases parodied are not found in conjunction in our Homer. That is no matter for surprise, but it is surprising to find them joined in the plus verses that follow Θ 202 in 3 a. PHeid. 1261 :

οἵ κεν δὴ κακὸν οἶτον ἀναπλήσαντες ὄλωνται
ἀνδρὸς ἑνὸς ῥιπῇ· ὁ δὲ μαίνεται οὐκέτ᾽ ἀνεκτῶς,
Ἕκτωρ, ὃς τάχα νῆας ἐνιπρήσει πυρὶ κηλέῳ,
δηιώσας Δαναοὺς παρὰ θῖν᾽ ἁλὸς ἀτρυγέτοιο.

At first blush that might tempt one to assume that the author of this interpolation had before him the text as known to Hipponax ; but Gerhard, who first observed the correspondence, was wiser, and hesitated to claim that the coincidence was anything more than accidental. In this he was clearly correct, for the plus verses are obviously patchwork. The first of the phrases parodied has a closer parallel in Γ 417 κακὸν οἶτον ὄληαι, while the second is familiar from Α 316, 327, κ 179, and it is upon these (or rather their forerunners) that Hipponax drew. There is no reason to believe even that he found the phrases in juxtaposition in his Homer.

(3) There is linguistic evidence for Ionic influence upon the text in post-Pisistratean times. Clearest and most widespread is the orthographic change from εο to ευ to designate the diphthong resulting from the contraction of ε and ο, a change which I have discussed in CP 18 (1923). 170–7, developing a suggestion of Meister. In Ionic inscriptions this orthography is not found until the fourth century, and in the Homeric text its beginnings can be placed no earlier. It must have started, more or less sporadically at first, in some MSS., and afterwards have been regularized—no doubt by Zenodotus. A number of forms ἑστεῶτα, -τε, -τες, εἰδέω adduced by Wackernagel (SU 72 f.), and πεπτεῶτα(ς), κτεῶμεν, ἑῶμεν cited by Meister (HK 189), are best taken as showing this late Ionic influence also, though they cannot be dated so closely. Finally there are a number of Ionicizing variants found only in a

part of the tradition—chiefly in the text of Zenodotus; of them Wackernagel cites ἐμεωυτόν, ἑωυτήν, ἐπιστέαται, πεποιέαται, ὦλλοι, δένδρει, γήρει.

Wackernagel's explanation is the use of MSS. 'die etwa aus ionischen Städten kamen'—a very probable explanation, and yet one that assumes more than it is strictly necessary to assume. From the fifth century onwards Ionic influences were strong enough at Athens (cf. Thumb, *HGD* 365 ff.) to leave their mark upon Attic language and literature; and it would be only natural for them to appear also in copies of an old Ionic document made in Athens. Still, I have neither wish nor need to question the existence of such Ionic MSS., but the problem of their source remains. Wackernagel (61) speaks of ' einen ionischen Nebenstrom der Überlieferung', but the question needs to be put more precisely. Are we to understand that a new affluent has joined the main stream, or has that current for a time divided, the channel of one branch running through foreign soil? The latter is in my opinion the correct view: these later Ionic MSS. will have come from the edition of Pisistratus.

(4) To show that, I may start from the opposite opinion of Kirchhoff[1], who has, in his discussion of λ 602–3, made use of the broadest argument that can be brought to bear against my position. The belief in 'Attic interpolations' can, he thinks, have been suggested only by the fact that they were to be found in Attic MSS. alone. But Lachmann (31 f.) had already anticipated and refuted that argument: no one of those who assumed 'Attic interpolations' could point to MSS. that were free of them. Afterwards Wilamowitz (*HU* 235 ff.) developed and clinched the proof: even in the fourth century Dieuchidas could find no version of the *Catalogue* except the Attic one. In Zenodotus the Ionic linguistic influence was at its height, but we do not hear that a single line[2]

---

[1] Compare p. 232 for his conviction ' dass die handschriftlichen Exemplare, über welche die alexandrinischen Kritiker verfügten, keinesweges ohne Ausnahme aus dem Pisistratischen geflossen waren, sondern dass unter ihnen sich auch solche befanden, welche auf eine von diesem unabhängige Quelle zurückgingen '.

[2] His variant in γ 307 ἀπὸ Φωκήων is ascribed by La Roche, *HTk* 15 f. to a source free from Attic influence, while Wilamowitz (*HU* 260) thinks it an emendation. The matter is obviously too small to require discussion in this connexion; nor do lines like A 265, B 558, that cannot be traced even to Aristarchus, come into consideration here.

of the 'Attic interpolations' was absent from his text; on the contrary he must have read *B* 546–56, as he athetized three lines from this section. Zenodotus' MSS. were tinged with late Ionicisms, but they were nevertheless descended from the Pisistratean edition. When, therefore, Zenodotus offers the original, Aristarchus an interpolated text, we must not believe with Wecklein (*ZAV* 5, *ZuA* 3, *et passim*) that the interpolation was brought into the tradition through the edition of Pisistratus, but assign it to some later period.

There remains then but one consideration that can be urged against the assumption of a single source for the tradition of our text; but that question is so large that it seems better to devote to it a separate section.

§ 3. The 'City' Editions.

The mention in the scholia[1] of certain editions that bore the names of cities must always have been a predisposing cause to a belief in the existence of non-Attic texts. It is probably because so little is known of these editions that they have made such an appeal to the imagination. They have been pictured as official documents made at public cost, or preserved in public archives; they have been dated before Pisistratus, shortly after his time, or somewhere between him and Zenodotus; they have been cited too as evidence for the energy with which the Alexandrian critics searched the Greek world from Marseilles to Sinope for MSS. of Homer. Protests against such views from Wolf onwards have not been lacking; but they have not carried conviction sufficiently to exempt me from a discussion of the question. Ludwich's conclusion that owing to the lack of information we must remain uncertain about the date and source of these editions would probably find to-day the most supporters, but I believe that it is possible to advance beyond it.

A good deal of the power exercised upon us by these city editions comes from the suggestive influence of their class name,

---

[1] The unfortunately scanty material has been collected by La Roche, *HTk* 16–49; Ludwich, *AHT* i. 3–15; add from the Ammonius commentary (POxy. 221) the citation (vi. 16) of ἡ κατ' Εὐριπίδην, and of the omission of Φ 290–2 in ἡ Κρητική, the latter on the authority of Seleucus.

αἱ κατὰ πόλεις, αἱ (ἀπό, διά, ἐκ) τῶν πόλεων, αἱ πολιτικαί. These phrases, I must recall, have no better authority than the epitomator of the scholia, who in the last books of the *Iliad* is at times too lazy to be more precise. The contrasting term is αἱ κατ᾽ ἄνδρα, to include the editions or manuscripts that were designated by the name of an individual. The texts of both classes must be considered together—for they seem to be on a par—and it is convenient to begin with the second.

It includes the editions of Aristophanes, of Rhianus (*c.* 250–200), and those of Sosigenes and Philemon, who are apparently somewhat later than Rhianus. The originals of all these were accessible to Aristarchus, but the edition of Zenodotus he seems to have known only through copies—τὰ Ζηνοδότεια, *sc.* ἀντίγραφα. That fact alone must make us wary of assuming that he could consult still earlier editions, and there are besides other indications to warrant such hesitation. The edition of the *Odyssey* by Aratus, a contemporary of Zenodotus, is never mentioned (cf. La Roche, *HTk* 43) in the scholia; nor is the edition by Aristotle. It is Plutarch (*Alex.* c. viii) and Strabo (xiii. 594) who speak of the latter; but what the Alexandrians knew of Aristotle's text came not from his edition, but from his other works; cf. La Roche, *HTk* 23 ff.; Ludwich, *AHT* ii. 433 n.

The remaining two of the κατ᾽ ἄνδρα editions seem to be earlier than Zenodotus, but in each case there are reasons which make such a dating difficult, to say the least.

There is the edition of Euripides which is ascribed not to the tragic poet but to his (or another's) nephew, and even then with a doubt—εἰ μὴ ἄρα ἑτέρου ἐστίν. All that we know of it is that it contained after B 848 and 866 plus verses—much the sort of interpolation found in Ptolemaic papyri, and suggestive of the idea that it was of no earlier date. The edition, which (cf. Ludwich, *AHT* i. 4) no evidence connects with Aristarchus, is never mentioned in the A scholia, but only in the other branch of the tradition. Finsler, *Homer*[2], i. 349, and Bassett, *Harvard Studies*, 31 (1920). 56, have already given reasons for believing that this branch of the scholia contains Pergamene elements; and I hope to show also that Pergamene work is the most probable source for the plus verses preserved in the T scholia. All of this points to Pergamum as the

abode of this edition ; we may suspect that it was one of the great treasures of its library—and a forgery.

The rival library at Alexandria possessed an edition[1] of Antimachus, which is of interest here only on the chance that it belonged to the famous poet Antimachus of Colophon. The scholia cite the poet,[2] as they would do of course in either event; but they neither indicate that the MS. was his, nor do they distinguish between two men of the same name. The need for a distinction seems greater to us than it would to Didymus and Aristonicus, for each of them was dealing chiefly with one man; and besides the epitomator would not have been likely to preserve such information, even if he had found it. It becomes then a question of probability whether we are simply confronted by homonyms, or whether one fifth-century text survived and was used by the Alexandrians apparently without recognition of the unique position it held among their sources.

Our experience with texts of this class cannot lead us to expect for the κατὰ πόλεις editions any great age. For one of them, ἡ Κρητική, the opposite is indicated. Ludwich (AHT i. 4), noting that the only citation of it (at A 381) came from Seleukos, was inclined to assume that it was not used by Aristarchus. Since then the discovery of the Ammonius commentary has brought us another citation of this text and again on the same authority, thus tending to strengthen Ludwich's assumption. Then ἡ Κρητική will best be dated about the time of Aristarchus.[3]

A study of the variants in the κατὰ πόλεις texts led Roemer, Zenod. 24, to declare that the belief an ihr ehrwürdiges Alter becomes more and more shaken the more one examines them. Nevertheless he concludes (p. 31) that ἡ Μασσαλιωτική, ἡ Χία, and perhaps ἡ Ἀργολική, were earlier than Zenodotus. I should ascribe to them a later date.

---

[1] The references in Ludwich, AHT i. 3, must be supplemented from La Roche, HTk 22 ; our information comes through Didymus.

[2] There is added: ὁ Κολοφώνιος A 1 (ς A), E 389 (ς D), and ἐν τῇ Λυδῇ Z 200 (ς B) ; other clear examples at B 2, Δ 439, Ε 499.

[3] Cf. Ludwich, AHT i. 7, for reasons to class with it ἡ πολύστιχος, ἡ κυκλική, and ἡ ἐκ Μουσείου. The scholia on a 424 might seem to indicate that ἡ Ἀργολική was later than Aristophanes ; but I do not believe the argument would hold.

In early texts from Ionia we should expect Ionicisms. We find not only nothing of the sort, but some features that are distinctly un-Ionic : thus iteratives are supplanted by other forms ὀτρύνεσκον Ω 109 (ὀτρύνουσιν, Chia, Mass.), νεικείεσκον T 86 (νεικείουσιν, Chia) ; for ἐρχθέντα Φ 282 is read εἰρχθέντα in the Massaliotike ; and for λωτοῦντα M 283 the hyper-Ionic λωτεῦντα by the same MS. Such variants are about on a par with the Atticisms of the Ptolemaic papyri (cf. Gerhard, 20 n.), and point perhaps to Alexandria as the place of origin. The orthography ὄρευς (Chia, Mass.) Γ 10 gives as a *terminus post quem* the fourth century ; while μῆς (Chia) T 117 is an example of the interchange of η and ει, which is not frequently attested (cf. Menrad, *Münch. Sitzb.* 1894, 176) until the second century, though an example in the third century (cf. Gerhard on X 99) is now quotable. A date towards the close of the third century seems therefore most probable.

If we look to the contents of these editions they seem also to hold an intermediate position between Aristarchus and Zenodotus. Every line in them [1] was read by Aristarchus except T 76-7, for which he had and preferred another version of equal length. Whenever, as at P 134-6, Σ 39-49, α 97–101, these texts differed, he followed the longer version, which seems also to have had the majority of them in its favour. As compared with Zenodotus they are longer texts, having every line of his and others besides. Only once (P 134-6), or perhaps twice (Σ 39-49), does one of them, and then only one of them, agree with Zenodotus in not attesting lines which were afterwards accepted by Aristarchus. In one passage (T 76 f.) we can watch the text grow. Zenodotus read a single line :

τοῖσι δ' ἀνιστάμενος μετέφη κρείων Ἀγαμέμνων.

The Massaliotike and Chia add a tasteless verse to recall that Agamemnon was wounded :

τοῖσι δ' ἀνιστάμενος μετέφη κρείων Ἀγαμέμνων
μῆνιν ἀναστενάχων καὶ ὑφ' ἕλκεος ἄλγεα πάσχων.

Aristophanes and Aristarchus preferred a version :

τοῖσι δὲ καὶ μετέειπε ἄναξ ἀνδρῶν Ἀγαμέμνων
αὐτόθεν ἐξ ἕδρης, οὐδ' ἐν μέσσοισιν ἀναστάς·

which proclaims itself as still younger by polemicizing against this.

---

[1] Only an emendation of Ludwich's—clever but erroneous—puts α 424ᵃ into ἡ Ἀργολική.

These facts seem to me to point all in one direction: the κατὰ πόλεις editions were the sort of text that would have been put out at Alexandria somewhat before 200 B.C. with the approbation of the Museum—parallels to the texts published on the basis of Aristarchus' edition in the next century. In PHibeh 20 I would recognize a text of this type ; cf. the editors' remark ' owing to the rarity of additional lines 20 can hardly be placed in the same class as the other Homeric papyri ' of the Ptolemaic period. No doubt they were carefully written texts, worthy to be consulted in matters of orthography and syntax ; and apparently these are the questions in which the Aristarcheans valued their testimony. Naturally enough we hear chiefly of the mistakes from which they would not be free—a fact that might easily lead to an undue depreciation of them.

Against these considerations nothing can be urged except the names given to these texts. It was a natural supposition of Wolf's (*Proll.* 177 f.) that the name was, in the absence of more definite information, that of the city from which the MS. came to Alexandria. But the supposition leads to difficulties : for either (1) the Alexandrians sent to the ends of the world and brought back MSS. such as they already had ; or (2) they brought home copies so overwhelmingly divergent that they disregarded them except in a few trivial matters ; or (3) the epitomator has recorded these, while consistently disregarding the greater variations. I am not prepared to accept any one of these alternatives.

If an explanation of the names be insisted upon it might be suggested that some editions were prepared for the export trade, and named accordingly. The absence of an Athenian edition could be explained on that basis as easily as (thanks to Ritschl) it is now done on the usual hypothesis.

§ 4. The relative Trustworthiness of the Witnesses.

We are thus brought back to our starting-point—the belief in a single fountain-head for our tradition, and to the problem of determining what are for it the best-attested lines. Then comes the difficulty of estimating the value of conflicting testimony. Mere

numbers will not decide, for usually it is simply witness against witness ; and, when not, we are ignorant of the relations between the witnesses, and how far they may be in collusion.

To say that Aristarchus is more apt to be right than Zenodotus, and then follow him through thick and thin, is an easy but dangerous course. The superiority of Aristarchus is not in his sources, for we have found none of them earlier than Zenodotus ; while a wider collation of later MSS. would be peculiarly likely to increase the number of interpolations. We may imagine as a modern parallel : an edition based on the *codex Venetus* A, and another derived from the later MSS. with their plus verses. Nor can we justify our procedure by our general estimate of the two men ; for our estimate is debatable, and at all events formed from information which is obviously partisan. It would be after all landing in Aristarcholatry, and aligning ourselves with the scholiasts who wrote : the rule is against it ἀλλ' ἐπειδὴ οὕτως δοκεῖ τονίζειν τῷ Ἀριστάρχῳ πειθώμεθα αὐτῷ ὡς πάνυ ἀρίστῳ γραμματικῷ (B 316) and καὶ μᾶλλον πειστέον Ἀριστάρχῳ ἢ τῷ Ἑρμαππία, εἰ καὶ δοκεῖ ἀληθεύειν (Δ 235). The MSS., to be sure, invariably support Aristarchus, but it would be most illogical to appeal to that fact ; for they are derived from Aristarchus, and as Wilamowitz (*Ilias* 8) very neatly puts it : ' Alle Handschriften besagen ja nur, dass Aristophanes[1] diese Fassung aufgenommen hat.'

Nor, on the other hand, can we simply take the earliest form of the tradition. I am not troubled a whit by the fact that it is often represented for us by Zenodotus, whom many would regard as peculiarly suspect. It is merely that we know as a matter of method that the age of a MS., while entitled to consideration, cannot be regarded as an infallible index of its correctness.

Help is to be gained, however, from our study of the later stage of the tradition. There conflicts of testimony were brought about not by the omission, but by the addition of verses. Mechanical blunders barred, each of our MSS. contains the text of Aristarchus together with more or less extraneous material. I would suggest, therefore,

---

[1] Wilamowitz considers Aristarchus as absolutely dependent in such matters on Aristophanes ; cf. 121 'Aristarch, d. h. Aristophanes'. We cannot often (but cf. K 497, O 33, Σ 10-11, 597-8, Ψ 332-3, β 51^{ab}) detect the difference, but that is no reason for obliterating it.

as a working hypothesis, that in the same way each of the pre-Aristarchean MSS. contained the text of Pisistratus, together with the addition of a greater or less number of other verses. If so, Leaf's assertion: 'There is no single case in Homer where the loss of a line can be assumed with reasonable probability; the tradition was wonderfully tenacious of all it had got as well as acquisitive of new matter,' is true in a fuller degree than he intended. His meaning was that every line has reached us in some fashion or other; my meaning is that every line of the genuine text was contained in every edition.

That needs two restrictions. It is the ordinary technique of the interpolators simply to add extra lines; at times, however, they sacrifice a bit of the original text in order to insert the longer version. An example is the sacrifice of *B* 55:

τοὺς ὅ γε συγκαλέσας πυκινὴν ἠρτύνετο βουλήν·

to make room for:

αὐτὰρ ἐπεί ῥ' ἤγερθεν ὁμηγερέες τ' ἐγένοντο
τοῖσι δ' ἀνιστάμενος μετέφη κρείων Ἀγαμέμνων.

Other examples will be collected in the index. In this way a few lines have been ousted from some texts.

This restriction is real, but limited in extent; the other is purely formal—the barring of mechanical blunders. Then, as in later times, there was surface corruption, but we should expect it to be sloughed off rapidly; for a corrector would set it right, or comparison with another MS. would soon lead to its elimination. Even if it persisted, it was not worth recording—unless it could be made to discredit Zenodotus. On him Aristonicus was waging a relentless war, and he has seen fit to note a number of omissions and transpositions of lines that can be due to no other cause. These too will be collected in the index, but I may here illustrate by *A* 446 f.:

ὣς εἰπὼν ἐν χερσὶ τίθει, ὁ δὲ δέξατο χαίρων
παῖδα φίλην. τοὶ δ' ὦκα θεῷ ἱερὴν ἑκατόμβην κτλ.,

where a copyist's eye slipped from the ν in one line to the ν below it, with the result that Zenodotus' text read:

ὣς εἰπὼν τοὶ δ' ὦκα θεῷ ἱερὴν ἑκατόμβην κτλ.,

arrant nonsense, but carefully recorded by Aristonicus.

Such blunders in Zenodotus can be accounted for in two ways.
My first idea was that the fault belonged to the antigraphon used
by Aristonicus, and in part that is no doubt true. Wecklein, however, has put upon the facts a different interpretation. According
to him the MSS. collated by Zenodotus contained the blunders ;
Zenodotus left the text exactly as he found it, and only the wider
collations of his successors brought to light the true readings. The
modern editions I have imagined above would again present parallels.
If my treatment of $\varGamma$ 333 ff. is sound, I have succeeded in verifying
this explanation by showing that a mechanical transposition of lines
passed from some common source both to PHibeh 19 and to
Zenodotus. The important corollary is that Zenodotus then worked
with περιττὴ εὐλάβεια—a quality not usually attributed to him ;
and if he did so work, we can feel more assured than ever of the
conservatism of our tradition, more hopeful of recovering, in its
broad outlines at least, the text of its fountain-head.

§ 5.   The Difficulties encountered by this Hypothesis.

The hypothesis proposed runs counter to certain widely held
opinions, and before proceeding to test it I must examine the
validity of those beliefs.

(1) In 1910 Dietrich Muelder published a noteworthy book *Die
Ilias und ihre Quellen*, in which he undertook to explain the composition of the *Iliad* without assuming that a single line of the
Wolfian vulgate was interpolated. Since then others have followed
more or less closely in his footsteps, some on the basis of one belief,
some on the basis of another ; and by many the interpolation theory
has been viewed as dead. But 'interpolation theory' is an ambi-
guous phrase. In the sense that an *Ur-Ilias* may be found in the
vulgate by the removal of interpolations it is indeed untenable ; but
equally untenable is the belief that the text has been transmitted
from Pisistratus to Ludwich without accretions. For the period
between Aristarchus and Ludwich it is, as I have already shown,
directly disproved by the testimony of the vulgate papyri ; while for
the period before Aristarchus the Ptolemaic papyri both show the
fact of interpolation, and give us the opportunity of forming at least
some idea of its extent.

The longest consecutive text from which an estimate can be formed is the Θ papyrus. Gerhard's table shows that in it ten columns or 300 verses correspond to Θ 8–258, an increase of practically 20 per cent. The Geneva papyrus with 83 lines, covering but 70 of the vulgate, shows a similar increase; in the shorter Dublin fragment (39:36) and in PHibeh 23 (30:28) the increment is only about half as great. The latter ratio (155:140) is found in the last five columns of PGerhard, and rises slightly (62:55) in columns xxv–xxvi, while in columns ii–v (124:118) it drops to 5 per cent. Gerhard's calculations for the intervening columns vi–xxiv, xxvii–xxxiii are based upon assumptions of the lowest possible increment, and are extremely uncertain. PHibeh 19 is composed almost entirely of short fragments, and as a whole (104:91) offers nothing surprising; but the difference between the fragments of B (45:44) and those of Γ (59:47) is a good illustration of the dangers in regarding scattered fragments as fair samples of the whole.

The enthusiasm with which the longer texts were welcomed, when the discoveries first began, encountered in Ludwich's *Die Homervulgata als voralexandrinisch erwiesen* (Leipzig, 1898) a strong opposition. Many ideas of the book require modification, but the point of interest here—the character of this increment—carried conviction rapidly. In 1906 Grenfell and Hunt already saw (*Hibeh Papyri*, i. 75) that 'the new lines are in many cases no doubt interpolated from other portions of the poems', and in the remaining cases 'are often due to the unconscious influence of parallel passages'. Five years later Gerhard (4) could speak more positively: 'Die schon früher konstatierte Wertlosigkeit der Plusverse wird durch das neue Material vollkommen bestätigt. Sie kennzeichnen sich durchweg als unecht und störend.' The matter needs at this point no further discussion, even though Grenfell, *JHS* 39 (1919). 18, has written: 'But even Homer sometimes nodded, and since the repetitions are already so numerous in his poems, a few more, though displeasing to our literary taste, may nevertheless be primitive.'

For those who would deny all interpolations there is then left but one line of argument: to maintain that in the midst of all this interpolation the text of Aristarchus alone remained unaffected. It is a counsel of desperation; for it ascribes to Aristarchus superhuman powers as a critic, and in the same breath denies his conclusions.

According to Geppert, *ap.* Drerup i. 85, the great Alexandrian athetized 851 lines in the *Iliad* and 315 in the *Odyssey*—K and ψ 297-ω 548 not being counted. These atheteses may possibly mean at times no more than the *cruces* of a modern text; cf. Ludwich, *RhM* 69 (1914). 710, 725; but in the main they indicate Aristarchus' belief that the lines athetized were interpolated.

(2) There is another belief which, without being formulated explicitly, permeates much of the criticism of the Homeric poems; the belief that the presumptions run regularly in favour of the longer text. It has two roots, of which the first is the practice, already criticized, of using the MSS. derived from Aristarchus to corroborate the testimony of Aristarchus. For in the large majority of the cases in dispute his text is the longer text, and there was thus created a fictitious preponderance of testimony in its favour. The second root was a belief that the Homeric text had been hacked at repeatedly in the course of its tradition. This hacking may, in my opinion, be denied.

(*a*) The charge is brought first against the Alexandrian critics, and its discussion must begin with the distinction between ἀθετεῖν and οὐ γράφειν. The confusion about the meaning of ἀθέτησις goes back at least to Heyne, but even forty years ago Ludwich could complain of the need of discussing it;[1] and in spite of the clearness of his discussion, the matter is not yet universally understood.[2] I see nothing to be gained, however, by a reiteration of the argument, and will merely state my understanding of the term: ἀθετεῖν is to put a mark (ὀβελός) before a line of the text to indicate that it was believed by the editor to be unhomeric. There was no intention to shorten the text (the obelus is not a mark of cancellation in that sense), nor is there reason to believe that a shortening ever resulted. Such shortenings were, however, assumed (cf. above, p. 5 f.), and those who did so expected, logically enough, that the

---

[1] Heyne, iii, pp. lv f.: 'qua voce quid sibi vellent, grammatici ne ipsi quidem notiones certas habuisse videntur.' Ludwich, *AHT* ii. 133 n.: 'Es sollte eigentlich unnötig sein dergleichen elementare Dinge noch besonders zur Sprache zu bringen; leider ist es das aber nicht.'

[2] Roemer's *Aristarchs Athetesen* (*passim*) and Allen's *Catalogue* will furnish examples. In the latter *om. Zen.* has supplanted at B 641-2, 686-94 the correct *ath. Zen.* of the Oxford text; consequently Zenodotus' reading is cited for a line (690) that 'was not in his text'. Conversely Aristarchus is said (p. 56) to have 'athetized' a line (B 558) known to have been absent from his text.

papyri would sometimes drop lines athetized by Aristarchus. The vulgate papyri discovered now cover a little over half of the two poems (some 15,000 lines), and have failed to produce a single example in accord with this expectation.

Something obviously different is meant when it is declared that an editor did not write (οὐκ ἔγραφεν) certain lines, or that they were not (οὐκ ἦσαν, οὐκ ἐφέροντο) in his text. Wolf saw this and very properly endeavoured to draw a distinction. But most unfortunately he coined a term [1] '*litura seu falx*' which suggests, and was meant to suggest, that the lines in question were first established in the text and afterwards pruned away by the critic. Clearly, as Wolf himself saw,[2] this is not the only possible explanation ; and a study of the question will, I believe, lead to the conclusion that it is not the correct one.

It is difficult enough to report with perfect objectivity the variants of a text. The trouble starts with the fact that words shift their meanings ; and so even the best of modern editors will (and should) write *omittunt* in cases for which, if taken *au pied de la lettre, non habent* would be a more precise expression. A taste for variety in style or for the strong language of polemics will increase the trouble enormously. In the statements about the Homeric text that have come down to us all of these factors are involved, and we must be on our guard against accepting them too naïvely.

A good illustration is furnished by the two cases in which it is Aristarchus who has thus been discredited. Plutarch (*poet. aud.* 26ᶠ) quotes four verses of which he says Ἀρίσταρχος ἐξεῖλε ταῦτα τὰ ἔπη φοβηθείς, and Athenaeus (v. 181ᶜ) introduces another quotation with the statement ὁ δ' Ἀρίσταρχος . . . τοῦ Κρητικοῦ χοροῦ τὸν ᾠδὸν ἐξεῖλεν ἐπιτεμὼν τὰ ποιήματα τὸν τρόπον τοῦτον. Both times the verses, I 458–61, Σ 604/5, said to have been 'removed' by Aristarchus, are found in none of our MSS. In these statements we must, however, distinguish between fact and theory. Plutarch

---

[1] *Proll.* 257 f., and cf. Wecklein's criticism, *ZAV* 63 n., of the term : 'ebenso schief wie der von Lehrs *eiecisse*.'

[2] *Proll.* 222 n. 93 Aristophanes added ' eos quoque versus quos Z. vel deleverat vel in codd. suis non invenerat ' ; of those who charged Zenodotus with altering the text (p. 210) 'nusquam satis distinguunt quid ipse de suo invexerit, quid olim vulgatum invenerit ' ; *ib.* n. 80 shows that he is not caught by their apparent definiteness of phraseology.

and Athenaeus knew evidently the vulgate text, perhaps also that
Aristarchus was responsible for it ; and besides, directly or indirectly,
they knew a longer text.   These are facts to which they are competent to testify, and we find that we have no reason[1] to dispute
them.   The rest, though stated as fact (ἐξεῖλεν, ἐξεῖλεν ἐπιτεμών),
can be nothing but theory—an effort to give a rational explanation
for the existence of the two texts.   Intrinsically it is no better
than an aitiological legend ; for it is inconsistent with the character
of Aristarchus, and with the treatment of δ 15–19 ascribed to him
by Athenaeus in this very passage.

Now the Aristarcheans, or at least one of them, did the same
sort of thing, only the target for their attack was not Aristarchus.
Zenodotus is the person against whom such charges are levelled in
the scholia, and only Zenodotus.   Whenever lines are ' omitted '
by Rhianus, or by Aristophanes, or by the κατὰ πόλεις texts, the
statements are purely objective.   Similar statements are made also
of Zenodotus, but by their side are others which assume that he had
before him the Aristarchean text and arbitrarily changed it.   In
the large majority of cases the statements of this type come to us
clearly from Aristonicus ; so much so that it is justifiable to ascribe
to him the others, holding the epitomator responsible for any apparent deviation.

The vocabulary used by Aristonicus in this polemic is rich and needs to be
examined in detail.

Porson (ѕ λ 525) defined περιγράφειν etymologically as ' lineis voces inclu-
dere et sic delendas monere ', noting also that it shifts to an equivalent of *delere*.
Heyne renders it (Θ 493) by *tollere*; while Wolf, *Proll.* 201, n. 72, Ludwich,
AHT ii. 134, Wecklein, *ZAV* 63, believe that it is a synonym for ἀθετεῖν.   The
difference lay according to them in the form of the mark, which was a sort of
bracket more convenient in dealing with long passages.   Still, as Ludwich noted,
the word is used also with reference to single lines; also it seems strange that
Aristarchus should not have taken over this symbol as well as the ὀβελός from
his predecessor, and perhaps still more strange that Aristonicus should have
recorded such a trivial matter.   I take the word to mean *delere*, ' cancel ', ' strike
out ', and regard its use by Aristonicus as a perfect parallel to that of ἐξεῖλεν by
Plutarch and Athenaeus.

One passage, Π 432–58, demands this interpretation, for to Aristonicus'

---

[1] Forty years ago Ludwich (*AHT* i. 439) could suggest that ἐξεῖλεν was carelessly
used for ἠθέτησεν ; but the suggestion runs counter to all that we now know of the
relationship between our MSS. and Aristarchus.

καθόλου περιγράφει corresponds an οὐκ ἦν in the report of Didymus; and it is unfortunately the only passage in which we can check one by the other. At B 156–67 Aristonicus' statement is so full and explicit (οὕτως ἐπισυντέτμηκεν . . . καθόλου τὸν τῆς "Ηρας λόγον περιγράψας) that it is difficult to believe that he is merely recording an athetesis. Yet this is supposed to be established by the fact that at line 161 Zenodotus' reading 'Αργείην θ' 'Ελένην is recorded : and at B 111 a similar argument is adduced to show that οὕτω συντέμνει cannot there attest an actual omission. I think there is a simple explanation: both times there are (B 177, I 18) later repetitions of the line, the Aristarcheans naturally wish to discuss the text at the first occurrence, part of the evidence is Zenodotus' text of the parallel passage, and the epitomator thinks the resulting precision of statement unnecessarily troublesome. The same principle will apply to Λ 799 = Π 41, and Ξ 95 = P 173; but in these passages there are further complications, due to corruptions of the scholia.

The examples at Θ 493–6, Λ 794–803 (if this be the extent of the passage), γ 400–1, require no comment. At B 489 the vagueness must be due to the epitomator, and no more can be understood than that Zenodotus ' omitted ' some lines in this neighbourhood. At σ 115–16 διὸ περιγράφονται is taken by Ludwich and Roemer (AAH 234) as merely equivalent to ἀθετοῦνται. I think it comes from a condensation of two statements that Zenodotus omitted (περιέγραψε), and Aristarchus athetized the lines. There remains one exception to prove the rule : of λ 525 Aristonicus says περιγραπτέον ὡς ἀπρεπῆ, meaning, not that the line should be athetized, but that it should be deleted. It did not stand in the text of Aristarchus, and we may compare his remark παραιτητέον ἐκεῖνον τὸν στίχον τὸν ἐν τῷ καταλόγῳ ὑπό τινων γραφόμενον about another line (B 558) of the same sort.

We can now discuss two emendations. For ὃς γράφει at δ 498 either περιγράφει or οὐ γράφει may be read without difference of meaning; the latter is to be preferred, as closer to the MS. reading. For the clearly corrupt excerpt from Didymus in the T-scholia at O 265, Hiller, Phil. 28 (1869). 106 read : Ζηνόδοτος τοῦτον μόνον ⟨περι⟩γράφει, 'Αρίσταρχος δὲ καὶ τοὺς ἄλλους γ'. The emendation, though widely approved, cannot be right : (1) Zenodotus is not usually more conservative than Aristarchus; (2) the epitomator usually excerpts Aristonicus for Aristarchus, but Didymus for Zenodotus and Aristophanes; (3) περιγράφειν is not used by Didymus; (4) nor is it applied by an Aristarchean to Aristarchus; (5) nor is it equivalent to ἀθετεῖν. Assume a corruption of a most frequent type and read : Ζηνόδοτος τοῦτον μόνον γράφει, 'Αριστοφάνης δὲ καὶ τοὺς ἄλλους γ'.

One other usage in the scholia [1] must be noted. If there is occasion to specu-

---

[1] Athenaeus (ii. 39ᵈ) says of Θ 231 ἐπεσημήνατο ὁ γραμματικὸς 'Αρίσταρχος περιγράφειν τὸν στίχον, that is polemical in tone and not cautiously phrased delendum notavit for ut spurium notavit. It seems to have tempted Eustathius to write περιγράφων ἀθετεῖ, which shows a lack of sensitiveness for the terms. When Athenaeus v. 180ᵉ writes Διόδωρος δ' ὁ 'Αριστοφάνειος ὅλον τὸν γάμον (δ 3–19) περιέγραψεν, what he means to assert must remain uncertain. Θ 231 is not quoted by sT at Υ 83, but I hesitate to attach importance to the fact.

late about the merits of a text without certain lines the last element can be expressed in a variety of ways: περιγραφομένων τῶν στίχων γ 244–6; αἱρομένου τούτου, etc. Α 110, Β 76, Γ 395, Ω 6; ἀθετουμένου αὐτοῦ ₅ Τ at Α 110; εἰκότως ⟨ἂν⟩ αὐτοὺς περιαιρεθῆναι η 311–16. So Hephaistion (*ap.* Porphyry, 177. 31 Schr.) could say: δεῖν περιγράφειν ἢ ... (Μ 131–40) ἢ ... (Μ 141–53). The greater freedom of expression is permitted because it is obvious that there is no question of anything but a mental deletion—no actual physical alteration of the text. Ludwich (*AHT* ii. 134) equated ἦρκε and ἠθέτηκε, while Wecklein (*ZAV* 63 n.) finds in οὐκ ἔγραφε its equivalent; the latter seems to me the correct view, if we add to it the recognition of the polemical tone. The clearest example is at Ι 23–31 ὅτι Ζηνόδοτος ἦρκε τοὺς στίχους πρὸς οὐδὲν ἀναγκαῖον, ἀλλ᾽ ἕνεκα τοῦ κατ᾽ ἄλλους τόπους φέρεσθαι. τοιοῦτος δέ ἐστιν ἐπὶ τῶν διφορουμένων. τὴν δὲ συνέπειαν οὕτως ποιεῖ·

> 22 δυσκλέα Ἄργος ἱκέσθαι ⟨ἐπεὶ πολὺν ὤλεσα λαόν⟩.
> * ἤτοι ὅ γ᾽ ὣς εἰπὼν κατ᾽ ἄρ᾽ ἕζετο, θυμὸν ἀχεύων,
> * τοῖσι δ᾽ ἀνιστάμενος μετέφη κρατερὸς Διομήδης.

As Aristophanes and Aristarchus athetized only lines 23–5, Didymus must have been forced to divide his treatment. Only his first note has reached us παρὰ τῷ Ζηνοδότῳ οὐκ ἐφέροντο οἱ τρεῖς (₅ Τ, cf. Αᵗ), and it proves that these lines were not in the text of Zenodotus. The note on Η 482, Θ 1 in ₅ Α Ζηνόδοτος δὲ καὶ τοῦτον καὶ τὸν πρῶτον τῆς ἑξῆς ῥαψῳδίας ἦρκε (Bekker, εἴρηκεν cod.) στίχον must also refer to an omission; for the notes at Θ 1 ὅτι Ζηνόδοτος μετατίθησι τὴν ἀνατολήν κάτω πρὸς τὸ " οἱ δ᾽ ἄρα δεῖπνον ἕλοντο" and at Θ 53 ὅτι πρὸ τούτου τὴν ἀνατολὴν τίθησι Ζηνόδοτος cannot naturally be made to mean that Zenodotus had the line in both places.

The remaining passages are at Π 89 ὅτι Ζηνόδοτος τοῦτον καὶ τὸν ἑξῆς ἦρκεν, πεποίηκε δὲ οὕτως " μὴ σύ γ᾽ ἀγαλλόμενος πολέμῳ καὶ δηϊοτῆτι" ἵν᾽ ἐπιβάλλῃ ἡ συνέπεια and at Π 93 ὅτι Ζηνόδοτος κατὰ τὸ ἑξῆς τέσσαρας ἀπὸ τούτου ἦρκε, γράφει δὲ ἀντὶ αὐτῶν τοῦτον·

> μή σ᾽ ἀπογυμνωθέντα λάβῃ κορυθαίολος Ἕκτωρ.

In both cases the phraseology points clearly to the absence of these lines from Zenodotus' text. In contradiction the T-scholia say: τοὺς β᾽ ἀθετεῖ Ζηνόδοτος and τοὺς δ᾽ ἀθετεῖ Ζηνόδοτος καὶ ἀντ᾽ αὐτῶν γράφει κτλ., which I regard as a later misuse of ἀθετεῖν. As a parallel I may cite ₅ Α at Τ 387 ὅτι ἐνταῦθα μὲν αὐτοὺς (388–91) Ζηνόδοτος καταλέλοιπεν, ἐπὶ δὲ Πατρόκλου (Π 141–4) ἠθέτηκεν. Here ἠθέτηκεν must be condensed or corrupted from ἦρκεν τὸν πρὸ αὐτῶν ἀθετήσας; not only is the antithesis to καταλέλοιπεν then properly expressed, but the statement is also in harmony with the facts as told (₅ Αᵗ at Π 140) by Didymus. Another example is to be found at Φ 195, which Aristonicus declares was not to be found in the text of Zenodotus: ὅτι Ζηνόδοτος οὐκ ἔγραφε (₅ Α), Ἀριστόνικος ὅτι Ζηνόδοτος οὐ γράφει τὸν στίχον (₅ G). Nevertheless another note in ₅ G runs, as emended by Nicole: ὅτι Ζηνόδοτος τοῦτον ἠθέτηκεν ἄρας which must be corrupt for τοῦτον ἦρκεν. There can be no question of an ὀβελός in the margin of Zenodotus' edition. Comparison should be made also with the περιγράφων ἀθετεῖ (Θ 231) of

Eustathius; and with ἀθετουμένου ƨ T, corresponding to αἱρομένου ƨ A at A 110. Then in spite of Aristonicus' ἠθέτηκε we may believe that Γ 334–5 were not read by Zenodotus and suspect the same of B 227–8.

Another of these polemical terms is περιῄρηκε (περιῄρει): in γ 230 f. οὗτος ὁ στίχος λαγαρός ἐστι· διὸ Ζηνόδοτος ἴσως μετέγραφε . . . τὸν δὲ δεύτερον περιῄρει τελέως the emphatic language suggests that we are dealing with an omission. Other examples occur at I 14–16, II 677; compare also the use of ἐξεῖλεν by Athenaeus and Plutarch, and of ἐξαιροῦντες by Crates (ƨ G. at Φ 195), all clearly referring to omissions.

I should include also (ἐπι)συντέμνειν, A 446 f., B 60–70, 111–18, 156–67, though Ludwich (AHT ii. 18, 134) and Wilamowitz (Ilias, 267 n.) are of the opposite opinion. I should note the combination with περιγράψας in B 156–67, and the use of ἐπιτεμών by Athenaeus; the chief difficulty (citation of Zenodotean readings at B 111, 161) I have already discussed.

Finally, I may note Aristonicus' statements at A 219–20, Ζηνόδοτος μεταγράφει . . . καὶ τοὺς δύο ἕνα ἐποίησεν, and at Γ 423–6, Ζηνόδοτος μετετίθει τὴν συνέπειαν οὕτως, which are less acid in tone.

One of these words supports the other: if they are merely innocent synonyms for ἀθετεῖν, it is impossible to explain why Aristonicus alone uses them, and why he uses them only of Zenodotus. If the polemical tone is recognized, the question narrows to whether the polemical spirit would be excited by atheteses as well as by omissions. The former is unlikely, for Aristonicus and his schoolmates were in no position to use harsh language about the use of the ὀβελός—to say that a man who applied it ' cancelled ', ' lifted ', ' took away ', lines, or ' cut down ' the text. Besides, whatever evidence there is (Didymus at I 23–5, II 141–4, 432–58, Aristonicus' own phraseology at A 219–20, 446–7, B 60–70, 111–18, 156–67, Γ 423–6, Θ 1, I 23–31, II 89, 93) points in the other direction. I consider it therefore best to understand that the lines of which Aristonicus speaks in this fashion were not to be found in the text of Zenodotus.

For Aristonicus we must make the same distinction that we have made for Plutarch and Athenaeus. To the readings of Zenodotus' text he is competent to testify—allowance being made for possible corruptions in his ἀντίγραφα; but about the origin of these readings he had no information, and on this question the competency of his testimony must be denied. For Zenodotus had left no commentary to his text,[1] and neither his Γλῶσσαι Ὁμηρικαί nor a verbal tradition through Aristophanes can be assumed to have filled the gap. In all the refutations of Zenodotus there is never an appeal[2] from

---

[1] Wolf, Proll. 215 n. 84; Duentzer, Zenod. 36; La Roche, HTk 50; Ludwich, AHT i. 53 n.

[2] Roemer, Zenod. 678 : ' nie auch nur eine leise Andeutung oder einen kurzen Hinweis auf eine Sünde gegen die maasgebenden Handschriften.'

him to the MSS.; and that means either that the tradition supported Zenodotus, or that the Aristarcheans lacked information
about it. Aristonicus' phraseology, for all its strength, can show
no more [1] than the manner in which he endeavoured to rationalize
the facts known to him.

For a time it imposed upon modern scholars, but recently they
have tended to emancipate themselves from its influence. Schwartz
(*Adversaria*, 4) first enunciated clearly and fully the correct principle : Zenodotus 'versus quos in codicibus legit sed spurios esse
iudicavit, non suppressit, sed in contextu reliquit'. Finsler, *Homer*[2],
i. 344 f., followed with the suggestion that the verses ' omitted ' by
Zenodotus and athetized by his successors were in the main interpolations of later date than Zenodotus. Finally Wecklein (*ZAV* 59)
showed that the Zenodotean text is in some forty passages
'ursprünglich und offenbar auf handschriftlicher Überlieferung
beruhend' ; its authority, therefore, must weigh heavily, even when
its superiority is not obviously manifest.

The charges against the Alexandrian critics of hacking at the
text are, then, not supported by competent testimony. They have
grown out of attempts—naïve if innocent—to account for the existence of longer and shorter texts on the assumption that the longer
text is the original. That assumption runs counter to our experience during the whole of the period in which we have more
copious materials for following the transmission of the text. There
are besides more general considerations which deprive these charges
of plausibility. To omit a line is possible in modern times, because
of the critical apparatus in which the line will be duly preserved.
Deprived of that opportunity, an ancient editor was compelled to
act more conservatively ; he could omit only the sort of thing
a modern editor would exclude even from his critical apparatus.
His own interests too would suggest that he should retain the line
and obelize it. His atheteses (recall the often quoted *mutanda
notabit*) made his reputation ; and to drop a line that could be
athetized with obvious propriety was no better than killing the
goose that laid the golden eggs.

(*b*) Schwartz would push the hacking back to the λυτικοί of the
fifth and fourth centuries whose texts were, in his opinion, followed

---

[1] Cf. Ludwich, *AHT* ii. 104 f.

at some points by Zenodotus, while Aristarchus recovered the original version. In antiquity, as far as I can recall, the charge was never laid against them. Aristonicus, to be sure, does charge οἱ βουλόμενοι πρόβλημα ποιεῖν with interpolating Υ 269–72 and with altering in Κ 372 the phraseology; but we cannot argue from this charge to the other, for interpolation is a well-established fact, but the proof of hacking is still to seek.

The *luculentum testimonium* adduced by Schwartz (5) fails to prove the point. Zenodotus, following his MSS., did not read Φ 195, and the behaviour of his MSS. is ascribed to the influence of Megaclides, who in the fourth century 'versum 195 quamvis traditum invenisset, damnavit'. This assertion rests solely on a false expansion of an abbreviation (παρέλῑ̄) of scholia G into παρέλιπον instead of παρέλιπε: cf. Nicole's supplement to the scholia on Φ. The quotation there made from Megaclides is then precisely the same as that made in the Ammonius commentary, ποῖον ῥεῖθρον μεῖζον Ἀχελώου " ἐξ οὗπερ πάντες ποταμοί ". What follows ὥστε παρέλιπε τὸν περὶ τοῦ ʼΩκεανοῦ is merely an inference of the scholiast; and we are left simply with the fact that Zenodotus, Megaclides, and the anonymous poet of the Ammonius commentary had texts in which the Oceanus line did not occur.

Nor can I believe that the λυτικοί would have regarded excision as a satisfactory λύσις; it is certainly not an exhibition of cleverness such as they desired, and would rather have appeared to them a confession of inability. At Κ 372 they are represented not as exposing the falsification of the text but as grappling with the spurious reading; Aristotle, too, gave a λύσις for the παλαιὸν ζήτημα (Κ 253), although he knew (*Poet.* xxv. 1461 a 25) texts that did not contain the line. Apparently the λυτικοί of Plato's time [1] were prepared to interpret anything that then circulated, just as to-day the good Unitarians are prepared to 'defend' any line that Wolf printed. To call Zenodotus *obeli inventor* is only a partial recognition of his service. He seems to have been the first to grasp fully the fact that the MSS. of Homer were interpolated, and that

---

[1] No argument can be based on the phraseology (ἐξαλείψομεν, διαγράφωμεν, ἀποβλητέα, ἀφαιρετέα, ἐξαιρήσομεν) used by Plato, *Rep.* iii. 386 c–387 e. He is speaking not as a critic but as a legislator.

the interpolation must be imagined away before Homer could be understood.

For the sake of argument let us assume that this was not the case and that the λυτικοί did speak and write freely about the need of ejecting or excising certain lines of the poems. It will still be necessary to show that the text was thereby affected. We do not hear of the λυτικοί as editors of Homer; but if they were they would not have stopped their own mouths by removing all traces of these lines which afforded them so easy a triumph. Their pupils and admirers may have written on the margins of their scrolls ἐξαιρετέον, ἀποβλητέον or περιγραπτέον; but the publishers and copyists would have remained unaffected. Verbal variants are on a different footing, since they may be taken for corrections; and it is therefore not surprising that Schwartz has been able to trace a number of readings to this source. The later tradition again offers an instructive parallel; readings of Alexandrine critics have filtered freely into our MSS., while the *obeli* of the same critics have not caused the omission of a single line.

(c) There remains the suspicion that [1] the text has suffered from bowdlerizing. The possibility cannot be denied, and there are cases in which the assumption seems plausible as long as they are considered separately; but when the tradition of the poems is viewed as a whole it seems to me that this plausibility dwindles and vanishes.

Wackernagel (*SU* 224-9) has recently given us an excellent description of the bounds of propriety observed in the Homeric poems; and we may begin by noting that passages the bowdlerizers are supposed to have cut (A 31, I 119 a, 458-61, Π 432-58, θ 334-43) go little if at all beyond these limits. If these lines in *I* are shocking, so is much else in the tale of Phoenix; if the jesting between Hermes and Apollo offends, then the whole lay of Demodocus is offensive. The supposed bowdlerizing shows its effects too sporadically to permit us to regard it as a *vera causa*.

The difficulty will increase on closer examination. Plato objected to the morals of numerous passages, but the tradition is regularly undisturbed; the exception being that Π 432-58 were not read by Zenodotus. Are we to assume that Plato's criticism remained else-

---

[1] Cf. among others Cobet, *MC* 231; Wilamowitz, *Ilias*, 66 n.; Schwartz, 6 f.

where ineffective, but resulted in an excision of this passage, which is one of the least offensive? Again, Plato knows nothing of A 31. Was the text bowdlerized so early and so effectively that the line had vanished without trace by the end of the fifth century, but was somehow resurrected for Aristarchus?

Such difficulties do not exist, if we assume that these lines are interpolated, and I hope to offer below evidence in support of this assumption. Here I may merely recall that there are other 'shocking' lines (Ξ 241^{ab}, 351^a, O 5^a, λ 245) found only in part of the tradition. In their case the disturbance is evidently caused not by bowdlerizing but by interpolation. We have no right to assume that interpolators were always proper, pure-minded people; yet without that assumption we cannot argue that a line is genuine because 'shocking'.

§ 6. The Conclusion.

I may sum up my argument as follows: All MSS. of which we know directly or indirectly descend from a single archetype, and the problem is to determine the lines that it contained. The analogy of other epics [1] leads us to expect repeated interpolations during the transmission of the text, and this expectation is seen to be amply fulfilled, whenever the evidence is full enough to permit us to see clearly. On the other hand, there is no evidence for any shortening of the text either by the Alexandrian critics, by the λυτικοί, or by bowdlers. It follows, therefore, that whenever there are known to have existed longer and shorter versions of a passage the difference between them must be due to interpolation.

If the reasoning is correct, an examination of the passages in the Homeric poems such as defined should show: (1) a number of cases in which the longer version confirms by internal evidence of various sorts our belief that it is interpolated; (2) a number of cases in which such internal evidence is lacking; for interpolators, especially interpolators working with borrowed material, will not always leave finger-prints; (3) a much smaller number of cases in

---

[1] Cf. above, p. 15, and the quotation from John Meier, 'Jeder Kopist ändert das Original wie es der Rezitator auch tut'.

which the shorter version is so obviously bad that it can be nothing but a mechanical blunder; and of these a number (not all) will reveal a reason for the blunder.

The rest of the work will be devoted to an examination of the poems from this point of view. In making it I shall, of course, be compelled to examine also those passages in which there seems to be, but is not, evidence for the existence of two versions.

PART III

THE INTERPOLATIONS IN THE ILIAD

A

THE text proper begins only in line 9 : ὁ γὰρ βασιλῆι χολωθείς, and we hear of various proemia by which it was introduced. These may be noted briefly, although the matter concerns not so much the transmission of the text, as rather its adaptation to various purposes.

The familiar proem of the vulgate is also the one with the earliest attestation—the criticism by Protagoras ὅτι εὔχεσθαι οἰόμενος ἐπιτάττει.[1] It is apparently the one that established itself before the *Iliad* as a separate composition, and is to be compared with the proem of the *Odyssey*. The question of its date will turn upon the interpretation of Διὸς δ᾽ ἐτελείετο βουλή and the relation of this phrase to the *Cypria*, and lies outside the scope of the present book.[2]

---

[1] Aristotle, *Poet.* xix 1456ᵇ 15. The date of the *Iliad* doubled by the insertion of pentameters is indeterminable. Its opening:

Μῆνιν ἄειδε, θεά, Πηληϊάδεω Ἀχιλῆος
Μοῦσα, σὺ γὰρ πάσης πείρατ᾽ ἔχεις σοφίης

is quoted by Hesychius of Miletus, and ascribed to Pigres. Whether Hesychius regarded Pigres as a contemporary of Xerxes or Mausolus is none too clear; but he ascribes to him also the *Batrachomyomachia*. Now as the latter poem cannot be much earlier than the time of Augustus (cf. Wackernagel, *SU*, pp. 188–99) it is obvious, at least, that we have no right to be positive about the date of the other poem. Its very existence is indeed debatable ; cf. Ludwich, *HV* 33 n., and the literature there cited. The similar artifacts of Timolaos and Idaios need not concern us, nor the later and still more curious ones of Nestor and Tryphiodoros.

[2] On Zenodotus' athetesis of lines 4–5 cf. Schwartz, *Advers.* 8 f.; Bethe, *Homer*, i. 311 n. It is difficult to see a reason for the athetesis unless it is due to the absence of the lines from some of the MSS. used by Zenodotus. If so this interpolation will have been made to allude to the Cypria. Schwartz' objection to the separation of ἐξ οὗ from ἄειδε seems well taken.

Two other beginnings of the poem are reported in Osann's *Anecdotum Romanum*. The one given on the authority of Aristoxenus :

Ἔσπετε νῦν μοι, Μοῦσαι Ὀλύμπια δώματ' ἔχουσαι
ὅππως δὴ μῆνίς τε χόλος θ' ἕλε Πηλείωνα
Λητοῦς τ' ἀγλαὸν υἱόν· ὁ γὰρ βασιλῆι χολωθείς

comes clearly from an edition in which *Cypria, Iliad,* and *Little Iliad* had been run together into a consecutive Tale of Troy. The juncture between the two last poems has been preserved also (cf. p. 204) :

ὣς οἵ γ' ἀμφίεπον τάφον Ἕκτορος· ἦλθε δ' Ἀμαζὼν
Ἄρηος θυγάτηρ μεγαλήτορος ἀνδροφόνοιο.

Bethe (*Homer,* ii. 380) well illustrates the former transition by comparing Π 112 f. :

Ἔσπετε νῦν μοι, Μοῦσαι Ὀλύμπια δώματ' ἔχουσαι
ὅππως δὴ πρῶτον πῦρ ἔμπεσε νηυσὶν Ἀχαιῶν.

The other form of opening, said on the authority of Nicanor and of Crates to have been found in ἡ δοκοῦσα ἀρχαία Ἰλιάς that belonged to Apellikon, is incompletely reported. It ran perhaps :

Μούσας ἀείδω καὶ Ἀπόλλωνα κλυτότοξον
⟨Λήτους καὶ Διὸς υἱόν· ὁ γὰρ βασιλῆι χολωθείς⟩

though the transition may have been spun out to greater length. The imitation of the proem of the *Little Iliad* :

Ἴλιον ἀείδω καὶ Δαρδανίην εὔπωλον
ἧς πέρι πολλὰ πάθον Δαναοὶ θεράποντες Ἄρηος.

is obvious, and has entailed the strange quantity of ἀείδω and the unhomeric emphasis on the personality of the poet.[1] It, too, must come from a cyclic edition, but one in which the fusion of the poems had not been carried so far.

The paraphrase of A 17–42 given by Plato (*Rep.* iii. 393 d) seems somewhat condensed, but through it we can see that Plato's text was not closer to Aristarchus than :

ἔνθ' ἄλλοι μὲν πάντες ἐπευφήμησαν Ἀχαιοὶ
αἰδεῖσθαί θ' ἱερῆα καὶ ἀγλαὰ δέχθαι ἄποινα·
ἀλλ' οὐκ Ἀτρείδῃ Ἀγαμέμνονι ἥνδανε θυμῷ,

---

[1] Cf. Bethe, *Homer,* ii. 340. It starts from imitation of the Thebaïs :
Ἄργος ἄειδε θεὰ πολυδίψιον ἔνθεν ἄνακτες.

25 ἀλλὰ κακῶς ἀφίει, κρατερὸν δ' ἐπὶ μῦθον ἔτελλε·
" μή σε, γέρον, κοίλῃσιν ἐγὼ παρὰ νηυσὶ κιχείω
ἢ νῦν δηθύνοντ' ἢ ὕστερον αὖτις ἰόντα,
μή νύ τοι οὐ χραίσμῃ σκῆπτρον καὶ στέμμα θεοῖο.
τὴν δ' ἐγὼ οὐ λύσω· πρίν μιν καὶ γῆρας ἔπεισιν
30 ἡμετέρῳ ἐνὶ οἴκῳ, ἐν Ἄργεϊ, τηλόθι πάτρης.
32 ἀλλ' ἴθι, μή μ' ἐρέθιζε, σαώτερος ὥς κε νέηαι."

31 ἱστὸν ἐποιχομένην καὶ ἐμὸν λέχος ἀντιόωσαν.

It is indeed possible that line 23 was also omitted. One cannot be positive, for it is so insignificant a line that Plato in paraphrasing may have dropped it. I may note, however, that we have no early testimony even for its presence in the vulgate. Papyrus evidence is lacking, and the allusion by Philodemos of Gadara (Ludwich, *HZAD* 7) may refer to A 377, which is possibly the source of our line.

The omission of line 31, however, cannot be ascribed to Plato, such an ἀπρεπές being grist for his mill. There is further evidence against it.[1]

Aristarchus is supposed ordinarily[2] to have athetized lines 29–31 ; cf. Aristonicus, ap. 5 A :

τὴν δ' ἐγὼ οὐ λύσω] ἀθετοῦνται ὅτι ἀναλύουσι τὴν ἐπίτασιν τοῦ νοῦ καὶ τὴν ἀπειλήν. ἡσμένισε γὰρ καὶ ὁ Χρύσης συνούσης (Cobet, εἰπούσης cod.) αὐτῆς τῷ βασιλεῖ. ἀπρεπὲς δὲ καὶ τὸ τὸν Ἀγαμέμνονα τοιαῦτα λέγειν.

Roemer (*AAH* 167 ff.) argues that the athetesis destroys the point of the speech and that the lines are elsewhere (5 Σ 283, Ω 551, γ 117, δ 254) treated as if genuine. The latter is true only of lines 29–30, and it is obvious that the omission of line 31 alone would not spoil the speech. It is also clear that it is solely against line 31 that the argument of the scholium is directed. Furthermore, the scholium stands after that on line 30, a fact which loses little of its significance because the note on line 28 is out of place. I conclude therefore that the lemma is corrupt and that the note began ἀθετεῖται ὅτι ἀναλύει.

---

1 Soph. *Ai.* 491 is not, as claimed by van Leeuwen, an imitation of it.
2 Wackernagel, *SU* 227 n. 3, seems to be an exception.

Combining Aristarchus' athetesis with Plato's omission of the line, I conclude that the critic was in this case guided by MS. evidence, which he then endeavoured to confirm by subjective reasoning. I am not called upon to defend his reasoning, but it is not so absurd as Cobet (*Misc. Crit.* 230) has made appear. Tecmessa found in her position some relief from the misery of the δούλιον ἦμαρ; and weaving (cf. Wolf, *Vorll.* 56) is not so distinctly a menial occupation as the drawing of water.

The interpolation betrays itself by certain verbal peculiarities: only here (cf. La Roche, *Hom. Stud.* § 62. 1) is ἀντιᾶν combined with the accusative; and only here, as Paley noted, is its participle used other than as a future. Contrast Υ 125, Φ 431, α 25, γ 436, ω 56.

69 Κάλχας Θεστορίδης·

Eustathios comments: ὅτι τινές φασιν ἐν τῇ τοῦ Κάλχαντος Ὁμηρικῇ γενεαλογίᾳ στίχους ἐκλελοιπέναι ὁ Πορφύριος ἱστορεῖ, ἐκτιθέμενος καὶ στίχους δύο, ἐν οἷς Εὐβοεύς τε φαίνεται εἶναι καὶ Ἄβαντος ἀπόγονος.

The verses were undoubtedly interpolations. I suspect also that they were to be found not at this point but in the *Catalogue*. Calchas is not there mentioned, and we shall later meet several supplements intended to put into that section all it might reasonably be expected to contain.

Cf. also *Herm.* 14 (1879). 234; Ludwich, *HV* 30; Wecklein, *ZAV* 5.

Achilles' speech to Athena:

> " χρὴ μὲν σφωίτερόν γε, θεά, ἔπος εἰρύσασθαι
> καὶ μάλα περ θυμῷ κεχολωμένον· ὡς γὰρ ἄμεινον.
> 218 ὅς κε θεοῖς ἐπιπείθηται, μάλα τ' ἔκλυον αὐτοῦ."
> *   ὡς εἰπὼν πάλιν ὦσε μέγα ξίφος, οὐδ' ἀπίθησε
> 221 μύθῳ Ἀθηναίης.

219 ἢ καὶ ἐπ' ἀργυρέῃ κώπῃ σχέθε χεῖρα βαρεῖαν,
220 ἂψ δ' ἐς κουλεὸν ὦσε μέγα ξίφος, οὐδ' ἀπίθησε.

The text adopted follows Zenodotus; cf. Aristonicus, ap. ꜱ A: Ζηνόδοτος μεταγράφει . . . καὶ τοὺς δύο ἕνα ἐποίησεν. It is free

from all difficulty ;[1] though Wecklein (ZAV 63) seems alone in his appreciation of it.

For older attempts at the interpretation of the vulgate cf. Chr. Heimreich, *Das erste Buch der Ilias*, Ploen, 1883, p. 9. Recent exegesis may be represented by Leaf, ' He said, and stayed his heavy hand on the silver hilt ', or by Ameis-Hentze-Cauer, ' er hemmte die (das Schwert langsam herausziehende) Hand am Griffe '. Neither fits the situation well ; for if Achilles has been drawing his sword ever since line 194 he has been moving very slowly. His action, I take it, stops at line 199 with his recognition of Pallas Athene ; at all events, he cannot keep on drawing his sword after line 216—the beginning of his submissive speech. But with the vulgate text σχέθε χεῖρα, whatever it may mean, is subsequent to the speech. Leaf's statement, that ' ἦ καὶ always introduces an action coincident with the words ' is a blunder ;[2] cf., for instance, Δ 192 ἦ καὶ Ταλθύβιον, θεῖον κήρυκα, προσηύδα, or Leaf's own note on H 242.

Unsatisfactory as the translation is, it does not give the natural meaning of the lines. With its compounds σχεθέειν is used three times (H 188, Ω 374, ι 294) with χεῖρα, and always in the sense of putting one's hand in such and such a position. This is true also of its use of other parts of the body ; for instance, ξ 494 ἦ καὶ ἐπ' ἀγκῶνος κεφαλὴν σχέθεν, εἶπέ τε μῦθον ; and (except θ 537, which comes under another category) of things, shields, sceptres, booty, held in the hands. The meaning must then be : ' he spoke, and on the silver hilt he laid his heavy hand ' ; and that is obviously unsuited to the context.

But if the vulgate is impossible here it is easy to imagine a context in which it is possible, and that may bring us to the source of the interpolation. In the quarrel over the arms of Achilles the sword of Odysseus is but half drawn when Agamemnon intervenes (cf. the Vienna cylix by Douris, Hoppin i. 269) ; after his speech the king may well have turned and thrust the sword of Odysseus (his

---

[1] We now know (cf. Brugmann-Thumb, p. 602 f.) that the aorist participle need not designate antecedent action.

[2] An inaccessible article by Wähmer, *Ueber ἦ, ὡς φάτο, ὡς εἰπών und verwandte epische Formeln*, Göttingen, 1893, is said to show that subsequent action is regularly indicated by this formula. I have tested the facts for A-M ; one might claim coincident action for Γ 447, E 416, but that would be about all.

intimate friend) back into its sheath:

ἢ καὶ ἐπ' ἀργυρέῃ κώπῃ σχέθε χεῖρα βαρεῖαν
ἂψ δ' ἐς κουλεὸν ὦσε μέγα ξίφος· αὐτὰρ 'Οδυσσεύς.

Furthermore, objection must be raised against ἐς κουλεόν. All other examples μέγα κουλεόν Γ 272, Τ 253, περὶ κουλεόν Λ 30, and κουλεῷ λ 98, at the beginning of the verse can be explained as metrical lengthening. I would follow Boisacq in so explaining it against Schulze, QE 117; Meister, HK 203. Solmsen could find no certain instance of words of the form — ∪ ∪ ∪ changed to — — ∪ ∪, and I could add (AJP 28 (1907). 407 n.), but few instances of word groups, and those from the Odyssey. The use of ἐς κουλεόν may then be regarded as surprising in the Iliad, but not in the Little Iliad.

The vulgate reading is thus not only the worse-attested text, but also intrinsically inferior.

Achilles speaking to Thetis:

ὅτ' ἔφησθα κελαινεφέι Κρονίωνι
οἴη ἐν ἀθανάτοισιν ἀεικέα λοιγὸν ἀμῦναι
ὁππότε μιν ξυνδῆσαι 'Ολύμπιοι ἤθελον ἄλλοι
400   "Ηρη τ' ἠδὲ Ποσειδάων καὶ Παλλὰς 'Αθήνη·
ἀλλὰ σὺ τόν γ' ἐλθοῦσα, θεά, ὑπελύσαο δεσμῶν
ὦχ' ἑκατόγχειρον καλέσασ' ἐς μακρὸν "Ολυμπον,
ὃν Βριάρεων καλέουσι θεοὶ ἄνδρες δέ τε πάντες
Αἰγαίων'· ὁ γὰρ αὖτε βίῃ οὗ πατρὸς ἀμείνων.

400 "Ηρη τ' ἠδὲ Ποσειδάων καὶ Φοῖβος 'Απόλλων. Zenod.
404 Αἰγαίων'· ὁ γὰρ αὖτε βίῃ πολὺ φέρτατος ἦεν
τῶν ὁπόσοι ναίουσ' ὑπὸ Τάρταρον εὐρώεντα. Zenod.

Against line 400 there is evidence that indicates but falls short of proving the existence of texts without it. First it is suspect διὰ τὸ καὶ ἑτέρως φέρεσθαι; then Porphyry (p. 13 Schr.) knew of texts in which it preceded line 399 just as if it had been brought in from the margin.[1]

Zenodotus' variant for line 404 is given as emended by Bentley (Leaf) or Cobet (Ludwich); for other emendations cf. Duentzer,

[1] No stress can be laid on the fact that Dionysius of Halicarnassus (Rhet. ix. 15) ends his quotation with line 399. Unless quoting at second hand he was using the vulgate, for which line 400 is attested by 3 p. PGr.-Eg. ii. 106, and by the Aristarcheans.

Zenod. 158; Ludwich, *AHT* i. 193. The extra line is clearly an interpolation—on a par with other plus verses. Free composition by Zenodotus (cf. Roemer, *Zenod.* 42) is not to be considered, as Wecklein (*ZAV* 73) has seen. The presence of the line accords so badly with what we know of Zenodotus' text as to suggest that the reading of some other scholar [1] has been foisted upon him, or that the copy of his text used by the Aristarcheans had suffered interpolation.

After Odysseus' speech to Chryses:

446 ὣς εἰπὼν ἐν χερσὶ τίθει, ὁ δὲ δέξατο χαίρων
παῖδα φίλην. τοὶ δ' ὦκα θεῷ ἱερὴν ἑκατόμβην
ἑξείης ἔστησαν ἐΰδμητον περὶ βωμόν.

446-7 ὣς εἰπὼν τοὶ δ' ὦκα θεῷ ἱερὴν ἑκατόμβην Zenod.

Wolf (*Proll.* 203) emended the reading of Zenodotus to ὣς εἶπεν. This, though accepted by Ludwich (*AHT* i. 197), Wecklein (*ZAV* 63), is a *Verschlimmbesserung*—ὣς εἶπεν being absolutely un-homeric; cf. Berger, *De Iliadis et Odysseae partibus recentioribus*, Marburg, 1908, p. 47. Zenodotus surely knew enough to produce ὣς ἄρ' ἔφη· τοὶ δ' ὦκα κτλ. had he wished to rewrite the passage—a thing for which (cf. Duentzer, *Hom. Abh.* 194 f.) he could have had no motive.

It is Aristonicus (ap. SA) who records that Zenodotus wrote οὕτως συντετμημένως. He has evidently quoted exactly what he found in his copy of Zenodotus, and that copy had suffered from haplography. The only question is whether he realized [2] that he was criticizing a purely mechanical blunder, and was willing to hawk at such small game. At A 491 a more striking example will be found.

The close of the return from Chryse:

αὐτὰρ ἐπεί ῥ' ἵκοντο κατὰ στρατὸν εὐρὺν Ἀχαιῶν,
485 νῆα μὲν οἵ γε μέλαιναν ἐπ' ἠπείροιο ἔρυσαν
ὑψοῦ ἐπὶ ψαμάθοις, ὑπὸ δ' ἔρματα μακρὰ τάνυσσαν,
αὐτοὶ δ' ἐσκίδναντο κατὰ κλισίας τε νέας τε.

A different text is to be found in 1 *p*. PVitelli; cf. Ludwich, *Phil.*

---

[1] Cf. H. Pusch, *Quaestiones Zenodoteae*, Halle, 1889, for instances of his confusion with Zenodorus, Zenodotus of Mallos, or Zenodotus of Alexandria.

[2] On the tone and unfairness of his polemic against Zenodotus cf. Roemer, *Zenod.* 6 ff., where the problem is broached of how far Aristarchus is implicated.

63 (1904). 473–5; Hefermehl, *Phil.* 66 (1907). 192–201; Cauer, *Grundfr.*³ 44–6. The fragment contains two lines foreign to the vulgate, followed by lines 486–94. Owing to the late date of the papyrus it might seem proper to regard it as a vulgate text that had absorbed from the margin two lines of a parallel passage. Such was apparently the position taken by van Leeuwen, who in his edition ignores this papyrus. It is, however, untenable; for the new lines correspond to Hom. Hymn. iii. 505–6; while our scholia (cf. Allen-Sikes, pp. l, liii f.) are surprisingly silent about the Homeric Hymns. Interpolation from that source (cf. below on o 295) must be earlier than Alexandrian times, and this papyrus must be regarded as a belated survival of a Ptolemaic text.

Disregarding small and practically certain restorations, Hefermehl believes the papyrus read:

484 ⟨αὐτὰρ ἐπεί ῥ' ἵκοντο κατὰ στρατὸν εὐρὺν Ἀχαιῶν
433 ἱστία μὲν στεῖλαντο, θέσαν δ' ἐν νηὶ μελαίνῃ ∽ iii. 503
434 ἱστὸν δ' ἱστοδόκῃ πέλασαν προτόνοισιν ὑφέντες = 504
435 καρπαλίμως, τὴν δ' εἰς ὅρμον προέρεσσαν ἐρετμοῖς.⟩
437 ∽ ἐκ δὲ καὶ αὐτοὶ βάντες ἐπὶ ῥηγμῖνι θαλάσσης ∽ 505
485 ∽ ἐξ ἁλὸς ἤπειρον δὲ θοὴν ἀνὰ νῆ' ἐρύσαντο ∽ 506
486 ∽ ὑψοῦ ἐπὶ ψαμάθῳ παρὰ δ' ἔρματα μακρὰ τάνυσσαν = 507
487 αὐτοὶ δ' ἐσκίδναντο κατὰ κλισίας τε νέας τε.

Cauer in the main agrees, and there is no reason to doubt that the papyrus—if presenting a fairly reasonable text—read something like this. Only, against Hefermehl, I should increase the correspondence to the Hymn by reading: ἱστία μὲν πρῶτον κάθεσαν, λύσαν δὲ βοείας (βοῆας), and by not restoring the equivalent of A 435, which clearly looks forward to the mooring of the ship, not the drawing of it up on the land.

Hefermehl further assumes that the papyrus contained a shorter account of the landing at Chryse—just what is not stated, and would have proved hard to define. His assumed text is supposed to possess two merits: (1) it is free from a feature—the dismantling of the ship for a one-night stop—which previous critics had found absurd;[1] (2) it furnishes a simpler explanation for the composition

---

[1] Cf. Haesecke, *Die Entstehung des ersten Buches der Ilias*, Rinteln, 1881, pp. 5 f.; Hinrichs, ' Die Homerische Chryseisepisode,' *Hermes*, 17 (1882). 108. Wiser views are now expressed by Bethe, *Homer*, i. 180; Cauer, *Grundfr.*³ 45.

of the Hymn to Apollo.   Hefermehl therefore claims that the papyrus has preserved the original Homeric text.

Against this Cauer argues briefly but convincingly, while Wilamowitz (*Ilias*, 257 n.) sees no need for argument.   I wish to point out that Hefermehl's view is in conflict with our knowledge of the transmission of the text : (1) no other papyrus has the value claimed for this one; (2) no papyrus presents a parallel for the assumed shorter account of the landing at Chryse ; (3) the cutting down of the vulgate *A* 484-7 from a longer and better text is also without parallel.

If the papyrus teaches us anything about the Homeric text it is in a roundabout fashion.   Wecklein (*ZAV* 38 f., 78 f.) has noted that in *A* 515, Θ 549, the vulgate has taken up lines which are known from other sources as portions of longer interpolations. I believe that other examples can be found, and would suggest that *A* 486 has thus intruded.   The original text :

αὐτὰρ ἐπεί ῥ' ἵκοντο κατὰ στρατὸν εὐρὺν Ἀχαιῶν,
νῆα μὲν οἵ γε μέλαιναν ἐπ' ἠπείροιο ἔρυσαν·
αὐτοὶ δ' ἐσκίδναντο κατὰ κλισίας τε νέας τε.

would be free from the repetition ἐπ' ἠπείροιο, ἐπὶ ψαμάθοις, and from the rhyme ἔρυσαν, τάνυσσαν.

Of Achilles during the absence of the gods in Ethiopia :

αὐτὰρ ὁ μήνιε νηυσὶ παρήμενος ὠκυπόροισι,
διογενὴς Πηλῆος υἱός, πόδας ὠκὺς Ἀχιλλεύς·
490   οὔτε ποτ' εἰς ἀγορὴν πωλέσκετο κυδιάνειραν
οὔτε ποτ' ἐς πόλεμον, ἀλλὰ φθινύθεσκε φίλον κῆρ
αὖθι μένων, ποθέεσκε δ' αὐτήν τε πτόλεμόν τε.

---

491 om. Zenodotus.

Aristonicus (5 A) declares that Zenodotus athetized lines 488-92 τὸν δὲ " οὔτε ποτ' ἐς πόλεμον " οὐδὲ ἔγραφεν.

I can see in this nothing but a case of haplography similar to that in *A* 446-7.   Wecklein (*ZAV* 48 f.) emends to οὐδέ ποτ' εἰς ἀγορήν, and believes that Zenodotus' text is then superior.   The emendation seems to me to spoil the appropriateness [1] of ποθέεσκε.

---

[1] On its meaning cf. *CP* 15 (1920). 387-9, valid in spite of Shewan, ib. 16 (1921). 195-7 and 18 (1923). 348.

B

We are told of Agamemnon:

βουλὴν δὲ πρῶτον μεγαθύμων ἷζε γερόντων
Νεστορέῃ παρὰ νηὶ Πυλοιγενέος βασιλῆος·
55 τοὺς ὅ γε συγκαλέσας πυκινὴν ἠρτύνετο βουλήν·
" κλῦτε, φίλοι κτλ."

---

55 αὐτὰρ ἐπεί ῥ' ἤγερθεν ὁμηγερέες τ' ἐγένοντο,
* τοῖσι δ' ἀνιστάμενος μετέφη κρείων 'Αγαμέμνων· Zenod.

The vulgate is to be preferred because it is possible to explain the motive for the expansion—the desire to bring an explicit *verbum dicendi* immediately before the speech. I have discussed the matter, 'On the Interpolation of certain Homeric Formulas', *CP* 17 (1922). 213-21. Compare also Roemer, *Zenod.* 46, 66; *AAH* 503; Wilamowitz, *Ilias*, 261 n.; Wecklein, *ZAV* 73.

The expanded text is again not what one would expect of Zenodotus of Ephesus.

To the βουλὴ γερόντων Agamemnon reports of the dream:

59 στῆ δ' ἄρ' ὑπὲρ κεφαλῆς, καί με πρὸς μῦθον ἔειπεν·
* " ἠνώγει σε πατὴρ ὑψίζυγος, αἰθέρι ναίων,
* Τρωσὶ μαχήσασθαι προτὶ "Ιλιον ". ὡς ὁ μὲν εἰπὼν
71 ᾤχετ' ἀποπτάμενος, ἐμὲ δὲ γλυκὺς ὕπνος ἀνῆκεν.

---

60 " εὕδεις 'Ατρέος υἱὲ δαΐφρονος ἱπποδάμοιο;   = 23
     οὐ χρὴ παννύχιον εὕδειν βουληφόρον ἄνδρα,   = 24
     ᾧ λαοί τ' ἐπιτετράφαται καὶ τόσσα μέμηλε.   = 25
     νῦν δ' ἐμέθεν ξύνες ὦκα· Διὸς δέ τοι ἄγγελός εἰμι,   = 26
     ὃς σεῦ ἄνευθεν ἐὼν μέγα κήδεται ἠδ' ἐλεαίρει.   = 27
65 θωρῆξαί σ' ἐκέλευσε καρηκομόωντας 'Αχαιοὺς   = 28 ᴠ11
     πανσυδίῃ· νῦν γάρ κεν ἕλοις πόλιν εὐρυάγυιαν   = 29 ᴠ12
     Τρώων· οὐ γὰρ ἔτ' ἀμφὶς 'Ολύμπια δώματ' ἔχοντες = 30 = 13
     ἀθάνατοι φράζονται· ἐπέγναμψεν γὰρ ἅπαντας   = 31 = 14
     "Ηρη λισσομένη, Τρώεσσι δὲ κήδε' ἐφῆπται   = 32 = 15
70 ἐκ Διός. ἀλλὰ σὺ σῇσιν ἔχε φρεσίν." ὡς ὁ μεν εἰπὼν κτλ. = 33

Except for Wolf's emendation ἠνώγει (ἀνώγει cod.) the shorter version is that of Zenodotus; cf. Aristonicus (5 A) Ζηνόδοτος συντέτμηκεν, οὕτως εἰπὼν " ἠνώγει . . . ἀποπτάμενος ".

Roemer (*Zenod.* 45) condemns the version of Zenodotus because of προτὶ "Ιλιον; I doubt if the objection is valid against the author of this section. But as Wecklein (*Z A V* 62) has noted, προτί may be merely a corruption of περί: cf. the same confusion in reporting Zenodotus' reading of Σ 210. As for its contents, Agamemnon tells (cf. Wilamowitz, *Ilias*, 261 n.) as much as his purpose demands. More would have led into the difficulties of indirect discourse.

The vulgate with its triple repetition is objectionable (cf. Lachmann, 12); or, as Leaf puts it, ' the third repetition of the message is really too much '. The Aristarchean defence is found in Aristonicus (5 A): τὰ δὲ ἀπαγγελτικὰ ἐξ ἀνάγκης δὶς καὶ τρὶς ἀναπολεῖται ταῖς αὐταῖς λέξεσιν. Finsler (*Homer*[2], ii. 22) glides over the difficulty in much the same fashion; while Roemer (*AAH* 271) is enthusiastic about such exegesis. Wilamowitz' objection that Agamemnon is not an ἄγγελος is unnecessarily technical. Instances of double repetition are irrelevant; while the only [1] triple repetition, though adduced by Roemer to support the vulgate, conforms in reality to the pattern of the Zenodotean text. It is Ω 146–58, Zeus to Iris, repeated *mutatis mutandis* by Iris to Priam (175–87), but condensed to two lines (195–6) when reported by Priam to Hecuba. That one condensation is verbally closer than the other is immaterial.

The unparalleled (cf. Berger, *op. cit.* 73) ὡς ὁ μὲν εἰπών at the end of a line is common to both versions. In that of Zenodotus it may be explained as a consequence of the struggle with the indirect discourse; for the vulgate there is no such explanation. The quotation breaks off suddenly in the eleventh line in the midst of a polar sentence which we would expect to be completed by the quotation of the twelfth and last line. After that the narrative could have proceeded normally:

ὡς εἰπὼν ἀπέβη, ἐμὲ δὲ γλυκὺς ὕπνος ἀνῆκεν.

For an interpolator, however, for whom

ὡς ὁ μὲν εἰπὼν
ᾤχετ' ἀποπτάμενος, ἐμὲ δὲ γλυκὺς ὕπνος ἀνῆκεν.

was a given quantity, no other procedure was possible.

---

[1] The chance for another (H 416) by Idaios is avoided; the section shows an advanced technique in handling τὰ ἀπαγγελτικά.

Agamemnon's speech in the assembly begins :

110 ὦ φίλοι, ἥρωες Δαναοί, θεράποντες Ἄρηος,   ῀ I 17
119 λώβη γὰρ τάδε γ' ἐστὶ καὶ ἐσσομένοισι πυθέσθαι,
μὰψ οὕτω τοιόνδε τοσόνδε τε λαὸν Ἀχαιῶν
ἄπρηκτον πόλεμον πολεμίζειν ἠδὲ μάχεσθαι
ἀνδράσι παυροτέροισι· τέλος δ' οὔ πώ τι πέφανται.

111   Ζεύς με μέγας Κρονίδης ἄτῃ ἐνέδησε βαρείῃ,   = I 18
      σχέτλιος, ὃς πρὶν μέν μοι ὑπέσχετο καὶ κατένευσεν   = I 19
      Ἴλιον ἐκπέρσαντ' εὐτείχεον ἀπονέεσθαι,   = I 20
      νῦν δὲ κακὴν ἀπάτην βουλεύσατο, καί με κελεύει   = I 21
115   δυσκλέα Ἄργος ἱκέσθαι, ἐπεὶ πολὺν ὤλεσα λαόν.   = I 22
      οὕτω που Διὶ μέλλει ὑπερμενέι φίλον εἶναι   = I 23
      ὃς δὴ πολλάων πολίων κατέλυσε κάρηνα   = I 24
118   ἠδ' ἔτι καὶ λύσει· τοῦ γὰρ κράτος ἐστὶ μέγιστον.   = I 25

The text adopted is that of Zenodotus on the testimony of Aristonicus (5 A) : ὅτι ἀπὸ τούτου (111) ἕως τοῦ " αἰσχρὸν γὰρ τόδε
γ' ἐστί" οὕτως συντέμνει " ὦ φίλοι . . . μὰψ οὕτω". For my solution of the contradiction with Aristonicus' other note : ὅτι Ζηνόδοτος
γράφει " Ζεύς με μέγας Κρονίδης ", cf. above, p. 49.

Wecklein (Z A V 61 ff.) has seen the superiority of the Zenodotean
text. It is necessary, however, to examine one apparent objection
to it. Allusion to lines 111–18 is found in Nestor's speech by
Wilamowitz (Ilias, 268) and by Bethe (Homer, i. 210). That is a
natural interpretation of the vulgate, but to prove the genuineness
of the lines more is required. It must be shown that Nestor's
speech cannot be understood without such an allusion; and this
seems to me not to be the case. Agamemnon's thought runs: 'It
is a disgrace to return without victory. The odds seem to be in our
favour, but are against us: nine years have gone, our ships have
rotted, those at home long for us. Let us flee—victory is unattain-
able.' To this Odysseus replies: 'A desire to return can be understood and pardoned; still, to return now is a disgrace: let us wait
and see whether the prophecy of Calchas is true or not.' Nestor
outdoes him: 'Away with the one or two who think to return to
Argos before learning whether the promise of Zeus was a lie or
not! Fight as I advise, and you will learn whether it is the will of
God or the fault of your soldiery that prevents the capture of Troy.'
The latter is a generality, the former a counterpart to the omen

told by Odysseus. All is perfectly natural without any complaint of Agamemnon against Zeus.

The vulgate, on the contrary, offers two difficulties. The γάρ in the Zenodotean text opens the speech in a characteristic fashion on which the Alexandrian critics often comment ; but in the vulgate it has been a thorn for the interpreters; cf. Wolf, *Vorlesungen*, ii. 20 ; Erhardt, 19 ; Duentzer, *Hom. Abh.* 105 f. ; Bethe, *Homer*, i. 207. In the ninth book the words of Agamemnon (*I* 18–22) are justified by the catastrophe of Θ ; in *B* they have no meaning—unless one assumes with Wilamowitz that *B* was an independent poem with a background of its own.

Agamemnon closes his speech :

ἀλλ' ἄγεθ', ὡς ἂν ἐγὼ εἴπω, πειθώμεθα πάντες·
140   φεύγωμεν σὺν νηυσὶ φίλην ἐς πατρίδα γαῖαν·
οὐ γὰρ ἔτι Τροίην αἱρήσομεν εὐρυάγυιαν.

Of the last line s T says : οὗτος ὁ στίχος ἀναιρεῖ τὴν ἀμφιβολίαν· διὸ ἔν τισιν οὐ φέρεται. Whether this means that the line was not to be found in some editions other than those of Aristarchus, or not to be found in some MSS. known to the scholiast, cannot be determined. If the latter, it is a case of haplography,[1] for the presence of the line in the vulgate is attested by three papyri. If the former, it may again be mere haplography, and so the external evidence cannot here help us to a decision. The propriety of the line can be debated interminably ; cf. most recently Wilamowitz, *Ilias*, 267 n.

When the soldiery rushes for the ships :

155 ἔνθα κεν Ἀργείοισιν ὑπέρμορα νόστος ἐτύχθη,
* εἰ μὴ Ἀθηναίη λαοσσόος ἦλθ' ἀπ' Ὀλύμπου.

156	εἰ μὴ Ἀθηναίην Ἥρη πρὸς μῦθον ἔειπεν·	
	"ὢ πόποι, αἰγιόχοιο Διὸς τέκος, Ἀτρυτώνη,	= Ε 714
	οὕτω δὴ οἶκον δὲ φίλην ἐς πατρίδα γαῖαν	= Β 174
	Ἀργεῖοι φεύξονται ἐπ' εὐρέα νῶτα θαλάσσης,	
160	κὰδ δέ κεν εὐχωλὴν Πριάμῳ καὶ Τρωσὶ λίποιεν	∽ 176
	Ἀργείην Ἑλένην, ἧς εἵνεκα πολλοὶ Ἀχαιῶν	= 177

---

[1] The omission in Allen's V³² is either an inheritance from such MSS, or haplography of its scribe.

169 εὗρεν ἔπειτ' Ὀδυσῆα Διὶ μῆτιν ἀτάλαντον,
ἑσταότ'· οὐδ' ὅ γε νηὸς ἐυσσέλμοιο μελαίνης
ἅπτετ', ἐπεί μιν ἄχος κραδίην καὶ θυμὸν ἵκανεν.
ἀγχοῦ δ' ἱσταμένη προσέφη γλαυκῶπις Ἀθήνη·

ἐν Τροίῃ ἀπόλοντο φίλης ἀπὸ πατρίδος αἴης.	= 178
ἀλλ' ἴθι νῦν κατὰ λαὸν Ἀχαιῶν χαλκοχιτώνων·	∽ 179
σοῖς ἀγανοῖς ἐπέεσσιν ἐρήτυε φῶτα ἕκαστον	= 180
165 μηδὲ ἔα νῆας ἅλα δ' ἑλκέμεν ἀμφιελίσσας.	= 181
ὣς ἔφατ'· οὐδ' ἀπίθησε θεά, γλαυκῶπις Ἀθήνη,	= E 719 H 43
167 βῆ δὲ κατ' Οὐλύμποιο καρήνων ἀίξασα.	= Δ 74

For the post-Aristarchean interpolation of 168 and Wilamowitz' ascription of
it to Zenodotus cf. above pp. 6, 16.

The text adopted is that of Zenodotus on the testimony of Aristonicus (ꙅ A): Ζηνόδοτος οὕτως ἐπισυντέτμηκεν " εἰ μὴ Ἀθηναίη
... εὗρεν ἔπειτ' Ὀδυσῆα ", καθόλου τὸν τῆς ῝Ηρας λόγον περιγράψας.
For my explanation of the apparent contradiction offered by Aristonicus' note on 161: Ζηνόδοτος γράφει Ἀργείην θ' Ἑλένην, cf.
above, p. 49. Aristotle's quotation, *Rhet.* i. 6, p. 1363ᵃ 6, κὰδ δέ κεν
εὐχωλὴν Πριάμῳ, is to be referred not to line 160 (so Ludwich,
HV 76) but to line 176.

The cento in the vulgate is so inappropriate that Aristarchus
must needs athetize lines 160–2, 164. It hardly requires discussion,
but one may cf. Bethe, *Homer*, i. 207; Wilamowitz, *Ilias*, 262 n.;
Wecklein, *ZAV* 42. Bethe antedates the passage in describing it
as 'ein Verbindungsstück des letzten Bearbeiters'. The external
evidence reveals it as the work of some Athenian rhapsodist who
wished to present the intervention of the gods in a more grandiose
fashion. The episode in *A* gave him a suggestion which he worked
out at the cost of little effort.

According to Xenophon (*Mem.* i. 2, 58) Polycrates urged against
Socrates his frequent quotation of lines 188–91, 198–202, as an
evidence of undemocratic feeling. The existence of a text lacking
lines 192–7 is suggested by this, but not established; for either
Polycrates or Socrates may have selected from the vulgate only
such portions as were adapted to his purpose. Furthermore,
Aristotle (*Rhet.* ii. 2, p. 1379ᵃ 4) quotes line 196 which was also
read by Zenodotus, and line 192 was in the text of Aristophanes;

facts that tend to throw doubt upon the existence of such a shorter
text. On the other hand Aristarchus athetized lines 193-7, ap-
proximately[1] the lines unquoted in Xenophon. Ludwich infers
that this athetesis was in part based on MS. evidence. I consider
it necessary to declare simply *non liquet*; a conclusion to be re-
gretted because of the importance of the lines; cf. Bethe (*Homer*,
i. 209) for the higher criticism.

Restoration of 3 *a*. PHibeh 19 fr. q. :

258 [εἴ κ' ἔτι σ' ἀφραίνοντα κιχήσομαι, ὥς νύ περ ὧδε,]
258ᵃ [ὀλλύντ' Ἀργείων πουλὺν στ]ρατὸν α[ἰχμητάων] = Θ 472
259 [μηκέτ' ἔπειτ' Ὀδυσῆϊ κάρη ὤ]μοισιν ἐπ[είη]

The only difficulty is my reading π for κ; it will require a new
examination of the papyrus to determine whether it is possible.
The plus verse is obviously worthless.

The close of the prodigy at Aulis:

αὐτὰρ ἐπεὶ κατὰ τέκν' ἔφαγε στρουθοῖο καὶ αὐτήν,
318 τὸν μὲν †ἀρίζηλον θῆκεν θεός, ὅς περ ἔφηνε·
320 ἡμεῖς δ' ἑσταότες θαυμάζομεν, οἷον ἐτύχθη.

———

319 λᾶαν γάρ μιν ἔθηκε Κρόνου παῖς ἀγκυλομήτεω
om. van Leeuwen : damnat Christ.

The existence of a text without line 319 is to be inferred from
Aristonicus' allegation that the line was added[2] by Zenodotus
(s A): ὅτι Ζηνόδοτος γράφει ἀρίδηλον καὶ τὸν ἐχόμενον (319)
προσέθηκεν.

The line is clearly, as Aristarchus saw (s AT), an interpolation
blocking the way to the understanding of 318, in which ἀειδέλιον
(cf. Bechtel, *Lexilogus*, 19) is to be read.

B 489. A note of Aristonicus (s A) reads:

οὐδ' εἴ μοι δέκα] ὅτι ἡ ἰδιότης τῆς ὑπερβολῆς Ὁμηρική. καὶ ἐν

———

[1] By an oversight Ludwich *HV* 76 says 'genau dieselben', but presents the case
correctly *AHT* ii. 137 n.
[2] Wecklein (*ZAV* 74) sees through the phraseology : 'Der Ausdruck des Aristonikos
προσέθηκεν hat nicht mehr Bedeutung als der entgegengesetzte ἦρκε'. In the present
case this can be shown, for line 319 was known to Aristotle, cf. Porphyry (i. 33³ Schr.).

Ὀδυσσείᾳ " οὐδ' εἴ οἱ χεῖρές τε ἐείκοσι καὶ πόδες εἶεν " (μ 78).   ἡ δὲ ἀναφορὰ πρὸς τοὺς περιγράφοντας τούτους τοὺς στίχους. This suggests that Zenodotus (cf. above, p. 51) 'omitted' some lines in this neighbourhood, but the statement is too vague to permit of further discussion.

In the *Catalogue* we read :
517   αὐτὰρ Φωκήων Σχεδίος καὶ Ἐπίστροφος ἦρχον,
        υἱέες Ἰφίτου μεγαθύμου Ναυβολίδαο,
        οἳ Κυπάρισσον ἔχον Πυθῶνά τε πετρήεσσαν.

According to Diodorus xvi. 23, 5 the first and last of these lines were quoted by Philomelus as if in succession. Line 518 can be spared, and sources for it indicated in P 306, θ 116 ; but it is obvious that no great stress should be laid on quotations which reach us so indirectly. The neglect of the digamma is, however, worth noting; cf. *AJP* 33 (1912). 422 f.

Again :
        Λοκρῶν δ' ἡγεμόνευεν Ὀιλῆος ταχὺς Αἴας,
        μείων, οὔ τι τόσος γε ὅσος Τελαμώνιος Αἴας,
        ἀλλὰ πολὺ μείων· ὀλίγος μὲν ἔην, λινοθώρηξ
530   ἐγχείῃ δ' ἐκέκαστο Πανέλληνας καὶ Ἀχαιούς·

According to Allen, *Catalogue*, the last line is omitted by P² and was not read by Strabo, 370. In the former fact there is certainly no significance ; the latter is argued *ex silentio*, and the extent of the 'omission' is too uncertain for discussion here.

The vulgate reads :
536   οἳ δ' Εὔβοιαν ἔχον μένεα πνείοντες Ἄβαντες
        Χαλκίδα τ' Εἰρέτριάν τε πολυστάφυλόν θ' Ἱστίαιαν.

According to Allen, *Catalogue*, this is condensed in Strabo 40, 453 to one line :

        οἳ δ' Εὔβοιαν ἔχον καὶ Χαλκίδα τ' Εἰρέτριάν τε.

Strabo, however, is probably quoting only as much as is useful for his argument : " οἳ δ' Εὔβοιαν ἔχον " καὶ " Χαλκίδα τ' Εἰρέτριάν τε ".

In the vulgate the section on Athens ends with line 557, and that I believe is also the original text. It makes Aias, as I have said—

AJP 37 (1916). 29—' but a tail to the Athenian kite ', thus appropriating to the city of Pisistratus the exploits of Aias and Teucer. The whole problem has been excellently discussed in a larger setting by Bethe, *Homer*, ii. 342–50. I have little [1] to add except that line 558 is not needed for his argument ; indeed, Bethe (p. 347) sees that himself.

An Athenian legend of the conquest of Salamis told of an attempt at arbitration in which both parties interpolated this text to suit their needs. The meaning is clearly that they recited as if genuine extra lines of their own composition, not that they forged and put into circulation copies of the lengthened text. The full form of the tale was known to Hermippus and Apollodorus ; some form of it (it is impossible to be more precise) was known to Dieuchidas and Aristotle.

The interpolation of the Megarians :

Αἴας δ' ἐκ Σαλαμῖνος ἄγεν νέας ἐκ τε Πολίχνης
ἔκ τ' Αἰγειρούσσης Νισαίης τε Τριπόδων τε.

never, as far as we know, made its way into any Homeric text. That of the Athenians was taken up by some editors known to Aristonicus. For its subsequent history cf. above, p. 16, and p. 14 for other instances of interpolations originating in anecdotes.

B 559–68 are quoted in the *Certamen* (p. 43 Wilam.) with three plus verses :

563 τῶν αὖθ' ἡγεμόνευε βοὴν ἀγαθὸς Διομήδης
  * Τυδείδης οὗ πατρὸς ἔχων μένος Οἰνεΐδαο,
564 καὶ Σθένελος, Καπανῆος ἀγακλειτοῦ φίλος υἱός·
565 τοῖσι δ' ἄμ' Εὐρύαλος τρίτατος κίεν, ἰσόθεος φώς,
566 Μηκιστέος υἱὸς Ταλαϊονίδαο ἄνακτος·
567 συμπάντων δ' ἡγεῖτο βοὴν ἀγαθὸς Διομήδης.
568 τοῖσι δ' ἄμ' ὀγδώκοντα μέλαιναι νῆες ἕποντο·
  * ἐν δ' ἄνδρες πολέμοιο δαήμονες ἐστιχόωντο
  * Ἀργεῖοι λινοθώρηκες, κέντρα πτολέμοιο.

Wecklein (*ZAV* 15) notes that the last is also cited from an oracle in Schol. *Theocr.* 14. 48.

[1] To discuss whether *der letzte Bearbeiter* added B 557, or found a longer section of which he allowed nothing except B 557 to stand, would lead too far beyond the scope of this book.

This form of the text has nothing to recommend it except the increase of symmetry produced by the insertion of 563ᵃ. On the other hand, that line contains a neglected digamma, and 568ᵇ an unhomeric phrase.

Lines 603-14.

Stentor is mentioned only once in the poems (*E* 785); according to Aristonicus (ꜱ Aⁱ) ὅτι ἐνταῦθα μόνον μνημονεύει τοῦ Στέντορος. Aristarchus must have insisted on the fact. That it could be debated (ꜱ AT) whether he was Thracian or Arcadian is an indication that he was not listed in the *Catalogue*. That omission could either be explained or rectified. The former course is followed in ꜱ B, where his Thracian nationality is supported by the allegation ἔθος δὲ Ὁμήρῳ τοῖς μὴ παροῦσιν εἰκάζειν τοὺς θεούς. In ꜱ T the same claim is rejected :[1] ἀλλ᾽ ἔθος Ὁμήρῳ τοῖς παροῦσιν εἰκάζειν τοὺς θεούς. Those who regarded him as an Arcadian made good the deficiency of the *Catalogue*: τινὲς δὲ Ἀρκάδα φασὶν εἶναι τὸν Στέντορα καὶ ἐν τῷ καταλόγῳ πλάττουσι περὶ αὐτοῦ στίχους (ꜱ AT).

In a Ptolemaic papyrus such lines would not surprise us, but the Homeric text has not suffered by their loss. It is interesting to note the effort to make the *Catalogue* tell all it ought to know.

3 *a*. PHibeh 19 fr. *o.* ᴗ 663 ff.

Λ]ι[κύμνιον ὄζον Ἄρηος
ἤδη γηρά]σαντ᾽· ὁ δὲ λα[ὸν πολλὸν ἀγείρας
βῆ φεύγων πόντον] δέ, πλέω[ν ἐπὶ νῶτα θαλάσσης
[αἶψα δὲ νῆας ἔπηξεν κτλ.]

The restoration may be mentioned as a possibility. It assumes a misspelling (πλέον) and syntax and metre that would date this manipulator of the text.

The trouble would have been started by an expansion of the account of the killing of Likymnios.

Νιρεὺς αὖ Σύμηθεν ἄγε τρεῖς νῆας ἐίσας,
Νιρεὺς Ἀγλαΐης υἱὸς Χαρόποιό τ᾽ ἄνακτος,

---

[1] For a continuation of the debate cf. Haupt, ap. Lachmann, *Betracht.* 109 ; Drerup, *Das fünfte Buch*, 303 n. 3.

673 Νιρεύς, ὃς κάλλιστος ἀνὴρ ὑπὸ Ἴλιον ἦλθεν·
675 ἀλλ' ἀλαπαδνὸς ἔην, παῦρος δέ οἱ εἴπετο λαός.

674 τῶν ἄλλων Δαναῶν μετ' ἀμύμονα Πηλείωνα = P 280, λ 470, 551, ω 18 damnat Nauck.

The text is that of Zenodotus on the testimony of Aristonicus (ƨ A) : ὅτι ἐκ τῶν τριῶν (673–5) τοὺς δύο ἠθέτηκε Ζηνόδοτος, τὸν δὲ μέσον οὐδὲ ἔγραφεν. The distinction, as Wecklein (ZAV 38) has seen, could be due to nothing but MS. evidence. Schulze (QE 350) has correctly inferred from Iph. Aul. 204 that the line was not known to Euripides, and has connected this interpolation with others of the same tendency.

An acquaintance with the interpolated line is ascribed by Ludwich, but on insufficient grounds, to Antisthenes the Cynic ;[1] cf. Olympiodorus at Plat. Alc. i, p. 28 Cr. At all events it is found in 3 a. PHibeh 19. There cannot be any significance in the omission of the line by Galen, Protrep. 8, unless he is quoting at second hand.

Of Philoctetes it is said :

ἀλλ' ὁ μὲν ἐν νήσῳ κεῖτο κρατέρ' ἄλγεα πάσχων,
Λήμνῳ ἐν ἠγαθέῃ, ὅθι μιν λίπον υἷες Ἀχαιῶν
ἕλκει μοχθίζοντα κακῷ ὀλοόφρονος ὕδρου·
ἔνθ' ὅ γε κεῖτ' ἀχέων· τάχα δὲ μνήσεσθαι ἔμελλον
725 Ἀργεῖοι παρὰ νηυσὶ Φιλοκτήταο ἄνακτος.
727 τοὺς δὲ Μέδων κόσμησεν, Ὀιλῆος νόθος υἱός,
τόν ῥ' ἔτεκεν Ῥήνη ὑπ' Ὀιλῆι πτολιπόρθῳ.

726 οὐδὲ μὲν οὐδ' οἱ ἄναρχοι ἔσαν, πόθεόν γε μὲν ἄρχον· = 703
727 ἀλλὰ Μέδων κόσμησεν, κτλ.

Following Friedlander, Ariston. 77, Duentzer, Zen. 37, Wecklein has shown (ZAV 49 f., 78) that this is the text of Zenodotus according to Aristonicus (ƨ A): ὅτι Ζηνόδοτος γράφει " τοὺς δὲ Μέδων κόσμησεν " ἵνα συνδήσῃ τὴν φράσιν ἠθετηκὼς τοὺς προειρημένους (724–5) στίχους. He has also shown the superiority of this version.

It is a reasonable suspicion that Zenodotus knew texts in which 724–5 were lacking. Line 724 is found in 3 a. PHibeh 19, which contains, however, 674, a line not included in Zenodotus' edition.

---

[1] The parody of Hermippus, Frag. 82, 4 κ, may refer to one of the parallel passages.

After the close of the *Catalogue*:

760   οὗτοι ἄρ' ἡγεμόνες Δαναῶν καὶ κοίρανοι ἦσαν.
        τίς ταρ τῶν ὄχ' ἄριστος ἔην, σύ μοι ἔννεπε Μοῦσα,
        αὐτῶν ἠδ' ἵππων, οἳ ἅμ' Ἀτρείδῃσιν ἔποντο.
        ἵπποι μὲν μέγ' ἄριστοι ἔσαν Φηρητιάδαο,
        τὰς Εὔμηλος ἔλαυνε ποδώκεας ὄρνιθας ὥς,
765   ὄτριχας, οἰέτεας, σταφύλῃ ἐπὶ νῶτον ἐίσας·
        τὰς ἐν Πηρείῃ θρέψ' ἀργυρότοξος Ἀπόλλων,
        ἄμφω θηλείας, φόβον Ἄρηος φορεούσας·
768   ἀνδρῶν αὖ μέγ' ἄριστος ἔην πόδας ὠκὺς Ἀχιλλεύς·
771   ἀλλ' ὁ μὲν ἐν νήεσσι κορωνίσι ποντοπόροισι
        κεῖτ' ἀπομηνίσας Ἀγαμέμνονι, ποιμένι λαῶν
        Ἀτρείδῃ· κτλ.

768   ἄριστος ἔην Τελαμώνιος Αἴας
        ὄφρ' Ἀχιλεὺς μήνῑεν· ὁ γὰρ πολὺ φέρτατος ἦεν,
        ἵπποι θ', οἳ φορέεσκον ἀμύμονα Πηλείωνα.

From a study of *Iph. Aul.* 206 ff. it has been shown by Schulze (*QE* 349–51) that the text here adopted was that known to Euripides. It is intrinsically superior. The interpolator has left in μήνῑεν his hall-mark.

The vulgate reads:

                ὅτε τ' ἀμφὶ Τυφωέι γαῖαν ἱμάσσῃ
783   εἰν Ἀρίμοις, ὅθι φασὶ Τυφωέος ἔμμεναι εὐνάς·

According to Strabo xiii. 626 some texts added

783ᵃ   χώρῳ ἐνὶ δρυόεντι, Ὕδης (ὕλης) ἐν πίονι δήμῳ ∽ Υ 385

The vulgate says of Iris:

        εἴσατο δὲ φθογγὴν υἷι Πριάμοιο Πολίτῃ,
        ὃς Τρώων σκοπὸς ἷζε, ποδωκείῃσι πεποιθώς,
        τύμβῳ ἐπ' ἀκροτάτῳ Αἰσυήταο γέροντος,
        δέγμενος ὁππότε ναῦφιν ἀφορμηθεῖεν Ἀχαιοί.
795   τῷ μιν ἐεισαμένη προσέφη πόδας ὠκέα ᾿Ιρις·

794ᵃ   εἰς πεδίον Τρώεσσι φόνον καὶ κῆρα φέροντες ∽ Β 352

The worthless line is added in 3 *a*. PHibeh 19. It may be noted that this papyrus is free of the post-Aristarchean interpolation 798ᵃ found in POxy. 20.

That Wilamowitz, *Ilias*, 278 n., likes the verse is merely a matter of taste.

The vulgate reads :

αὐτὰρ Πυραίχμης ἄγε Παίονας ἀγκυλοτόξους,
τηλόθεν ἐξ Ἀμυδῶνος, ἀπ' Ἀξίου εὐρυρέοντος,
850 Ἀξίου, οὗ κάλλιστον ὕδωρ ἐπικίδναται αἶαν.

At Φ 140 the T-scholia say : καὶ οἱ μὲν ὑποτάσσουσι στίχον ἐν τῷ τῶν Παιόνων καταλόγῳ·

αὐτὰρ Πυραίχμης ἄγε Παίονας ἀγκυλοτόξους,
Πηλεγόνος θ' υἱὸς περιδέξιος Ἀστεροπαῖος,

ὃν καὶ ἐν πολλαῖς τῶν Ἰλιάδων φέρεσθαι. Ammonius (POxy. 221, vi. 16 ff.) now says more precisely in the edition of Euripides and some others.

Wilamowitz, *Ilias*, 85, favours the longer text ; but like Ludwich, *HV* 25, Wecklein, *ZAV* 6, I can regard it only as an interpolation— a belated effort to make the *Catalogue* correspond exactly to the poem.

Of the Paphlagonians was said :

851 Παφλαγόνων δ' ἡγεῖτο Πυλαιμένεος λάσιον κῆρ
ἐξ Ἐνετῆς, ὅθεν ἡμιόνων γένος ἀγροτεράων.

853 οἳ ῥα Κύτωρον ἔχον καὶ Σήσαμον ἀμφενέμοντο
ἀμφί τε Παρθένιον ποταμὸν κλυτὰ δώματ' ἔναιον,
855 Κρῶμνάν τ' Αἰγιαλόν τε καὶ ὑψηλοὺς Ἐρυθίνους.

The text adopted is that read by Eratosthenes and Apollodorus, Strabo 298, 553 being the source of our information. The interpretation of the passage is due to Allen, *Catalogue*, 156 ff. His ascription of the lines to the *Cypria* must, however, be rejected since Bethe's proof (*Homer*, ii. 212) that there was no *Catalogue of the Trojans* in the *Cypria*.[1] Another explanation can now be offered.

In the vulgate the *Catalogue* makes no mention of the Kaukones. Verses intruded to repair this omission are cited by the T-scholiast at Υ 329 : τινὲς δὲ καὶ φέρουσι τὸ

Καύκωνας ⟨δ'⟩ αὖτ' ἦγε Πολυκλέος υἱὸς Ἄμειβος
οἳ περὶ Παρθένιον ποταμὸν κλυτὰ δώματα ναῖον·

---

[1] Nor is there any need to discuss his views (p. 157) of the origin of the vulgate.

Eustathius, who knows them (cf. Neumann, p. 213) with a variant Ἄμειβος ἢ ἀμύμων, locates them correctly as 855ᵃᵇ. They furnish another illustration of the tendency to make the *Catalogue* complete. The interpolation is betrayed partly by its kinship to line 854 of the interpolation just discussed, partly (cf. Wecklein *ZAV* 6) by the form Πολυκλέος.

From Strabo 542 the interpolation can be taken as far back as Callisthenes;[1] while Strabo 678 (cf. Allen, *Catalogue*, 159) shows that it was read also by Apollodorus. The latter fact is another indication of a connexion between the 'plus verses' of the T-scholia and Pergamum.

I think we may picture the development somewhat as follows :

(*a*) The original text :

851   Παφλαγόνων δ' ἡγεῖτο Πυλαιμένεος λάσιον κῆρ
852   ἐξ Ἐνετῆς, ὅθεν ἡμιόνων γένος ἀγροτεράων.
856   αὐτὰρ Ἁλιζώνων κτλ.

which reached Zenodotus, and after him was used by Eratosthenes.

(*b*) By its side a text expanded by the use of an old Argonaut epos, perhaps :

851   Παφλαγόνων δ' ἡγεῖτο Πυλαιμένεος λάσιον κῆρ
852   ἐξ Ἐνετῆς, ὅθεν ἡμιόνων γένος ἀγροτεράων·
853   οἵ ῥα Κύτωρον ἔχον καὶ Σήσαμον ἀμφενέμοντο.
855ᵃ Καύκωνας δ' αὖτ' ἦγε Πολυκλέος υἱὸς Ἄμειβος·
855ᵇ οἳ περὶ Παρθένιον ποταμὸν κλυτὰ δώματα ναῖον, ∽854
855   Κρῶμνάν τ' Αἰγιαλόν τε καὶ ὑψηλοὺς Ἐρυθίνους.
856   αὐτὰρ Ἁλιζώνων κτλ.

I had written so far, and was hesitating how to suggest the idea that I should expect in a Ptolemaic papyrus a continuation of this text, when I turned again to PHibeh 19. The restoration of fragm. *p* :

   ] . υκων [
   ] περι π . [

as 855ᵃᵇ at once[2] became clear. It is tantalizing that not a letter can be made out above or below it. Now it is no more surprising

---

[1] Misprinted Callimachus, Duentzer, *Zenod.* 159 n.
[2] I had previously tried κηρ]ύκων in vain.

that Callisthenes should have used such a text [1] than that his contemporary Aeschines should have used a forerunner of PGerhard. Next come MSS. of (*a*) interpolated from (*b*) with more or less confusion, and from these and their understanding of the geography Aristophanes and Aristarchus get the vulgate 851-6 and Crates 851, 852, 855[ab], 856. The latter text is employed by Apollodorus.

The vulgate reads:

Μῃόσιν αὖ Μέσθλης τε καὶ Ἄντιφος ἡγησάσθην,
865 υἷε Ταλαιμένεος, τὼ Γυγαίη τέκε λίμνη,
οἳ καὶ Μῇόνας ἦγον ὑπὸ Τμώλῳ γεγαῶτας.

Strabo 626 knew of texts with an additional line:

Τμώλῳ ὕπο νιφόεντι, Ὕδης ἐν πίονι δήμῳ = Υ 385

Eustathius (cf. Neumann, 213) locates the line as 866[a], and gives its source as the edition of Euripides. For its connexion with Pergamum cf. above, p. 38. The line was probably intended at first as a variant to line 866, not as an addition to it.

At line 872 Aristonicus (s A) reports Aristarchus as criticizing Simonides: ὅτι ἐπὶ τοῦ Ἀμφιμάχου ἐστὶ τὸ " ὃς καὶ χρυσὸν ἔχων " ὁ δὲ Σιμωνίδης ἐπὶ τοῦ Νάστου λέγει. καὶ ὅτι οὐ λέγει ὅπλα αὐτὸν ἔχειν χρυσᾶ, ὡς καὶ πάλιν ὁ Σιμωνίδης ἐξέλαβεν, ἀλλὰ κόσμον χρυσοῦν· λέγει γὰρ " ἠΰτε κούρη ". LMueller, *Phil.* 11 (1856). 175 f., suggested that Simonides did not have lines 870-1 in his text. Acting on this Nauck and Christ bracket the lines, while van Leeuwen omits them. The solution is possible but not probable: (1) as not solving the whole difficulty, (2) because the lines do not resemble the other interpolations in the *Catalogue.* Simonides' allusion was doubtless to some incident either in the *Cypria* or the *Little Iliad,* or perhaps more exactly to the poems on which these epics were based.

The whole section 867-75 is full of difficulties, but at present we seem to have only internal evidence for their solution.

Γ

Plato, *Rep.* iii. 389 e, gives as examples of noble sentiments : οἷα καὶ Ὁμήρῳ Διομήδης λέγει·

---

[1] There is no reason to believe that he fabricated it, *pace* Wolf, *Proll.* 261 n. 46 ; Leaf, *Troy,* 283.

τέττα, σιωπῇ ἧσο, ἐμῷ δ' ἐπιπείθεο μύθῳ,
καὶ τὰ τούτων ἐχόμενα, τὰ
ἴσαν μένεα πνείοντες Ἀχαιοί,
σιγῇ δειδιότες σημάντορας,
καὶ ὅσ' ἄλλα τοιαῦτα.

It is difficult to make out the text used by Plato because of the ambiguity of τὰ τούτων ἐχόμενα. If it means *following* literally, his text must have had after Δ 421 three plus verses:

⟨καρπαλίμως δ' ἄρ'⟩ ἴσαν μένεα πνείοντες Ἀχαιοί, ∽ Γ 8
σιγῇ δειδιότες σημάντορας· ἀμφὶ δὲ πᾶσι   = Δ 431
τεύχεα ποικίλ' ἔλαμπε, τὰ εἱμένοι ἐστιχόωντο   = Δ 432

But the phrase may mean *of similar feeling*, and then (*a*) either Γ 8–9 were so modified, or (*b*) Plato's text has been corrupted from

ἴσαν ⟨σιγῇ⟩ μένεα πνείοντες Ἀχαιοί,
⟨καὶ⟩
σιγῇ δειδιότες σημάντορας.

The latter is palaeographically easy, and I consider it the most probable solution.

Hector speaking to Paris :

Δύσπαρι, εἶδος ἄριστε, γυναιμανές, ἠπεροπευτά,
40 αἴθ' ὄφελες ἄγονός τ' ἔμεναι ἄγαμός τ' ἀπολέσθαι.
καί κε τὸ βουλοίμην, καί κεν πολὺ κέρδιον ἦεν
ἢ οὕτω λώβην τ' ἔμεναι καὶ ὑπόψιον ἄλλων.

According to Eustathius (cf. Neumann, 214) Dionysius Skutobrachion was said to have had a longer text containing :

40ᵃ μηδέ τι γούνασιν οἷσιν ἐφέσσασθαι φίλον υἱὸν ∽ Ι 455
40ᵇ Δάρδανον . . .

The combination of the old phraseology and the new romantic mythology is a sufficient condemnation of this text.

In Agamemnon's oath the vulgate reads :

εἰ μέν κεν Μενέλαον Ἀλέξανδρος καταπέφνῃ,
αὐτὸς ἔπειθ' Ἑλένην ἐχέτω καὶ κτήματα πάντα,
283 ἡμεῖς δ' ἐν νήεσσι νεώμεθα ποντοπόροισιν·

283ᵃ Ἄργος ἐς ἱππόβοτον καὶ Ἀχαιίδα καλλιγύναικα = 75, 258

εἰ δέ κ' Ἀλέξανδρον κτείνῃ ξανθὸς Μενέλαος,
Τρῶας ἔπειθ' Ἑλένην καὶ κτήματα πάντ' ἀποδοῦναι,

The additional line is found in 3 a. PHibeh 19. It is harmless, but no one can claim that it is needed.

On the other hand line 283 is essential, as naming the advantage to result to the Trojans from the victory of their champion. For the vulgate the line is attested by PMus.Br. 126, PBerol. 263, so that its omission by some MSS. must be regarded as accidental; cf. AJP 37 (1916). 7.

After the prayer of the Achaeans and Trojans:

302 ὣς ἔφαν, οὐ δ' ἄρα πώ σφιν ἐπεκραίαινε Κρονίων.
303 τοῖσι δὲ Δαρδανίδης Πρίαμος μετὰ μῦθον ἔειπε·

302 ὣς ἔφαν εὐχόμενοι, μέγα δ' ἔκτυπε μητίετα Ζεὺς   ∽ Ο 377
*   ἐξ Ἴδης βροντῶν, ἐπὶ δὲ στεροπὴν ἐφέηκεν·
*   θησέμεναι γὰρ ἔμελλεν ἔτ' ἄλγεα στοναχάς τε   = Β 39
*   Τρωσί τε καὶ Δαναοῖσι διὰ κρατερὰς ὑσμίνας.   = Β 40
*   αὐτὰρ ἐπεί ῥ' ὅμοσέν τε τελεύτησέν τε τὸν ὅρκον,   = Ξ 280 etc.
303 τοῖσι δὲ Δαρδανίδης κτλ.

The only value of this longer version in 3 a. PHibeh 19 is to show the sort of thing that was then being done in the way of interpolation.

The text continues:

304 κέκλυτέ μευ, Τρῶες καὶ ἐυκνήμιδες Ἀχαιοί·

304 κέκλυτέ μευ, Τρῶες καὶ Δάρδανοι ἠδ' ἐπίκουροι,   = Η 348 etc.
304ᵃ ὄφρ' εἴπω τά με θυμὸς ἐνὶ στήθεσσιν ἀνώγει·   ∽ Η 349 etc.

The addition is again from 3 a. PHibeh 19.

No comment is needed beyond noting that the line here interpolated remains a favourite with the interpolators of later times; cf. Γ 86ᵃ, Η 369, Θ 6, θ 27, φ 276.

The description of Paris donning his armour:

328 αὐτὰρ ὅ γ' ἀμφ' ὤμοισιν ἐδύσετο τεύχεα καλὰ
329 δῖος Ἀλέξανδρος, Ἑλένης πόσις ἠυκόμοιο.
330 κνημῖδας μὲν πρῶτα περὶ κνήμῃσιν ἔθηκε

331 καλάς, ἀργυρέοισιν ἐπισφυρίοις ἀραρυίας·
332 δεύτερον αὖ θώρηκα περὶ στήθεσσιν ἔδυνεν
333 οἷο κασιγνήτοιο Λυκάονος· ἥρμοσε δ' αὐτῷ.
  * ἀμφὶ δ' ἄρ' ὤμοισιν βάλετ' ἀσπίδα τερμιόεσσαν·
336 κρατὶ δ' ἐπ' ἰφθίμῳ κυνέην εὔτυκτον ἔθηκεν,
337 ἵππουριν· δεινὸν δὲ λόφος καθύπερθεν ἔνευεν.
338 εἵλετο δ' ἄλκιμον ἔγχος, ὅ οἱ παλάμηφιν ἀρήρει.
339 ὣς δ' αὔτως Μενέλαος ἀρήιος ἔντε' ἔδυνεν.

---

334 ἀμφὶ δ' ἄρ' ὤμοισιν βάλετο ξίφος ἀργυρόηλον,
335 χάλκεον, αὐτὰρ ἔπειτα σάκος μέγα τε στιβαρόν τε·
Zenodotus :
333 οἷο κασιγνήτοιο Λυκάονος· ἥρμοσε δ' αὐτῷ.
336 κρατὶ δ' ἐπ' ἰφθίμῳ κυνέην εὔτυκτον ἔθηκεν,
337 ἵππουριν· δεινὸν δὲ λόφος καθύπερθεν ἔνευεν.
  * ἀμφὶ δ' ἄρ' ὤμοισιν βάλετ' ἀσπίδα τερμιόεσσαν
PHibeh 19 :
  * [ἀμφὶ δ' ἄρ' ὤμοισιν βάλετ' ἀσπίδα τερμιόεσσαν]
  * [καλήν, ἀμφιβρό]την, [πολυδαίδαλον, ὀμφαλόεσσαν.]
338 εἷλε[το δ' ἄλκιμα] δοῦρε δύ[ω, κεκορυθμένα χαλκῷ.   = Λ 43
339 ὣς δ' α[ὔτως Μεν]έλαος ἀρήια [τεύχε' ἔδυνεν·
  * ἀσπίδα κα[ὶ πήλη]κα φαεινή[ν καὶ δύο δοῦρε.
  * καὶ καλὰ[ς κνη]μῖδας ἐπισφ[υρίοις ἀραρυίας.
  * ἀμφὶ δ' ἄ[ρ' ὤμοισι]ν βάλετο ξί[φος ἀργυρόηλον.
vss. 332-3 om. van Leeuwen.

The basis for the reconstruction of the text is a note of Aristonicus. Its form in ς A is very corrupt :

ἀμφὶ δ' ἄρ' ὤμοισιν] ὅτι Ζηνόδοτος ἀμφοτέρους ἠθέτηκε καὶ μετὰ τὸν " οἷο κασιγνήτοιο " ὑποτάσσει·

κρατὶ δ' ἐπ' ἰφθίμῳ κυνέην εὔτυκτον ἔθηκεν,
ἵππουριν· δεινὸν δὲ λόφος καθύπερθεν ἔνευεν.
εἵλετο δ' ἄλκιμον ἔγχος·

ἀμφὶ δ' ἄρ' ὤμοισιν βάλετ' ἀσπίδα †τερσανόεσσαν] ὥστε ἐναντίως τῷ Ὁμηρικῷ ὁπλισμῷ ἔχειν· πρὸ τῆς ἀσπίδος γὰρ φανήσεται ἀναλαμβάνων τὴν περικεφαλαίαν καὶ ξίφος μὴ ἔχων.

The correction began when Cobet saw that one note had been split into two, the second lemma being in reality part of the Zenodotean text. But Villoison's correction of τερσανόεσσαν to θυσανόεσσαν, though approved by Dindorf and Roemer, who scolded

(*Zenod.* 45) Zenodotus for foisting it upon the text, was a *Verschlimmbesserung*. It was Robert (*Stud.* 3) who found the correct solution τερμιόεσσαν. Another *Verschlimmbesserung* was Dindorf's " addendum ὅ οἱ παλάμηφιν ἀρήρει ", which has not hitherto been questioned. The solution is: *delendum* εἵλετο δ' ἄλκιμον ἔγχος. Otherwise the picking up of the spear before putting on the shield is another contradiction τῷ Ὁμηρικῷ ὁπλισμῷ, and Aristonicus would never have let it pass unnoticed. Besides, this renders it possible to fit 3 *a*. PHibeh 19 to the Zenodotean text. Furthermore, the use of ὑποτάσσει shows that in Zenodotus' text line 336 followed line 333 ; the epitomator must therefore be charged with substituting ἠθέτηκεν for ἦρκεν.

Robert (*Stud.* 51 f.) saw that transposition of one line had taken place in the Zenodotean text, and that with that corrected we reach a text obviously superior to the vulgate. For (1) it preserves in τερμιόεσσαν, a rare word ; and (2) it is appropriate to this particular situation in not mentioning the sword. Paris had come to the field as an archer, and as such wearing a sword. The arming of Teucer (*O* 479–482) affords a perfect parallel.[1] The vulgate is either a mistaken effort to supply the sword, or a thoughtless slipping into the formula of Π and T.

The new lines of the papyri are interpolations, but ones from which we may perhaps learn. The first is a gloss, and a bad one, on τερμιόεσσαν ; furthermore, it must have been inserted after the mechanical corruption—the transposition started by haplography ἀμφὶ δ', κρατὶ δ'—had been made. In line 338 I suspect that the papyrus has preserved a Zenodotean reading. My reason is that in Zenodotus' text (cf. on *H* 255–7) Aias and Hector had two spears ;[2] but I have no suggestion to make (but cf. Bethe, *Homer*, i. 260) about the second spears in this duel. The three last lines make no reference to a corslet, and van Leeuwen argues that lines 332–3 could not have stood in the papyrus. If we look closer we must be struck by the confused order in which the weapons are mentioned, and by the differences in the lines. The two last are

---

[1] Robert rejected O 481 because of MS. evidence ; reference to Part I will show how it has since strengthened.

[2] Cf. also Aristonicus on Λ 43 ὅτι ⟨παρὰ Ζηνοδότῳ⟩ καὶ ἐπὶ τῆς Ἀλεξάνδρου μονομαχίας τὸ ὅμοιον—the note on Λ 41 being aimed also at Zenodotus.

commonplaces of arming scenes, while the first is adapted from α 256 with some ingenuity. I would suggest that the text grew in somewhat the following fashion. Lines 330–3 were lacking, the next beginning ἀμφὶ μὲν ὤμοισιν : then 339ᵃ is interpolated as an exact parallel to the arming of Paris. Next, 330–1 were introduced (entailing the change to ἀμφὶ δ' ἄρ' ὤμοισιν) and 339ᵇ added. Then 339ᶜ put on the shoulders of Menelaos the sword he uses in the sequel.

I believe, therefore, that lines 330–3 are interpolated, but as the argument goes beyond the direct external evidence, I have not removed them from the text given above. It confirms Robert's view that the equipment is ' Mycenaean ' in this section.

The same papyrus expands slightly the description of the combat :

361   Ἀτρείδης δ' ἄορ ὀξὺ ἐρυσσάμενος παρὰ μηροῦ   ∽ Φ 173
      πλῆξεν ἐπαΐξας κόρυθος φάλ[ον ἱπποδασείης
  *   χαλκείης· δεινὸν [δὲ κόρυς λάκεν· ἀμφὶ δ' ἄρ' αὐτῇ
      τριχθά τε καὶ τετραχθὰ διατρυφὲν ἔκπεσε χειρός.
      Ἀτρείδης δ' ᾤμωξεν ἰδὼν εἰς οὐρανὸν εὐρύν·
365   " Ζεῦ πάτερ, οὔ τις σεῖο θεῶν ὀλοώτερος ἄλλος.
      ἦ τ' ἐφάμη[ν τίσασθαι Ἀλέξανδρον κακότητος,
  *   δῖον Ἀλέξανδρον, Ἑλένης πόσιν ἠυκόμοιο·   ∽ Γ 329
      νῦν δέ μοι ἐν χείρεσσιν ἄγη ξίφος κτλ."

Only supplements that affect my problem are here indicated.

The inferiority of this to the vulgate is sufficiently obvious. The first interpolation ἱπποδασείης . . . λάκεν is noteworthy as not consisting of an even line. The editors consider Ἀλέξανδρον κακό-τητος a ' very doubtful ' restoration. I do not fully share these doubts, otherwise it would be easy to suggest ὅ με πρότερος κάκ' ἔοργε. That may, however, be improving upon the work of the interpolator.

The omission of the superfluous speech formula :

389   τῇ μιν ἐεισαμένη προσεφώνεε δῖ' Ἀφροδίτη.

by 3 a. PHibeh 20 can no longer be cited as a divergence from the vulgate ; for that line (cf. above, Part I) is nothing but a post-Aristarchean interpolation.

ILIAD Γ

85

The return of Helen to her palace is described :

421 αἱ δ' ὅτ' Ἀλεξάνδροιο δόμον περικαλλέ' ἵκοντο,
422 ἀμφίπολοι μὲν ἔπειτα θοῶς ἐπὶ ἔργα τράποντο,
* αὐτὴ δ' ἀντίον ἷζεν Ἀλεξάνδροιο ἄνακτος,
427 ὄσσε πάλιν κλίνασα, πόσιν δ' ἠνίπαπε μύθῳ·

423 ἡ δ' εἰς ὑψόροφον θάλαμον κίε δῖα γυναικῶν.
424 τῇ δ' ἄρα δίφρον ἑλοῦσα φιλομμειδὴς Ἀφροδίτη
425 ἀντί' Ἀλεξάνδροιο θεὰ κατέθηκε φέρουσα·
426 ἔνθα κάθιζ' Ἑλένη, κούρη Διὸς αἰγιόχοιο,

The text is that of Zenodotus on the testimony of Aristonicus
(5 A) at 423 : ἀπὸ τούτου ἕως τοῦ " ἔνθα κάθιζ' Ἑλένη " στίχοις
τέσσαρσι παράκεινται διπλαῖ περιεστιγμέναι, ὅτι Ζηνόδοτος μετετίθει
τὴν συνέπειαν οὕτως "ἀμφίπολοι . . . ἠνίπαπε μύθῳ".
The text of Zenodotus offers no difficulty. Aphrodite has played
her part and is dropped by the poet. The interpolator thought
differently and sought to give her a formal dismissal. His attempt
was unsuccessful, for he, too (cf. Wecklein, ZA V 47), simply drops
her at the end. He alone has applied the phrase κούρη Διὸς αἰγιόχοιο
to Helen.

Δ

Zeus' speech to Athena begins :
70 αἶψα μάλ' ἐς στρατὸν ἐλθὲ μετὰ Τρῶας καὶ Ἀχαιούς·
In 3 a. PHibeh 20 is prefixed :
69ᵃ ὄρσε' Ἀθηναίη κ]υδί[στη Τριτογένεια.
The line furnishes an instance of the vocative interpolations such
as can be found (cf. above, p. 9 n.) in post-Aristarchean times.

After the descent of Athena to the battle-field :
ἡ δ' ἀνδρὶ ἰκέλη Τρώων κατεδύσεθ' ὅμιλον,
Λαοδόκῳ Ἀντηνορίδῃ, κρατερῷ αἰχμητῇ,
88 Πάνδαρον ἀντίθεον διζημένη· εὗρε δὲ τόνδε
90 ἑσταότ', ἀμφὶ δέ μιν κρατεραὶ στίχες ἀσπιστάων
λαῶν, οἵ οἱ ἕποντο ἀπ' Αἰσήποιο ῥοάων.

88 Πάνδαρον ἀντίθεον διζημένη, εἴ που ἐφεύροι, ᴥ E 168
89 εὗρε Λυκάονος υἱὸν ἀμύμονά τε κρατερόν τε = E 169
814276   G

According to Aristonicus (ѕ A) the text adopted is that of Zenodotus : ὅτι Ζηνόδοτος τούτου μὲν τὸ ἀκροτελεύτιον οὕτως γράφει " εὗρε δὲ τόνδε ", τὸν δὲ δεύτερον οὐδὲ γράφει. Roemer (*AAH* 322 n.) doubts the trustworthiness of this statement—an excess of suspicion after the publication of 3*a*. PHibeh 20 that contains the same reading.

The shorter text offers no difficulty, and Wecklein (*ZAV* 63) can indeed claim for it certain advantages. As for Leaf's observation that εὗρε 'is commonly found beginning a sentence asyndetically', such conformity of usage is in part brought about by the assimilation of varying passages. It is no sufficient reason to make us depart in this case from the better attested text.

After Pandaros had made his vows to Apollo :

122 ἕλκε δ' ὁμοῦ γλυφίδας τε λαβὼν καὶ νεῦρα βόεια·
124 αὐτὰρ ἐπεὶ δὴ κυκλοτερὲς μέγα τόξον ἔτεινε,
λίγξε βιός, νευρὴ δὲ μέγ' ἴαχεν, ἆλτο δ' ὀιστὸς
ὀξυβελής, καθ' ὅμιλον ἐπιπτέσθαι μενεαίνων.

123 νευρὴν μὲν μαζῷ πέλασεν, τόξῳ δὲ σίδηρον.

At line 123 ѕ A, which goes back to Aristonicus, reads :

ὅτι Ζηνόδοτος πρὸ τούτου τὸν ἑξῆς τέταχεν οὕτως ποιήσας·
ἕλκε δ' ὁμοῦ γλυφίδας ⟨τε λαβὼν⟩ καὶ νεῦρα βόεια
εἶτα·
αὐτὰρ ἐπεὶ δὴ κυκλοτερὲς μέγα τόξον ἔτεινε,
νευρὴν μὲν μαζῷ πέλασεν, τόξῳ δὲ σίδηρον.
εἶτα·
λίγξε βιός·

This arrangement of lines is obviously impossible, and the scholiast goes on to point it out with delight.

Now it would be easy to suppose that this was a purely mechanical defect of the Zenodotean antigrapha, and that Aristonicus was again hawking at small game. That supposition, however, is barred. Zenodotus (and others, if we may trust the ἔν τισιν of A¹) reads ἄρα χαλκός in line 139 instead of the ἄρ' ὀιστός of the vulgate. That reading guarantees a text without line 123, as was first seen by Naber; cf. Ameis-Hentze, *Anh.* ii. 35.

The interpolation of the line from the margin is shown also by

its varying position. The only question is the date at which it was inserted. Wecklein (*ZAV* 66) believes that Zenodotus found it in the margin of a MS. and brought it into the text at the wrong point. I think it much more probable that he did not read the line at all, which was afterwards interpolated in the copy of his work used by Aristonicus.

The superiority of the shorter text is evident. The vulgate departs from the picture of life given in the rest of the poems. Arrows elsewhere are always χαλκήρεις. More generally the poems seem to describe a period of bronze weapons but iron tools.[1] There are three exceptions : the proverb in the *Odyssey* (π 294, τ 13), αὐτὸς γὰρ ἐφέλκεται ἄνδρα σίδηρος, which Lang would eject; the iron mace of Areïthoos mentioned as an oddity ; and this arrow-head, for which there is (*pace* Belzner) no similar explanation. It would be too curious a coincidence for both internal and external evidence to point against this line, if it were an original part of the text.

Line 123 is superfluous ; but its phrasing is original, its rhetoric forceful, and the details it adds picturesque. The interpolator did not fabricate it; he lifted it from another epos. The *Little Iliad* had two famous scenes in which an arrow-shot was the chief incident—the death of Achilles, and the death of Paris. Our verse will have come from one or the other.

The close of Machaon's surgery is described :

218 αἷμ' ἐκμυζήσας ἐπ' ἄρ' ἤπια φάρμακα εἰδὼς
219 πάσσε, τά οἵ ποτε πατρὶ φίλα φρονέων πόρε Χείρων.

Plato (*Rep.* iii. 408 a) applies to both the sons of Aisklepios a line adapted from this passage :[2]

αἷμ' ἐκμυζήσαντ' ἐπί τ' ἤπια φάρμακ' ἔπασσον.

The playful humour of the philosopher makes it impossible to be certain of his text. To pluralize both lines would have been difficult, and with our text before him he may simply have chosen

---

[1] Cf. A. Lang, *Homer and his Age*, 176 ff. ; *The World of Homer*, 96 ff. ; Belzner, *Homerische Probleme*, i. 32 ff. The theory that this is a true picture of the transition from the Mycenaean age I must leave to the archaeologist. It does not seem to harmonize with D. Fimmen, *Die Kretisch-Mykenische Kultur*, 145. Are not the poems written in an Iron Age with formulae for weapons inherited from the Bronze Age ?

[2] Because of τε Plato must have meant ἐκμυζήσαντο—the unusual voice being ' Homeric '.

the easiest course. It is possible also that he did not have line 219, a tag suggested by $\varDelta$ 832 and $\varPi$ 143 = T 390, line 218 ending φάρμακ' ἔπασσεν. In that case the interpolation will recall the post-Aristarchean manipulation of E 900 [901].

E

Pandaros speaking to Aeneas :

> ἵπποι δ' οὐ πάρεασι καὶ ἅρματα, τῶν κ' ἐπιβαίην·
> ἀλλά που ἐν μεγάροισι Λυκάονος ἔνδεκα δίφροι
> 194/5 πρωτοπαγεῖς· παρὰ δέ σφιν ἑκάστῳ δίζυγες ἵπποι
> ἑστᾶσι κρῖ λευκὸν ἐρεπτόμενοι καὶ ὀλύρας.

194 καλοί, πρωτοπαγεῖς, νεοτευχέες· ἀμφὶ δὲ πέπλοι
195 πέπτανται· παρὰ δέ σφιν ἑκάστῳ δίζυγες ἵπποι.

The text is that of Zenodotus as restored by Ludwich, *AHT* i. 253. The basis is an obviously corrupt note[1] of Aristonicus (s A) ὅτι Ζηνόδοτος μετέθηκεν ⟨οὕτως . . .⟩ ὡς ταυτολογοῦντος "πρωτοπαγεῖς νεοτευχέες".

The use of πέπλος for anything but a woman's garment is unusual : Ebeling cites $\varOmega$ 229, 796, η 96, of which the two first are doubtful examples.

The interpolation consists of two glosses, the line being filled out as $\varTheta$ 441 suggested.

The Danaoi feared not the Trojans:

> ἀλλ' ἔμενον νεφέλῃσιν ἐοικότες, ἅς τε Κρονίων
> νηνεμίης ἔστησεν ἐπ' ἀκροπόλοισιν ὄρεσσιν
> ἀτρέμας, ὄφρ' εὕδῃσι μένος Βορέαο καὶ ἄλλων
> ζαχρειῶν ἀνέμων, οἵ τε νέφεα σκιόεντα
> 526 πνοιῇσιν λιγυρῇσι διασκιδνᾶσιν ἀέντες.
> 528 Ἀτρείδης δ' ἀν' ὅμιλον ἐφοίτα πολλὰ κελεύων·

527 ὡς Δαναοὶ Τρῶας μένον ἔμπεδον οὐδὲ φέβοντο = O 622

The shorter text is found in 3 a. PHibeh 20. It is open to no objection, and I believe we should accept it as the better-attested reading.

---

[1] No variant in s G except Ζηνόδωρος. Heyne's conjecture ἠθέτηκεν is impossible.

On coming to the battlefield:

> ἔνθα στᾶσ' ἤυσε θεά, λευκώλενος *Ήρη,
785 Στέντορι εἰσαμένη μεγαλήτορι, χαλκεοφώνῳ·
787 " αἰδώς, Ἀργεῖοι, κάκ' ἐλέγχεα, κτλ."

786 ὃς τόσον αὐδήσασχ' ὅσον ἄλλοι πεντήκοντα
damnat Nauck.

Such was the reading of certain texts other than Aristarchus. The authority is a greatly condensed note (5 ABT) ἔν τισιν οὐκ ἦν ὁ στίχος διὰ τὴν ὑπερβολήν : Eustathius (p. 228, Neumann) reports to the same effect. The line is merely a gloss on χαλκεοφώνῳ. When Drerup, *Das fünfte Buch*, 304 n., speaks of the *Tilgung* of the verse it is a *petitio principii*. There is no early evidence for the line. Aristotle, *Pol.* vii. 4: 1326ᵇ 7, is only an allusion to the concept of Stentor as a loud-voiced herald ; it gives no indication that Homer is the source, still less that line 786 was known to the philosopher.

Athena telling Diomedes of Tydeus' exploit :

> δαίνυσθαί μιν ἄνωγον ἐνὶ μεγάροισιν ἔκηλον·
> αὐτὰρ ὁ θυμὸν ἔχων ὃν καρτερόν, ὡς τὸ πάρος περ,
807 κούρους Καδμείων προκαλίζετο, πάντα δ' ἐνίκα.
809 σοὶ δ' ἤτοι μὲν ἐγὼ παρά θ' ἵσταμαι ἠδὲ φυλάσσω
> καί σε προφρονέως κέλομαι Τρώεσσι μάχεσθαι·
> ἀλλά σευ ἢ κάματος πολυάιξ γυῖα δέδυκεν,
> ἤ νύ σέ που δέος ἴσχει ἀκήριον. οὐ σύγ' ἔπειτα
> Τυδέος ἔκγονός ἐσσι δαΐφρονος Οἰνεΐδαο.

808 ῥηιδίως· τοίη οἱ ἐγὼν ἐπιτάρροθος ἦα ∽ Δ 390
omittunt Bekker, van Leeuwen ; damnant Nauck, Christ, Ludwich.

In *AJP* 37 (1916). 25 I endeavoured to show that line 808 was to be found both in the texts of Zenodotus and Aristarchus; similar conclusions have been reached by Wecklein, *ZAV* 73, *ZuA* 92 f. I believe that I can now strengthen the argument. At *B* 318 Aristonicus declares that Zenodotus added (προσέθηκε) the following line, which was, however, read also by Aristarchus. Therefore, when he declares at line 807 Ζηνόδοτος ὑποτάσσει τούτῳ στίχον " ῥηιδίως ... ἦα ", we are not entitled to infer that the line was not

read by Aristarchus. In each case Aristonicus must have known of 'some' texts that lacked the line.

These texts were right: the line spoils the following argument, and contains in ἐπιτάρροθος a difficulty from which Δ 390 with ἐπίρροθος is free.

Z

Andromache meets Hector:

> ἥ οἱ ἔπειτ' ἤντησ', ἅμα δ' ἀμφίπολος κίεν αὐτῇ
> 400 παῖδ' ἐπὶ κόλπῳ ἔχουσ' ἀταλάφρονα, νήπιον αὔτως,
>   Ἑκτορίδην· ἀγαπητόν, ἀλίγκιον ἀστέρι καλῷ,
>   τόν ῥ' Ἕκτωρ καλέεσκε Σκαμάνδριον, αὐτὰρ οἱ ἄλλοι
>   Ἀστυάνακτ'· οἶος γὰρ ἐρύετο Ἴλιον Ἕκτωρ.

In the *Cratylus* 392 c Plato writes: οὐκοῦν οἶσθα ὅτι Ὅμηρος τὸ παιδίον τὸ τοῦ Ἕκτορος ὑπὸ τῶν Τρώων φησὶ καλεῖσθαι Ἀστυάνακτα, Σκαμάνδριον δὲ δῆλον ὅτι ὑπὸ τῶν γυναικῶν, ἐπειδὴ οἵ γε ἄνδρες αὐτὸν Ἀστυάνακτα ἐκάλουν; At its face value this means that Homer says the child was called Astyanax by the men (Τρώων) of Troy, but Skamandrios by other unnamed persons, whom Plato infers to be the women of Troy. This, as Ludwich (*HV* 89) saw, is in contradiction to lines 402-3. Gilbert Murray (*RGE*[2] 307) emends τὸν μήτηρ καλέεσκε; but that is impossible, for Plato plainly indicates that his ὑπὸ τῶν γυναικῶν is merely an inference. Leaf sees that the allusion is to X 506, Ἀστυάναξ ὃν Τρῶες ἐπίκλησιν καλέουσι, the passage in Z being ignored. But is it intentional, playful ignoring, or were these lines actually unknown to Plato? On the latter supposition Σκαμάνδριος as the child's name disappears from the poems in contradiction to Plato; cf. also 392 b: ὁ δὲ Σκαμάνδριός τε καὶ ὁ Ἀστυάναξ ἀνθρωπινώτερον διασκέψασθαι, ὡς ἐμοὶ δοκεῖ, καὶ ῥᾷον, ἅ φησιν ὀνόματα εἶναι τῷ τοῦ Ἕκτορος υἱεῖ. The difficulty could be met in two ways: (1) Homer = the Cycle, which for Plato is not probable; (2) a slip of memory by which the name known from other sources was thought of as in the *Iliad*.

My decision would be that the absence of lines 402-3 from the text of Plato may be suspected, but cannot be rendered very probable.

H

After describing the first spear-casts:

255 τὼ δ' ἐκσπασσαμένω δολίχ' ἔγχεα χερσὶν ἄμ' ἄμφω—
258 Πριαμίδης μὲν ἔπειτα μέσον σάκος οὔτασε δουρί·
οὐ δ' ἔρρηξεν χαλκός, ἀνεγνάμφθη δέ οἱ αἰχμή.
Αἴας δ' ἀσπίδα νύξεν ἐπάλμενος· ἡ δὲ διὰ πρὸ
ἤλυθεν ἐγχείη, στυφέλιξε δέ μιν μεμαῶτα·
τμήδην δ' αὐχέν' ἐπῆλθε, μέλαν δ' ἀνεκήκιεν αἷμα.

256 σύν ῥ' ἔπεσον, λείουσιν ἐοικότες ὠμοφάγοισιν   ⌒ E 782
257 ἢ συσὶ κάπροισιν, τῶν τε σθένος οὐκ ἀλαπαδνόν.   = E 783
The transition 255–6 modelled on Ψ 686–7.

Certainty as to what Zenodotus[1] and others read in this context is precluded by the self-confessed laziness of the epitomator, who has reduced the notes of Didymus and Aristonicus to the following form (s A): τοὺς στίχους τούτους οὐ προσίενται ἔνιοι, ὥσπερ οὐδὲ Ζηνόδοτος, ἀλλὰ τὸ τῆς συνεπείας οὕτως ἔχει παρ' αὐτῷ ⟨. . .⟩. ὥσπερ καὶ ὁ Ἀριστόνικος ἐκτίθησιν, ἣν πέριττον ἐνομίσαμεν γράψαι.

This note is referred to lines 255–7 by its lemma, and the text thus obtained is approved by Wecklein, ZAV 58 f., citing an inaccessible work, A. Clausing, Kritik und Exegese d. hom. Gleichn. im Altertum, Parchim, 1913. It is then necessary to understand that the heroes were equipped with two spears. That is not necessarily incompatible with line 213, and if it is in conflict with Γ, that is a problem which must be left to the higher criticism. However, 3 a. PHibeh 19 gives two spears to the champions in Γ, and we have seen reasons for believing that in this it is closely allied to the Zenodotean text. The three lines may have been taken directly from a cyclic epic.

But the authority of the lemmata is none too great, and the note would still stand in its proper order were it referred to lines 256–7. Even that change is unnecessary, for line 255 (with or without variants) may have stood in the omitted συνέπεια. According to Ludwich (AHT i. 279) this was the solution that Lehrs adopted; and he was followed by Fick (Ilias, 440). It seems to me the more probable; because there is then a tangible reason for the interpola-

---

[1] I can understand Leaf's note only if it is a confusion for 'rejected 256–7 (and perhaps 255)'.

tion, a wish to do away with the distributive apposition, and its gratification by the ordinary cento technique.

For the construction Fick compares σ 95, to which I may add *H* 306, *M* 400 ff., and a reference to Leaf's note on *Γ* 211. The use of ἔπειτα (Wecklein objects to it in the vulgate) may be compared with *Δ* 730, but that is itself unusual; cf. my *Participle in Hesiod*, 433 f.

I think we may feel sure that lines 256–7 were interpolated, but we must remain uncertain as to just what preceded them.

The bearing upon the Homeric text of a passage in Thucydides i. 11. 1—ἐπειδὴ δὲ ἀφικόμενοι μάχῃ ἐκράτησαν (δῆλον δέ· τὸ γὰρ ἔρυμα τῷ στρατοπέδῳ οὐκ ἂν ἐτειχίσαντο) κτλ.—was first seen by Hermann (*Opuscula*, viii. 387) and then forgotten. La Roche (*HTk* 37) shows no acquaintance with it, nor does Ameis-Hentze[2] (*Anhang*, iii. 22) cite Hermann. It was necessary for M. L. Earle (*Collected Essays*, 142–4) to re-make the discovery. It is again disregarded by Wilamowitz and Bethe, but Gilbert Murray (*RGE*[2] 313) has appreciated its importance, and restated it in classic form: ' This shows that Thucydides (1) knew of the wall round the camp so frequently mentioned in our *Iliad*, and (2) surmised [1] that it must have been built at the beginning of the war after the first battle. Now in our *Iliad* (*H* 337 ff., 436 ff.) the building of this wall and the exact circumstances which led to it are fully described, and are not what Thucydides conjectures they "must have been ".' And p. 315: ' On the whole it seems to me probable that Thucydides used, or learnt at school, or heard recited at the Panathenaea, an *Iliad* without the account of the *Wall-building*.'

I see only two lines along which this argument could be attacked, but in neither case successfully. It might be argued that Thucydides is reproducing the view of some earlier writer,[2] whose testimony could apply only to some pre-Pisistratean stage of the poem. But even if that could be established, the fact that Thucydides could

---

[1] Or rather knew from another source. Thucydides is making an inference, but I think it is merely about the issue of the battle.

[2] Wilamowitz, *Ilias*, 338 n., suggests Hellanicus. Hecataeus might also be considered. D. S. Robertson, *Class. Rev.* 38 (1924). 7 emends very cleverly οὐκ ἂν ⟨ἔτει ι'⟩ ἐτειχίσαντο—but I cannot see that the text of Thucydides becomes thereby any more logical.

repeat the argument would still indicate that the Pisistratean text also lacked the *Wall-building*. It might also be claimed that Thucydides had in mind not the *Iliad* but the *Cypria*. That is true; but since Bethe (*Homer*, ii. 207–23) has shown that the poems of the *Cycle* do not overlap, it follows that if the *Wall-building* stood in the *Cypria*, it is an interpolation in the *Iliad*. That is what is indicated by Thucydides.

If Thucydides attests the *Wall-building* in the *Cypria*, it then becomes a problem to explain the absence of all allusion to it in the hypothesis of Proklos. It is easy to assume that it has been cut out to avoid a contradiction with the interpolated text of the *Iliad*; but (cf. Bethe, *ibid.* 204) the case is perhaps not so simple. There is confusion in our sources, Proklos and Apollodorus putting the embassy at different times. In opposition to Bethe 238 I think that the account of Proklos is intrinsically superior,[1] but the question is decided by a passage in Herodotus (ii. 118) that will go back ultimately[2] to the *Cypria*: ἐκβᾶσαν δὲ ἐς γῆν καὶ ἱδρυθεῖσαν τὴν στρατιὴν πέμπειν ἐς τὸ Ἴλιον ἀγγέλους, σὺν δέ σφι ἰέναι καὶ αὐτὸν Μενέλεων. τοὺς δ' ἐπείτε ἐσελθεῖν ἐς τὸ τεῖχος, ἀπαιτέειν Ἑλένην τε καὶ τὰ χρήματα τά οἱ οἴχετο κλέψας Ἀλέξανδρος, τῶν τε ἀδικημάτων δίκας αἰτέειν.

We must then regard as our best source the story told by Proklos: ἔπειτα ἀποβαίνοντας αὐτοὺς εἰς Ἴλιον εἴργουσιν οἱ Τρῶες, καὶ θνῄσκει Πρωτεσίλαος ὑφ' Ἕκτορος. ἔπειτα Ἀχιλλεὺς αὐτοὺς τρέπεται ἀνελὼν Κύκνον τὸν Ποσειδῶνος. καὶ τοὺς νεκροὺς ἀναιροῦνται. καὶ διαπρεσβεύονται πρὸς τοὺς Τρῶας τὴν Ἑλένην καὶ τὰ κτήματα ἀπαιτοῦντες. ὡς δὲ οὐχ ὑπήκουσαν ἐκεῖνοι, ἐνταῦθα δὴ τειχομαχοῦσιν. ἔπειτα τὴν χώραν ἐπεξελθόντες πορθοῦσι καὶ τὰς περιοίκους πόλεις. It is at first sight tempting to put the *Wall-building* with the *Burial of the Dead*,[3] as in the *Iliad*, but logically

---

[1] In Apollodorus the Greeks send their embassy not from Tenedos but from the fleet hovering off the Trojan coast (ἀναχθέντες δὲ ἀπὸ τῆς Τενέδου προσπλέουσι Τροίᾳ καὶ πέμπουσιν κτλ.); in Proklos the invaders force a landing and establish themselves in the country first. Being then in a position to exert pressure by threats of ravaging the countryside, they make a final demand for submission, all in accordance with Greek military practice.

[2] Cf. Aly, *Volksmärchen*, 66 f.

[3] The arrangements for this truce must have been such as to make Thucydides feel it necessary to argue that the Greeks did win the battle.

that is not its place, and I would suggest that τειχομαχοῦσιν has supplanted τειχοποιοῦσιν; when and with how much consciousness need not be decided.[1]

In defining the text used by Thucydides I would follow the delimitation of the interpolation made by Wilamowitz, *Ilias*, 52 ff., which differs only slightly from that of Robert, *Stud.* 168.

After the duel of Aias and Hector the Achaeans :

320 δαίνυντ', οὐδέ τι θυμὸς ἐδεύετο δαιτὸς ἐίσης.
321 νώτοισιν δ' Αἴαντα διηνεκέεσσι γέραιρεν
322 ἥρως Ἀτρείδης, εὐρυκρείων Ἀγαμέμνων.
345 Τρώων αὖτ' ἀγορὴ γένετ' Ἰλίου ἐν πόλει ἄκρῃ,
     δεινή, τετρηχυῖα, παρὰ Πριάμοιο θύρῃσι.

323 αὐτὰρ ἐπεὶ πόσιος καὶ ἐδητύος ἐξ ἔρον ἕντο,
     τοῖς ὁ γέρων πάμπρωτος ὑφαίνειν ἤρχετο μῆτιν,
325 Νέστωρ, οὗ καὶ πρόσθεν ἀρίστη φαίνετο βουλή·
     ὅ σφιν ἐϋφρονέων ἀγορήσατο καὶ μετέειπεν·
     "'Ατρείδη τε καὶ ἄλλοι ἀριστῆες Παναχαιῶν·
     πολλοὶ γὰρ τεθνᾶσι καρηκομόωντες Ἀχαιοί,
     τῶν νῦν αἷμα κελαινὸν εὔρροον ἀμφὶ Σκάμανδρον
330 ἐσκέδασ' ὀξὺς Ἄρης, ψυχαὶ δ' Ἄϊδος δὲ κατῆλθον·
     τῶ σε χρὴ πόλεμον μὲν ἅμ' ἠοῖ παῦσαι Ἀχαιῶν,
     αὐτοὶ δ' ἀγρόμενοι κυκλήσομεν ἐνθάδε νεκροὺς
     βουσὶ καὶ ἡμιόνοισιν· ἀτὰρ κατακείομεν αὐτοὺς
     τυτθὸν ἀπὸ πρὸ νεῶν, ὥς κ' ὀστέα παισὶν ἕκαστος
335 οἴκαδ' ἄγῃ, ὅτ' ἂν αὖτε νεώμεθα πατρίδα γαῖαν.
     τύμβον δ' ἀμφὶ πυρὴν ἕνα χεύομεν ἐξαγαγόντες
     ἄκριτον ἐκ πεδίου· ποτὶ δ' αὐτὸν δείμομεν ὦκα
     πύργους ὑψηλούς, εἶλαρ νηῶν τε καὶ αὐτῶν·
     ἐν δ' αὐτοῖσι πύλας ποιήσομεν εὖ ἀραρυίας,
340 ὄφρα δι' αὐτάων ἱππηλασίη ὁδὸς εἴη.
     ἔκτοσθεν δὲ βαθείαν ὀρύξομεν ἐγγύθι τάφρον,
     ἥ χ' ἵππον καὶ λαὸν ἐρυκάκοι ἀμφὶς ἐοῦσα,
     μή ποτ' ἐπιβρίσῃ πόλεμος Τρώων ἀγερώχων."
344 ὣς ἔφαθ', οἱ δ' ἄρα πάντες ἐπήνησαν βασιλῆες.

[1] The relation between the *Cypria* and B-H resulting from the use of the same underlying *epe* is too large a question to be broached here. I suspect that originally the *Embassy* resulted in arrangements for a duel between Paris and Menelaos. The author of the *Cypria* finding that no longer available made the *Embassy* end with the Trojans refusing to agree to the demands made of them, and the Achaeans fortifying the position they were to hold for the next ten years.

τοῖσιν δ' Ἀντήνωρ πεπνυμένος ἦρχ' ἀγορεύειν·
"κέκλυτέ μευ, Τρῶες καὶ Δάρδανοι ἠδ' ἐπίκουροι,
ὄφρ' εἴπω, τά με θυμὸς ἐνὶ στήθεσσι κελεύει.

350 δεῦτ' ἄγετ', Ἀργείην Ἑλένην καὶ κτήμαθ' ἅμ' αὐτῇ
δώομεν Ἀτρείδῃσιν ἄγειν· νῦν δ' ὅρκια πιστὰ
ψευσάμενοι μαχόμεσθα· τῷ οὔ νύ τι κέρδιον ἧμιν
ἔλπομαι ἐκτελέεσθαι, ἵνα μὴ ῥέξομεν ὧδε."
ἤτοι ὅ γ' ὡς εἰπὼν κατ' ἄρ' ἕζετο· τοῖσι δ' ἀνέστη

355 δῖος Ἀλέξανδρος, Ἑλένης πόσις ἠυκόμοιο,
ὅς μιν ἀμειβόμενος ἔπεα πτερόεντα προσηύδα·
"Ἀντῆνορ, σὺ μὲν οὐκέτ' ἐμοὶ φίλα ταῦτ' ἀγορεύεις·
οἶσθα καὶ ἄλλον μῦθον ἀμείνονα τοῦδε νοῆσαι.
εἰ δ' ἐτεὸν δὴ τοῦτον ἀπὸ σπουδῆς ἀγορεύεις,

360 ἐξ ἄρα δή τοι ἔπειτα θεοὶ φρένας ὤλεσαν αὐτοί.
αὐτὰρ ἐγὼ Τρώεσσι μεθ' ἱπποδάμοις ἀγορεύσω.
ἀντικρὺ δ' ἀπόφημι· γυναῖκα μὲν οὐκ ἀποδώσω·
κτήματα δ', ὅσσ' ἀγόμην ἐξ Ἄργεος ἡμέτερον δῶ,
πάντ' ἐθέλω δόμεναι καὶ ἔτ' οἴκοθεν ἄλλ' ἐπιθεῖναι."

365 ἤτοι ὅ γ' ὡς εἰπὼν κατ' ἄρ' ἕζετο· τοῖσι δ' ἀνέστη
Δαρδανίδης Πρίαμος, θεόφιν μήστωρ ἀτάλαντος,

367 ὅ σφιν ἐυφρονέων ἀγορήσατο καὶ μετέειπε·

370 "νῦν μὲν δόρπον ἕλεσθε κατὰ πτόλιν, ὡς τὸ πάρος περ,
καὶ φυλακῆς μνήσασθε καὶ ἐγρήγορθε ἕκαστος·
ἠῶθεν δ' Ἰδαῖος ἴτω κοίλας ἐπὶ νῆας
εἰπέμεν Ἀτρείδῃς, Ἀγαμέμνονι καὶ Μενελάῳ,
μῦθον Ἀλεξάνδροιο, τοῦ εἵνεκα νεῖκος ὄρωρε.

375 καὶ δὲ τόδ' εἰπέμεναι πυκινὸν ἔπος, αἴ κ' ἐθέλωσι
παύσασθαι πολέμοιο δυσηχέος, εἰς ὅ κε νεκροὺς
κείομεν· ὕστερον αὖτε μαχησόμεθ', εἰς ὅ κε δαίμων
ἄμμε διακρίνῃ, δώῃ δ' ἑτέροισί γε νίκην."

379 ὡς ἔφαθ', οἱ δ' ἄρα τοῦ μάλα μὲν κλύον ἠδὲ πίθοντο.

381 ἠῶθεν δ' Ἰδαῖος ἔβη κοίλας ἐπὶ νῆας.
τοὺς δ' εὖρ' εἰν ἀγορῇ Δαναούς, θεράποντας Ἄρηος,
νηὶ πάρα πρυμνῇ Ἀγαμέμνονος· αὐτὰρ ὁ τοῖσι

384 στὰς ἐν μέσσοισιν μετεφώνεεν ἠπύτα κῆρυξ·

386 "ἠνώγει Πρίαμός τε καὶ ἄλλοι Τρῶες ἀγαυοὶ
εἰπεῖν, αἴ κέ περ ὕμμι φίλον καὶ ἡδὺ γένοιτο,
μῦθον Ἀλεξάνδροιο, τοῦ εἵνεκα νεῖκος ὄρωρε·

κτήματα μέν, ὅσ᾽ Ἀλέξανδρος κοίλης ἐνὶ νηυσὶν
390 ἠγάγετο Τροίην δ᾽—ὡς πρὶν ὤφελλ᾽ ἀπολέσθαι—
πάντ᾽ ἐθέλει δόμεναι καὶ ἔτ᾽ οἴκοθεν ἄλλ᾽ ἐπιθεῖναι·
κουριδίην δ᾽ ἄλοχον Μενελάου κυδαλίμοιο
οὔ φησιν δώσειν· ἦ μὴν Τρῶές γε κέλονται.
καὶ δὲ τόδ᾽ ἠνώγεον εἰπεῖν ἔπος, αἴ κ᾽ ἐθέλητε
395 παύσασθαι πολέμοιο δυσηχέος, εἰς ὅ κε νεκροὺς
κείομεν· ὕστερον αὖτε μαχησόμεθ᾽, εἰς ὅ κε δαίμων
ἄμμε διακρίνῃ, δώῃ δ᾽ ἑτέροισί γε νίκην."
ὣς ἔφαθ᾽, οἱ δ᾽ ἄρα πάντες ἀκὴν ἐγένοντο σιωπῇ.
ὀψὲ δὲ δὴ μετέειπε βοὴν ἀγαθὸς Διομήδης·
400 "μήτ᾽ ἄρ τις νῦν κτήματ᾽ Ἀλεξάνδροιο δεχέσθω
μήθ᾽ Ἑλένην· γνωτὸν δέ, καὶ ὃς μάλα νήπιός ἐστιν,
ὡς ἤδη Τρώεσσιν ὀλέθρου πείρατ᾽ ἐφῆπται."
ὣς ἔφαθ᾽, οἱ δ᾽ ἄρα πάντες ἐπίαχον υἷες Ἀχαιῶν
μῦθον ἀγασσάμενοι Διομήδεος ἱπποδάμοιο.
405 καὶ τότ᾽ ἄρ᾽ Ἰδαῖον προσέφη κρείων Ἀγαμέμνων·
"Ἰδαῖ᾽, ἤτοι μῦθον Ἀχαιῶν αὐτὸς ἀκούεις,
ὥς τοι ὑποκρίνονται· ἐμοὶ δ᾽ ἐπιανδάνει οὕτως.
ἀμφὶ δὲ νεκροῖσιν κατακαιέμεν οὔ τι μεγαίρω·
οὐ γάρ τις φειδὼ νεκύων κατατεθνηώτων
410 γίνετ᾽, ἐπεί κε θάνωσι, πυρὸς μειλισσέμεν ὦκα.
ὅρκια δὲ Ζεὺς ἴστω, ἐρίγδουπος πόσις Ἥρης."
ὣς εἰπὼν τὸ σκῆπτρον ἀνέσχεθε πᾶσι θεοῖσιν·
ἄψορρον δ᾽ Ἰδαῖος ἔβη προτὶ Ἴλιον ἱρήν.
οἱ δ᾽ ἔατ᾽ εἰν ἀγορῇ Τρῶες καὶ Δαρδανίωνες
415 πάντες ὁμηγερέες, ποτιδέγμενοι, ὁππότ᾽ ἄρ᾽ ἔλθοι
Ἰδαῖος. ὁ δ᾽ ἄρ᾽ ἦλθε καὶ ἀγγελίην ἀπέειπε
στὰς ἐν μέσσοισιν· τοὶ δ᾽ ὁπλίζοντο μάλ᾽ ὦκα,
ἀμφότερον, νέκυάς τ᾽ ἀγέμεν, ἕτεροι δὲ μεθ᾽ ὕλην.
Ἀργεῖοι δ᾽ ἑτέρωθεν ἐϋσσέλμων ἀπὸ νηῶν
420 ὠτρύνοντο νέκυς τ᾽ ἀγέμεν, ἕτεροι δὲ μεθ᾽ ὕλην.
Ἤλιος μὲν ἔπειτα νέον προσέβαλλεν ἀρούρας,
ἐξ ἀκαλαρρείταο βαθυρρόου Ὠκεανοῖο
οὐρανὸν εἰσανιών· οἱ δ᾽ ἤντεον ἀλλήλοισιν.
ἔνθα διαγνῶναι χαλεπῶς ἦν ἄνδρα ἕκαστον·
425 ἀλλ᾽ ὕδατι νίζοντες ἄπο βρότον αἱματόεντα,
δάκρυα θερμὰ χέοντες, ἀμαξάων ἐπάειραν.

οὐ δ' εἴα κλαίειν Πρίαμος μέγας· οἱ δὲ σιωπῇ
νεκροὺς πυρκαϊῆς ἐπενήνεον ἀχνύμενοι κῆρ,
ἐν δὲ πυρὶ πρήσαντες ἔβαν προτὶ Ἴλιον ἱρήν.
430 ὣς δ' αὔτως ἑτέρωθεν ἐυκνήμιδες Ἀχαιοὶ
431 νεκροὺς πυρκαϊῆς ἐπενήνεον ἀχνύμενοι κῆρ,
432 ἐν δὲ πυρὶ πρήσαντες ἔβαν κοίλας ἐπὶ νῆας.
466 βουφόνεον δὲ κατὰ κλισίας καὶ δόρπον ἕλοντο.

_____

433 ἦμος δ' οὔτ' ἄρ πω ἠώς, ἔτι δ' ἀμφιλύκη νύξ,
τῆμος ἄρ' ἀμφὶ πυρὴν κριτὸς ἔγρετο λαὸς Ἀχαιῶν,
435 τύμβον δ' ἀμφ' αὐτὴν ἕνα ποίεον ἐξαγαγόντες
ἄκριτον ἐκ πεδίου, ποτὶ δ' αὐτὸν τεῖχος ἔδειμαν
πύργους θ' ὑψηλούς, εἶλαρ νηῶν τε καὶ αὐτῶν.
ἐν δ' αὐτοῖσι πύλας ἐνεποίεον εὖ ἀραρυίας,
ὄφρα δι' αὐτάων ἱππηλασίη ὁδὸς εἴη.
440 ἔκτοσθεν δὲ βαθεῖαν ἐπ' αὐτῷ τάφρον ὄρυξαν,
εὐρεῖαν, μεγάλην, ἐν δὲ σκόλοπας κατέπηξαν.
[ὣς οἱ μὲν πονέοντο καρηκομόωντες Ἀχαιοί·
οἱ δὲ θεοὶ πὰρ Ζηνὶ καθήμενοι ἀστεροπητῇ
θηεῦντο μέγα ἔργον Ἀχαιῶν χαλκοχιτώνων.
445 τοῖσι δὲ μύθων ἦρχε Ποσειδάων ἐνοσίχθων·
"Ζεῦ πάτερ, ἦ ῥά τίς ἐστι βροτῶν ἐπ' ἀπείρονα γαῖαν,
ὅς τις ἔτ' ἀθανάτοισι νόον καὶ μῆτιν ἐνίψει;
οὐχ ὁράᾳς, ὅτι δ' αὖτε καρηκομόωντες Ἀχαιοὶ
τεῖχος ἐτειχίσσαντο νεῶν ὕπερ, ἀμφὶ δὲ τάφρον
450 ἤλασαν, οὐ δὲ θεοῖσι δόσαν κλειτὰς ἑκατόμβας;
τοῦ δ' ἤτοι κλέος ἔσται, ὅσον τ' ἐπικίδναται ἠώς·
τοῦ δ' ἐπιλήσονται, τὸ ἐγὼ καὶ Φοῖβος Ἀπόλλων
ἥρῳ Λαομέδοντι πολίσσαμεν ἀθλήσαντε."
τὸν δὲ μέγ' ὀχθήσας προσέφη νεφεληγερέτα Ζεύς·
455 "ὢ πόποι, ἐννοσίγαι' εὐρυσθενές, οἷον ἔειπες.
ἄλλος κέν τις τοῦτο θεῶν δείσειε νόημα,
ὃς σέο πολλὸν ἀφαυρότερος χεῖράς τε μένος τε·
σὸν δ' ἤτοι κλέος ἔσται, ὅσον τ' ἐπικίδναται ἠώς.
ἄγρει μάν, ὅτ' ἂν αὖτε καρηκομόωντες Ἀχαιοὶ
460 οἴχωνται σὺν νηυσὶ φίλην ἐς πατρίδα γαῖαν,
τεῖχος ἀναρρήξας τὸ μὲν εἰς ἅλα πᾶν καταχεῦαι,
αὖτις δ' ἠιόνα μεγάλην ψαμάθοισι καλύψαι,
ὥς κέν τοι μέγα τεῖχος ἀμαλδύνηται Ἀχαιῶν."
ὣς οἱ μὲν τοιαῦτα πρὸς ἀλλήλους ἀγόρευον.]
465 δύσετο δ' ἠέλιος, τετέλεστο δὲ ἔργον Ἀχαιῶν.
For lines 368 f., 380, 385 cf. p. 18.

The lines of which we are thus freed have always been one of the chief causes of offence in the criticism of the end of *H*, itself generally regarded as one of the latest portions of the *Iliad*. Into this there is no need to go in detail.[1] Apart from more general and more debatable matters, the shorter text frees us from two glaring faults of the vulgate: (1) the dawn of two days (421, 433) without the mention of nightfall between; (2) the disappearance of the Trojans for a whole day, whereas in the older text they feast (477) like the Achaeans after the labour of burying the dead. It remains to be seen whether other passages imply the building of the wall during the action of the poem.[2]

In the Thucydidean text we come to the wall first at Θ 177, where Hector in the full tide of victory expects to sweep over it unchecked. Its sudden appearance need occasion no difficulty: hitherto the fighting has been further inland, and when we are driven back with the Achaeans to the camp, we accept the fact of its fortification as a matter of course. For the vulgate the sequence is not so easy: the outmarch of the Achaeans is suggested rather than described (Θ 53-4), with never a word about the fortifications that have just been built—a thing to be expected all the more because it would parallel the mention (Θ 58) of the Trojan walls. After Θ 177 we hear a great deal of the Achaean wall (cf. Bethe, *Homer*, i. 120-43), but only in *I* 348 ff. is there any indication of the time of its building. There Achilles has refused his aid, Agamemnon must do the best he can with Odysseus and the others:

> ἦ μὲν δὴ μάλα πολλὰ πονήσατο νόσφιν ἐμεῖο,
> καὶ δὴ τεῖχος ἔδειμε καὶ ἤλασε τάφρον ἐπ' αὐτῷ
> 350 εὐρεῖαν, μεγάλην, ἐν δὲ σκόλοπας κατέπηξεν·
> ἀλλ' οὐδ' ὣς δύναται σθένος Ἕκτορος ἀνδροφόνοιο
> ἴσχειν.

Wilamowitz (*Ilias*, 64 n.) considers it necessary to get rid of this, and therefore ascribes *I* 346-56 to the redactor of the *Presbeia*.

---

[1] The linguistic faults of the interpolation (cf. Leaf; Robert, *l.c.*; Bechtel, *Vocal-contr.* 126, 165, 217), and the violation (337 ∽ 436) of Wernicke's law (*AJP* 34 (1913). 171; Hermann, *Silbenbildung* 97) cannot be pressed because of the lateness of the context.

[2] Ⲏ 30-2 have often been cited as contradicting such a concept, but Leaf disputes the interpretation. In neither case is there a difficulty for the solution I am advocating.

That seems to me (so also to Cauer, *GGA* 179 [1917]. 219) impossible : the *schöne Zusammenhang* is anything but good ; [1] lines 346–7 are reported at 680–1 ; the lines are too beautiful, and too characteristically in the style of *I*. Bethe's judgement (p. 130) is correct ; we have here an indication of the presuppositions on which *I* as an independent poem was based.

That, however, is not sufficient to show that the author of Θ must have composed the *Wall-building*. To be sure he was trying to take up the suggestions of *I* and *K*, but we have no right to assume that he succeeded in embodying them all. On that point we must be guided by the external evidence, and it shows that this [2] piece of harmonizing was not his. I think well enough of the man to believe also, that had he attempted it, he would have done it better.[3]

As for the date of the interpolation, we cannot prove from Aristotle's remark (Strabo 598), ὁ δὲ πλάσας ποιητὴς ἠφάνισεν, that he was acquainted with it. According to Didymus (ς A at 452, ς T at 443), Zenodotus, Aristophanes, and Aristarchus καθόλου τὴν τῶν θεῶν ἀγορὰν ἠθέτουν, that will mean lines 442–64.[4] This unusual consensus of opinion (not to mention the probability that the epitomator has obliterated a distinction ; 'omisit Zenodotus, obelis notaverunt Aristophanes et Aristarchus') suggests the existence of MS. evidence against these lines, even at a time when the rest of the interpolation was firmly established. If so, the interpolation was not all of one piece.

The evening after the burial of the dead :

476   παννύχιοι μὲν ἔπειτα καρηκομόωντες Ἀχαιοὶ
      δαίνυντο, Τρῶες δὲ κατὰ πτόλιν ἠδ' ἐπίκουροι·
      παννύχιος δέ σφιν κακὰ μήδετο μητίετα Ζεὺς
      σμερδαλέα κτυπέων. τοὺς δὲ χλωρὸν δέος ᾕρει·

[1] I object to the sudden coming in of the second persons singular without the Ὀδυσσεῦ of 346 ; to the difficulty of ῥέξας, νηήσας without construction, which in the vulgate is eased by the presence of line 356.

[2] Later we shall see that the exchange of armour was not carried originally into the description of the arming of Patroclus.

[3] Bethe's argument (p. 218 n.) against such a view is based chiefly on an understanding of the text tradition which I have tried to show is untenable.

[4] Aristonicus (ς A at 443) says 443-64, but that was a slip on which the scholars of Pergamum (ς T at 464) seem to have pounced vigorously.

480   οἶνον δ' ἐκ δεπάων χαμάδις χέον, οὐδέ τις ἔτλη
πρὶν πιέειν, πρὶν λεῖψαι ὑπερμενέι Κρονίωνι.

482   κοιμήσαντ' ἄρ' ἔπειτα καὶ ὕπνου δῶρον ἕλοντο. ∽ I 713, τ 427.

The additional line was lacking in the text of Zenodotus according
to Aristonicus (s A): Ζηνόδοτος δὲ καὶ τοῦτον καὶ τὸν πρῶτον
τῆς ἐξῆς ῥαψῳδίας ἦρκε (Bekker; εἴρηκεν cod.) στίχον.

I am not, like Wecklein, _Z A V_ 65, impressed by a contradiction
between the παννύχιοι of 476 and the plus verse of the vulgate.
The latter is perfectly useless, the source of its interpolation is
evident, and we have no reason to add it against the external
evidence. The case may be allowed to rest there.

Duentzer's belief (_Zenod._ 154, 163) that Zenodotus had himself
removed the line is improbable in itself, and opposed to certain facts
which will be presented in connexion with the following line.

Θ

I   'Ηὼς μὲν κροκόπεπλος ἐκίδνατο πᾶσαν ἐπ' αἶαν.

The edition of Zenodotus (cf. _AJP_ 42 (1921). 258 f.) will be best
thought of as written continuously, like the Ptolemaic papyri, without book division. The note of Aristonicus quoted on _H_ 482
informed us that Θ I was missing from the text of Zenodotus.
Notes of the same scholar preserved in s A: ὅτι Ζηνόδοτος
μετατίθησι τὴν ἀνατολὴν κάτω πρὸς τὸ " οἱ δ' ἄρα δεῖπνον ἕλοντο ",
and at line 53: ὅτι πρὸ τούτου τὴν ἀνατολὴν τίθησι Ζηνόδοτος, show
that it stood between lines 52–3 of the vulgate.

The absence of any statement about the text of Zenodotus renders
it natural to suppose that in his edition the sunrise was told in the
same verse. That has been the general assumption, but Schultz—
GGA 174 (1912). 63—assumes that it was extended by a passage
modelled on γ 1–3. I think, however, that I can offer a restoration
of PHibeh 21 preferable to that suggested by Schultz, which will
show the papyrus in exact agreement with the Zenodotean text as
usually understood.

There are then, for the transposition of Θ I, four possible explanations : (1) There was a mechanical blunder in some source common
to Zenodotus and the papyrus. (2) The line is an interpolation
betrayed by its varying position. (3) The _Council of the Gods_

(lines 2–52) is an interpolation for the same reason. (4) Zenodotus
has preserved the original text. Of these (2) may be set aside at
once: in *BAT* the opening of the day is formally stated, and there
is no reason to doubt that the author of Θ followed the same pattern.
We must also discard (3), though it is suggested by Leaf: the
Council of the Gods is an interpolation in the *Iliad*, but in the
section $H^2Θ$ it is decidedly no interpolation. Wecklein (*ZAV* 65)
decides in favour of (4), but Leaf's objection seems valid against it.
We are thus left with (1), for which a parallel has already been adduced in the discussion of Paris' arming for his duel with Menelaos.

Zeus' speech to the Gods:

εἰ δ' ἄγε πειρήσασθε, θεοί, ἵνα εἴδετε πάντες,
σειρὴν χρυσείην ἐξ οὐρανόθεν κρεμάσαντες—
20 πάντες δ' ἐξάπτεσθε θεοὶ πᾶσαί τε θέαιναι—
ἀλλ' οὐκ ἂν ἐρύσαιτ' ἐξ οὐρανόθεν πεδίον δὲ
Ζῆν' ὕπατον μήστωρ', οὐδ' εἰ μάλα πολλὰ κάμοιτε.
ἀλλ' ὅτε δὴ καὶ ἐγὼ πρόφρων ἐθέλοιμι ἐρῦσαι,
αὐτῇ κεν γαίῃ ἐρύσαιμ' αὐτῇ τε θαλάσσῃ·
25 σειρὴν μέν κεν ἔπειτα περὶ ῥίον Οὐλύμποιο
δησαίμην, τὰ δέ κ' αὖτε μετήορα πάντα γένοιτο.
27 τόσσον ἐγὼ περί τ' εἰμὶ θεῶν περί τ' εἴμ' ἀνθρώπων."
41 ὣς εἰπὼν ὑπ' ὄχεσφι τιτύσκετο χαλκόποδ' ἵππω,
ὠκυπέτα, χρυσέῃσιν ἐθείρῃσιν κομόωντε,
χρυσὸν δ' αὐτὸς ἔδυνε περὶ χροΐ, γέντο δ' ἱμάσθλην
χρυσείην, εὔτυκτον, ἑοῦ δ' ἐπεβήσετο δίφρου.

28 ὣς ἔφαθ'· οἱ δ' ἄρα πάντες ἀκὴν ἐγένοντο σιωπῇ = Ι 430 = 693
μῦθον ἀγασσάμενοι· μάλα γὰρ κρατερῶς ἀγόρευσεν. ∽ Ι 431 = 694
30 ὀψὲ δὲ δὴ μετέειπε θεά, γλαυκῶπις Ἀθήνη· = Ι 432 = 696 + a 44
"ὦ πάτερ ἡμέτερε Κρονίδη, ὕπατε κρειόντων, = a 45
εὖ νυ καὶ ἡμεῖς ἴδμεν, ὅ τοι σθένος οὐκ ἐπιεικτόν· ∽Θ 463
ἀλλ' ἔμπης Δαναῶν ὀλοφυρόμεθ' αἰχμητάων, = Θ 464
οἵ κεν δὴ κακὸν οἶτον ἀναπλήσαντες ὄλωνται. = Θ 465
35 ἀλλ' ἤτοι πολέμου μὲν ἀφεξόμεθ', ὡς σὺ κελεύεις·
βουλὴν δ' Ἀργείοις ὑποθησόμεθ', ἥ τις ὀνήσει,
ὡς μὴ πάντες ὄλωνται ὀδυσσαμένοιο τεοῖο."
τὴν δ' ἐπιμειδήσας προσέφη νεφεληγερέτα Ζεύς· ∽ Χ 182
"θάρσει, Τριτογένεια, φίλον τέκος· οὔ νύ τι θυμῷ = Χ 183
40 πρόφρονι μυθέομαι, ἐθέλω δέ τοι ἤπιος εἶναι." = Χ 184
om. Bekker², damnat Christ.

814276   H

Of the two questions involved, the first may be dismissed briefly. [Arist.] περὶ ζῴων κιν. 4. 699ᵇ 35 quotes line 20 as following lines 21–22; while PHibeh 21 confirms the order of the vulgate. The varying position may betray the fact that the line is interpolated, but more probably it is merely the result of a clerical blunder.

The lines I have not included in my text were read but athetized by Aristarchus; the evidence being given by Aristonicus (ş A): ἐντεῦθεν (28) ἕως τοῦ " πρόφρονι μυθέομαι " ἀθετοῦνται στίχοι ιγ´. The Hibeh papyrus no doubt contained these verses, lines 28–32, 38–40 being still extant. It contained also instead of line 38:

> ὣς φάτο· μείδησεν δὲ πατὴρ ἀνδρῶν τε θεῶν τε
> χειρί τέ μιν κατέρεξεν, ἔπος τ᾽ ἔφατ᾽ ἔκ τ᾽ ὀνόμαζεν·

As Gerhard (8 n.) has observed, similar verses were read for Ξ 263 by some editors according to the T scholia.

Zenodotus, I believe—and Wecklein (ZAV 52) is of the same opinion—did not read these verses. The evidence was given by Didymus, but it has reached us in very corrupt form (ş T on Θ 37): τε οὐ σθένουσιν· οὐδὲ ἐν τῇ Ζηνοδότου δὲ ὁ φέρων· τότε γὰρ κτλ.: for various emendations cf. Maass; Ludwich, AHT i. 283; Roemer, AAH 232. The most probable solution seems to be : ἀθετοῦνται ⟨. . . . .⟩ οὐδὲ ἐν τῇ Ζηνοδότου ἐφέροντο, although ἀθετοῦσιν . . . . . . ἐφέρετο is not impossible. In the latter case the statement refers to line 37 alone, in which τεοῖο = σοῦ is singled out for criticism; but we are now coming to a series of passages in which Aristonicus testifies that Aristarchus athetized certain lines, and Didymus adds the information that Aristophanes had previously athetized the verses, and Zenodotus did not read them. It is most likely that the same relation existed here. The occurrence of the lines in PHibeh is no valid counter-argument; for we have seen in Γ a papyrus akin to Zenodotus, but containing interpolations from which his text was free.

If the short version is Zenodotean, there is no ground to question its superiority. The earlier literature is copiously cited in the Ameis-Hentze, Anhang, iii. 87, to which may be added that Lentz 30 approves Aristarchus' athetesis of the passage. Wilamowitz (Ilias, 42 n.) has pointed out that the interpolation is an unnecessary

and unsuccessful attempt to prepare for Hera's action in Θ 218 ; and also that it spoils the effectiveness of the present scene. Rothe (*Ilias*, 226) finds in Zeus' last words a ' feine Ironie des Dichters ', the intention being that Zeus shall here make ' eher einen komischen als einen furchtbaren Eindruck '. That is a *reductio ad absurdum* of the ' defence ' of the interpolation.

It is possible, I believe, to restore the Hibeh papyrus so that from Θ 17–73 it shall read without break. Except for the intrusion of line 38ᵃ, as just mentioned, Θ 17–48, 68–73 are in agreement with the vulgate, and reference to Grenfell and Hunt will suffice. For the rest I would read :

49   ἔνθ' ἵππους ἔστησε Κρόνου πάις ἀγκυλομ]ήτεω
50   λύσας ἐξ ὀχέων, κατὰ δ' ἠέρα πουλὺν ἔχευ]εν,
50ᵃ   [τοῖσιν δ' ἀμβροσίην Σιμόεις ἀνέτειλε νέμεσθαι·]
51   αὐτὸς δ' ἐν κορυφῇσι καθέζετο κύδεϊ γαί]ων,
51ᵃ   ["Ἴδης ἐν κορυφῇσι πολυπτύχου, ὑληέσσης,]
52   [εἰσορόων Τρώων τε πόλιν καὶ νῆας Ἀχαιῶν]
52ᵃ   [χαλκοῦ τε στεροπὴν ὀλλύντας τ' ὀλλυμένους τε.]
52ᵇ   ['Ηὼς μὲν κροκόπεπλος ἐκίδνατο πᾶσαν ἐπ' αἶαν,]
53   οἱ δ' ἄρα δεῖπνον ἕλοντο καρηκομόωντες Ἀχαιο]ὶ
54   ῥίμφα κατὰ κλισίας, ἀπὸ δ' αὐτοῦ θωρήσσον]το.
54ᵃ   ⟨τοὺς διεκόσμεον πάντες, ὅσοι πάρος ἦσαν ἄριστοι,⟩
54ᵇ   πάντη ἐποιχόμενοι· μετὰ δὲ κρείων] Ἀγαμέμνων,
54ᶜ   ὄμματα καὶ κεφαλὴν ἴκελος Διὶ τερ]πικεραύνῳ,
54ᵈ   Ἄρει] δὲ ζ[ώνην, στέρνον δὲ Ποσειδάω]νι.
55   Τρῶες δ' [αὖθ' ἑτέρωθεν ἀνὰ πτόλι]ν ὡπλί[ζο]ντο
55ᵃ   Ἕκτορά τ' [ἀμφὶ μέγαν καὶ ἀμύμον]α Που[λυ]δάμαντα
55ᵇ   Αἰνεία[ν θ', ὃς Τρωσὶ θεὸς ὣς τίετο δήμῳ,
55ᶜ   τρεῖς τ' Ἀ[ντηνορίδας, Πόλυβον καὶ Ἀγήνορα δῖον
55ᵈ   ἠίθεόν τ' Ἀκά[μαντ', ἐπιείκελον ἀθανάτοισιν,
56   παυρότεροι· μέμ[ασαν δὲ καὶ ὣς ὑσμῖνι μάχεσθαι,
57   χρήῃ ἀναγκα[ίῃ, πρό τε παίδων καὶ πρὸ γυναικῶν.
58   πᾶσαι δὲ ὤίγο[ντο πύλαι, ἐκ δ' ἔσσυτο λαός,
59   πεζο[ί θ' ἱ]ππῆ[ές τε· πολὺς δ' ὀρυμαγδὸς ὀρώρει
60   οἱ δ' ὅτε [δή] ῥ' ἐ[ς] χ[ῶρον ἕνα ξυνιόντες ἵκοντο,
61   σύρ ῥ' ἔβ[α]λον ῥ[ινούς, σὺν δ' ἔγχεα καὶ μένε' ἀνδρῶν
62   χαλκ[εοθ]ωρήκ[ων· ἀτὰρ ἀσπίδες ὀμφαλόεσσαι

63 ἔπλη[ντ' ἀλλ]ή[λῃσι, πολὺς δ' ὀρυμαγδὸς ὀρώρει.
64 ἔνθα δ' [ἄμ'] οἰμω[γή τε καὶ εὐχωλὴ πέλεν ἀνδρῶν
65 ὀλλύντων τ[ε καὶ ὀλλυμένων, ῥέε δ' αἵματι γαῖα.
65ᵃ ἐν δ' Ἔρις, [ἐ]ν δὲ Κ[υδοιμὸς ὁμίλεον, ἐν δ' ὀλοὴ Κήρ,
65ᵇ ἄλλον ζωὸν ἔχ[ουσα νεούτατον, ἄλλον ἄουτον,
65ᶜ ἄλλον τε[θ]ν[ηῶτα κατὰ μόθον ἕλκε ποδοῖιν·
65ᵈ ν[εκρούς τ' ἀνθρώπων ἔρυον κατατεθνηώτων.
65ᵉ [ὦρσε δὲ τοὺς μὲν Ἄρης, τοὺς δὲ γλαυκῶπις Ἀθήνη]
65ᶠ [Δεῖμός τ' ἠδὲ Φόβος καὶ Ἔρις, ἄμοτον μεμαυῖα,]
65ᵍ [Ἄρεος ἀνδροφόνοιο κασιγνήτη ἑτάρη τε,]
65ʰ [ἥ σφιν καὶ τότε μέσσῳ ὁμοίιον ἧκ]εν ὄλεθρο[ν
65ⁱ [ἐρχομένη καθ' ὅμιλον, ὀφέλλουσ'] εὖ στόν[ον ἀνδρῶν.
66 ὄφρ[α] μὲ[ν ἠὼ]ς ἦν [καὶ ἀέξετο ἱ]ε[ρὸν ἦμαρ,
67 τόφρα μά[λ' ἀ]μφοτ[έρων βέλε' ἥπτετο, πῖπτε δὲ λαός.
68 ἦμος δ' ἠέ[λιο]ς κτλ.

Line 50 corresponds to E 776, and I have restored E 777 as 50ᵃ. If the geography produced by the transplanting of these verses shocked the interpolator (a thing by no means certain) he may have substituted ποταμός, or taken instead :

Ξ 347 τοῖσι δ' ὑπὸ χθὼν δῖα φύεν νεοθηλέα ποίην.

For line 51ᵃ I have taken Φ 449, modifying it in accordance with X 171.

Line 52 is identical with Λ 82, and I have placed Λ 83 after it. This makes the present participle εἰσορόων express purpose, but that certainly would not have troubled the interpolator.

Line 52ᵇ = Θ 1 is attested in this place for Zenodotus, and the editors considered the possibility of its occurrence. At the time of their publication it 'was not possible to be so definite about the number of lines as it now is—thanks to Gerhard. That there is even any uncertainty about the location of these plus verses is due to the fact that]ων may be the end either of line 51 or of line 52.

The editors restored 54ᵇ μετὰ δὲ ... 54ᵈ corresponding to B 477–9. My reading of 54ᵃ (cf. B 476 and Λ 825) cannot claim to restore more than the sense, being too long for what was in the papyrus. The slight traces have been printed]ιϲεϲ . [. .] ι, but perhaps]ιοϲ . [.] ι would describe them better. The ι is quite certainly the end of the line. The beginning of 54ᵇ [16 letters] is exactly filled by πάντη ἐποιχόμενοι, which I have taken from Z 81, K 167.

From here to line 65^c I have followed the editors; lines 55^{a-d} being Δ 57–60, and 65^{a-c} (as recognized by Blass) Σ 535–7. What is needed is a line to close the picture, and I have taken Σ 540 with slight (and perhaps unnecessary) variations. The editors suggest τ for the fourth letter, but doubtfully.

If we turn now to the unidentified fragment _o_ we can soon convince ourselves that the second line cannot be restored from Homer except by the use of Δ 445. The variant ὀφέλλουσ' εὖ is not only in accord with the tendency of Ptolemaic papyri to strengthen the language, but fits nicely with the Homeric practice of placing εὖ after a participle, νηήσας εὖ I 358, φρίξας εὖ τ 446, the only other example in such a position being οἶδα γὰρ εὖ ρ 563. If this is so, it can hardly be preceded by anything except Δ 444 in variant form. It is also clear that ὄλεθρο[ν must come from the end of the line to accord with Homeric usage. Then νεῖκος must drop and μέσσῳ will naturally take its place. Whether the text read ὁμοίιον ἧκ]εν or ἀδευκέα βάλλ]εν is uncertain, but the former variant seems to meet better the spatial requirements and I have given it the preference. Now this distich could not be used without what precedes it; and remembering how the interpolator took Σ 535–7, 540, I have taken Δ 439–41, 444–5 with a similar break. The resulting five lines are exactly the number of lines required as 65^{e-i}, and the subject-matter suits admirably. Nor do I see in Θ any other place suitable for the interpolation of such a passage, except perhaps after line 252, where fortunately the papyrus is extant.

The difficulty comes with the attempt to fit fragment _o_ into what follows. It is not clear that the fragment is from the foot of a column, nor does the general appearance of the papyrus forbid the juncture. In line 66 ι]ερον may be reconciled with the slight traces; in line 67 λε seems reasonably sure, but an ι or ν before it would suit the ink-marks best.

Four columns (Θ 76–179) are completely missing. They contained 16 plus verses—supposing the interpolated line 123 to have been present. Of these no more can be said than that they may perhaps have included the plus verses about to be mentioned from other sources.

After Diomedes slays Hector's charioteer :

> ἔνθα κε λοιγὸς ἔην καὶ ἀμήχανα ἔργα γένοντο

131 καί νύ κε σήκασθεν κατὰ Ἴλιον ἠύτε ἄρνες,
     εἰ μὴ ἄρ' ὀξὺ νόησε πατὴρ ἀνδρῶν τε θεῶν τε.

131ᵃ Τρῶες ὑπ' Ἀργείων ἔλιπον δέ κεν Ἕκτορα δῖον
131ᵇ χαλκῷ δηιόωντα, δάμασσε δέ μιν Διομήδης.

The verses are preserved in the T scholia: ἔν τισι τῶν παλαιῶν φέρονται δύο στίχοι " Τρῶες . . . Διομήδης ". The authorship of the scholium is uncertain, the introductory formula not being (cf. Ludwich, AHT i. 285) one of those used by Didymus. La Roche's emendation δῃωθέντα seems unnecessary.

Wecklein (ZAV 78) makes the attractive suggestion that line 131 itself is part of the interpolation. The question must be decided on internal evidence; for the line which is found in PMus. Br. 736 is certainly a part of the vulgate, its omission by the first hand of M and by Xᵇ being accidental.

After Hector's taunt:

      ὣς φάτο· Τυδείδης δὲ διάνδιχα μερμήριξεν,
168 ἵππους τε στρέψαι καὶ ἐναντίβιον μαχέσασθαι.

168ᵃ ἢ μήτε στρέψαι μήτ' ἀντίβιον μαχέσασθαι.

It is Aristonicus (ꜱ A) who records: ὅτι ὑποτάσσουσιν " ἢ . . . μαχέσασθαι ".

The addition (cf. Ludwich, HV 24; Wecklein, ZAV 7) needs no discussion.

The ninth column (Θ 180–202) has been completed by the addition of PHeid. 1261. The first thing to note is the presence of line 183, which (cf. Part I) was originally foreign to the vulgate. Next, I would suggest that there is more in the substitution for φώνησέν τε of φαίδιμος Ἕκτωρ than has hitherto been suspected. The purpose was to permit the adding of

184ᵃ [καί σφεας φωνήσας ἔπεα πτερόεντα προσηύδα.]

The importance of this is the shortening by one verse of the long interpolation at the end of the column.

For the next plus verses [1] it will be sufficient to record Gerhard's supplements:

---

[1] Of small matters I should prefer κ' ἐνὶ θυμῷ for κεν ἔπειτα in line 196. Space could be saved in line 199 by reading σείσθη for σείσατο, if that would suffice.

197ᵃ ὀλλυμένο]υς· μάλα γάρ κε[ν ἐμεῦ γευσαίατο δουρός
199ᵃ χερσὶν δ᾽ ἀ]μφοτέραισιν ἑ[ὼ πεπλήγετο μηρώ.

Gerhard's recovery of the plus verses at the end of the column is a brilliant piece of work; and yet I think all must feel that the last verse

δῃώσας Δαναοὺς παρὰ θῖν᾽ ἁλός· αὐτὰρ Ἀχιλλεὺς
ἐσθλὸς ἐὼν Δαναῶν οὐ κήδεται οὐδ᾽ ἐλεαίρει

is unsuited to this place. The restoring of line 184ᵃ enables us to do without it, reading:

202ᵃ οἵ κεν δὴ κ]ακὸν οἶτον [ἀναπλήσαντες ὄλωνται
202ᵇ ἀνδρὸς ἐν]ὸς ῥιπ[ῇ· ὁ δὲ μαίνεται οὐκέτ᾽ ἀνεκτῶς,
202ᶜ [Ἕκτωρ, ὃς τάχα νῆας ἐνιπρήσει πυρὶ κηλέῳ]
202ᵈ [δῃώσας Δαναοὺς παρὰ θῖν᾽ ἁλὸς ἀτρυγέτοιο.]

On Wilamowitz (*Ilias*, 30 n.) these lines make 'durchaus den Eindruck der Echtheit'; I cannot understand the feeling, but find them typical representatives of this class of interpolation.

In the reconstruction of the next two columns (Θ 203–58) difficulty comes with the question raised by Gerhard whether the lines printed as 206ᵃ, 255ᵃ are in reality plus verses, or possibly mere interlinear variants. He does not make clear (p. 8) the grounds for his suspicion, and I can find no warrant for it in the papyrus. Of 206ᵃ little is left, but I am inclined to believe that the true decipherment is to be found not in the text but in the notes '[. . .]α κ[' of the English editors. I think we may restore it as:

207 [ἔνθ]α κ[άθοιτ᾽ αὐτοῦ ἀκαχήμενος οἷος ἐν Ἴδῃ.

The κε is not essential for the syntax, and the restored text would be akin to Zenodotus' reading:

αὐτοῦ κ᾽ ἔνθα κάθοιτ᾽ ἀκαχήμενος οἷος ἐν Ἴδῃ.

For line 255ᵃ [21 letters] . κειν[I have nothing to suggest; but if I have followed Gerhard's computation aright, he employs it as a plus verse, and I shall do likewise.

In the tenth column (Θ 203–30) two plus verses:

204ᵃ [. . . . . . .] και μ[
216ᵃ [ἔνθα κε λοιγὸς ἔην καὶ ἀμήχαν]α ἔργ᾽ ἐγένοντο

are extant. Verses 217 ff. stand opposite lines 251 ff., and this can best be brought about by assuming that there were three plus verses

between 207–16ᵃ, and that lines 224–6 (on which cf. Part I) were not contained in the papyrus. The last is Gerhard's suggestion, and I think we now have more reason than ever for accepting it.

In the last column (Θ 231–58), for the same reason, one verse before line 249 must be missing. It is again a brilliant suggestion of Gerhard's that line 235, which he has restored as Θ 202ᶜ, is the line in question.[1] If so, the athetesis by Aristophanes and Aristarchus rested in part at least on MS. evidence; it is regrettable that we cannot raise that to a certainty. I should follow van Leeuwen in restoring:

252ᵃ Ζεὺς δὲ πατὴρ ὤτρυνε φ[όβον Τρώεσσιν ἐνόρσας
252ᵇ εἶξαν δὲ Τρῶες τυτθὸν Δα[ναοῖσιν ὀπίσσω.

Ludwich's φ[άλαγγας κύδεϊ γαίων, though approved by the English editors, and now by van Leeuwen himself, sins against Wernicke's law—the sort of mistake that would not be expected of the interpolator.

Agamemnon speaks:

" Τεῦκρε, φίλη κεφαλή, Τελαμώνιε, κοίρανε λαῶν,
βάλλ' οὕτως, αἴ κέν τι φόως Δαναοῖσι γένηαι
283 πατρί τε σῷ Τελαμῶνι, ὅ σ' ἔτρεφε τυτθὸν ἐόντα·
285 τὸν καὶ τηλόθ' ἐόντα ἐυκλείης ἐπίβησον.

----

284 καί σε, νόθον περ ἐόντα, κομίσσατο ᾧ ἐνὶ οἴκῳ
om. van Leeuwen.

The text is that of Zenodotus; the plus verse was read, but athetized, by Aristophanes and Aristarchus. The evidence is given by Didymus: παρὰ Ζηνοδότῳ οὐδὲ ἦν· ἠθέτητο δὲ καὶ παρὰ Ἀριστοφάνει (ς A), or παρὰ Ζηνοδότῳ οὐκ ἦν· ἠθέτει δὲ καὶ Ἀριστοφάνης (ς T).

The short version is obviously superior. Wilamowitz (*Ilias*, 49 n.) and Wecklein (*ZAV* 50) have set forth the faults of the vulgate both in regard to legend and style. The line simply foists upon Homer the later mythology of which there is no trace in the *Iliad*. The question raised by Roemer (*AAH* 52 f.) whether lines 283–5 are not all interpolated falls outside the scope of this book.

----

[1] 235 om. Bekker; damn. Nauck, Ludwich. An improbable alternative would be line 231, which is not quoted in ς T at Υ 83.

Athena speaking to Hera:

εἰ γὰρ ἐγὼ τάδε ᾔδε' ἐνὶ φρεσὶ πευκαλίμῃσιν,
εὖτέ μιν εἰς Ἀίδαο πυλάρταο προύπεμψεν
ἐξ Ἐρέβευς ἄξοντα κύνα στυγεροῦ Ἀίδαο,
οὐκ ἂν ὑπεξέφυγε Στυγὸς ὕδατος αἰπὰ ῥέεθρα.
370 νῦν δ' ἐμὲ μὲν στυγέει, Θέτιδος δ' ἐξήνυσε βουλάς.
373 ἔσται μὰν ὅτ' ἂν αὖτε φίλην γλαυκώπιδα εἴπῃ.

371   ἦ οἱ γούνατ' ἔκυσσε καὶ ἔλλαβε χειρὶ γενείου
372   λισσομένη τιμῆσαι Ἀχιλλῆα πτολίπορθον.   = O 77

The text is that of Zenodotus, the plus verses were read but athetized by Aristarchus. The evidence is given partly by Aristonicus (s A) ἀθετοῦνται δύο στίχοι, partly by Didymus (s Aᵗ) οὐδὲ παρὰ Ζηνοδότῳ ἦσαν, or (s T) παρὰ Ζηνοδότῳ οὐκ ἦσαν οἱ δύο. This difference of form is not so significant as Roemer (*AAH* 145) represents it; if any supplement is to be made it should be ἠθέτει δὲ καὶ Ἀριστοφάνης. The parallelism with the note on Θ 284 would then be exact (cf. also Wecklein, *ZAV* 54).

The short version is perfectly satisfactory, the longer one offers difficulties. The γούνατ' ἔκυσσε recalls ξ 279 καὶ κύσα γούναθ' ἐλών, but that is man and man, while kissing between man and woman is in Homer most unusual; cf. most recently Wackernagel, *SU* 229. Unusual also is the application of πτολίπορθος to Achilles. In two (Θ 372 = O 77) of the four passages in which it occurs the lines are disposed of by the *recensio*; in a third (Φ 550) there was an ancient variant Ἀχιλλέα Πηλείωνα, while Ω 108 is from a portion of the poem for which our scholia flow less freely. Aristarchus probably athetized the last as well as the two first examples, since Aristonicus (s A) says of the epithet in Φ 550 νῦν δὲ ἅπαξ ἐπ' Ἀχιλλέως. His note (s A) at O 56 contains too sweeping a statement, probably because the epitomator has cut away the needed qualification. I should ascribe to a Pergamene source the counterargument in s T which Roemer (*AAH* 54) has successfully rewritten. Why should we bring into the *Iliad* these peculiarities in order to be told things evident to every one—except perhaps a schoolboy?

The interpolation was late enough to draw upon O 64-77.

After Athena's speech :

ὡς ἔφατ', οὐδ' ἀπίθησε θεά, λευκώλενος "Ηρη. ∽ E 719
382   ἡ μὲν ἐποιχομένη χρυσάμπυκας ἔντυεν ἵππους·   = E 720
384   αὐτὰρ Ἀθηναίη, κούρη Διὸς αἰγιόχοιο,   = E 733
388   τεύχεσιν ἐς πόλεμον θωρήσσετο δακρυόεντα·   = E 737
ἐς δ' ὄχεα φλόγεα ποσὶ βήσετο, λάζετο δ' ἔγχος = E 745
βριθὺ μέγα στιβαρόν, τῷ δάμνησι στίχας ἀνδρῶν = E 746
ἡρώων, τοῖσίν τε κοτέσσεται ὀβριμοπάτρη.   = E 747

383 cf. Part I.
385   πέπλον μὲν κατέχευεν ἑανὸν πατρὸς ἐπ' οὔδει   = E 734
ποικίλον, ὅν ῥ' αὐτὴ ποιήσατο καὶ κάμε χερσίν, = E 735
387   ἡ δὲ χιτῶν' ἐνδῦσα Διὸς νεφεληγερέταο   = E 736

The text is that of Zenodotus, the plus verses were read but athetized by Aristophanes and Aristarchus. The evidence is in a note of the A scholia that combines Aristonicus and Didymus: ἀθετοῦνται στίχοι τρεῖς ... ἠθέτει δὲ καὶ Ἀριστοφάνης· Ζηνόδοτος δὲ οὐδὲ ἔγραφεν. In the T scholia we have Didymus alone: Ἀριστοφάνης ἠθέτει τοὺς τρεῖς· Ζηνόδοτος δὲ οὐδὲ ἔγραψεν. Duentzer (*Zenod.* 164) already rejected as an error the contradictory statement of Aristonicus (s A) at E 734 : οἱ ἀστερίσκοι ὅτι ἐνταῦθα μὲν καλῶς κεῖνται, ἐν δὲ τῇ κόλῳ μάχῃ μηδεμιᾶς φαινομένης ἀριστείας οὐ δεόντως. ὁ δὲ Ζηνόδοτος τούτους μὲν ἀθετεῖ, ἐκείνους δὲ καταλείπει. Ludwich (*AHT* i. 293) saw that all that was required was emendation to παραλείπει, and Wecklein (*ZAV* 46 f.) approves the change.

The merits of the shorter version are obvious. Roemer (*AAH* 264 f.) gives a good presentation of the case. Surely there can be no question of intruding the lines.

Aristarchus athetized lines 390–1 also, and it is possibly due only to the epitomator that we do not hear of their absence from the edition of Zenodotus.

After the battle :

Τρώων αὖτ' ἀγορὴν ποιήσατο φαίδιμος "Εκτωρ,
490   νόσφι νεῶν ἀγαγὼν ποταμῷ ἐπὶ δινήεντι,
ἐν καθαρῷ, ὅθι δὴ νεκύων διεφαίνετο χῶρος.

492   ἐξ ἴππων δ' ἀποβάντες ἐπὶ χθόνα μῦθον ἄκουον·
497   " κέκλυτέ μευ, Τρῶες καὶ Δάρδανοι κτλ.

493 τόν ῥ' Ἕκτωρ ἀγόρευε διίφιλος· ἐν δ' ἄρα χειρὶ ᴠZ 318
     ἔγχος ἔχ' ἐνδεκάπηχυ· πάροιθε δὲ λάμπετο δουρὸς = Z 319
     αἰχμὴ χαλκείη, περὶ δὲ χρύσεος θέε πόρκης·   = Z 320
496 τῷ ὅ γ' ἐρεισάμενος ἔπεα Τρώεσσι μετηύδα·   ᴠB 109

The text is that of Zenodotus on the testimony of Aristonicus
(ς A): ὅτι Ζηνόδοτος περιγράφει ἀπὸ τούτου (493) τέσσαρας στίχους
κατὰ τὸ ἐξῆς. On the meaning of περιγράφειν cf. p. 48 f.; Wecklein (ZAV 41), misinterpreting this, ends by advocating (so also
Lentz, 16 f.) the rejection of the parallel passage. Zenodotus'
reading can be nothing but the reading of his MSS., since for an
excision of the passage there would be no rational motive.

Duentzer (Zenod. 164) maintained that the short version was
impossible : ' post μῦθον ἄκουον, nullo versu interposito, ipsa oratio
sequi nequit'. The Ameis-Hentze (Anhang, iii. 103) quotes
him, however, as demanding the rejection of these lines. His
second opinion is the wiser, as a comparison of Δ 137 ᴠ Φ 98
shows.

Against the external evidence arguments such as those adduced
by Wilamowitz (Ilias, 33) cannot prevail; at the most they can
show only how well the interpolator worked. His motive—to get
an explicit verbum dicendi before the speech—I have explained
and paralleled in CP 17 (1922). 213-21. He achieved his result
with a certain cleverness, but at the cost of little labour.

Zenodotus having read ἄας for ἠοῦς in Θ 470 would be expected
to show in Θ 525 the same text. There is no record of the variant,
and Wecklein (ZuA 33) very acutely suggests that lines 524-5 were
not in the text of Zenodotus.

Evidence of this sort lies outside the plan of my book, but I may
note that these lines contain the only example of ὑγιής in the
poems. The word is an unpoetic equivalent of σάος, and Aly
(Volksmärchen, 34 n.) has already concluded that Herodotus did
not get his λόγον οὐχ ὑγιέα from this passage of Homer.

Bekker² omits lines 523-41.

Hector speaking to the Trojans :

ἔλπομαι εὐχόμενος Διί τ' ἄλλοισίν τε θεοῖσιν
527   ἐξελάαν ἐνθένδε κύνας κηρεσσιφορήτους.

528   οὓς κῆρες φορέουσι μελαινάων ἐπὶ νηῶν.
om. Bekker[1], van Leeuwen ; damn. Nauck, Christ, Ludwich.

The text is that of Zenodotus ; the plus verse was read but
athetized by Aristarchus. The evidence is given by Aristonicus
and Didymus (ṣ A): ἀθετεῖται ... ὁ δὲ Ζηνόδοτος οὐδὲ ἔγραφεν
αὐτόν. In the T scholia Didymus alone is excerpted : Ζηνόδοτος
οὐδὲ γράφει τοῦτον.
The extra line is obviously a gloss and (cf. Wecklein, ZAV 52)
a bad one. Wilamowitz (Ilias, 29 n.) well says that it was 'fast
übertriebene Vorsicht' to admit it to the text. Aristarchus'
athetesis shows his appreciation of the situation.

Hector's speech continues :

ἀλλ' ἤτοι ἐπὶ νυκτὶ φυλάξομεν ἡμέας αὐτούς,
530   πρωὶ δ' ὑπηοῖοι σὺν τεύχεσι θωρηχθέντες
νηυσὶν ἔπι γλαφυρῇσιν ἐγείρομεν ὀξὺν Ἄρηα.
εἴσομαι, εἴ κέ μ' ὁ Τυδεΐδης, κρατερὸς Διομήδης,
πὰρ νηῶν πρὸς τεῖχος ἀπώσεται, ἤ κεν ἐγὼ τὸν
534   χαλκῷ δῃώσας ἔναρα βροτόεντα φέρωμαι
• 538   ἠελίου ἀνιόντος ἐς αὔριον. εἰ γὰρ ἐγὼν ὣς
•   εἴην ἀθάνατος καὶ ἀγήρως ἤματα πάντα,
• 540   τιοίμην δ' ὡς τίετ' Ἀθηναίη καὶ Ἀπόλλων,
ὡς νῦν ἡμέρη ἥδε κακὸν φέρει Ἀργείοισιν."

ɔ 535   αὔριον ἦν ἀρετὴν διαείσεται, εἴ κ' ἐμὸν ἔγχος
٠ɔ 536   μείνῃ ἐπερχόμενον· ἀλλ' ἐν πρώτοισιν, ὀίω,
ɔ 537   κείσεται οὐτηθείς, πολέες δ' ἀμφ' αὐτὸν ἑταῖροι
532-4 damn. Ludwich ; 535-41 damn. Christ.

The text is, in my opinion, that of Zenodotus ; but thanks to the
self-confessed laziness of the epitomator—τὰ αὐτὰ δὲ λέγει περὶ
τῶν στίχων τούτων ὁ Δίδυμος ἃ καὶ ὁ Ἀριστόνικος· διὸ οὐκ ἐγράψαμεν
τὰ Διδύμου—we have one of the worst tangles in the scholia. The
note of Aristonicus as it has reached us in ṣ A is : ὅτι ἢ τούτους δεῖ
τοὺς τρεῖς στίχους (535-7) μένειν, οἷς τὸ ἀντίσιγμα παράκειται, ἢ
τοὺς ἑξῆς τρεῖς, οἷς αἱ στιγμαὶ παράκεινται· εἰς γὰρ τὴν αὐτὴν

γεγραμμένοι εἰσὶ διάνοιαν. ἐγκρίνει δὲ μᾶλλον ὁ Ἀρίσταρχος τοὺς δευτέρους διὰ τὸ καυχηματικωτέρους εἶναι τοὺς λόγους. ὁ δὲ Ζηνόδοτος τοὺς πρώτους τρεῖς οὐδὲ ἔγραφεν. The marks of the codex Venetus I have printed in the margin.

Now there is here clearly corruption, for the second doublet consists in reality not of three but of four (538–41) verses. The solution of the difficulty has been sought along three lines.

(1) Wolf (*Prolegg.* 257 n. 43) moved the notes and marks up, so that lines 532–4, 535–7 should be the ones in question. This is the most violent of the changes suggested, but it has been approved by Ludwich (*AHT* ii. 141), and followed in his edition. The result is also most unsatisfactory ; the text read by Zenodotus and wished by Aristarchus being then obviously defective. Wecklein (*ZAV* 52 f.), seeing this, seeks to save the situation by assuming that τοὺς δευτέρους and τοὺς πρώτους have been interchanged.

(2) Pluygers suggested that Θ 540 = N 827 was an interpolation so late that it was not known to Aristarchus and his followers : lines 538, 539, 541 being the ones to which the στιγμαί originally belonged. The solution is easy and ingenious ; and has commended itself to many—to Wilamowitz (*Ilias*, 29 n.) most recently. If it were true I should expect, however, some disturbance in our MS. tradition. Of course it is possible that the line was interpolated early enough to make its way into all MSS. ; and to that extent the question must remain open, pending the discovery of early papyri.

(3) Bekker in his second edition of the *Iliad* emended the scholium to ἢ τοὺς ἐξῆς τέσσαρας, and the same result can be reached still more simply by reading ἢ τοὺς ἐξῆς.

Of these solutions the pre-Wecklein form of (1) may be pronounced untenable. All others agree on what for me is the main point—that Zenodotus did not read Θ 535–7, and that Aristarchus athetized the same lines. The two remaining questions are : (*a*) did Aristarchus condemn these lines as a doublet to 532–4 or as a doublet to 538–41 ; and (*b*) is line 540 Aristarchean or not ? Neither need be discussed further in this book.

The superiority of the short version is again obvious ; a text with both doublets is intolerable, nor is there any doubt which of the two is to be preferred.

These interpolators, however, usually work with the idea of lengthening the text, not of supplanting one passage with another. I am inclined therefore to believe with Christ that the original text ended with line 534, and was interpolated in two fashions, some adding 538–41, others 535–7 ; while the vulgate is a conflation of both.

After Hector's speech :

οἱ δ' ἵππους μὲν λῦσαν ὑπὸ ζυγοῦ ἱδρώοντας,
δῆσαν δ' ἱμάντεσσι παρ' ἅρμασιν οἷσιν ἕκαστος·
545 ἐκ πόλιος δ' ἄξαντο βόας καὶ ἴφια μῆλα
καρπαλίμως, οἶνον δὲ μελίφρονα οἰνίζοντο
547 σῖτόν τ' ἐκ μεγάρων, ἐπὶ δὲ ξύλα πολλὰ λέγοντο·
549 κνίσην δ' ἐκ πεδίου ἄνεμοι φέρον οὐρανὸν εἴσω.
553 οἱ δὲ μέγα φρονέοντες ἐπὶ πτολέμοιο γεφύρας
εἴατο παννύχιοι, πυρὰ δέ σφισι καίετο πολλά.

Sic Bekker[1], Leaf, Ludwich, van Leeuwen; sic voluit La Roche. 549 om. Bekker[2]; damn. Nauck.

This was the text of Aristarchus, on the testimony of all our MSS. ; cf. also Ludwich, *HV* 21 ; Wecklein, *ZAV* 68.

In [Plato] *Alc.* ii. 149 d is quoted in *oratio obliqua* a passage from ' Homer' which may be restored as :

ἔρδον δ' ἀθανάτοισι τεληέσσας ἑκατόμβας.　∽ *A* 315 *B* 306
κνίσην δ' ἐκ πεδίου ἄνεμοι φέρον οὐρανὸν εἴσω　= Θ 549
ἡδεῖαν· τῆς δ' οὔ τι θεοὶ μάκαρες δατέοντο,
οὐδ' ἔθελον· μάλα γάρ σφιν ἀπήχθετο "Ιλιος ἱρὴ ∽ Ω 27
καὶ Πρίαμος καὶ λαὸς ἐϋμμελίω Πριάμοιο.　= Δ 47

The quotation may be either from a Cyclic poem, or from a text of the *Iliad* contaminated with such a poem ; cf. Σ 608[a-d] for the contamination of Homer and Hesiod. Unfortunately Barnes used the lines for the padding of our vulgate, and was followed in this by Wolf.

Wecklein (*ZAV* 78 f.) would regard line 549 as a part of the interpolation ; but against this idea, which goes back to Bekker, Wilamowitz (*Ilias*, 30 n.) has argued effectively. We are then not told of the meal, and the οἱ δὲ in line 553 without change of subject makes a bad connexion.

Wilamowitz sees that the description of this unwelcome hecatomb does not belong here, and assigns it to the *Little Iliad* with great probability. But when he suggests that the interpolation was made by the author of Θ, I cannot follow him. The external evidence is against it, since there is nothing to suggest a lacuna in the vulgate. His belief in a longer text of Θ must also be rejected. We now have better material for judging the Ptolemaic text of Θ, and can see that, like other Ptolemaic texts, it has grown large through interpolation.

There follows the famous simile :

ὡς δ' ὅτ' ἐν οὐρανῷ ἄστρα φαεινὴν ἀμφὶ σελήνην
556 φαίνετ' ἀριπρεπέα, ὅτε τ' ἔπλετο νήνεμος αἰθήρ·
560 τοσσὰ μεσηγὺ νεῶν ἠδὲ Ξάνθοιο ῥοάων
Τρώων καιόντων πυρὰ φαίνετο Ἰλιόθι πρό.

557 ἔκ τ' ἔφανεν πᾶσαι σκοπιαὶ καὶ πρώονες ἄκροι   = Π 299
558 καὶ νάπαι· οὐρανόθεν δ' ἄρ' ὑπερράγη ἄσπετος αἰθήρ, = Π 300
559 πάντα δὲ εἴδεται ἄστρα, γέγηθε δέ τε φρένα ποιμήν.
557-8. om. Bekker ; damn. Ludwich.

The text is that of Zenodotus, the plus verses were read but athetized by Aristophanes and Aristarchus. The confusion in the scholia renders it uncertain whether two or three lines are in question. The clearest statement is that of Didymus (ꙅ T) : οὐκ ἐφέροντο τὰ γ' παρὰ Ζηνοδότῳ· ἠθέτει δὲ καὶ Ἀριστοφάνης τὰ γ'. But in ꙅ A at line 557 Aristonicus is abstracted : ἀθετεῖται ὅτι . . . καὶ ὁ ἑξῆς δὲ συναθετεῖται αὐτῷ . . ., and Didymus' statement is appended in abbreviated form : οὐκ ἐφέροντο δὲ οὐδὲ παρὰ Ζηνοδότῳ. ἠθέτει δὲ καὶ Ἀριστοφάνης. Aristonicus' note on Π 299–300 (ꙅ A) : ὅτι ἐνταῦθα οἰκείως κεῖνται . . . ἐν δὲ τῇ Θ κακῶς naturally throws no light on our question ; since he can there speak only of the lines taken from Π, regardless of the borrowing from other sources.

Roemer (*AAH* 248 f.) accepts the statement of Didymus ; Wecklein (*ZAV* 53) does the same, apparently without noting that it had been contradicted. I follow, not merely because the resulting text is better—in being free of the ' painfully prominent repetition ' of ἄστρα that kept Leaf from regarding 557-8 as interpolated ; but also because I think it is then easier to understand how the contradiction arose. Aristonicus treated each line separately, and two-thirds of the material was enough for the epitomator.

Wecklein observes that the interpolation must have led to a corruption of the text—ὡς δ' ὅτ' ἐν (555) for ὅσσα δ' ἐν. After that correction I do not see how any fault can be found with the short version. As for the additional lines of the vulgate the two first are Π 299–300, while the third gets its inspiration from Δ 279, its phraseology from ζ 106, Δ 683, N 493. That contrasts strongly with the originality of the immediate (553–65) context. The question of taste is (as always) debatable. Here it must be remembered that the short text has generally been wrongly defined—a heavy handicap. Even so Fränkel—intimately acquainted with the style of the similes and exceedingly conservative—leaves it an open question (p. 34 n.) whether lines 557–8 are not an interpolation. Ludwich and Lentz (26) affirm it positively ; they are Aristarcheans *strengster Observanz*, and Cauer (*GGA* 179 (1917). 528 n., *Grundfr.*[3] 472 n.) believes that no other type of scholar would to-day demand the ' Streichung der beiden störenden Verse '. But that is not the question. Roemer and Wecklein—who have defined the plus verses correctly—see that there is no need for their insertion, and that position seems irrefutable. I can agree most heartily with Cauer's emark ' Den Dichter der κόλος μάχη muss man nehmen wie er ist '—only that does not mean as he is in Wolf's edition.

I

The Argives are summoned to an assembly :

13   ἷζον δ' εἰν ἀγορῇ τετιηότες· ἂν δ' Ἀγαμέμνων
 *   ἵστατο δάκρυ χέων μετὰ δ' Ἀργείοισιν ἔειπεν·
17   "ὦ φίλοι, Ἀργείων ἡγήτορες ἠδὲ μέδοντες,
      Ζεύς με μέγα Κρονίδης ἄτῃ ἐνέδησε βαρείῃ,
      σχέτλιος, ὃς τότε μέν μοι ὑπέσχετο καὶ κατένευσεν
20   Ἴλιον ἐκπέρσαντ' εὐτείχεον ἀπονέεσθαι,
      νῦν δὲ κακὴν ἀπάτην βουλεύσατο, καί με κελεύει
22   δυσκλέα Ἄργος ἱκέσθαι, ἐπεὶ πολὺν ὤλεσα λαόν."
 *   ἤτοι ὅ γ' ὣς εἰπὼν κατ' ἄρ' ἕζετο θυμὸν ἀχεύων·

---

14 ἵστατο δάκρυ χέων ὥς τε κρήνη μελάνυδρος,   ∽ Π 3
15 ἥ τε κατ' αἰγίλιπος πέτρης δνοφερὸν χέει ὕδωρ·   = Π 4
16 ὡς ὁ βαρὺ στενάχων ἔπε' Ἀργείοισι μετηύδα·   = Σ 323 + B 109

* τοῖσι δ' ἀνιστάμενος μετέφη κρατερὸς Διομήδης·
32 "'Ατρείδη, σοὶ πρῶτα μαχήσομαι κτλ.

---

23 οὕτω που Διὶ μέλλει ὑπερμενέι φίλον εἶναι,   = B 116
24 ὃς δὴ πολλάων πολίων κατέλυσε κάρηνα   = B 117
25 ἠδ' ἔτι καὶ λύσει· τοῦ γὰρ κράτος ἐστὶ μέγιστον.   = B 118
26 ἀλλ' ἄγεθ', ὡς ἂν ἐγὼ εἴπω, πειθώμεθα πάντες·   = B 139
27 φεύγωμεν σὺν νηυσὶ φίλην ἐς πατρίδα γαῖαν·   = B 140
28 οὐ γὰρ ἔτι Τροίην αἱρήσομεν εὐρυάγυιαν."   = B 141
29   ὡς ἔφαθ', οἱ δ' ἄρα πάντες ἀκὴν ἐγένοντο σιωπῇ.   = I 693
30 δὴν δ' ἄνεῳ ἦσαν τετιηότες υἷες 'Αχαιῶν·   = I 695
31 ὀψὲ δὲ δὴ μετέειπε βοὴν ἀγαθὸς Διομήδης·   = I 696
23–5 om. Bekker²; damn. Nauck, Ludwich.

Aristonicus (ⓢ A) testifies that this is the text of Zenodotus:
ὥστε κρήνη μελάνυδρος] ὅτι Ζηνόδοτος γράφει "μετὰ δ' Ἀργείοισιν
ἔειπεν, ὦ φίλοι Ἀργείων". περιῄρηκε δὲ πάντα τὰ κατὰ τὴν παρά-
θεσιν (15–16) and again: ὅτι Ζηνόδοτος ἦρκε τοὺς στίχους (23–31)
πρὸς οὐδὲν ἀναγκαῖον, ἀλλ' ἕνεκα τοῦ κατ' ἄλλους τόπους φέρεσθαι.
τοιοῦτος δέ ἐστιν ἐπὶ τῶν διφορουμένων. τὴν δὲ συνέπειαν οὕτως
ποιεῖ "δυσκλέα . . . Διομήδης". For lines 23–5 this is confirmed
by Didymus (ⓢ T, cf. ⓢ Aᵗ): παρὰ τῷ Ζηνοδότῳ οὐκ ἐφέροντο οἱ τρεῖς·
καὶ Ἀριστοφάνης δὲ ἀθετεῖ. There is an instructive contrast between
Didymus' simple statement of fact and the polemical mixture of
fact and inference in Aristonicus.

There are here three interpolations which it is best to handle
separately:

(1) Lines 14–15: the inappropriate borrowing of the simile from
Π 3–4 is obvious; cf. Wilamowitz, *Ilias*, 33; Wecklein, *ZAV* 41 f.;
note also the awkwardness with which line 16 strives but fails to
resume the point of the simile.[1] Wilamowitz thinks the interpolation was made by the author of Θ; of him I have a better opinion,
but the external evidence removes the necessity for discussion.[2]

(2) The expansion of Agamemnon's speech. Wilamowitz declares
that the text of Zenodotus is unintelligible, a verdict with which
I cannot agree. Agamemnon simply lays the case before the

---

[1] According to Aristonicus, 'some' Zenodotus, *pace* Roemer, not included, read ὡς ὅ
γε δακρυχέων. The emendation shows a proper feeling for the difficulty, but a lamentable
indifference to cacophony.

[2] For an ingenious piece of special pleading for the lines, see Fraenkel, 21.

assembly ; but his statement of it—God has deceived me, and bids me return to Argos in disgrace—indicates sufficiently the proposal he expects and desires. That is a sufficient basis for Diomedes' reply.

In the main we have simply a supplement from *B* ; but three lines, *I* 23-5 = *B* 116-18, have proved to be original in neither place. These lines are here athetized by Aristophanes and Aristarchus, Roemer (*AAH* 233) agreeing. It is probable that they had less MS. support than the other lines—in other words, that the interpolation had been made piecemeal. The interpolator got them no doubt from a cyclic poem.

(3) The substitution of a more grandiose for a simpler form of transition. In addition to the closest parallel,[1] *I* 693 ff., compare *H* 398 f., *I* 430 ff., *K* 219 f., and especially its use (Θ 28 ff.) by an interpolator. Surely, had the vulgate been original, no one would have disturbed it.

Agamemnon replying to Nestor's suggestion that he should make amends :

$$\mathring{a}\lambda\lambda' \ \mathring{\epsilon}\pi\epsilon\mathring{\iota} \ \mathring{a}a\sigma\acute{a}\mu\eta\nu \ \phi\rho\epsilon\sigma\mathring{\iota} \ \lambda\epsilon\upsilon\gamma\alpha\lambda\acute{\epsilon}\eta\sigma\iota \ \pi\iota\theta\acute{\eta}\sigma\alpha\varsigma,$$
120 $\mathring{a}\psi \ \mathring{\epsilon}\theta\acute{\epsilon}\lambda\omega \ \mathring{a}\rho\acute{\epsilon}\sigma\alpha\iota \ \delta\acute{o}\mu\epsilon\nu\alpha\acute{\iota} \ \tau' \ \mathring{a}\pi\epsilon\rho\epsilon\acute{\iota}\sigma\iota' \ \mathring{a}\pi\omega\nu\alpha.$

119ᵃ ἢ οἴνῳ μεθύων, ἤ μ' ἔβλαψαν θεοὶ αὐτοί.

According to Athenaeus (i. 11ᵃ) the plus verse was quoted by Dioskourides, a pupil of Isocrates. Following Eustathius (1176, 11 ff.) Barnes printed the line after *T* 137, but Wolf did not follow him in this.

The line is no more than a gloss, the first half suggested by Achilles' taunt, *A* 225.

Wilamowitz' inclination (*Ilias*, 66 n.) to accept the line is based on the belief that the text has been bowdlerized. That idea I have discussed, p. 54 f. above.

Agamemnon winds up his offer of Trojan booty :

$$\Tau\rho\omega\iota\acute{a}\delta\alpha\varsigma \ \delta\grave{\epsilon} \ \gamma\upsilon\nu\alpha\hat{\iota}\kappa\alpha\varsigma \ \mathring{\epsilon}\epsilon\acute{\iota}\kappa\omega\sigma\iota\nu \ \alpha\mathring{\upsilon}\tau\grave{o}\varsigma \ \mathring{\epsilon}\lambda\acute{\epsilon}\sigma\theta\omega,$$
140 $\alpha\mathring{\iota} \ \kappa\epsilon \ \mu\epsilon\tau' \ \mathring{A}\rho\gamma\epsilon\acute{\iota}\eta\nu \ \mathring{E}\lambda\acute{\epsilon}\nu\eta\nu \ \kappa\acute{a}\lambda\lambda\iota\sigma\tau\alpha\iota \ \mathring{\epsilon}\omega\sigma\iota\nu.$

140ᵃ τὴν γὰρ ἀπ' αὖτις ἐγὼ δώσω ξανθῷ Μενελάῳ.

The plus verse is known from a note of Aristonicus (ș A): ὅτι ἔνιοι ὑποτάσσουσι στίχον " τὴν . . . Μενελάῳ ". On the surface this

---

[1] It will appear below that the missing line (694) is a still later interpolation.

means that Aristarchus knew the verse but did not include it in his text ; its attestation must then have been exceedingly weak. I am inclined to believe that here, as at Θ 168ᵃ, Aristonicus has added a comment of his own, and that the interpolation is even post-Aristarchean. That will account for the severity of Aristonicus' criticism εὐήθως πάνυ better than Wecklein's assumption (*ZAV* 8) that this was the text of Zenodotus.

Agamemnon speaking of Achilles :

> δμηθήτω—Ἀίδης τοι ἀμείλιχος ἠδ' ἀδάμαστος·
> τοὔνεκα καί τε βροτοῖσι θεῶν ἔχθιστος ἁπάντων—
> 160 καί μοι ὑποστήτω, ὅσσον βασιλεύτερός εἰμι
> ἠδ' ὅσσον γενεῇ προγενέστερος εὔχομαι εἶναι.

158ᵃ (159ᵃ) οὕνεκ' ἐπεί κε λάβῃσι πέλωρ ἔχει οὐδ' ἀνίησιν.

The line is known from a note of Didymus that has reached us in two forms : φησὶν ὁ Ἀρίσταρχος ὅτι ἔνιοι ὑποτάσσουσι τούτῳ (159) " οὕνεκ' . . . ἀνίησιν " (ⓢ A); and at line 158 (ⓢ T) ἔνιοι τοῦτο ὑποτάσσουσιν " οὕνεκ' . . . ἀνίησιν ".

The variation in the position of the line may well indicate that it was intended as a substitute for line 159. As Wilamowitz has seen, there can be no question of adding the line ; and indeed a period οὕνεκα . . . τοὔνεκα such as he prints (*Ilias*, 67 n.) is hardly Homeric ; cf. Lehrs, *Aristarchus* ³, 58 n.; Wecklein, *ZAV* 78. The feature πέλωρ applied to Hades, for which Wilamowitz values the line, is none too certain, Nauck's emendation λάβῃσιν ἕλωρ being most attractive.

Line 159 is thus to a certain extent discredited διὰ τὸ καὶ ἑτέρως φέρεσθαι. Agamemnon's meaning is plain enough without it.

On the surface, line 159ᵃ was known to Aristarchus, but not included in his edition; it may, however, be judged like Θ 168ᵃ, *I* 140ᵃ.

Disregarding minor variants, Plato read (*Hipp. Min.* 365 a) :

> " Διογενὲς Λαερτιάδη, πολυμήχαν' Ὀδυσσεῦ,
> χρὴ μὲν δὴ τὸν μῦθον ἀπηλεγέως ἀποειπεῖν,
> 310 ᾗ περ δὴ φρονέω τε καὶ ὡς τετελεσμένον ἔσται·

---

311 ὡς μή μοι τρύζητε παρήμενοι ἄλλοθεν ἄλλος cf. σ 231

312   ἐχθρὸς γάρ μοι κεῖνος ὁμῶς Ἀίδαο πύλῃσιν,
ὅς χ᾽ ἕτερον μὲν κεύθῃ ἐνὶ φρεσίν, ἄλλο δὲ εἴπῃ.
αὐτὰρ ἐγὼν ἐρέω, ὥς μοι δοκεῖ εἶναι ἄριστα.

Plato's text seems to me superior, and I see no reason why we should depart from it. The verb τρύζειν is not found elsewhere in the poems.

Aristotle (*Rhet.* iii. 11 : 1413ª 28) quotes as instances of ὑπερβολαὶ μειρακιώδεις lines 385, 388–90. I think the quotations are meant as two examples, for line 385 by itself produces an impression of completeness. There is thus no proof (cf. Roemer, *SB d. Münchn. Akad.* 1884, 275) that lines 386–7 were not in the text of Aristotle. Nauck was inclined to reject them, but line 386 at least seems necessary. Helbig (*RhM* xvi. (1861) 308 ff.; cf. Duentzer, *Aristarch.* 156) rejected line 387 alone. This is possible, but takes the discussion to questions of internal evidence.

Achilles describes the alternatives before him :

εἰ μέν κ᾽ αὖθι μένων Τρώων πόλιν ἀμφιμάχωμαι,
ὤλετο μέν μοι νόστος, ἀτὰρ κλέος ἄφθιτον ἔσται·
εἰ δέ κεν οἴκαδ᾽ ἵκωμι φίλην ἐς πατρίδα γαῖαν,
415   ὤλετό μοι κλέος ἐσθλόν, ἐπὶ δηρὸν δέ μοι αἰών.

416   ἔσσεται, οὐδέ κε μ᾽ ὦκα τέλος θανάτοιο κιχείη.
om. Bekker ; damn. Nauck, Christ, Ludwich.

According to Didymus this plus verse was not in the edition of Zenodotus (s Aᵗ T) : οὐδὲ παρὰ Ζηνοδότῳ ἐφέρετο. It was read but athetized by Aristarchus.

Interpolation of this type is frequent (cf. also Wecklein, *ZAV* 53), the purpose being to supply the construction for a clause which needs no supplement. Notice also how the line upsets the balance of the period.

Phoenix after telling of his mother's plot :

τῇ πιθόμην καὶ ἔρεξα· πατὴρ δ᾽ ἐμὸς αὐτίκ᾽ ὀισθεὶς
πολλὰ κατηρᾶτο, στυγερὰς δ᾽ ἐπεκέκλετ᾽ Ἐρινῦς,
455   μή ποτε γούνασιν οἷσιν ἐφέσσεσθαι φίλον υἱὸν
ἐξ ἐμέθεν γεγαῶτα· θεοὶ δ᾽ ἐτέλειον ἐπαράς,
457   Ζεύς τε καταχθόνιος καὶ ἐπαινὴ Περσεφόνεια.

458   τὸν μὲν ἐγὼ βούλευσα κατακτάμεν ὀξέι χαλκῷ·

462 ἔνθ' ἐμοὶ οὐκέτι πάμπαν ἐρητύετ' ἐν φρεσὶ θυμὸς
πατρὸς χωομένοιο κατὰ μέγαρα στρωφᾶσθαι.

459 ἀλλά τις ἀθανάτων παῦσεν χόλον, ὅς ῥ' ἐνὶ θυμῷ
460 δήμου θῆκε φάτιν καὶ ὀνείδεα πόλλ' ἀνθρώπων,
461 ὡς μὴ πατροφόνος μετ' 'Αχαιοῖσιν καλεοίμην.

ex. Plut. *Poet. aud.* 26ᶠ addunt Barnes, Wolf, Bekker, Nauck; et unc. secl. La Roche, Christ.

Plutarch's story—that Aristarchus removed (ἐξεῖλε) these lines, being shocked by their impropriety—has been discussed by Lehrs, *Arist.*³ 335; Duentzer, *Hom. Fr.* 193; Ludwich, *AHT* i. 73 (ii. 479), *HV* 40; Amoneit, *de Plutarchi stud. hom.* 48 f.; E. Meyer, *Hermes*, 27 (1892). 371; Murray, *RGE*² 142; Roemer, *AAH* 448 ff.; Finsler, *Homer*² ii. 95; Wilamowitz, *Ilias*, 66 n.; Wecklein, *ZAV* 68.

From Plutarch's statement we must infer that (1) he had observed that the lines were not in the vulgate MSS. of his day; (2) he believed that these MSS. depended on the edition of Aristarchus; (3) he knew, directly or indirectly, of a pre-Aristarchean text or texts in which these lines were contained; (4) he generalized and believed this of all early texts; (5) he drew the conclusion that Aristarchus had removed the lines, and proceeded to guess at his motives. Roemer, misinterpreting Porphyry, claims that the lines were in Aristarchus and rightly regarded by him as genuine. Ludwich admits that they may have stood in Aristarchus' edition, and been athetized—ἐξεῖλε being misused for ἠθέτησεν. Neither position can be maintained; had the lines been in the text of Aristarchus they would be in our manuscripts.

To return and criticize Plutarch: (1) we have every reason to believe this observation accurate, and may confidently expect papyri when discovered to confirm it; (2) I have argued in Part I for such a view—the interesting thing would be to know on what grounds Plutarch based his beliefs; (3) such texts would resemble the Ptolemaic papyri, and their existence is in nowise improbable; (4) the generalization is rash and opposed to what we know of Aristarchus; had he known any MS. evidence worthy of consideration he would have written the lines, athetizing them had it seemed desirable; with (4) falls (5) also.

Wilamowitz claims that this is merely pushing the responsibility for the bowdlerizing back one step. That assumes the lines to be

genuine, and the text bowdlerized.   I have already (p. 54 f.) made
my argument against a belief in bowdlerizing.   Had there been a
successful bowdler at work on the Homeric poems, it is obvious
that we would never have got the story of Phoenix in its present
shape.   The external evidence is against the lines, and the only
question is whether their insertion is necessary.   That they are not
as bad as other interpolations (cf. Leaf, Roemer, Wilamowitz) may
be conceded ; but even on internal evidence alone Finsler has made
a good case for refusing to regard them as genuine.

Phoenix argues :

> ἀλλ', Ἀχιλεῦ, δάμασον θυμὸν μέγαν· οὐδέ τί σε χρὴ
> 497   νηλεὲς ἦτορ ἔχειν· στρεπτοὶ δέ τε καὶ θεοὶ αὐτοί.
> 499   καὶ μὲν τοὺς θυέεσσι καὶ εὐχωλῆς ἀγανῆσι
> λοιβῇ τε κνίσῃ τε παρατρωπῶσ' ἄνθρωποι
> λισσόμενοι, ὅτε κέν τις ὑπερβήῃ καὶ ἁμάρτῃ.

> 498   τῶν περ καὶ μείζων ἀρετὴ τιμή τε βίη τε.

Apart from minor verbal variants, the passage is so quoted by
Plato, *Rep.* ii. 364 d.   The additional line simply emphasizes
unnecessarily that the argument is *a fortiori*.   Even its position in
the vulgate may be doubted : Dion. Hal., *Rh.* ix. 14 (Ludwich,
HZAD 30), quotes only lines 496–7, and papyrus evidence is still
lacking.

In the story of Meleager :

> ἡ δὲ χολωσαμένη, δῖον γένος, ἰοχέαιρα,
> ὦρσεν ἔπι χλούνην, σῦν ἄγριον, ἀργιόδοντα,
> 540   ὃς κακὰ πόλλ' ἔρδεσκεν ἔθων Οἰνῆος ἀλωήν.

Aristotle (*Hist. An.* vi. 28 : 578ᵃ 33) quotes :

> 539   θρέψεν ἔπι χλούνην, σῦν ἄγριον· οὐδὲ ἐῴκει ωι 190
> θηρί γε σιτοφάγῳ, ἀλλὰ ῥίῳ ὑλήεντι   ωι 191

Eustathius (p. 252 Neumann) ascribes the same variant to Strabo,
who derived it from Aristotle.

The contamination with the *Odyssey* is obvious, but we have no
reason to doubt (cf. Duentzer, *Zenod.* 159 n. ; Wecklein, *ZAV* 8)
that Aristotle has quoted his text correctly.

ILIAD *I* 123

After the close of Odysseus' report:

693   ὣς ἔφαθ'· οἱ δ' ἄρα πάντες ἀκὴν ἐγένοντο σιωπῇ.
695   δὴν δ' ἄνεῳ ἦσαν τετιηότες υἷες Ἀχαιῶν·
     ὀψὲ δὲ δὴ μετέειπε βοὴν ἀγαθὸς Διομήδης·

694 μῦθον ἀγασσάμενοι· μάλα γὰρ κρατερῶς ἀγόρευσε ∽ I 431
om. Bekker, van Leeuwen; damn. Nauck, Christ, Ludwich.

On the testimony of Didymus (s AA^{t}T) this is the text of Zenodotus: Ζηνόδοτος δὲ τὸν στίχον οὐκ ἔγραφεν (οὐ γράφει AT), Ἀριστοφάνης (Ἀρίσταρχος AT) δὲ ἠθέτει (ἀθετεῖ AT). Cf. Ludwich, *AHT* i. 170 f.

Some MSS. read ἀπέειπεν exactly as in *I* 431, and that was no doubt the earliest form of this interpolation, ἀγόρευσε being an ancient *Verschlimmbesserung*, found only here and in the interpolation Θ 29. Of the worth of the interpolated line there need be no discussion[1]: its date is shown by the fact that it was unknown to the interpolators of *I* 23–31. The relation between these passages was observed but misinterpreted by Duentzer, *Hom. Fragen*, 195.

K

The opening of B is quoted by mistake instead of the opening of K by Aristotle, *Poet.* xxv: 1461^a 16. The philosopher then continues: ἅμα δέ φησιν·

     ἤτοι ὅτ' ἐς πεδίον τὸ Τρωικὸν ἀθρήσειεν
     αὐλῶν συρίγγων θ' ὅμαδον

The preceding blunder—be it in the MS. tradition or in the quoter's memory—discredits to a certain extent the quotation that follows it. If it be regarded as accurate then Aristotle's MS. must have read:

11   ἤτοι ὅτ' ἐς πεδίον τὸ Τρωικὸν ἀθρήσειεν
13   αὐλῶν συρίγγων θ' ὅμαδον ἐνοπήν τ' ἀνθρώπων,
12   θαύμαζεν πυρὰ πολλά, τὰ καίετο Ἰλιόθι πρό.

This variation admits of three explanations:

(1) It is a clerical blunder, destitute of all significance. This is the easiest solution, but by no means certain.

(2) It is the original text; and some Alexandrian, being troubled by the isolated use of ἀθρήσειεν as a verb of intellectual perception,

[1] Cf. also Wecklein, *ZAV* 53, 75 n., with whose treatment of the scholia I cannot agree.

eased the situation by transposing the lines,[1] and assuming (cf. the scholia) a location of the king's tent that would permit the verb to have its usual meaning.

(3) The varying position of line 13 may indicate that it is interpolated. Duentzer (*Hom. Abh.* 308, 321) wished to reject the verse on other grounds; and so did (cf. Ameis-Hentze, *Anh.* iv. 16) Nauck, and van Leeuwen and Mendes da Costa. The line shows, however, more originality than would be expected in an interpolation. Nestor in waking Diomedes :

$$\text{`` } \xi\gamma\rho\epsilon o, \text{ } T\upsilon\delta\epsilon os \text{ } \upsilon i\epsilon\cdot \text{ } \tau i \text{ } \pi\alpha\nu\nu\upsilon\chi o\nu \text{ } \upsilon\pi\nu o\nu \text{ } \alpha\omega\tau\epsilon\hat{\iota}s \text{ ;}$$

160   οὐκ ἀίεις, ὡς Τρῶες ἐπὶ θρωσμῷ πεδίοιο
       εἴαται ἄγχι νεῶν, ὀλίγος δέ τε χῶρος ἐρύκει ; ''

Eustathius (p. 254 Neumann) has preserved in corrupt form an additional (159ᵃ) line : ὁ Νέστωρ τῷ Διομήδῃ κειμένῳ πού φησιν·

       ἔγρεο,
       μή τίς τοι [καθ]εύδοντι μεταφρένῳ ἐν δόρυ πήξῃ ∽ Θ 95

The matter is of interest because it shows how lines crawled from anecdotes to the text. Diog. La. (vi. 53) tells the following story of a quotation of Homer by Diogenes Cynicus : μειράκιον εὔμορφον ἀφυλάκτως ἰδὼν κοιμώμενον, νύξας " ἐπέγειραι " ἔφη

       " μή τις σοι εὔδοντι μεταφρένῳ ἐν δόρυ πήξῃ "

The story, probably, was told also with ἔγρεο substituted for ἐπέγειραι. With or without this aid some one stupidly inserted the line in his MS., and Eustathius was uncritical enough to make use of it.

After Diomedes has expressed his wish for a comrade :

       ὣς ἔφαθ'· οἱ δ' ἔθελον Διομήδεϊ πολλοὶ ἕπεσθαι·
       ἠθελέτην Αἴαντε δύω, θεράποντες Ἄρηος,
       ἤθελε Μηριόνης, μάλα δ' ἤθελε Νέστορος υἱός,
230   ἤθελε δ' Ἀτρείδης δουρικλειτὸς Μενέλαος,
       ἤθελε δ' ὁ τλήμων Ὀδυσεὺς καταδῦναι ὅμιλον
       Τρώων· αἰεὶ γάρ οἱ ἐνὶ φρεσὶ θυμὸς ἐτόλμα.
       τοῖσι δὲ καὶ μετέειπεν ἄναξ ἀνδρῶν Ἀγαμέμνων·
       " Τυδείδη Διόμηδες, ἐμῷ κεχαρισμένε θυμῷ,
235   τὸν μὲν δὴ ἕταρόν γ' αἱρήσεαι, ὅν κ' ἐθέλησθα,
       φαινομένων τὸν ἄριστον, ἐπεὶ μεμάασί γε πολλοί.

[1] One may assume that they had MSS. in which the transposition had occurred as a *mechanical blunder.*

μηδὲ σύ γ' αἰδόμενος σῇσι φρεσὶ τὸν μὲν ἀρείω
καλλείπειν, σὺ δὲ χείρον' ὀπάσσεαι αἰδοῖ εἴκων,
239 ἐς γενεὴν ὁρόων, μηδ' εἰ βασιλεύτερός ἐστιν."
241 τοῖς δ' αὖτις μετέειπε βοὴν ἀγαθὸς Διομήδης·

240 ὣς ἔφατ', ἔδδεισεν δὲ περὶ ξανθῷ Μενελάῳ.

The text is that of Zenodotus on the testimony of Didymus
(s AT): οὐδὲ ἐν τῇ Ζηνοδότου ἦν (δὲ ἦν A). About Aristophanes
we have no information, while Aristarchus' position is uncertain,
because of the confused form of Aristonicus' note.[1]

The line gives a correct but totally superfluous explanation of
Agamemnon's motive. That Wilamowitz likes the line is a matter
of taste, with which its interpolator would agree. Shewan (*Dolon*,
223) has no perception of the question; Duentzer (*Zenod.* 165)
claims that the line is essential, but on grounds that are not valid.
The αὖτις simply marks this as the second speech of Diomedes;
while the single verse between two speeches is (cf. Berger, 90) the
favourite type of formula in the *Doloneia*. Excellent parallels are
λ 342 (λ 343 is one of the post-Aristarchean interpolations), σ 405.

Not only is the version of Zenodotus in this way more in harmony
with its context, but the added line (cf. Berger, 90), by continuing
the same subject after ὣς ἔφατ', departs from ordinary Homeric
usage.

Under these circumstances there can be no question of bringing
the line into the text.

In accepting his appointment Odysseus says:

"Τυδεΐδη, μήτ' ἄρ με μάλ' αἴνεε μήτε τι νείκει·
250 εἰδόσι γάρ τοι ταῦτα μετ' Ἀργείοις ἀγορεύεις.
ἀλλ' ἴομεν· μάλα γὰρ νὺξ ἄνεται, ἐγγύθι δ' ἠώς·
ἄστρα δὲ δὴ προβέβηκε, παροίχωκεν δὲ πλέων νύξ."

253 τῶν δύο μοιράων, τριτάτη δ' ἔτι μοῖρα λέλειπται.
om. Bekker².

Didymus (s A) tells us that the plus verse was not in the text of
Zenodotus: Ζηνόδοτος οὐδὲ ἔγραφεν, and also (s AT) that it was

[1] Varying solutions by Roemer, *AAH* 203 f. ; Wilamowitz, *Ilias*, 61 n. ; Wecklein,
ZAV 58. Wilamowitz' attempt to establish a connexion with the omission of line 230
in a couple of medieval MSS. is discussed above, p. 6 f.

athetized by Aristophanes: Ἀριστοφάνης ἠθέτει (ἀθετεῖ T). Aristonicus (s A) says that Aristarchus athetized the line—a statement that Roemer (*AAH* 157 ff.) rejects.

Both texts were known to Aristotle. He quotes *Poet.* xxv : 1461ᵃ 25 παρῴχηκεν δὲ πλέω νύξ as an example of ἀμφιβολία ; an example that would have been destroyed by the addition of line 253. On the other hand, Porphyry (p. 149 Schr.) cites a λύσις by Aristotle for this famed problem. Wilamowitz (*Ilias*, 60 n.), agreeing with Bywater, says that this cannot be reconciled with the passage in the *Poetics*. I think (cf. above, p. 53) that the solution is that the λυτικός would accept as a basis for discussion any text the ἐνστατικός offered.

The external evidence must be decisive, though Wilamowitz will not so regard it. The speech of Odysseus is complete, and loses symmetry by the addition. The cause of the interpolation is to be found in the ἀμφιβολία for which Aristotle cites the passage.

Against the meaning there is nothing to be urged. The interpolator has filled out the passage in the language of common sense, and has fallen victim to pedantry. The criticism of his line is quite on a par with the remark attributed to a great astronomer, that Tennyson's lines,

> Every moment dies a man,
> Every moment one is born,

are false, for otherwise the population of the world would remain constant.

His language has required much explaining.[1] Aristarchus, according to Aristonicus, urged that there was no other example of δύο as genitive or dative in Homer. Leaf and Roemer cite in rebuttal δύω ποταμῶν κ 515, δύω κανόνεσσι Ν 407, but Cauer (*Grundfr.*³ 53 f.) and Wecklein (*ZAV* 55) have made the necessary reply.

Wecklein has approved an idea of Ludwich's (*AHT* i. 315) that the uninterpolated text was known even to the scholiast. It was a venturesome conjecture at the start, and I think has not hit the mark. The line was read by Philodemus of Gadara (Ludwich, *HZAD* 11), is attested by two papyri, and all our MSS. We have no reason to doubt that it has been firmly seated in the text ever

---

[1] For other points cf. Shewan, *Dolon*, 223, and the literature there cited.

since Aristophanes, no matter how clearly critics may have seen that it did not belong there.

Odysseus calls the attention of Diomedes to Dolon ; and then although Odysseus alone has spoken :

349   ὣς ἄρα φωνήσαντε παρ' ἐξ ὁδοῦ ἐν νεκύεσσι
      κλινθήτην· ὁ δ' ἄρ' ὦκα παρέδραμεν ἀφραδίῃσιν.

Didymus (s A, and with greater condensation s TV) defends this reading by adducing *Φ* 298, which will prove to be support of doubtful value. He also reports : ἐν μέντοι τῇ Ἀριστοφάνους καὶ ἄλλαις ἑτέρως ἐφέρετο·

      ὣς ἔφατ', οὐδ' ἀπίθησε βοὴν ἀγαθὸς Διομήδης·
      ἐλθόντες δ' ἑκάτερθε παρὲξ ὁδοῦ ἐν νεκύεσσι
      κλινθήτην.

Obviously the shorter version is to be preferred—the motive for the expansion being patent. In a Ptolemaic papyrus the longer text would occasion no surprise ; but it is curious that Aristophanes should have accepted it, and that Aristarchus should have reversed the judgement of his predecessor. Under ἄλλαις I should think first of the city editions and that of Rhianus ; cf. Wolf, *Proll.* 221 n. 97, and above, p. 41. Like Wecklein (*ZAV* 72 f.), I see no reason for believing, with Duentzer (*Zenod.* 159 f.), that we have here an emendation made by Zenodotus. Compare also Wackernagel, *KZ* 23 (1877). 307.

The slaughter of the sleeping Thracians ends :

      ἀλλ' ὅτε δὴ βασιλῆα κιχήσατο Τυδέος υἱός,
495   τὸν τρισκαιδέκατον μελιηδέα θυμὸν ἀπηύρα
      ἀσθμαίνοντα· κακὸν γὰρ ὄναρ κεφαλῆφιν ἐπέστη.

497 τὴν νύκτ', Οἰνείδαο πάις, διὰ μῆτιν Ἀθήνης.
om. Bekker, Nauck ; damn. Christ, Ludwich.

The text given is that of Zenodotus and Aristophanes on the testimony of Didymus (s Aᵗ): οὔτε ἐν ⟨τῇ⟩ Ζηνοδότου οὔτε ἐν τῇ Ἀριστοφάνους ἐφέρετο. Aristarchus received the plus verse into his text, but according to Aristonicus (s A) athetized it.

As Wilamowitz (*Ilias*, 60 n.) and Wecklein (*ZAV* 55) have seen, the external evidence is decisive. Whatever may be thought of Shewan, *Dolon*, 226, as a ' defence' of the line, it is no proof that

the line must be inserted. The bitter irony is in line 496 itself and requires no interpretation. This the interpolator attempted ; to expect him to regard the digamma is too much, but he has slipped in his syntax ; cf. Leaf, and van Leeuwen's correction to τῇ νυκτί.

The awakening of Hippokoon :

ὁ δ' ἐξ ὕπνου ἀνορούσας,
520   ὡς ἴδε χῶρον ἐρῆμον, ὅθ' ἔστασαν ὠκέες ἵπποι,
ἄνδρας τ' ἀσπαίροντας ἐν ἀργαλέῃσι φονῇσιν,
ὤμωξέν τ' ἄρ' ἔπειτα φίλον τ' ὀνόμηνεν ἑταῖρον.

According to Aristonicus (s A) the order of lines was different in the text of Zenodotus : ὅτι Ζηνόδοτος τὸ⟨ν ἕνα⟩ ἐναλλὰξ τῷ τόπῳ τούτῳ τίθησιν·

ὁ δ' ἐξ ὕπνου ἀνορούσας,
ὤμωξέν τ' ἄρ' ἔπειτα ⟨φίλον τ' ὀνόμηνεν ἑταῖρον⟩
ὡς ἴδε χῶρον ἐρῆμον, ⟨ὅθ' ἔστασαν ὠκέες ἵπποι,⟩
ἄνδρας τ' ἀσπαίροντας.

This is obviously impossible, but Wecklein (ZAV 66) seems to take the matter too seriously. It is simply a mechanical blemish started by the similarity of ⲰС and ⲰΙ at the beginning of the verses. It may have happened in the MSS. used by Zenodotus, or more probably in the antigraphon of his work used by Aristonicus.

In passing I may notice a matter that concerns the higher criticism. Line 522 is twice repeated (Ψ 178, Ω 591), and each time introduces a speech ; the longer formula beginning ὤμωξέν τ' ἄρ' ἔπειτα is also used O 397 f., ν 198 f., only in this way. Probably, therefore, as an independent lay K contained at this point a lamentation. In the *Iliad* it would have been inappropriate, as the scholiast felt, and it has accordingly been sacrificed.

As the heroes approach, Nestor speaks :

533   ὦ φίλοι, Ἀργείων ἡγήτορες ἠδὲ μέδοντες,
535   ἵππων μ' ὠκυπόδων ἀμφὶ κτύπος οὔατα βάλλει.

---

534   ψεύσομαι ἦ ἔτυμον ἐρέω; κελέται δέ με θυμός = δ 140

The line was not read by Zenodotus (s T) παρὰ δὲ τῷ Ζηνοδότῳ οὐκ ἦν ὁ στίχος.

Leaf and Shewan (*Dolon*, 227) discuss the line on the assumption

that it was excised by Zenodotus. As Wilamowitz (*Ilias*, 60 n.) has seen, this line is so inoffensive that no one would ever have been impelled to remove it. More generally (cf. also Wecklein, *ZAV* 59 f.) we have found that such assumptions are untenable.

Λ

Eris comes to the ships of the Achaeans:

10 ἔνθα στᾶσ' ἤυσε θεὰ μέγα τε δεινόν τε
 ὄρθι', Ἀχαιοῖσιν δὲ μέγα σθένος ἔμβαλ' ἑκάστῳ
12 καρδίῃ, ἄλληκτον πολεμίζειν ἠδὲ μάχεσθαι. = Β 452
15 Ἀτρείδης δ' ἐβόησεν ἰδὲ ζώννυσθαι ἄνωγεν

13 τοῖσι δ' ἄφαρ πόλεμος γλυκίων γένετ' ἠὲ νέεσθαι = Β 453
14 ἐν νηυσὶ γλαφυρῇσι φίλην ἐς πατρίδα γαῖαν. = Β 454
om. Bekker; damn. Nauck, Christ, Ludwich.

The text is that of Zenodotus; the additional lines were read, but athetized by Aristophanes and Aristarchus. The evidence is given partly by Aristonicus (ς A): οὗτος καὶ ὁ ἑξῆς ἀθετοῦνται, partly by Didymus (ς A): παρὰ Ἀριστοφάνει δὲ ἠθετοῦντο, παρὰ Ζηνοδότῳ ⟨δὲ⟩ οὐδὲ ἦσαν, or (ς T) Ζηνόδοτος οὐκ οἶδεν· Ἀριστοφάνης ἀθετεῖ.

The superiority of the shorter version is easily to be recognized (cf. Lentz, 5; Roemer, *AAH* 233; Bethe, *Homer*, i. 161 f.). Wilamowitz (*Ilias*, 183 n.) and Wecklein (*ZAV* 55) set a just value upon the external evidence.

The general description of the battle closed:

Ἔρις δ' ἄρ' ἔχαιρε πολύστονος εἰσορόωσα·
 οἴη γάρ ῥα θεῶν παρετύγχανε μαρναμένοισιν,
75 οἱ δ' ἄλλοι οὔ σφιν πάρεσαν θεοί, ἀλλὰ ἕκηλοι
 σφοῖσιν ἐνὶ μεγάροισι καθείατο, ἧχι ἑκάστῳ
 δώματα καλὰ τέτυκτο κατὰ πτύχας Οὐλύμποιο.

πάντες δ' ἠτιόωντο κελαινεφέα Κρονίωνα,
 οὕνεκ' ἄρα Τρώεσσιν ἐβούλετο κῦδος ὀρέξαι.
80 τῶν μὲν ἄρ' οὐκ ἀλέγιζε πατήρ· ὁ δὲ νόσφι λιασθεὶς
 τῶν ἄλλων ἀπάνευθε καθέζετο κύδεϊ γαίων,
 εἰσορόων Τρώων τε πόλιν καὶ νῆας Ἀχαιῶν
 χαλκοῦ τε στεροπὴν ὀλλύντας τ' ὀλλυμένους τε.
om. Bekker; damn. Nauck, Ludwich.

The text adopted is that of Zenodotus; the six following lines were read but athetized by Aristophanes and Aristarchus. The evidence is furnished partly by Aristonicus (ᔕ A): ἀθετοῦνται στίχοι ἕξ, partly by Didymus (ᔕ A): τούτους καὶ Ἀριστοφάνης ἠθέτει, παρὰ δὲ Ζηνοδότῳ οὐδὲ ἐγράφοντο, or (ᔕ T) τούτους δὲ Ζηνόδοτος οὐκ οἶδεν, Ἀριστοφάνης δὲ ἀθετεῖ. The six additional lines are a cento, and their worthlessness is easy to recognize. Those who wish to connect with them the lines that precede run counter to the external evidence, which indicates that even if all these be interpolated the interpolation is not of one piece. Roemer (*Zenod.* 38 ff., *AAH* 303), though looking at the problem from the wrong angle, saw that lines 78–83 must be 'rejected'. Bethe (*Homer*, i. 162) and Finsler (*Homer*² ii. 106) recognize the interpolation, though dating it too early. Wilamowitz (*Ilias*, 184) and Wecklein (*ZAV* 55) properly accept the external evidence as conclusive. When Rothe (*Ilias*, 250) denies the right 'diese Verse zu beseitigen' he is simply stating the question wrongly. We should ask what right have we to insert these verses in the face of this external evidence ?

The description of the Trojan flight closed :

ὡς τοὺς Ἀτρείδης ἔφεπε κρείων Ἀγαμέμνων,
178   αἰὲν ἀποκτείνων τὸν ὀπίστατον, οἱ δὲ φέβοντο.

179   πολλοὶ δὲ πρηνεῖς τε καὶ ὕπτιοι ἔκπεσον ἵππων
Ἀτρείδεω ὑπὸ χερσί· περὶ πρὸ γὰρ ἔγχεϊ θῦεν   ᔕ Π 699
om. Bekker, van Leeuwen ; damn. Ludwich.

The text is that of Zenodotus ; his successors read the two extra lines, but how they applied their obeli is uncertain. The scholia are greatly confused, and we seem to be left with contradictory statements of Didymus and Aristonicus. The note of the former in ᔕ T reads : Ἀριστοφάνης τοὺς δύο ἀθετεῖ· Ζηνόδοτος οὐ ⟨γράφει⟩, which should not be corrected by substituting as Maass did Ἀρίσταρχος for Ἀριστοφάνης. In ᔕ A a fuller form of this note has been preserved but it has suffered haplography : Ζηνόδοτος οὐκ ἔγραφεν· Ἀριστοφάνης δὲ ἠθέτει ⟨τοὺς δύο· Ἀρίσταρχος δὲ μόνον ἀθετεῖ⟩ τὸν "Ἀτρείδεω ὑπὸ χερσίν". That is, I believe, a correct statement of the facts, and shows the gradual growth of the text.

Aristonicus' note (5 A) is: ἀθετοῦνται ἀμφότεροι, καὶ ἀστερίσκοι παράκεινται, ὅτι κατὰ τὴν Πατρόκλου ἀριστείαν τάξιν ἔχουσι νῦν δὲ οὔ. The latter statement is erroneous, as a doublet for line 179 cannot be found. Bekker suggested the widely different Π 379, but Roemer (AAH 254 f.) has shown the impossibility of that suggestion. Friedländer, followed by Lentz (23), believed that Aristonicus had before Π 699 a plus verse ∽ Δ 179 ; to-day the suggestion is manifestly impossible. Consequently, as Roemer has seen, only line 180 could have been marked with an asterisk. That harmonizes with my restoration of Didymus, according to which Aristarchus athetized line 180 alone. Whether the inclusion of line 179 in his athetesis is a blunder of Aristonicus or of the epitomator may be left undecided.

At all events the lines were not in the text of Zenodotus, and that bit of evidence (cf. Wilamowitz, Ilias, 187 n. ; Wecklein, ZAV 55 f.) is decisive. Lentz (27) disregards it in order to reject lines 163–80. Whether the lines can be tolerated (Roemer, AAH 255) is not the question, but whether they must be inserted.

The form πρηνεῖς (cf. Bechtel, Vocalcontr. 49) is an indication of the date of the poem from which the line containing it has been lifted.

After Diomedes' speech to Odysseus :

ἦ ῥα καὶ ἀμπεπαλὼν προΐει δολιχόσκιον ἔγχος,
350 καὶ βάλεν, οὐδ' ἀφάμαρτε, τιτυσκόμενος κεφαλῆφιν,
ἄκρην κὰκ κόρυθα· πλάγχθη δ' ἀπὸ χαλκόφι χαλκὸς
οὐδ' ἵκετο χρόα καλόν· ἐρύκακε γὰρ τρυφάλεια
τρίπτυχος αὐλῶπις, τήν οἱ πόρε Φοῖβος Ἀπόλλων.
354 Ἕκτωρ δ' ὢκ' ἀπέλεθρον ἀνέδραμε, μίκτο δ' ὁμίλῳ.
357 ὄφρα δὲ Τυδείδης μετὰ δούρατος ᾤχετ' ἐρωὴν
τῆλε διὰ προμάχων, ὅθι οἱ καταείσατο γαίης,
τόφρ' Ἕκτωρ ἄμπνυτο, καὶ ἂψ ἐς δίφρον ὀρούσας
360 ἐξέλασ' ἐς πληθὺν καὶ ἀλεύατο κῆρα μέλαιναν.

355 στῆ δὲ γνὺξ ἐριπὼν καὶ ἐρείσατο χειρὶ παχείῃ ∽ E 309
356 γαίης· ἀμφὶ δὲ ὄσσε κελαινὴ νὺξ ἐκάλυψεν. = E 310

The text is adopted in the belief that it was that of Zenodotus, although such is not the statement of the Alexandrians as it has

reached us ; for, taking their statements at their face value, we should have to believe that line 356 alone was in question. Didymus tells us (s T) : Ζηνόδοτος οὐ γράφει, Ἀρίσταρχος δ' ἀθετεῖ, and more fully and correctly (s A¹) : προηθέτει Ἀριστοφάνης· Ζηνόδοτος δὲ οὐδὲ ἔγραφεν. According to the lemma of s T this refers to line 356, and that is confirmed by the note of Aristonicus (s A) : ὁ ὀβελὸς καὶ ὁ ἀστερίσκος ὅτι ἐν ἄλλῳ τόπῳ ὀρθῶς κεῖται, followed by a discussion that touches line 356 alone. However, without the line that follows line 355 is impossible, as Heyne, Nauck, Roemer (AAH 253), and Wecklein (ZAV 56) have seen, though Ludwich (AHT i. 329) is not convinced. There are, then, two alternatives : (1) to believe with Roemer that the athetesis of line 356 was a silly idea against which Aristarchus argued (without making the decisive point that it was needed to supplement line 355) and that our tradition is all topsy-turvy ; or (2) extend the statements to both lines. The latter involves much less correction of the tradition, and is in itself more probable.

Not only is the shorter text perfectly satisfactory, but the motive for the interpolation is clear. Some one overpressed the meaning of ἄμπνυτο and understood that Hector had swooned.[1] Naturally he felt that the fact should be stated, and he supplied the statement at the cost of little effort.

In s A is preserved a note beginning ὡς φιλοψευδὴς ὁ τυφλός, ὅτι καὶ ἄπιστα ψεύδεται, that brings out the contradictions between these lines and their context. It has been ascribed to Zoilus, but with doubtful right (cf. Friedländer, Zoilus, 63), so that it cannot be used to date the interpolation.

In describing the wounding of Machaon 3/2 a PDublin reads :

504   οὐδ' ἄν πω χάζοντο κελεύθου δῖοι Ἀχαι]οί,
  *   οὐδ' εἶξαν πολέμοιο δυσηχέος ὀλλύμε]νοί περ,
505   εἰ μὴ Ἀλέξανδρος, Ἑλένης πόσις ἠ]υκόμοιο,
506   παῦσεν ἀριστεύοντα Μαχάονα, ποιμέ]να λαῶν,
507   ἰῷ τριγλώχινι βαλὼν κατὰ δεξιὸν ὦμ]ον.

504ᵃ ΝΟΥΠΕΡ : οὐδ' εἶξαν πολέμοιο πεφυζότες οὐλομένου περ Ludwich ; ἀλλὰ καὶ ὡς κρατερῶς ἀντεῖχον τειρόμενοί περ van Leeuwen in violation of Wernicke's law.

[1] Lentz (6) and Roemer fall into the same error.

508 τῷ ῥα περίδεισαν μένεα πνείοντες] Ἀχαιοί,
509 μή πώς μιν πολέμοιο μετακλινθέν]τος ἔλοιεν
* Τρῶες ὑπέρθυμοι καὶ ἀπὸ κλυτὰ τεύ]χη ἔλοιντο.

509ᵃ : supplevit Robert.

The worthlessness of the plus verses is obvious. If not, the form
ἔλοιντο would indicate sufficiently the date; cf. Wackernagel, *S U*
89–96.

The speech of Idomeneus to Nestor:

511 "ὦ Νέστορ Νηληιάδη, μέγα κῦδος Ἀχαιῶν,
ἄγρει, σῶν ὀχέων ἐπιβήσεο, πὰρ δὲ Μαχάων
βαινέτω· ἐς νῆας δὲ τάχιστ' ἔχε μώνυχας ἵππους·
ἰητρὸς γὰρ ἀνὴρ πολλῶν ἀντάξιος ἄλλων."

515 ἰούς τ' ἐκτάμνειν ἐπί τ' ἤπια φάρμακα πάσσειν ῳ Λ 829 f.
om. Bekker, van Leeuwen; damn. Nauck, Ludwich. PDublin reads:

513 ἐς νῆας δὲ τάχιστ' ἔχε μών]υχας ἵππους
* νόσφιν ἀπὸ Τρώων τε καὶ Ἕκτορος ἀνδροφό]νοιο·
514 ἰητρὸς γὰρ ἀνὴρ πολλῶν ἀντάξιος ἄλ]λων·
* εἷς γὰρ ἐπιστάμενος πολλοὺς ἐσάωσε καὶ] ἄλλους
515 ἰούς τ' ἐκτάμνων, ἐπί τ' ἤπια φάρμα]κα πάσσων.

following for the new lines Robert and van Leeuwen.

The text preferred is that of Zenodotus; the additional line was
read but athetized by Aristophanes and Aristarchus. The evidence
comes partly from Aristonicus (s A): ἀθετεῖται, and partly from
Didymus (s A): καὶ Ἀριστοφάνης προηθέτει· Ζηνόδοτος δὲ οὐδὲ
ἔγραφεν, or (s T): Ζηνόδοτος δὲ οὐ γράφει· Ἀριστοφάνης δὲ ἀθετεῖ.
The text used by Plato probably agreed with that of Zenodotus;
for thrice (*Symp.* 214 b, *Pol.* 297 e, *Laws*, v. 730 d) he alludes to
line 514, but without ever a hint at the existence of the additional
line of the vulgate. The simpler interpolation of the vulgate I
regard as the more original: it is a loosely appended remark to
call attention to the services of the physician, which is more fully
elaborated in the papyrus. Wecklein (*Z A V* 38 f., 79) thinks that
the interpolations were made in the reverse order.

There can be no doubt of the superiority of the shorter version.
Its meaning is indeed spoiled (cf. Fick, *Ilias*, 483) by the interpolation. The sense is that the life of a physician is worth more to the

community than the lives of many laymen; not that a physician is better skilled than many laymen at cutting out arrows and using drugs.

After Idomeneus' speech:

> ὣς ἔφατ᾽, οὐδ᾽ ἀπίθησε Γερήνιος ἱππότα Νέστωρ·
> αὐτίκα δ᾽ ὧν ὀχέων ἐπεβήσετο, πὰρ δὲ Μαχάων
> βαῖν᾽, Ἀσκληπιοῦ υἱὸς ἀμύμονος ἰητῆρος.
> 519 μάστιξεν δ᾽ ἵππους· τὼ δ᾽ οὐκ ἄκοντε πετέσθην.
> 521 Κεβριόνης δὲ Τρῶας ὀρινομένους ἐνόησεν.

> 520 νῆας ἔπι γλαφυράς· τῇ γὰρ φίλον ἔπλετο θυμῷ.
> * ὣς ο[ἱ μὲν μάρναντο δέμας πυρὸς αἰθομένοιο·
> or ὣς ο[ἱ μεν σεύοντο θοὰς ἐπὶ νῆας Ἀχαιῶν·

The alternative to line 520 is found in 3/2 a PDublin; the restorations are those of van Leeuwen and of Robert, the former being the more probable.

Neither verse is needed, and I have regarded both as intruders διὰ τὸ καὶ ἑτέρως φέρεσθαι. Line 520 we have already met as an interpolation at K 531. It does not occur as a whole elsewhere in the Homeric poems. The phrases joined in it are common; cf. Δ 281 and Ξ 337 among others.

Kebriones speaking to Hector:

> ἀλλὰ καὶ ἡμεῖς
> κεῖσ᾽ ἵππους τε καὶ ἄρμ᾽ ἰθύνομεν, ἔνθα μάλιστα
> 529 κοῦροί τ[ε ἱππῆές τε κακὴν ἔριδα προφέρονται.

> 529 ἱππῆες πεζοί τε, κακὴν ἔριδα προβαλόντες,
> 530 ἀλλήλους ὀλέκουσι, βοὴ δ᾽ ἄσβεστος ὄρωρεν.

The text given is that of 3/2 a PDublin as restored by van Leeuwen.

The variant at the beginning need not be insisted upon, but that at the end restores the correct phrase. Nauck had seen the difficulty, and his προφέροντες was at least on the right track. The added line is composed from Σ 172 and Δ 500.

Of Hector after he comes to the rescue of the Trojans:

> 540 αὐτὰρ ὁ τῶν ἄλλων ἐπεπωλεῖτο στίχας ἀνδρῶν = Δ 264

ἔγχεῖ τ' ἄορί τε μεγάλοισί τε χερμαδίοισιν, = Λ 265
Αἴαντος δ' ἀλέεινε μάχην Τελαμωνιάδαο.

543 Ζεὺς γάρ οἱ νεμέσασχ' ὅτ' ἀμείνονι φωτὶ μάχοιτο
om. Bekker, Leaf, Ludwich, Monro-Allen, van Leeuwen; damn. La Roche
Nauck 540-3 damn. Christ.

The additional line is quoted (v. l. νεμέσησ') by Aristotle, *Rhet.*
ii. 9: 1387ᵃ 35, by Plutarch (*Poet. aud.* 24 c) and also (νεμεσᾶθ')
by [Plut.] *Vit. Hom.* ii. 132. It is unknown to the scholiasts, and is
found in no papyrus or manuscript. Barnes adapted it as P 99ᵃ, and
Wolf placed it here in accordance with Aristotle.

That it is an interpolation cannot be doubted. Wilamowitz
(*Ilias*, 192 n.) has located its source a *sententia* Ζεὺς γάρ τοι νεμεσᾶ,
ὅτ' ἀμείνονι φωτὶ μάχοιο preserved by Plutarch (*Poet. aud.* 36 a).
An echo of this or a similar *sententia* may be noted in [Plato]
Minos, 319 a : νεμεσᾶ γὰρ ὁ θεός, ὅταν τις ψέγῃ τὸν ἑαυτῷ ὅμοιον ἢ
ἐπαινῇ τὸν ἑαυτῷ ἐναντίως ἔχοντα.

Line 541 is well attested for the vulgate by two papyri ; its
omission by the first hand of Yᶜ (Wecklein, *ZAV* 30) must be therefore purely accidental. Plutarch (*Poet. aud.* 24 c), in a passage
derived according to Wilamowitz from Chrysippus, omits the line.
If he has preserved the text of his source the line is a late interpolation. Lentz (5 f.) has shown that it is unsuited to this context ;
but whether that tells against the single line or against lines 540-2
is a question not to be discussed in this book.

Nestor telling how Neleus disposed of the booty :

τῶν ὁ γέρων ἐπέων κεχολωμένος ἠδὲ καὶ ἔργων
704 ἐξέλετ' ἄσπετα πολλά· τὰ δ' ἄλλ' ἐς δῆμον ἔδωκε.

705 δαιτρεύειν, μή τίς οἱ ἀτεμβόμενος κίοι ἴσης ᵘ ι 42 = 549
om. Bekker; damn. Nauck, Ludwich.

The text is that of Zenodotus, according to Didymus (ẟ AAᶜT),
Ζηνόδοτος οὐδὲ ἔγραφεν (γράφει T). According to Aristonicus
(ẟ A) the line was athetized by Aristarchus.

Lentz (20) thought it necessary to eject the line ; at all events
there is no reason to insert it. Wecklein (*ZAV* 55) sees that the
shorter text is satisfactory.

Nestor after quoting the instructions of Menoitios:

790 ὡς ἐπέτελλ' ὁ γέρων, σὺ δὲ λήθεαι. ἀλλ' ἔτι καὶ νῦν
 ταῦτ' εἴποις Ἀχιλῆι δαΐφρονι, αἴ κε πίθηται.
 τίς δ' οἶδ', εἴ κέν οἱ σὺν δαίμονι θυμὸν ὀρίναις
793 παρειπών; ἀγαθὴ δὲ παραίφασίς ἐστιν ἑταίρου."

794	εἰ δέ τινα φρεσὶν ἦσι θεοπροπίην ἀλεείνει	ꟙ Π 36
795	καί τινά οἱ πὰρ Ζηνὸς ἐπέφραδε πότνια μήτηρ,	ꟙ Π 37
*	ἀργυρόπεζα Θέτις, θυγάτηρ ἁλίοι]ο γέροντος,	= Α 538
*	αὐτὸς μὲν μενέτω νηῶν ἐν ἀγ]ῶνι θοάων·	cf. Π 239
796	ἀλλὰ σέ περ προέτω, ἅμα δ' ἄλλος λαὸς ἐπέσθω	ꟙ Π 38
	Μυρμιδόνων, αἴ κέν τι φόως Δαναοῖσι γένηαι.	ꟙ Π 39
	καί τοι τεύχεα καλὰ δότω πόλεμον δὲ φέρεσθαι,	ꟙ Π 40
	αἴ κέ σε τῷ ἴσκοντες ἀπόσχωνται πολέμοιο	ꟙ Π 41
800	Τρῶες, ἀναπνεύσωσι δ' ἀρήιοι υἷες Ἀχαιῶν	= Π 42
	τειρόμενοι· ὀλίγη δέ τ' ἀνάπνευσις πολέμοιο.	= Π 43
	ῥεῖα δέ κ' ἀκμῆτες κεκμηότας ἄνδρας αὐτῇ	= Π 44
	ὤσαισθε προτὶ ἄστυ νεῶν ἄπο καὶ κλισιάων.	ꟙ Π 45

795ᵃᵇ add. 2 a. PGenav. 6, suppl. Nicole. 802–3 om. Bekker.

In presenting this text I believe that I am following Zenodotus. No note of Didymus has reached us, and that of Aristonicus (5 A): ὅτι Ζηνόδοτος ἐκ τούτου καὶ τὸν ἑξῆς περιέγραψεν, ἀναγκαίους ὄντας εἰς ἐρεθισμὸν Ἀχιλλέως is obviously corrupt. His only other note is on lines 802–3: ἀθετοῦνται ἀμφότεροι καὶ ἀστερίσκοι παράκεινται. The emendation began with Cobet reading καὶ τοῦτον καὶ τὸν ἑξῆς, which was later altered to οὐκ εὖ τοῦτον καὶ τὸν ἑξῆς by Lehrs. Roemer (AAH 75 f.) saw that without lines 794–5 the following lines could not stand; and Wilamowitz (Ilias, 204 n.) and Wecklein (ZAV 65) have since taken the same position.[1] For reasons already

---

[1] The exact emendation is difficult as three questions are entangled: the text of Zenodotus, the statement of Aristonicus, and the form given to it by the epitomator. Roemer and Wecklein have further complicated it by not noting that ἐκ τούτου must be included in the count so that the numbers they suggest (ἑπτά and ἐννέα) are one too low. At first sight it seems strange that Roemer should have extended Zenodotus' περίγραψις only to lines 794–801, for it is obvious that Zenodotus could not have wished to read 793, 802, 803 in succession. But it is perfectly possible that Aristonicus chose to divide his notes in this fashion: blaming Zenodotus for 'cancelling' 794–801, and mentioning the fact that his edition did not contain 802–3 (if he noted it at all) as a support for the Aristarchean athetesis of the lines. Palaeographically the confusion of η' with β' is easy, even if it lacks the dazzling quality of Wilamowitz' δ = either δύο or δίκα; and so on this ground there is little choice between the emendations. Both

given (p. 48 f.), I must understand from περιέγραψεν that Zenodotus did not read the lines in question ;[1] but I agree with Wilamowitz and Wecklein in believing 794–803 to be the lines meant. The comparative merits of the two versions require no long discussion. Wilamowitz, not seeing that the *recensio* disposes of the lines, argues convincingly for their ejection ; they are not merely superfluous, they are a positive offence in the *Iliad*. Similar opinions may be found in Heyne, Fick (83), Leaf, and Wecklein. Bethe (*Homer*, i. 150) sees that the passage in Π is the original, but dates the insertion of the lines here too early.

Looking at it from the point of internal evidence, Aristarchus (followed by Lentz, 7) seems to have swallowed a camel (794–801) only to strain at a gnat (802–3). His MSS. must have given support to these lines in different degrees—lines 802–3 being a still later interpolation than the lines that precede. In corroboration note how line 801, the end of the first interpolation, comes back to the same type of sentence as is found in line 793, the end of the original text.

In the remainder of the book PGenav. 6 shows also an expanded text :

804   ὡς φάτο, τῷ δ' ἄρα θυμὸν ἐνὶ στήθ]εσσιν ὄρινε·
*   τεῖρε γὰρ αἰνὸν ἄχος κραδίην, ἀ]κάχησε δὲ θυμό[ν. cf. Π 52
805   βῆ δὲ θέειν παρὰ νῆας ἐπ' Αἰακίδη]ν Ἀχιλῆα,
*   ἀγγελίην ἐρέων αὖτίς τ'] ἔνδυνε φάλα[γγας. cf. Ξ 355
806   ἀλλ' ὅτε δὴ κατὰ νῆας Ὀδυσσῆ]ος θείοιο
807   ἷξε θέων Πάτροκλος, ἵνα σφ' ἀγορή] τε θέμις τε
*   καὶ κλισίαι προπάροιθε νεῶν ὀρθ]οκραιράων
808   [ἦσαν,]

804ᵃ suppl. Nicole ; 805ᵃ Diels ; 807ᵃ Nicole.

suffer, however, from the fact that the counter-argument ἀναγκαίους ὄντας εἰς ἐρεθισμὸν Ἀχιλλέως applies (cf. ς BT) to lines 794–5 alone. It is possible to say that this is merely a stray fragment of the Aristarchean justification of lines 794–801 ; but it seems to me more probable that Aristonicus split his statement according to this defence. Then Lehrs is right, and our difficulties are due to the epitomator, who suppressed the notes on lines 796–801 ; or to the copyist who lost them. The curious note in ς T αἵ κέν τι φόως Δαναοῖσι] ὡς νῦν αὐτῶν ἐν σκότῳ ὄντων suggests that Aristonicus may have explained Zenodotus' omission of lines 796–7 much as he did his athetesis of Φ 538–9 : ἠθέτηκε γελοῖον ἡγούμενος διὰ πύλης φωτίζεσθαι τὴν πόλιν, τοῦ παντὸς τόπου ἐναιθρίου ὄντος.

[1] His spelling ἴσκοντες, cited by ς T, was to be found in Π 41.

M

The Trojans attack :

<blockquote>

ἐν δὲ πύλῃσι δύ' ἀνέρας εὗρον ἀρίστους,
υἷας ὑπερθύμους Λαπιθάων αἰχμητάων,
τὸν μὲν Πειριθόου υἷα, κρατερὸν Πολυποίτην,
130 τὸν δὲ Λεοντῆα, βροτολοιγῷ ἶσον Ἄρηϊ.

</blockquote>

130ᵃ υἱὸν ὑπερθύμοιο Κορώνου Καινείδαο ᴨ B 46

The plus verse is known from s T: τινὲς ἐπάγουσιν τῷ "ἶσον Ἄρηϊ" "υἱὸν . . . Καινείδαο". There can be no question of adding the verse. The method of citation is unusual, unless it is mere haplography: τῷ ⟨τὸν δὲ Λεοντῆα βροτολοιγῷ⟩ ἶσον Ἄρηϊ. The long note in s T praising the style of the passage is based on the interpolated text, which I suspect to be that approved by Crates.

After Asios has upbraided Zeus :

<blockquote>

ὣς ἔφατ', οὐ δὲ Διὸς πεῖθε φρένα ταῦτ' ἀγορεύων·
174 Ἕκτορι γάρ οἱ θυμὸς ἐβούλετο κῦδος ὀρέξαι.
182 ἔνθ' αὖ Πειριθόου υἱός, κρατερὸς Πολυποίτης,
δουρὶ βάλεν Δάμασον κυνέης διὰ χαλκοπαρῄου·

</blockquote>

<blockquote>

175 ἄλλοι δ' ἀμφ' ἄλλῃσι μάχην ἐμάχοντο πύλῃσιν· ᴨ Ο 414
ἀργαλέον δέ με ταῦτα θεὸν ὡς πάντ' ἀγορεῦσαι·
πάντῃ γὰρ περὶ τεῖχος ὀρώρει θεσπιδαὲς πῦρ
λάϊνον· Ἀργεῖοι δέ, καὶ ἀχνύμενοί περ, ἀνάγκῃ   cf. Ο 133
νηῶν ἠμύνοντο· θεοὶ δ' ἀκαχείατο θυμὸν
180 πάντες, ὅσοι Δαναοῖσι μάχης ἐπιτάρροθοι ἦσαν.   cf. Ρ 339
181 σὺν δ' ἔβαλον Λαπίθαι πόλεμον καὶ δηϊοτῆτα.   cf. Δ 447

</blockquote>

om. Bekker ; damn. Nauck, Christ, Ludwich ; 175–80 om. van Leeuwen.

The shorter version is that of Zenodotus ; the extra lines were read but athetized by Aristophanes and Aristarchus. Our authorities differ as to whether line 181 was or was not one of the plus verses. According to Aristonicus (s A) ἀπὸ τούτου (175) ἕως τοῦ "πάντες ὅσοι Δαναοῖσιν" ἀθετοῦνται στίχοι ϛ', but the BT scholia cite as one of Aristarchus' objections the use of Λαπίθαι in line 181. The line is attested by two papyri and the MSS., so that a reconciliation of these statements by supposing that Aristarchus did not read the line would be improbable. It being necessary to choose between the

two, the error made by Aristonicus seems to me the easier to understand.[1] The information about the earlier editors is given by Didymus (s A): ἠθετοῦντο δὲ καὶ παρὰ Ἀριστοφάνει· παρὰ Ζηνοδότῳ δὲ οὐδὲ ἐγράφοντο or (s T) Ζηνόδοτος οὐδὲ γράφει, Ἀριστοφάνης δὲ ἀθετεῖ.

The objections to the interpolation are well stated by Leaf, and a just verdict is rendered also by Wilamowitz, *Ilias*, 213; cf. Finsler, *Homer*², ii. 119.

The short version is again justified most clearly.

The famous speech of Sarpedon closes :

νῦν δ'—ἔμπης γὰρ κῆρες ἐφεστᾶσιν θανάτοιο
μυρίαι, ἃς οὐκ ἔστι φυγεῖν βροτὸν οὐδ' ὑπαλύξαι—
328   ἴομεν, ἠέ τῳ εὖχος ὀρέξομεν, ἠέ τις ἡμῖν.

328ᵃ   δώσει ἀποκτάμενος κλυτὰ τεύχεα καὶ δόρυ μακρόν.

The additional line was read by some according to Aristonicus (s A): τινὲς ὑποτιθέασι στίχον " δώσει ... μακρόν ".

It is a familiar type of interpolation, and this time the interpolator has betrayed the fact, cf. Wecklein (*ZAV* 9), that he did not understand the form ὀρέξομεν.

The Trojans swarm up the wall :

445   Ἕκτωρ δ' ἁρπάξας λᾶαν φέρεν, ὅς ῥα πυλάων
ἑστήκει πρόσθε, πρυμνὸς παχύς, αὐτὰρ ὕπερθεν
ὀξὺς ἔην· τὸν δ' οὔ κε δύ' ἀνέρε δήμου ἀρίστω
ῥηιδίως ἐπ' ἄμαξαν ἀπ' οὔδεος ὀχλίσσειαν,
449   οἷοι νῦν βροτοί εἰσ'· ὁ δέ μιν ῥέα πάλλε καὶ οἷος.
451   ὡς δ' ὅτε ποιμὴν ῥεῖα φέρει πόκον ἄρσενος οἰὸς
χειρὶ λαβὼν ἑτέρῃ, ὀλίγον τέ μιν ἄχθος ἐπείγει,
ὡς Ἕκτωρ ἰθὺς σανίδων φέρε λᾶαν ἀείρας.

450   τόν οἱ ἐλαφρὸν ἔθηκε Κρόνου παῖς ἀγκυλομήτεω ᴗ B 319
om. Bekker, van Leeuwen ; damn. Nauck, Christ, Ludwich.

The plus verse was not found in the edition of Zenodotus ; it was read, but athetized by Aristophanes and Aristarchus. The evidence is in the A scholia : ⟨ἀθετεῖται⟩ ὅτι ἐκλύει τὴν τοῦ βαστάζοντος

---

[1] But Wecklein (*ZAV* 55) follows Aristonicus.

δύναμιν (Aristonicus). καὶ Ἀριστοφάνης ἠθέτει, Ζηνόδοτος δὲ οὐδὲ ἔγραφεν (Didymus).

There can be no question of inserting the line in the face of the external evidence against it. Indeed, opinions differed even when there was supposed to be a question of ejecting it, but inclined in the main to a recognition of its worthlessness. Heyne, to be sure, countered the Aristarchean argument in a way that commended itself to Leaf, and Lachmann (46) would retain line 450 but remove 449 ∽ 383. Heyne, however, appreciated the weight of the external evidence, and so did Fick (*Ilias*, 491). Paley brackets the line, and Wecklein (*ZAV* 55) gives it short shrift. Bethe (*Homer*, i. 29) seems to ignore it, as do Wilamowitz (*Ilias*, 217) and Finsler (*Homer*, ii. 124). Roemer (*AAH* 175 n.) approves the rejection of the line, and collects other instances in which national partisanship has influenced the tradition. We shall meet examples of this on a larger scale.

It may be noted that the corresponding line B 319 has already turned out an interpolation.

N

At line 254 the T scholia report : ἔν τισι μετὰ τοῦτον φέρεται·

Ἰδομενεῦ, Κρητῶν βουληφόρε χαλκοχιτώνων.

The verse made its way into some MSS., and as line 255 into the Wolfian vulgate. It has consequently been discussed in Part I ; cf. also Wecklein, *ZAV* 30.

Othryoneus asked for Cassandra in marriage :

ὑπέσχετο δὲ μέγα ἔργον,
367 ἐκ Τροίης ἀέκοντας ἀπωσέμεν υἷας Ἀχαιῶν.

367ᵃ φοιτῶν ἔνθα καὶ ἔνθα θοὰς ἐπὶ νῆας Ἀχαιῶν

The plus verse is reported by ﹩ T : τινὲς δὲ ἐπάγουσι· "φοιτῶν ... Ἀχαιῶν". The verse is there admired, but in modern times no demonstration of its worthlessness is needed ; cf. Ludwich, *HV* 25.

I suspect that we are again dealing with Pergamene material.

After describing the good qualities of Hippodameia :

$$τοὔνεκα καί μιν$$
433   γῆμεν ἀνὴρ ὤριστος ἐνὶ Τροίῃ εὐρείῃ.

433ᵃ   πρὶν Ἀντηνορίδας τραφέμεν καὶ Πανθόου υἷας
    ᵇ   Πριαμίδας θ', οἳ Τρωσὶ μετέπρεπον ἱπποδάμοισιν,
    ᶜ   αὐτόν τ' Αἰνείαν ἐπιείκελον ἀθανάτοισιν,
    ᵈ   ἔως ἔθ' ἥβην εἶχεν, ὄφελλε δὲ κούριον ἄνθος.

The TV scholia introduce a quotation of three (a, b, d) of these
lines with the words τινὲς ἄλλους ὑποτάσσουσιν, and according to
Neumann (p. 271) Eustathius knew the interpolation in the same
form. According to Ludwich (AHT i. 360, HV 25), who is followed
by Wecklein (ZAV 10), the remaining line was interpolated by
Bekker². That cannot be entirely right, as Wolf (Proll. 259, n. 45)
already speaks of four lines in Eustathius.

The value of the interpolation needs no discussion. The ultimate
source is, no doubt, a cyclic poem, which would be expected (cf.
Bethe, Homer, ii. 257, 317) to show partiality for these heroes. The
immediate source is probably a Pergamene text.

The T scholia report : Ζηνόδοτος δὲ ὁ Μαλλώτης προστίθησιν·
ἄλλῳ δ' ὀρχηστύν, ἑτέρῳ κίθαριν καὶ ἀοιδήν.

The line (731) made its way into some MSS. and into the Wolfian
vulgate. It has consequently been discussed in Part I ; cf. also
Duentzer, Zenod. 23 f. ; Ludwich, HV 25 ; Wecklein, ZAV 68.

Here we have definitely attested a Pergamene origin for one of
these plus verses known from the T scholia.

In the description of Hector's advance :

πάντῃ δ' ἀμφὶ φάλαγγας ἐπειρᾶτο προποδίζων,
εἴ πώς οἱ εἴξειαν ὑπασπίδια προβιβῶντι·
808   ἀλλ' οὐ σύγχει θυμὸν ἐνὶ στήθεσσιν Ἀχαιῶν.
Αἴας δὲ πρῶτος προκαλέσσατο, μακρὰ βιβάσθων·

808ᵃ   λίην γάρ σφιν πᾶσιν ἐκέκριτο θάρσεϊ πολλῷ.

The extra line is introduced by Aristonicus with the phrase
(ⅎ A) ὅτι Ζηνόδοτος ὑποτάσσει, or (ⅎ T) μετὰ τοῦτον Ζηνόδοτος
γράφει. Didymus (ⅎ A) says with greater fullness : καὶ ὁ Ἀρίσταρχος
περὶ τοῦ στίχου οὕτως λέγει ὅτι ἐν τοῖς Ζηνοδοτείοις ἐφέρετο. The

line should follow line 807, as Friedländer noted. That may be the fault of the epitomator, and as such could be corrected without even a transposition of notes. It is equally probable, however, that the position in which the Aristarcheans found the line has been reported correctly; and if so, it must have been an interpolation in their antigrapha. This is all the more probable because, from the form of his statement, Didymus evidently had before him a report —of Ptolemaeus Epithetes; cf. Ludwich, *AHT* i. 48—that contradicted the statement of Aristarchus.

I do not see how the line can be satisfactorily interpreted. Duentzer (*Zenod.* 158) noted that θάρσεϊ πολλῷ is an unhomeric phrase, and it is perhaps worth noting that in our poems the perf. pass. of κρίνω is confined to the participle. Wecklein (*ZAV* 73) is of the opinion that we have not the long version complete, another line with a verb (μάχεσθαι for instance) being required. Be that as it may, we have no reason to suspect a lacuna in the vulgate.

Ξ

The conclusion of Odysseus' speech :

90   σίγα, μή τίς τ' ἄλλος Ἀχαιῶν τοῦτον ἀκούσῃ,
     μῦθον, ὃν οὔ κεν ἀνήρ γε διὰ στόμα πάμπαν ἄγοιτο,
     ὅς τις ἐπίσταιτο ᾗσι φρεσὶν ἄρτια βάζειν
     σκηπτοῦχός τ' εἴη, καί οἱ πειθοίατο λαοὶ
94   τοσσοίδ', ὅσσοισιν σὺ μετ' Ἀργείοισιν ἀνάσσεις·
96   ὃς κέλεαι πολέμοιο συνεσταότος καὶ αὐτῆς
     νῆας ἐυσσέλμους ἅλα δ' ἑλκέμεν, ὄφρ' ἔτι μᾶλλον
     Τρωσὶ μὲν εὐκτὰ γένηται ἐπικρατέουσί περ ἔμπης,
     ἡμῖν δ' αἰπὺς ὄλεθρος ἐπιρρέπῃ· οὐ γὰρ Ἀχαιοὶ
100 σχήσουσιν πόλεμον νηῶν ἅλα δ' ἑλκομενάων,
     ἀλλ' ἀποπαπτανέουσιν, ἐρωήσουσι δὲ χάρμης.
     ἔνθα κε σὴ βουλὴ δηλήσεται, ὄρχαμε λαῶν."

95   νῦν δέ σευ ὠνοσάμην πάγχυ φρένας, οἷον ἔειπες = P 173
om. Bekker ; damn. Nauck, Ludwich.

The A scholia offer a blend of Aristonicus and Didymus : ἀθετεῖται ὅτι ... (Aristonicus), Ζηνόδοτος δὲ γράφει "νῦν δέ σε ὠνοσάμην πάγχυ φρένας". καὶ Ἀριστοφάνης δὲ προηθέτει (Didymus). The T scholia contain only the statement of Didymus : Ζηνόδοτος "νῦν δέ σε "· Ἀριστοφάνης δὲ ἀθετεῖ.

On the surface this does not concern me, but on account of the ordinary relation of the three editors I believe the epitomator is at fault. The full statement would have been that Zenodotus here omitted the line, but read νῦν δέ σε at P 173. Roemer (*AAH* 243 n.) sees that the omission in Zenodotus is to be expected ; but is put off the track by the report of the variant, for which I have found (cf. p. 49) another explanation. It is also worth noting that Plato (*Laws*, iv. 706 e) quotes lines 96–102 ; though line 95, had it been in his text, would have been a more natural starting-point.

Reasons for 'retaining' the verse are collected by Benicken (*Stud.* i. 54 f.), reasons for 'rejecting' it are given by Lentz (20) and by Leaf. I do not see how there can be any question of inserting it.

Diomedes' speech begins :

110 ἐγγὺς ἀνήρ—οὐ δηθὰ ματεύσομεν—αἴ κ' ἐθέλητε
πείθεσθαι καὶ μή τι κότῳ ἀγάσησθε ἕκαστος,
οὕνεκα δὴ γενεῆφι νεώτατός εἰμι μεθ' ὑμῖν·
113 πατρὸς δ' ἐξ ἀγαθοῦ καὶ ἐγὼ γένος εὔχομαι εἶναι.
115 Πορθεῖ γὰρ τρεῖς παῖδες ἀμύμονες ἐξεγένοντο,
ᾤκεον δ' ἐν Πλευρῶνι καὶ αἰπεινῇ Καλυδῶνι,
Ἄγριος ἠδὲ Μέλας, τρίτατος δ' ἦν ἱππότα Οἰνεύς,
πατρὸς ἐμοῖο πατήρ· ἀρετῇ δ' ἦν ἔξοχος αὐτῶν.
ἀλλ' ὁ μὲν αὐτόθι μεῖνε, πατὴρ δ' ἐμὸς Ἄργεϊ νάσθη
120 πλαγχθείς· ὡς γάρ που Ζεὺς ἤθελε καὶ θεοὶ ἄλλοι.
Ἀδρήστοιο δ' ἔγημε θυγατρῶν, ναῖε δὲ δῶμα
ἀφνειὸν βιότοιο, ἅλις δέ οἱ ἦσαν ἄρουραι
πυροφόροι, πολλοὶ δὲ φυτῶν ἔσαν ὄρχατοι ἀμφίς,
πολλὰ δέ οἱ πρόβατ' ἔσκε· κέκαστο δὲ πάντας Ἀχαιοὺς
125 ἐγχείῃ· τὰ δὲ μέλλετ' ἀκουέμεν, εἰ ἐτεόν περ.

114 Τυδέος, ὃν Θήβῃσι χυτὴ κατὰ γαῖα κάλυψε cf. Ζ 464
om. Bekker ; damn. Nauck, Christ, Ludwich.

The scholia are in great confusion, but we can still see that some text or texts lacked this plus verse. Aristonicus (5 A) says: ὅτι "χυτὴ" γῆ ἡ ἐπὶ τοῖς νεκροῖς ἐπιχεομένη, οὐ καθολικῶς, ὡς "μέλαινα" καὶ "φερέσβιος". Didymus reports (5 A): Ζηνόδοτος δὲ ἠθέτει

παρὰ Ἀριστοφάνει δὲ οὐκ ἦν, or (5 T): Ζηνόδοτος ἠθέτει· παρὰ δὲ Ἀριστοφάνει οὐδὲ ἦν. There is also a note in 5 T on line 115: ἐπίτηδες δέ, εἰ μὴ εὐκαίρως, οὐ μέμνηται Τυδέως ὁ ποιητής.

The form of Aristonicus' note leaves the position taken by Aristarchus uncertain; Ludwich (*AHT* i. 369) asserts, and Roemer (*AAH* 206) denies, that he athetized the line. The former seems to me more probably correct, but from the standpoint of this book Aristarchus' verdict is the matter of least interest. The relation of Aristophanes to Zenodotus, as presented by Didymus, is most unusual; according to Wolf (*Proll.* 222, n. 98) entirely without parallel. Nauck restored the normal relationship by interchanging the names, so also Duentzer, *Zenod.* 168 n.; Wecklein, *ZAV* 56 f. It might be less violent to assume a defect in the antigraphon of Aristophanes, and thus accomplish the same result. The T scholium would still be left, however, attesting a text without the line.

The line is superfluous and clumsy rather than objectionable; the text printed will show, I think, that it is not indispensable, even when the genealogy follows. It is necessary therefore to be guided by the external evidence. Other discussions will be found in Benicken, *Stud.* i. 51 ff., and in Leaf. Robert (*Oidipus*, ii. 43) argues unconvincingly that the line could not have been interpolated after Aeschylus.

Strabo (x. 463) quotes line 117 before 116, but probably intentionally; cf. HBidder, 36—the source is Poseidonios.

The chiefs move towards the battle:

οὐδ' ἀλαὸς σκοπιὴν εἶχε κλυτὸς ἐννοσίγαιος,
136 ἀλλὰ μετ' αὐτοὺς ἦλθε παλαιῷ φωτὶ ἐοικώς,
δεξιτερὴν δ' ἕλε χεῖρ' Ἀγαμέμνονος Ἀτρεΐδαο,
καί μιν φωνήσας ἔπεα πτερόεντα προσηύδα·

136ᵃ ἀντιθέῳ Φοίνικι, ὀπάονι Πηλείωνος ∽ Ψ 360

The plus verse is cited by Aristonicus (5 A) from Zenodotus: ὅτι Ζηνόδοτος ὑποτάσσει " ἀντιθέῳ ... Πηλείωνος ". It is commented upon also in the T scholia : τὸ γὰρ προστιθέναι τὸν στίχον ἐκεῖνον " ἀντιθέῳ ... Πηλείωνος " περίεργον.

It would be impossible to maintain that the text contains a lacuna ; on the contrary Wilamowitz, *Ilias*, 231, finds a special

beauty in the anonymity of the god's disguise. Be that as it may, the external evidence is against the line, and it is too typically like the plus verses of the Ptolemaic papyri to permit us to regard it as anything but an interpolation. The interpolator must be credited with seeing that the vagueness of the god's disguise is 'unhomeric'. The attempt in s T to disprove this breaks down: θ 194 being extremely late, while δέμας δ' ἤικτο γυναικί is not (as Roemer, *AAH* 19, takes it) from δ 796, where the name follows, but from ν 288, π 157, υ 31. These passages are also irrelevant, because in them Athena appears not in disguise, but in her divine majesty.

It is surprising to find this line in the text of Zenodotus of Ephesus. Wecklein (*ZAV* 73) lists it among interpolated lines that Zenodotus found in his sources; cf. above, p. 44, for the possibility of other explanations.

Hera goes to Lemnos:

231   ἔνθ' Ὕπνῳ ξύμβλητο, κασιγνήτῳ Θανάτοιο,
  ἔν τ' ἄρα οἱ φῦ χειρὶ ἔπος τ' ἔφατ' ἔκ τ' ὀνόμαζεν·

231ᵃ   ἐρχομένῳ κατὰ φῦλα βροτῶν ἐπ' ἀπείρονα γαῖαν.

The plus verse is attested by the T scholia: τινὲς δὲ ⟨προσ⟩-γράφουσιν· " ἐρχομένῳ ... γαῖαν ".
It made its way also into PMorgan, and consequently has been treated in Part I; cf. also Ludwich, *HV* 25.

Hera speaking to Hypnos:

" κοίμησόν μοι Ζηνὸς ὑπ' ὀφρύσιν ὄσσε φαεινώ,
αὐτίκ' ἐπεί κεν ἐγὼ παραλέξομαι ἐν φιλότητι.
δῶρα δέ τοι δώσω καλὸν θρόνον, ἄφθιτον αἰεί,
χρύσεον· Ἥφαιστος δέ κ', ἐμὸς παῖς, ἀμφιγυήεις
240   τεύξει ἀσκήσας, ὑπὸ δὲ θρῆνυν ποσὶν ἥσει,
τῷ κεν ἐπισχοίης λιπαροὺς πόδας εἰλαπινάζων."

241ᵃ   αὐτὰρ ἐπὴν δὴ νῶι κατευνηθέντε ἴδηαι
ᵇ   ἀγγεῖλαι τάδε πάντα Ποσειδάωνι ἄνακτι.

The plus verses are quoted in the T scholia (κατευνηθέντες cod.) τινὲς ἐπάγουσιν· " αὐτὰρ ... ἄνακτι ". The verses, if genuine,

should have come after line 237 ; whether that is secondary confusion, or an indication that they came in *via* the margin, must be
left undecided.

We can follow the short version without hesitation ; cf. Ludwich,
HV 25 ; Wecklein, *ZAV* 10. The lines are indelicate, and with
them, as the scholiast points out, Hera perjures herself (*O* 41) in
the sequel. Still, no one, as far as I know, has ever suggested that
our text has here been bowdlerized. We have then a clear example
of an interpolator inserting the sort of thing a bowdler would have
cut out ; cf. also above, p. 55.

The purpose of the interpolation is clear ; to account for the
subsequent action of Hypnos, which in reality needs no explanation.
There is no reason (cf. Duentzer, *Zenod.* 159 n.) to suppose that
the lines come from Zenodotus. We are hearing through s T of a
longer text, which we may well suspect is that of Pergamum.

Hypnos speaking to Hera :

"῞Ηρη, πρέσβα θεά, θύγατερ μεγάλοιο Κρόνοιο,
ἄλλον μέν κεν ἔγωγε θεῶν αἰειγενετάων
245 ῥεῖα κατευνήσαιμι, καὶ ἂν ποταμοῖο ῥέεθρα
Ὠκεανοῦ, ὅς περ γένεσις πάντεσσι τέτυκται·

246ᵃ ἀνδράσιν ἠδὲ θεοῖς, πλείστην ⟨δ'⟩ ἐπὶ γαῖαν ἵησιν

According to Plutarch, *de Facie*, xxv. 4 : 938 d (cf. Amoneit, 30,
48), the additional line was read by Crates.

Plutarch likes the line, but it is merely an unnecessary interpretation of πάντεσσι filled out in a limping fashion. No one is likely
to claim that it must be introduced in spite of the external evidence ;
cf. also Duentzer, *Zenod.* 24 n. ; Wecklein, *ZAV* 10. It seems
to me fully on a par with the plus verses that the T scholia are
quoting.

After the speech of Hypnos :

263   τὸν δ' αὖτε προσέειπε βοῶπις πότνια ῞Ηρη·

263   ὡς φάτο· μείδησεν δὲ θεά, λευκώλενος ῞Ηρη,
*   χειρί τέ μιν κατέρεξεν ⟨ἔπος τ' ἔφατ' ἔκ τ' ὀνόμαζεν·⟩

The variant (γράφεται) is preserved in the T scholia. No dis-

cussion is needed; cf. Wecklein, *ZAV* 10; *CP* 17 (1922). 220; and on Θ 38, where the same interpolation is found in a Ptolemaic papyrus.

After Hypnos demands an oath:

277   ὡς ἔφατ'· οὐδ' ἀπίθησε θεά, λευκώλενος "Ηρη,

*   ὤμνυε δ' ἐκ πέτρηφι κατειβόμενον Στυγὸς ὕδωρ.

280   αὐτὰρ ἐπεί ῥ' ὄμοσέν τε κτλ.

278 ὤμνυε δ', ὡς ἐκέλευε, θεοὺς δ' ὀνόμηνεν ἅπαντας
279 τοὺς ὑποταρταρίους, οἳ Τιτῆνες καλέονται.

πέτρηφι Barnes, πέτρης codd.; πέτρης καταειβόμενον vel καταλειβόμενον Bekker.

The line is preserved in the TV scholia as a variant (τινὲς δὲ γράφουσιν), which in V is attached to line 278 but in T to line 279. Eustathius (Neumann, 278) understood that the line was added: ἐν δὲ τῷ " οἳ Τιτῆνες καλέονται " προσγράφουσί τινες καὶ ἕτερον στίχον, and to match this ⟨προσ⟩γράφουσιν has been foisted upon the scholia. The variant has been given too short shrift by Ludwich, *HV* 25; Wecklein, *ZAV* 10. For line 278 the T scholia have preserved a variant θεὸν δ' ὀνόμηνεν ἕκαστον, evidently the older reading which was afterwards altered to permit line 279 to follow. The latter is an adaptation of Hesiod, *Th.* 851, and is the only place in which either ὑποταρτάριος or Τιτῆνες is found in Homer. Between the line of the scholia and line 278 in its earlier form the choice is slight. I have decided against line 278 because of the bad company in which it is found.

Plato's criticism (*Rep.* iii. 390 c) of Zeus—καὶ οὕτως ἐκπλαγέντα ἰδόντα τὴν "Ηραν, ὥστε μηδ' εἰς τὸ δωμάτιον ἐθέλειν ἐλθεῖν, ἀλλ' αὐτοῦ βουλόμενον χαμαὶ ξυγγίγνεσθαι, καὶ λέγοντα ὡς οὕτως ὑπὸ ἐπιθυμίας ἔχεται, ὡς οὐδ' ὅτε τὸ πρῶτον ἐφοίτων πρὸς ἀλλήλους φίλους λήθοντε τοκῆας—strongly suggests that he had some such text as:

315   οὐ γάρ πώ ποτέ μ' ὧδε θεᾶς ἔρος οὐδὲ γυναικὸς
316   θυμὸν ἐνὶ στήθεσσι περιπροχυθεὶς ἐδάμασσεν,

*   οὐδ' ὅτε τὸ πρῶτόν περ ἐμισγόμεθ' ἐν φιλότητι

*   εἰς εὐνὴν φοιτῶντε φίλους λήθοντε τοκῆας,

327   ὡς σέο νῦν ἔραμαι καί με γλυκὺς ἵμερος αἱρεῖ.

However, the impossibility of excluding the supposition that Plato's allusion is inexact renders further discussion futile.

After the description of the bed of flowers:

350   τῷ ἔνι λεξάσθην, ἐπὶ δὲ νεφέλην ἔσσαντο
καλήν, χρυσείην· στιλπναὶ δ'. ἀπέπιπτον ἔερσαι.

351ᵃ δή ῥα τότ' ὀφθαλμοῖσι Διὸς χύτο νήδυμος ὕπνος.

The TV scholia record the addition (ἐπάγουσι δέ τινες) of this line, but differ as to its position; it being located after line 350 in the T scholia.

The scholiasts approve the expanded text τοῦτο γὰρ δεῖ δηλω-θῆναι, just as they approved of N 367ᵃ. I suspect therefore that it is the Pergamene text. Modern taste will hardly agree; nor will it, I hope, suspect bowdlerizing. Ludwich (HV 25) and Wecklein (ZAV 10) are content merely to register the interpolation. I may note that the plus verse contains probably an example of νήδυμος : cf. below on Π 432-58.

The speech of Poseidon closes:

370 ἀλλ' ἄγεθ', ὡς ἂν ἐγὼ εἴπω, πειθώμεθα πάντες.
ἀσπίδες ὅσσαι ἄρισται ἐνὶ στρατῷ ἠδὲ μέγισται,
ἑσσάμενοι, κεφαλὰς δὲ παναίθῃσιν κορύθεσσι
κρύψαντες, χερσὶν δὲ τὰ μακρότατ' ἔγχε' ἑλόντες,
ἴομεν· αὐτὰρ ἐγὼν ἡγήσομαι, οὐδ' ἔτι φημὶ
375 Ἕκτορα Πριαμίδην μενέειν, μάλα περ μεμαῶτα."

376 ὃς δέ κ' ἀνὴρ μενέχαρμος, ἔχει δ' ὀλίγον σάκος ὤμῳ,
377 χείρονι φωτὶ δότω, ὁ δ' ἐν ἀσπίδι μείζονι δύτω.
om. Bekker; damn. Nauck, Christ, Ludwich.

The text adopted is that of Zenodotus; the plus verses were read, but athetized by Aristophanes and Aristarchus. The evidence comes partly from Aristonicus (s A): οὗτος καὶ ὁ ἑξῆς ἀθετοῦνται, and partly from Didymus (s T): τοὺς δύο Ζηνόδοτος μὲν οὐδὲ γράφει, Ἀριστοφάνης δὲ ἀθετεῖ, mutilated in s A: Ζηνόδοτος ⟨. . .⟩ δὲ προηθέτει.

Criticism has long attacked this section on internal grounds, for which reference to Ameis-Hentze (Anhang, v. 90) must here suffice. Leaf well calls 376-7 and 381-2 'the climax of absurdity'. Against the latter lines there is no external evidence, a reminder probably of the fragmentary nature of the scholia. Robert (Stud. 119 ff.) includes 376-7 in his Ur-Ilias, but the result he wishes could be

obtained without coming into this conflict with the external evidence. Wilamowitz (*Ilias*, 234 n.) sees clearly that the lines are interpolated. Aristarchus observed that μενέχαρμος is without parallel in Homer. It is under the analogy of μενεπτόλεμος, and elsewhere (*I* 529, *Δ* 122, 303, *N* 396, *O* 582, *Ψ* 419) μενεχάρμης is always employed. We have no right to import such a form, and must regard the shorter text as clearly superior.

According to Aristonicus (ş A at 394) ὅτι Ζηνόδοτος τούτων τῶν ὁμοιώσεων τὴν πρώτην τρίτην τέταχεν that editor must have read:

δή ῥα τότ᾽ αἰνοτάτην ἔριδα πτολέμοιο τάννσσαν
390 κυανοχαῖτα Ποσειδάων καὶ φαίδιμος Ἕκτωρ,
ἤτοι ὁ μὲν Τρώεσσιν, ὁ δ᾽ Ἀργείοισιν ἀρήγων.
ἐκλύσθη δὲ θάλασσα ποτὶ κλισίας τε νέας τε
393 Ἀργείων· οἱ δὲ ξύνισαν μεγάλῳ ἀλαλητῷ.
396 οὔτε πυρὸς τόσσος γε πέλει βρόμος αἰθομένοιο
οὔρεος ἐν βήσσῃς, ὅτε τ᾽ ὤρετο καιέμεν ὕλην·
οὔτ᾽ ἄνεμος τόσσον γε περὶ δρυσὶν ὑψικόμοισιν
399 ἠπύει, ὅς τε μάλιστα μέγα βρέμεται χαλεπαίνων·
394 οὔτε θαλάσσης κῦμα τόσον βοάᾳ ποτὶ χέρσον,
395 ποντόθεν ὀρνύμενον πνοιῇ Βορέω ἀλεγεινῇ,
400 ὅσση ἄρα Τρώων καὶ Ἀχαιῶν ἔπλετο φωνὴ
δεινὸν ἀυσάντων, ὅτ᾽ ἐπ᾽ ἀλλήλοισιν ὄρουσαν.

It is impossible to overlook the probability that this is merely haplography, started by the recurrence of οὔτε at the beginning of three lines, and imperfectly corrected. The question then passes into one of internal evidence. Wecklein (*ZAV* 66) is in favour of rejecting 394–5, which he compares with *Δ* 123 (q. v.), a misplaced interpolation. It is, however, equally probable that the transposition is no more than a mechanical defect in the antigraphon used by Aristonicus, and that he is again hawking at small game.

O

The Trojans were in desperate plight:

ἔγρετο δὲ Ζεὺς
5 Ἴδης ἐν κορυφῇσι παρὰ χρυσοθρόνου Ἥρης.

5ᵃ ἕζετο δ᾽ ὀρθωθείς, μαλακὸν δ᾽ ἔνδυνε χιτῶνα = B 42.

The plus verse is known from the T scholia προστιθέασι δὲ καὶ τὸ
" ἕζετο . . . χιτῶνα ".
Wecklein (ZAV 10) and Ludwich (HV 26) are content to record
the interpolation. Its absence from our texts is surely not due to
bowdlerizing.

The speech of Zeus to Hera :

" ἦ μάλα δὴ κακότεχνος, ἀμήχανε, σὸς δόλος, "Ηρη,
15 "Εκτορα δῖον ἔπαυσε μάχης, ἐφόβησε δὲ λαούς.
οὐ μὰν οἶδ', εἰ αὖτε κακορραφίης ἀλεγεινῆς
17 πρώτη ἐπαύρηαι καί σε πληγῆσιν ἱμάσσω·
32 ὄφρα ἴδῃ, ἤν τοι χραίσμῃ φιλότης τε καὶ εὐνή."
34 ὣς φάτο· ῥίγησεν δὲ βοῶπις πότνια "Ηρη.

18 ἦ οὐ μέμνῃ, ὅτε τε κρέμω ὑψόθεν, ἐκ δὲ ποδοῖιν
   ἄκμονας ἧκα δύω, περὶ χερσὶ δὲ δεσμὸν ἴηλα
20 χρύσεον, ἄρρηκτον; σὺ δ' ἐν αἰθέρι καὶ νεφέλῃσιν
   ἐκρέμω· ἠλάστεον δὲ θεοὶ κατὰ μακρὸν "Ολυμπον,
   λῦσαι δ' οὐκ ἐδύναντο παρασταδόν· ὃν δὲ λάβοιμι,
   ῥίπτασκον τεταγὼν ἀπὸ βηλοῦ, ὄφρ' ἂν ἴκηται
   γῆν ὀλιγηπελέων· ἐμὲ δ' οὐδ' ὣς θυμὸν ἀνίει
25 ἀζηχὴς ὀδύνη Ἡρακλῆος θείοιο,
   τὸν σὺ ξὺν Βορέῃ ἀνέμῳ πεπιθοῦσα θυέλλας
   πέμψας ἐπ' ἀτρύγετον πόντον, κακὰ μητιόωσα,
   καί μιν ἔπειτα Κόων δ' εὐναιομένην ἀπένεικας.
   τὸν μὲν ἐγὼν ἔνθεν ῥυσάμην καὶ ἀνήγαγον αὖτις
30 "Αργος ἐς ἱππόβοτον, καὶ πολλά περ ἀθλήσαντα.
   τῶν σ' αὖτις μνήσω, ἵν' ἀπολλήξῃς ἀπατάων
habent omnes.
   33 ἢν ἐμίγης ἐλθοῦσα θεῶν ἄπο καί μ' ἀπάτησας.
damn. Nauck.

To begin with the shorter interpolation : it was found neither in
the text of Zenodotus nor of Aristophanes. The evidence is given
by Didymus (5 A^t) : οὔτε παρὰ Ζηνοδότῳ οὔτε παρ' Ἀριστοφάνει ἦν,
or (5 T) οὐδὲ παρὰ τοῖς περὶ Ζηνόδοτον ἦν.
These editors must have been following their MSS., for they
could have had no possible reason for excluding it. It is a common
type of interpolation—the filling out of an idea already sufficiently
expressed—and we have no right to insert it against the external
evidence.

The longer interpolation also was not read by Zenodotus on the testimony of Didymus (ⓈAᵗ): Ζηνόδοτος οὐδὲ ὅλως τὴν κόλασιν τῆς Ἥρας γράφει.

That the κόλασις Ἥρας has run the gauntlet of criticism as well as it has is due to its intrinsic interest. It completes for us the story from the Herakles epos—part of which has been told by Hypnos in the preceding book. That the two parts do not overlap is natural—it lay in the plan of the interpolator that they should not. How a demand can be maintained that Zeus *must* tell of his previous brutality—and that is what is needed to shake the authority of the older and better-attested version—I do not see.

Besides, the sequence 31-2 is impossible, as Ameis-Hentze (*Anh.* v. 125 f.) has shown. This difficulty is felt by Leaf, who also calls attention to the emptiness of αὖτις in line 31 ; Finsler's attempt (*Homer²*, ii. 149) to make τῶν σ' αὖτις μνήσω = ' I will repeat your punishment' is ingenious rather than convincing. The linguistic oddities of the passage (cf. Leaf) cannot be pressed too hard, as they can be paralleled from late but genuine sections of the poem. Still the accumulation is remarkable, and it is worth noting that Fick (*Ilias*, 496) assigns these lines to the *Ionische Redaction*, while its context is regarded as part of the *Erweiterung der Menis*. Bechtel (*Vocalcontr.* 166) treats O 1-63, 72-7, as a unit ; but, except for the neglected digamma αἷμ' ἐμέων, all the marks of lateness noted fall within this interpolation. Witte (*Glotta*, 2 (1910). 18 f.) calls attention to the fact that O 25 and Λ 398 (for which he gives a sufficient explanation) are the only examples of ὀδύνη in contrast to twenty-three examples of ὀδύναι.

Finally, the interpolation seems to have had a rival. Eustathius (Neumann, p. 280) and ⓈT at line 21 quote two plus verses. Barnes (cf. Ludwich, *AHT* i. 384, *HV* 22) brought them into the vulgate as 30ᵃᵇ—an obvious impossibility. Duentzer (*Zenod.* 159 n.) doubted whether they could be ascribed to Zenodotus, but it was left to Erhardt (280) to find the solution. They are from a shorter version of the interpolation :

18 ἦ οὐ μέμνῃ, ὅτε τε κρέμω ὑψόθεν, ἐκ δὲ ποδοῖιν
19 ἄκμονας ἧκα δύω, περὶ χερσὶ δὲ δεσμὸν ἴηλα
20 χρύσεον, ἄρρηκτον ; σὺ δ' ἐν αἰθέρι καὶ νεφέλῃσιν
21 ἐκρέμω· ἠλάστεον δὲ θεοὶ κατὰ μακρὸν Ὄλυμπον,

* πρὶν τότε δή σ᾽ ἀπέλυσα πεδῶν, μύδρους δ᾽ ἐνὶ Τροίῃ
* κάββαλον, ὄφρα πέλοιτο καὶ ἐσσομένοισι πυθέσθαι.
31 τῶν σ᾽ αὖτις μνήσω, ἵν᾽ ἀπολλήξῃς ἀπατάων.

The existence of two versions (cf. Didymus at T 327) tends to discredit each.

The κόλασις Ἥρας is not as obviously unfit as are many other interpolations. But the shorter text can be followed without difficulty; Wecklein (ZAV 57) also prefers it, and in view of the many cases in which it has proved superior we have no right to depart unnecessarily from it. The motive of the interpolation is readily comprehensible. The original appealed to its hearers by an allusion which was expected to be and was familiar to them. As circumstances shifted some rhapsodist found it convenient to supply what experience had shown was no longer generally known.

The speech of Zeus after Hera has made her submission ends:

ἀλλ᾽ εἰ δή ῥ᾽ ἐτεόν γε καὶ ἀτρεκέως ἀγορεύεις,
ἔρχεο νῦν μετὰ φῦλα θεῶν καὶ δεῦρο κάλεσσον
55   Ἶρίν τ᾽ ἐλθέμεναι καὶ Ἀπόλλωνα κλυτότοξον,
ὄφρ᾽ ἡ μὲν μετὰ λαὸν Ἀχαιῶν χαλκοχιτώνων
ἔλθῃ καὶ εἴπῃσι Ποσειδάωνι ἄνακτι
παυσάμενον πολέμοιο τὰ ἃ πρὸς δώμαθ᾽ ἱκέσθαι,
Ἕκτορα δ᾽ ὀτρύνῃσι μάχην ἐς Φοῖβος Ἀπόλλων,
60   αὖτις δ᾽ ἐμπνεύσῃσι μένος, λελάθῃ δ᾽ ὀδυνάων,
αἳ νῦν μιν τείρουσι κατὰ φρένας, αὐτὰρ Ἀχαιοὺς
αὖτις ἀποστρέψῃσιν, ἀνάλκιδα φύζαν ἐνόρσας,
φεύγοντες δ᾽ ἐν νηυσὶ πολυκλήισι πέσωσι."

Πηλείδεω Ἀχιλῆος· ὁ δ᾽ ἀνστήσει ὃν ἑταῖρον
65   Πάτροκλον· τὸν δὲ κτενεῖ ἔγχεϊ φαίδιμος Ἕκτωρ
Ἰλίου προπάροιθε, πολέας ὀλέσαντ᾽ αἰζηοὺς
τοὺς ἄλλους, μετὰ δ᾽ υἱὸν ἐμὸν Σαρπηδόνα δῖον.
τοῦ δὲ χολωσάμενος κτενεῖ Ἕκτορα δῖος Ἀχιλλεύς.
ἐκ τοῦ δ᾽ ἄν τοι ἔπειτα παλίωξιν παρὰ νηῶν
70   αἰὲν ἐγὼ τεύχοιμι διαμπερές, εἰς ὅ κ᾽ Ἀχαιοὶ
Ἴλιον αἰπὺ ἕλοιεν Ἀθηναίης διὰ βουλάς.
τὸ πρὶν δ᾽ οὔτ᾽ ἄρ᾽ ἐγὼ παύω χόλον οὔτε τιν᾽ ἄλλον
ἀθανάτων Δαναοῖσιν ἀμυνέμεν ἐνθάδ᾽ ἐάσω,
πρίν γε τὸ Πηλείδαο τελευτηθῆναι ἐέλδωρ,

ILIAD O 153

75 ὣς οἱ ὑπέστην πρῶτον, ἐμῷ δ' ἐπένευσα κάρητι,
ἤματι τῷ, ὅτ' ἐμεῖο θεὰ Θέτις ἥψατο γούνων,
λισσομένη τιμῆσαι Ἀχιλλῆα πτολίπορθον.
56–77 om. Bekker²; 63–77 damn. Christ; 64–77 om. van Leeuwen.

The text adopted is that of Zenodotus; the additional lines were read but obelized by Aristophanes and Aristarchus, by whom lines 56–63 were also athetized. The verdict of Aristarchus is reported at line 56 by Aristonicus (s A): ἀπὸ τούτου ἕως τοῦ "λισσομένη τιμῆσαι" ἀθετοῦνται στίχοι κβ', or (s BT): ἀθετοῦνται ὡς περιττοὶ εἴκοσι καὶ δύο στίχοι. To this Didymus (s Aᵗ) adds καὶ παρὰ Ἀριστοφάνει ἠθέτηντο. It is also Didymus who at line 64 gives us the information about Zenodotus (s A): Ζηνόδοτος δὲ ἀπὸ τοῦ "Πηλείδεω Ἀχιλῆος" ἕως τοῦ "λισσομένη τιμῆσαι" οὐδ' ὅλως ἔγραφεν, or (s T) Ζηνόδοτος ἐνθένδε ἕως τοῦ "λισσομένη" οὐδὲ ἔγραφεν. To this is appended in s T a very remarkable note: ἐοίκασι γὰρ Εὐριπιδείῳ προλόγῳ ταῦτα· ἐναγώνιος δέ ἐστιν ὁ ποιητὴς καί, ἐὰν ἄρα, σπέρμα μόνον τίθησιν· "κακοῦ δ' ἄρα οἱ πέλεν ἀρχή" (Δ 604)· τάχα δὲ ὁ ταῦτα ποιήσας ⟨ἐποίησε⟩ καὶ τὸ "ᾠχόμεθ' ἐς Θήβην" (Α 366–92) καὶ τὸ "ἤρξατο δ' ὡς πρῶτον Κίκονας δάμασε" (ψ 310–43).

On the surface this would seem to be Zenodotus' explanation of his reasons for omitting the line; and it is so taken by Duentzer (Zenod. 24) and by Leaf. The idea is inadmissible, for Zenodotus (cf. above, p. 51) had left no commentary; and Aristarchus and his followers could do no more than guess at his reasons. I am glad that this can be shown independently, for on my own line of reasoning the Zenodotean origin of this scholium must be denied. Zenodotus could not have given such an explanation, for the simple reason that he had nothing to explain, lines 64–77 being for him non-existent. Roemer (AAH 297) claims that the criticism is by Aristarchus, because it is so excellent; against that a plea of non sequitur must be entered. Eustathius (Neumann, p. 282) names Zenodotus of Mallos as the source; and Heyne (vii. 19), though reasoning badly, probably divined the ultimate source when he named Crates of Mallos. Traces of Pergamene tradition crop out in the T scholia, and I should include this among them. Very likely these scholars here reverted to the text of Zenodotus; their defence of lines 56–63 has been lost, but their attack on lines 64–77 has survived.

Of modern scholars Wilamowitz (*Ilias*, 233 n.) has approached the problem correctly—lines 64–77 are disposed of by the *recensio*. His defence of lines 56–63 (they are not intended for Hera, but the poet has every reason to explain to his hearers how Zeus will act) shows at least that the two passages are not of one piece. That is as far as the present book need go into the problem.

Other scholars have made their approach in the belief that the burden of proof must be borne by him who denies the genuineness of the passage. Yet many of them have ended by agreeing either with Aristarchus or Zenodotus. The older writings are summarized in the Ameis-Hentze, *Anhang*, v. 99 ff., 127 f., and copious extracts are printed in Benicken, *Stud*. i. 161 ff. The view of Lachmann (54 f.) and of Benicken, that the passage must be genuine because it is so incompatible with our *Iliad* that no man could have been foolish enough to interpolate it in that poem, must be rejected. According to these scholars the passage was part of an independent lay, so old that the story then had, or could then be imagined to have, a different ending. But the forms κτενεῖ, πολέας (cf. Bechtel, *Vocalcontr.* 59, 229) are characteristic of the very latest strata of the poems, and consequently render any such dating impossible. Duentzer (*Hom. Abh.* 77) and Friedländer (*Hom. Krit.* 51 n.) endeavoured to meet the difficulty raised by Lachmann by supposing that the interpolation was made not in the *Iliad* but in the song of a rhapsodist who was using this part of the poem separately. The explanation does not explain ; and, besides, it is worth noting that interpolations to adapt a part of the poem to separate recitation, though frequently assumed, are not revealed by our external evidence. We must simply recognize that it is impossible to set in advance a limit to human folly,[1] and accept the external evidence as showing how foolish some man actually was.

Bergk endeavoured to restrict the interpolation to lines 64–71, its worst part, and was followed by Ameis-Hentze and by Bechtel. The forms with which Bechtel deals are, to be sure, restricted to these lines, but that is insufficient to prove the remainder genuine.

[1] The limits of possibility will vary at different periods, and it must be remembered that these scholars dated the interpolations much earlier than I do. The Athenian of the fifth century must have found his Homer as difficult as the modern Englishman his Chaucer. An interpolation quite as foolish in Chaucer—perhaps even in Shakespeare— could be safely read before a modern audience.

The objections to Bergk's idea are: (1) τὸ πρίν = πρίν, according
to Leaf without parallel ; and (2) the gods, in contradiction to the
sequel, are thus given permission to interfere as soon as the Greeks
are driven to their ships.   On the other hand, Lentz (28) and Fick
(*Ilias*, 496) follow Aristarchus; while Lang (*Homer and the Epic*,
171) agrees with Zenodotus, acknowledging, ' however regretfully ',
that lines 64–77 ' do look like an interpolation '.   In more
recent times Roemer (*AAH* 296–300) defends the Aristarchean
athetesis in its entirety.   Wecklein (*ZAV* 44) recognizes the break
between 56–63 and 64–77, but regards each piece as an interpolation ; the former on linguistic evidence that is not to be discussed
in this book. Rothe (*Ilias*, 272 n.) regards the interpolation—*ganz
oder zum grössten Teile*—as proved completely.   Cauer (*Grundfr.*³
237 f.) regards the whole passage as a misfit, but seems content to
classify it as late.   Drerup (*Hom. Poet.* i. 359) accepts the vulgate
text, and thus gives one more proof of his inability to discriminate
between Homer and the Pseudohomerica ; Finsler too (*Homer*², ii.
150) gives a short and unsatisfactory defence of the passage.

Bethe (*Homer*, i. 290–3) discusses the passage carefully with a
view to establish its genuineness in the sense that it is the work of
the *Verfasser unserer Ilias*.   I cannot concede that it is an interpolation of so early a date, and must examine his arguments. Bethe
admits the linguistic difficulties (or rather those discussed by
Roemer, *Münchn. SB*, 1907, 515 ff.), but maintains that an Athenian
of the sixth century could have perpetrated them. The position is
sound, but there still remains the feeling of the author's helplessness
that one gets in the reading of this passage.   Bethe claims also
that the passage is necessary because of Hera's speech (93–9) to
Themis.   Granting for the sake of argument that Hera must have
been told more than she could guess from the looks (13) and threats
(17) of Zeus, it is clear that lines 56–63 abundantly satisfy the
claim.   The difficulties in what follow do not seem to be fully
appreciated by Bethe : if the author means what he says, or can
say what he means, then Hector falls at the ships, and the Greeks
sweep on in an unbroken victory to the capture of Troy.   That
contradicts both the *Iliad* and the *Cycle*.

The motive for the interpolation is chauvinism.[1]   Some one could

---

[1] Cf. also on O 610-14, where the trick of connexion is the same.

not allow the fears aroused by lines 56–63 to remain for a moment unallayed. The poet was proceeding on another principle, that of arousing suspense. The interpolation spoils that intention, and also the diplomatic manœuvre of Zeus. Hera's protestations he meets simply with an acid test : if you mean what you say, do thus and so ; the result will be that Poseidon will quit the battle and Hector will rout the Achaeans.

The merit of the shorter version is shown by its presenting this idea unspoiled by the intrusion of a passage that wavers between cajoling and exasperating Hera—especially a passage so strangely worded and in such flagrant contradiction with ideas found elsewhere in the epos.

After the close of Zeus' speech :

78 ὣς ἔφατ'· οὐδ' ἀπίθησε θεά, λευκώλενος "Ηρη.

78ᵃ Ζῆν' ὑποταρβήσασα· νόος δέ οἱ ἄλλα μενοίνα.

The T scholia introduce the plus verse with the phrase τινὲς μετὰ τοῦτον γράφουσι. They also corrupt Ζῆν' to Ζηνόδοτος : that may be a piece of pure stupidity, or may conceal the source, Zenodotus of Mallos.

There is obviously no need (cf. Ludwich, *HV* 26 ; Wecklein, *ZAV* 11) to depart from the shorter and better-attested version. I may compare the similar expansion of Ξ 263 that reaches us in the same fashion.

After his cure by Apollo Hector returns to the battle :

ὡς δ' ὅτε τις στατὸς ἵππος, ἀκοστήσας ἐπὶ φάτνῃ,	= Z 506
δεσμὸν ἀπορρήξας θείῃ πεδίοιο κροαίνων,	Z 507
265 [εἰωθὼς λούεσθαι ἐυρρεῖος ποταμοῖο,]	Z 508
269 ὡς "Εκτωρ λαιψηρὰ πόδας καὶ γούνατ' ἐνώμα	
ὀτρύνων ἱππῆας, ἐπεὶ θεοῦ ἔκλυεν αὐδήν.	

266 κυδιόων· ὑψοῦ δὲ κάρη ἔχει, ἀμφὶ δὲ χαῖται	= Z 509
267 ὤμοις ἀίσσονται· ὁ δ' ἀγλαΐηφι πεποιθώς,	= Z 510
268 ῥίμφα ἑ γοῦνα φέρει μέτα τ' ἤθεα καὶ νομὸν ἵππων·	= Z 511

The text is offered in the belief that it is that of the Zenodotean antigraphon. Aristophanes and Aristarchus read the plus verses, the latter at least athetizing them and the line that precedes them.

Aristonicus (s A) gives clear testimony : ἀπὸ τούτου (265) ἕως τοῦ "ῥίμφα ἓ γοῦνα φέρει" ἀθετοῦνται στίχοι δ' καὶ ἀστερίσκοι παράκεινται, ὅτι οἰκειότερον ἐπ' Ἀλεξάνδρου. That is not contradicted by his note on Ζ 506–11: καὶ τούτοις ὁμοίως ἀστερίσκοι παράκεινται, ὅτι τὴν παραβολὴν ὅλην ἐπὶ "Εκτορος βληθέντος λίθῳ ὑπ' Αἴαντος μετήνεγκεν ἐντεῦθεν, this being merely a statement of the lines contained in Aristarchus.

The note of Didymus (s T) is admittedly corrupt; for reasons already given, p. 49, I emend: Ζηνόδοτος τοῦτον (265) μόνον γράφει, Ἀριστοφάνης (Ἀρίσταρχος cod.) δὲ καὶ τοὺς ἄλλους γ'. Hiller's emendation ⟨περι⟩γράφει has set the critics upon the wrong trail.

The text ascribed to Zenodotus can be understood only if we assume that line 265 is the abortive beginning of an interpolation. Wecklein has shown that this sort of thing has elsewhere taken place in the vulgate, and we may believe that it was here present in the MSS. used by Zenodotus. It is also possible, however, that the copy of his work used by the Aristarcheans had suffered interpolation. I have consequently bracketed the line.

There is no occasion to rehearse the discussions of the passage, which have generally issued in the belief that Ζ is the original seat of the simile, and have sought to explain its presence here partly on the assumption of the same, partly on the assumption of a different author. Bethe (*Homer*, i. 295) shows the use of borrowed material throughout this section, but without citing anything approaching this repetition of six consecutive lines. One who wished to borrow the simile—whether it was his own or another's—was of course under no compulsion to take it in its entirety. The external evidence indicates[1] that he was content with the two first lines, and that copyists made the borrowing complete.

The ways of Zeus are set forth and then:

τὰ φρονέων νήεσσιν ἔπι γλαφυρῇσιν ἔγειρεν
"Εκτορα Πριαμίδην, μάλα περ μεμαῶτα καὶ αὐτόν.
605 μαίνετο δ', ὡς ὅτ' Ἄρης ἐγχεσπάλος ἢ ὀλοὸν πῦρ
οὔρεσι μαίνηται βαθέης ἐν τάρφεσιν ὕλης·

[1] Shewan's discussion, CP 6 (1911). 274 f., is based on the customary inversion of the evidence. 'The burden of proof is on him who seeks' to insert.

ἀφλοισμὸς δὲ περὶ στόμα γίνετο, τὼ δέ οἱ ὄσσε
λαμπέσθην βλοσυρῆσιν ὑπ' ὀφρύσιν, ἀμφὶ δὲ πήληξ
609 σμερδαλέον κροτάφοισι τινάσσετο μαρναμένοιο.
615 καί ῥ' ἔθελεν ῥῆξαι στίχας ἀνδρῶν, πειρητίζων,
ᾗ δὴ πλεῖστον ὅμιλον ὅρα καὶ τεύχε' ἄριστα·

610 Ἕκτορος· αὐτὸς γάρ οἱ ἀπ' αἰθέρος ἦεν ἀμύντωρ
Ζεύς, ὅς μιν πλεόνεσσι μετ' ἀνδράσι μοῦνον ἐόντα
τίμα καὶ κύδαινε· μινυνθάδιος γὰρ ἔμελλεν
ἔσσεσθ'· ἤδη γάρ οἱ ἐπώρνυε μόρσιμον ἦμαρ
614 Παλλὰς Ἀθηναίη ὑπὸ Πηλείδαο βίηφι.

om. Bekker, van Leeuwen ; damn. Nauck, Ludwich.

The text given is that of Zenodotus ; the five plus verses were read, but obelized, by Aristarchus. The evidence is given by Aristonicus (ⵣ AB): ἀθετοῦνται στίχοι ε', and by Aristonicus combined with Didymus (ⵣ T) ἀθετοῦνται στίχοι ε' ὡς περιττοί· οὐδὲ παρὰ Ζηνοδότῳ δὲ ἦσαν οἱ ε'.

Critics have often (Finsler, *Homer*², ii. 158 is a recent exception) thought it necessary to ' eject ' these verses. When it is recognized that they are not present in the oldest and best tradition, no claim can be made (cf. Wilamowitz, *Ilias*, 157 n.) for their insertion. The trick of connexion (cf. also Wecklein, *ZAV* 45) recalls the interpolation of lines 64–77, and we find here the same chauvinistic motive. The hearers will be more comfortable if reminded that Hector is doomed to death. There is also the same helplessness of expression—cf. ἀπ' αἰθέρος, μοῦνον ἐόντα, and ὑπὸ Πηλείδαο βίηφι.

In the attack on the ships :

οὐδὲ μὲν Ἕκτωρ
689 μίμνεν ἐνὶ Τρώων ὁμάδῳ πύκα θωρηκτάων·
ἀλλ' ὥς τ' ὀρνίθων πετεηνῶν αἰετὸς αἴθων
ἔθνος ἐφορμᾶται, κτλ.

689ᵃ ἀλλὰ πολὺ προθέεσκε, τὸ ὃν μένος οὐδενὶ εἴκων = Χ 459 λ 515

The plus verse is introduced in the T scholia by the phrase : τινὲς ἐπισυνάπτουσι τούτῳ τόδε.

This at least half mechanical addition needs no discussion ; cf. Ludwich, *HV* 26 ; Gerhard, 84 n. ; Wecklein, *ZAV* 11.

Π

Achilles speaking to Patroclus:

ἀλλὰ καὶ ὣς, Πάτροκλε, νεῶν ἀπὸ λοιγὸν ἀμύνων
ἔμπεσ' ἐπικρατέως, μὴ δὴ πυρὸς αἰθομένοιο
82 νῆας ἐνιπρήσωσι, φίλον δ' ἀπὸ νόστον ἕλωνται.
πείθεο δ', ὥς τοι ἐγὼ μύθου τέλος ἐν φρεσὶ θείω, κτλ.

82ᵃ τοὺς ἄλλους ἐνάριζ', ἀπὸ δ' Ἕκτορος ἴσχεο χεῖρας.

The verse was added by Barnes from the story told of Diogenes
Cynicus by Diog. La. vi. 2. 63: ἐρανόν ποτε αἰτούμενος, πρὸς τὸν
ἐρανάρχην ἔφη,

"τοὺς ἄλλους ἐνάριζ', ἀπὸ δ' Ἕκτορος ἴσχεο χεῖρας."

Achilles' instructions to Patroclus:

    ἐκ νηῶν ἐλάσας ἰέναι πάλιν· εἰ δέ κεν αὖ τοι
    δώῃ κῦδος ἀρέσθαι, ἐρίγδουπος πόσις Ἥρης,
89/91 μὴ σύ γ' ἀγαλλόμενος πολέμῳ καὶ δηιοτῆτι,
92 Τρῶας ἐναιρόμενος, προτὶ Ἴλιον αἰπὺν ἴεσθαι,
* μή σ' ἀπομουνωθέντα λάβῃ κορυθαίολος Ἕκτωρ·
95 ἀλλὰ πάλιν τροπάασθαι, ἐπὴν φάος ἐν νήεσσι
    θήῃς, τοὺς δέ τ' ἐᾶν πεδίον κάτα δηριάασθαι.
    αἲ γάρ, Ζεῦ τε πάτερ καὶ Ἀθηναίη καὶ Ἀπολλον,
    μήτε τις οὖν Τρώων θάνατον φύγοι, ὅσσοι ἔασι,
    μήτε τις Ἀργείων, νῶιν δ' ἐκδῦμεν ὄλεθρον,
100 ὄφρ' οἶοι Τροίης ἱερὰ κρήδεμνα λύωμεν."

---

89 μὴ σύγ' ἄνευθεν ἐμεῖο λιλαίεσθαι πολεμίζειν
90 Τρωσὶ φιλοπτολέμοισιν· ἀτιμότερον δέ με θήσεις.
91 μηδ' ἐπαγαλλόμενος πολέμῳ καὶ δηιοτῆτι,
92 Τρῶας ἐναιρόμενος, προτὶ Ἴλιον ἡγεμονεύειν,
93 μή τις ἀπ' Οὐλύμποιο θεῶν αἰειγενετάων
94 ἐμβήῃ· μάλα τούς γε φιλεῖ ἑκάεργος Ἀπόλλων·
vss. 97–100 om. Bekker; damn. Nauck, Christ, Ludwich.

The text is adopted in the belief that it is the text of Zenodotus,
except that in line 92 instead of his προτὶ Ἴλιον αἰπὺ δίεσθαι
(Aristonicus, ṣ A) I have followed Wecklein's emendation. The
scholia are, however, in great confusion.

Aristonicus (s A) makes the statement: ὅτι Ζηνόδοτος τοῦτον (89) καὶ τὸν ἑξῆς ἦρκεν, πεποίηκε δὲ ⟨τὸν τρίτον⟩ οὕτως "μὴ σύ γ' ἀγαλλόμενος πολέμῳ καὶ δηιοτῆτι". The corresponding statement in s T: τοὺς β′ (89–90) ἀθετεῖ Ζηνόδοτος, is in flat contradiction. The difficulty is to be solved by recognizing that the T scholiast has substituted ἀθετεῖ for ἦρκεν—in the next note he does the same, as his own language shows—and has dropped the statement about the third line.

Aristonicus (s A) then says: ὅτι Ζηνόδοτος κατὰ τὸ ἑξῆς τέσσαρας ἀπὸ τούτου (93) ἦρκε, γράφει δὲ ἀντὶ αὐτῶν τοῦτον "μή σ' ἀπογυμνωθέντα λάβῃ κορυθαίολος Ἕκτωρ". The corresponding note in s T is: τοὺς γ′ ἀθετεῖ Ζηνόδοτος καὶ ἀντ' αὐτῶν γράφει "μή σ' ἀπομουνωθέντα λάβῃ κορυθαίολος Ἕκτωρ", ὃν παρῳδεῖ Διονύσιος ὁ Θρᾷξ ἀντὶ τοῦ (" ἀπομουνωθέντα" "ἀπογυμνωθέντα" καὶ ἀντὶ τοῦ) "λάβῃ" "δάκῃ" λέγων. Here the substitution of ἀθετεῖ for ἦρκε is unmistakable, because of the following ἀντ' αὐτῶν γράφει, but ἀπομουνωθέντα is clearly the Zenodotean text. The supplement is needed both to account for the ἀπογυμνωθέντα in A, and to perfect the joke perpetrated by Dionysius. Roemer (AAH 429) enjoys this jest hugely without understanding it. The Alexandrians smelt paiderasty in this speech, and Dionysius must have said what a pity that Zenodotus did not read μή σ' ἀπογυμνωθέντα δάκῃ κορυθαίολος Ἕκτωρ. What he meant should be clear ; but if not, one may meditate on the motives that lead Hindu writers on the technique of the drama to include kissing, biting, and scratching under one and the same taboo. Compare also the Kāmasūtra, and the jest from the same sphere quoted on K 159ᵃ.

The most serious difficulty remains—the conflict of the numerals. The γ′ in T is impossible, and was emended to δ′ by Maass ; that harmonizes with A, and the text after the omission of lines 93–6 is readable. But Wilamowitz (Ilias, 121) has shown that lines 97–100 were composed to follow lines 95–6 ; and I have therefore assumed that δ′ is a corruption of δύο.

Of the relative merits of the two versions little need be said. To me as to Wecklein (ZA V 62) the text of Zenodotus seems superior to lines 89–91 of the vulgate. It is necessary, however, to note that it may be merely a case of haplography ; a copyist's eye wandering from μὴ σύ γ' ἀγαλλόμενος to μηδ' ἐπαγαλλόμενος. Wecklein

hesitates to follow Zenodotus in reading for lines 93-4 μή σ'
ἀπομουνωθέντα λάβῃ κορυθαίολος "Εκτωρ. I think we should do so
without hesitation, because the motive for the interpolation is clear.
It is chauvinism : Patroclus must fear not Hector, but the intervention of a god. The interpolation clashes also with lines 97-100,
as Lachmann (66) felt. Unfortunately he chose the wrong solution.
Lines 97-100 were athetized by Aristarchus according to Aristonicus (s A): ἀθετοῦνται στίχοι τέσσαρες. s T has preserved a
remarkable note, which I would assign to its Pergamene source : παν-
τελῶς ἐκβλητέον τοὺς δ' στίχους. . . . καλῶς οὖν φησιν Ἀρίσταρχος
Ζηνόδοτον ὑπωπτευκέναι, ὡς εἶεν παρεντεθέντες οἱ στίχοι ὑπὸ τῶν ἀρ-
σενικοὺς ἔρωτας λεγόντων εἶναι παρ' 'Ομήρῳ καὶ ὑπονοούντων παιδικὰ
εἶναι Ἀχιλλέα Πατρόκλου (Ἀχιλλέως Πάτροκλον Roemer). The
foundation of Aristarchus' remark is unknown. It need have been
nothing more than the obelizing of these lines by Zenodotus ; and
in that case their discussion falls outside the limits set for this book.

The arming of Patroclus :

130 ὣς φάτο, Πάτροκλος δὲ κορύσσετο νώροπι χαλκῷ.
    κνημῖδας μὲν πρῶτα περὶ κνήμῃσιν ἔθηκε
    καλάς, ἀργυρέοισιν ἐπισφυρίοις ἀραρυίας·
    δεύτερον αὖ θώρηκα περὶ στήθεσσιν ἔδυνε
    ποικίλον ἀστερόεντα, κακῶν βελέων ἀλεωρήν.
135 ἀμφὶ δ' ἄρ' ὤμοισιν βάλετο ξίφος ἀργυρόηλον
    χάλκεον, αὐτὰρ ἔπειτα σάκος μέγα τε στιβαρόν τε·
    κρατὶ δ' ἐπ' ἰφθίμῳ κυνέην εὔτυκτον ἔθηκεν,
    ἵππουριν· δεινὸν δὲ λόφος καθύπερθεν ἔνευεν.
    εἵλετο δ' ἄλκιμα δοῦρε, τά οἱ παλάμηφιν ἀρήρει.
140 [ἔγχος δ' οὐχ ἕλετ' οἶον ἀμύμονος Αἰακίδαο.]
145 ἵππους δ' Αὐτομέδοντα θοῶς ζευγνῦμεν ἄνωγε,
    τὸν μετ' Ἀχιλλῆα ῥηξήνορα τῖε μάλιστα,
    πιστότατος δέ οἱ ἔσκε μάχῃ ἔνι μεῖναι ὁμοκλήν.

134 sic τινές ap. T, Aristophanes, Vesp. 615 ; ποδώκεος Αἰακίδαο ceteri.

141 βριθύ, μέγα, στιβαρόν· τὸ μὲν οὐ δύνατ' ἄλλος 'Αχαιῶν = T 388
    πάλλειν, ἀλλά μιν οἶος ἐπίστατο πῆλαι Ἀχιλλεύς,   = T 389
    Πηλιάδα μελίην, τὴν πατρὶ φίλῳ τάμε Χείρων   = T 390
    Πηλίου ἐν κορυφῆς, φόνον ἔμμεναι ἡρώεσσιν.   = Γ 391

In line 134 I have followed without hesitation the earlier-attested

text. When it is recognized that the variant is later than Pisistratus there can be no doubt as to which is variant and which is original text. I regard the line as very important,[1] because it shows that the Pisistratean text did not carry the exchange of armour into this section, but that some person or persons afterwards tampered with the text for the purpose of rendering the poem more consistent. We have seen the same sort of thing being done in the *Catalogue*, and on a large scale in the *Wall-building*.

In lines 140–4 the text printed is that which I believe to be the text of Zenodotus, although the statements in the scholia are greatly confused. The most definite statement, and the one most worthy of credence, is that of Didymus (ﬅ A^t): Ζηνόδοτος τοῦτον (140) ἀθετήσας τοὺς ἑξῆς τέσσαρας οὐκ ἔγραφεν. Then the note of Aristonicus (ﬅ A) at T 387 : ἀθετοῦνται στίχοι τέσσαρες, ὅτι ἐκ τοῦ Πατρόκλου ὁπλισμοῦ μετάκεινται. ἡ δὲ περιεστιγμένη διπλῆ, ὅτι ἐνταῦθα μὲν (T 388–91) αὐτοὺς Ζηνόδοτος καταλέλοιπεν, ἐπὶ δὲ Πατρόκλου (Π 141–4) ἠθέτηκεν must be corrected by applying it to the following line (so Ludwich, *AHT* i. 448 f.; Roemer, *AAH* 266), and not by emending τέσσαρες to πέντε with Cobet. We must also believe that the epitomator has substituted ἠθέτηκεν for ἦρκεν, and that is confirmed by the antithetic word καταλέλοιπεν, and also by the fact that the epitomator must have found something like ἀθετήσας . . . ἦρκε (cf. Didymus' report), which would have seemed to him unnecessarily explicit. This explains also why the note is placed one line too soon, that being the point where Aristonicus' discussion began. A note of Aristonicus in ﬅ T (abbreviated in ﬅ B), referred by its lemma to Π 141–2 but applying undoubtedly to the following lines also, ἀστερίσκους ἔχουσι κακῶς ὄντες ἐν τῇ T, presents the facts in the same light.

One other question may best be considered at this point—whether T 388–91 is the source of the interpolation, or whether both passages are interpolated from some cyclic poem. The latter idea is suggested by a note in ﬅ A^t at T 387 : οὐδὲ ἐν ταῖς ἄλλαις ἦσαν οἱ ἀθετούμενοι (388–91). Ultimately the note will go back to Didymus; but as the lines are explicitly attested for Zenodotus by Aristonicus it is

---

[1] Niese (93 f.), writing before the publication of the T scholia, was greatly troubled by this line as read in the vulgate. I may note also that Γ 332 f., which he draws into the question, have at least proved objects of suspicion.

clear that the epitomator has here done his worst. I suspect that
Didymus gave a statement of the facts for Π 140-4, and that the
epitomator, finding it burdensome, threw the scholarship overboard.
If so, there is no external evidence against T 388-91 ; if, on the
other hand, one prefers to believe that this remark must have been
started by the omission of T 388-91 in some text, we shall have
another case (cf. B 116-18 = I 23-5, X 133-5 = 316^{a-e}) of what
Gerhard (80 n.) well terms 'freifliegende Einschubverse', suggesting
that these lines were also used as X 320^{a-d} in his papyrus.

In the shorter version line 140 is clearly an interpolation—
especially since Wecklein (ZAV 43) has made the point that if
genuine it must have stood before line 139—and I have followed
Zenodotus in athetizing it. He must have found it in some manuscripts, and that he wrote it at all must be regarded as a mani-
festation of περιττὴ εὐλάβεια.

As for a choice between the versions, the $recensio$, as Wilamowitz
($Ilias$, 124; cf. $Hermes$, 35 (1900). 564) has seen, settles the
question. But Wilamowitz does the interpolation too much honour
when he makes it 'so jung, dass er die Asteropaiosgeschichte
voraussetzt'; Bethe ($Homer$, i. 84 f.) also dates the interpolation too
early. On the other hand, Robert ($Studien$, 93) tries to avoid the
force of the external evidence:[1] 'Der Umstand, dass Zenodot sie
nicht las und vielleicht in einigen seiner Handschriften nicht fand,
wird reichlich aufgewogen durch die Thatsache, dass bereits der
Dichter des T diese Verse gekannt und nachgeahmt hat.' But that
is the point at issue, and the external evidence indicates that these
verses have been taken from T at a time so late that Zenodotus'
MSS. were essentially free from the interpolation.

Apart from the external evidence we may claim that the shorter
version is superior, for those who have started with the longer
version have often demanded the excision of the passage. For the
older literature cf. Ameis-Hentze, $Anhang$, vi. 44 f., and also Leaf.
Of more recent writers Roemer (AAH 266) follows Aristarchus ;[2]
Rothe ($Ilias$, 282) and Finsler ($Homer$, ii. 164) retain the lines,
being impressed by the leisurely movement of the section—a

---

[1] This is a corollary to his belief that the exchange of armour was an original
motif; cf. AJP 42 (1921). 278 f.

[2] For T 388-91 refusing to believe that Aristarchus athetized the lines.

leisureliness which we have neither reason nor right to increase by intruding lines not in the earliest and best tradition. Ameis-Hentze, after a close interpretation of the language, conclude that lines 140-4 must go unless a distinction can be drawn between ἔγχος = *Stosslanze* and δοῦρε = *Wurfspeeren* ; I think (cf. Seymour, *Life in the Hom. Age*, 664 f.) that the distinction is impossible.

Finally, I must notice a passage in the B scholia at 141 which at first blush seems to be a quotation from Zenodotus. It runs φησὶ γὰρ Ζηνόδοτος ὅτι ποῖόν τι ἦν ὡς μὴ δύνασθαι αὐτὸ αἴρειν τοὺς ἥρωας ; As Duentzer (*Zenod.* 37) has seen, such an argument is incompatible with the retention in T of the lines. I would associate this passage with the one already discussed at *O* 64, and one that will be mentioned at *Π* 467. All three come through the BT scholia ; in one place (*O* 64) Eustathios ascribes the note to Zenodotus of Mallos, and all should be looked upon as Pergamene. In the *Odyssey* (at δ 353, π 281) similar fragments are found.

Achilles prayer begins :

" Ζεῦ ἄνα, Δωδωναῖε, Πελασγικέ, τηλόθι ναίων,
  Δωδώνης μεδέων δυσχειμέρου· ἀμφὶ δὲ Σελλοὶ
235 σοὶ ναίουσ᾽ ὑποφῆται ἀνιπτόποδες, χαμαιευνᾱι.
236 ἠμὲν δή ποτ᾽ ἐμὸν ἔπος ἔκλυες εὐξαμένοιο,   ∪ *A* 453
238 ἠδ᾽ ἔτι καὶ νῦν μοι τόδ᾽ ἐπικρήηνον ἐέλδωρ·   = *A* 455

237 τίμησας μὲν ἐμέ, μέγα δ᾽ ἴψαο λαὸν Ἀχαιῶν = A 454

The text is that of Zenodotus ; Aristophanes and Aristarchus read, but obelized, the additional line.

The evidence comes partly from Aristonicus (ṣ A) : ὁ μὲν ὀβελὸς πρὸς τὴν προειρημένην ἀθέτησιν, ὁ δὲ ἀστερίσκος, ὅτι ἐκ τῆς τοῦ Χρύσου εὐχῆς μετενήνεκται, with which is to be compared a corrupt scholium in T on *O* 75 as emended by Roemer (*AAH* 148 n.) : Ἀρίσταρχος ἀθετεῖ ⟨ὡς καὶ⟩ τὸ "τίμησας μὲν ἐμέ" (τιμήσαμεν εἴη cod.). In part it is given by Didymus (ṣ T) : Ζηνόδοτος οὐδὲ γράφει· Ἀριστοφάνης ἀθετεῖ.

Here I shall not venture to claim intrinsic superiority for the shorter text. The longer version seems to me strangely expressed ; but the objections have not carried general conviction (cf. Ameis-Hentze, *Anhang*, vi. 48 ; Lentz, 4 ; and Leaf), and they may

possibly be no more than pressing too literally the wording. On
the other hand, Duentzer's claim that the line is necessary 'quum
Achilles hoc loco Iovis ultionem, clade Graecis immissa sibi com-
paratam, non commemorare non posset' seems clearly exaggerated.
The special beauties discovered in the line by Finsler (*Homer*[2], ii.
165) and Wilamowitz (*Ilias*, 119 n.), the contrast between the
former prayer for vengeance and the present prayer for the sparing
of Patroclus, are read into the longer version. They could be read
equally well into the shorter text; indeed, a still greater beauty
might then be claimed, on the ground that we are allowed to feel
this contrast for ourselves. At all events these beauties cannot be
made a basis for claiming that there is a lacuna in the shorter text.
Our choice must follow the external evidence.

That, however, is not so simple because of the nature of the
Chryseis episode. It is composed so largely of borrowed lines that
it is the simplest hypothesis (cf. Leaf and Wilamowitz) to believe
that its author found Π 236–8 as in our vulgate and used them as
A 453–5 for his own ends. It is then surprising, as Wecklein
(*ZAV* 54) has felt, that his use of the line should have been so
successful. We must furthermore assume that just this line was
lost in some MSS. through a mechanical blunder of a rather rare
type—the accidental skipping of a line even without haplographic
temptation. That would be a curious coincidence, too curious to
accept. Besides, there are in the Chryseis episode (cf. Ameis-
Hentze, *Anhang*, i. 17) a few verses for which no source can be
indicated. I should regard A 454 as an example of this kind, and
ascribe the complete assimilation of the passages to an interpolator.[1]

The meeting of Sarpedon and Patroclus:

    οἱ δ' ὥς τ' αἰγυπιοὶ γαμψώνυχες, ἀγκυλοχεῖλαι,
    πέτρῃ ἐφ' ὑψηλῇ μεγάλα κλάζοντε μάχωνται,
    ὣς οἱ κεκλήγοντες ἐπ' ἀλλήλοισιν ὄρουσαν.
431 τοὺς δὲ ἰδὼν ἐλέησε Κρόνου παῖς ἀγκυλομήτεω·
459 αἱματοέσσας δὲ ψιάδας κατέχευεν ἔραζε
    παῖδα φίλον τιμῶν, τόν οἱ Πάτροκλος ἔμελλε
    φθίσειν ἐν Τροίῃ ἐριβώλακι, τηλόθι πάτρης.

---

[1] A similar position was taken by Fick, *Ilias*, 78, 86, and less distinctly 499.

432 Ἥρην δὲ προσέειπε κασιγνήτην ἄλοχόν τε·   ᛋ Σ 356
"ὥμοι ἐγών, ὅ τε μοι Σαρπηδόνα, φίλτατον ἀνδρῶν,
μοῖρ' ὑπὸ Πατρόκλοιο Μενοιτιάδαο δαμῆναι.   ᛋ Π 420
435 διχθὰ δέ μοι κραδίη μέμονε φρεσὶν ὁρμαίνοντι,   cf. Κ 4
ἤ μιν ζωὸν ἐόντα μάχης ἄπο δακρυοέσσης
θείω ἀναρπάξας Λυκίης ἐν πίονι δήμῳ,
ἢ ἤδη ὑπὸ χερσὶ Μενοιτιάδαο δαμάσσω."
τὸν δ' ἠμείβετ' ἔπειτα βοῶπις πότνια Ἥρη·   = Α 551
440 "αἰνότατε Κρονίδη, ποῖον τὸν μῦθον ἔειπες.   = Α 552
ἄνδρα θνητὸν ἐόντα, πάλαι πεπρωμένον αἴσῃ,   = Χ 179
ἂψ ἐθέλεις θανάτοιο δυσηχέος ἐξαναλῦσαι;   = Χ 180
ἔρδ'· ἀτὰρ οὔ τοι πάντες ἐπαινέομεν θεοὶ ἄλλοι.   = Χ 181
ἄλλο δέ τοι ἐρέω, σὺ δ' ἐνὶ φρεσὶ βάλλεο σῇσιν·   = Α 297
445 αἴ κε ζὼν πέμψῃς Σαρπηδόνα ὃν δὲ δόμον δέ,
φράζεο, μή τις ἔπειτα θεῶν ἐθέλησι καὶ ἄλλος
πέμπειν ὃν φίλον υἱὸν ἀπὸ κρατερῆς ὑσμίνης·   cf. Σ 243
πολλοὶ γὰρ περὶ ἄστυ μέγα Πριάμοιο μάχονται   cf. Χ 251
υἱέες ἀθανάτων· τοῖσιν κότον αἰνὸν ἐνήσεις.   cf. Θ 449
450 ἀλλ' εἴ τοι φίλος ἐστί, τεὸν δ' ὀλοφύρεται ἦτορ,   cf. Χ 169
ἤτοι μέν μιν ἔασον ἐνὶ κρατερῇ ὑσμίνῃ   cf. Φ 207
χέρσ' ὕπο Πατρόκλοιο Μενοιτιάδαο δαμῆναι·   ᛋ Π 420
αὐτὰρ ἐπεὶ δὴ τόν γε λίπῃ ψυχή τε καὶ αἰών,   cf. ι 523
πέμπειν μιν Θάνατόν τε φέρειν καὶ νήδυμον Ὕπνον,   cf. Π 671 f.
455 εἰς ὅ κε δὴ Λυκίης εὐρείης δῆμον ἵκωνται,   cf. Π 673
ἔνθα ἑ ταρχύσουσι κασίγνητοί τε ἔται τε   = Π 674
τύμβῳ τε στήλῃ τε· τὸ γὰρ γέρας ἐστὶ θανόντων."   = Π 675
458 ὣς ἔφατ', οὐδ' ἀπίθησε πατὴρ ἀνδρῶν τε θεῶν τε.   = Δ 68

The text adopted is that of Zenodotus. The evidence is given
partly by Aristonicus (ᛋ A) at line 432 : ὅτι Ζηνόδοτος καθόλου
περιγράφει τὴν ὁμιλίαν τοῦ Διὸς καὶ τῆς Ἥρας, and partly by
Didymus (ᛋ T) ibid. : παρὰ Ζηνοδότῳ οὐκ ἦν ὁ διάλογος τῆς Ἥρας
καὶ τοῦ Διός. This language, although explicit, has been misinterpreted : not to mention Roemer, Zenod. 66, one may compare
Ludwich, HV 103, ' athetierte ' ; Wilamowitz, Ilias, 137, ' als unecht
bezeichnet ' ; Wecklein, ZAV 64, 'als unecht erklärt '.

The extent of the omission is not precisely described, but Heyne
(vii. 215 f.) defined it correctly. Unfortunately Bekker[2] made
431–61 the omitted lines, and the suggestion has remained as a
trap for the unwary ; even Leaf at line 666 and Ludwich (HV 103)
have fallen into it, after avoiding it elsewhere. Lachmann (72 f.)

re-established the correct definition, but his criticism should have fallen on Bekker instead of Zenodotus.

The external evidence gives us an *entweder-oder* that cannot be avoided; and so a compromising solution like that of Robert (*Studien*, 395) need not be considered. The criticism that has started from the longer version has frequently (cf. Ameis-Hentze, *Anhang*, vi. 23 f., 54 f.) ended by demanding the 'ejection' of these lines. Wilamowitz (*Ilias*, 137) voices it excellently when he contrasts the perfect sequence 431/59 with the absurd juncture 458/9 of the vulgate. However, in ascribing the passage to the *Bearbeiter* of the *Patrocleia* he gives it much too early a date. There can be no question of inserting such a passage in the face of the external evidence.

There is also linguistic evidence against it. Bechtel (*Lexil.* 150 f.) has shown that νήδυμος is a ghost-word, a spook born in the tradition of the Homeric poems. Of it there are thirteen examples regularly spelled with a ν-, so regularly that the variants cited at Κ 91, δ 793, μ 311 must be regarded merely as secondary accidents. That is the spelling of Aristarchus, but it was, as we shall see, by no means uncontested. Apollonius Rhodius, who wrote (2. 407) οὐ κνέφας ἥδυμος ὕπνος, evidently did not approve of it; and it is in opposition both to the etymology of the word and to the usage outside Homer.

Aristonicus (cf. below) cites for ἥδυμος both Simonides and Antimachus. Epicharmus (fr. 179) has λόγων ἀκούσας ἀδύμων, the *Etymologicum Magnum* (420. 47) knows ἡδυμέστερος, -έστατος citing Alcman. Bechtel cites examples of ἄδυμος as a proper name from inscriptions. The metre guarantees ἥδυμος for *Hom. Hymn* iv. 241, 449, and yet νήδυμος is written by one family (*p*) of manuscripts. In the only other cases (v. 171, xix. 16) νήδυμος is written apparently without variant at the head of the verse; whether the ν comes from the end of the preceding line [1] or is due to the influence of the Homeric text need not be decided. For νήδυμος I know of only late examples: the inscriptions cited by van Leeuwen, *EDE* 141 g, and Nonnus cited by Liddell and Scott.

In Homer ἥδυμος can be restored without difficulty in eleven out

---

[1] Elision at the end of the line, on which cf. Wackernagel, *SU* 160 ff., implies the necessary continuity of pronunciation.

of the thirteen passages. In seven there is not even question of emendation, but merely of the interpretation of the earliest form of writing:[1] five (B 2, K 91, Ξ 242, δ 793, μ 311) as noted by Buttmann are of the type *EXENEΔΥΜΟΣ*, the other two (K 187, Ξ 354) of the type *ΤΟΝΕΔΥΜΟΣ*. In the remaining four (Ξ 253, Ψ 63, μ 366, ν 79) the correct spelling ἥδυμος is the only change required ; the passages from the *Odyssey* being examples of *hiatus licitus*, and no indication of a digamma. In this passage (454), however, νήδυμος is guaranteed [2] by the metre :

πέμπειν μιν Θάνατόν τε φέρειν καὶ νήδυμον Ὕπνον

and very probably for the interpolator of Ξ 351ᵃ :

δή ῥα τότ᾽ ὀφθαλμοῖσι Διὸς χύτο νήδυμος ὕπνος.

The discussion of νήδυμος gives us incidentally an insight into the way in which the Aristarcheans presented their results. It has been slightly obscured (a note moved from Ξ 253 to Ξ 242 in Aᵗ, and notes on μ 366, ν 79, lost) in later times, but that is no more than the fragmentary nature of the scholia would lead us to expect.

The question is discussed at the first occurrence of the word in each poem. Aristonicus (ß A) at B 2 : ὅτι τὸ νήδυμος μετὰ τοῦ ν̄, καὶ οὐχὶ ἥδυμος, ὡς ἔνιοι, παρὰ τὸ ἡδύς, ὡς δῆλον ἐκ τοῦ " νήδυμος ἀμφιχυθείς " (Ξ 253, Ψ 63). οἱ δὲ μεθ᾽ Ὅμηρον καὶ χωρὶς τοῦ ν̄ λέγουσι· καὶ Ἀντίμαχος " ἐπεί ῥά οἱ ἥδυμος ἐλθών " καὶ Σιμωνίδης " οὗτος δέ τοι ἥδυμον ὕπνον ἔχων ". ἴσως οὖν ἐνόμισαν ἀπὸ τοῦ ἡδὺς εἶναι παραγωγὸν τὸ ἥδυμος, ὡς ἔτυμος ἐτήτυμος. The true etymology being thus rejected, the scholiast continues with other suggestions that need not detain us. On this passage the BGT scholia have similar etymological notes, the question of text criticism being greatly reduced : for instance (ß T) ὅτι δὲ μετὰ τοῦ ν̄· φησὶ " νήδυμος ἀμφιχυθείς ". The long note at δ 793 is largely etymological, but begins with the question of spelling : ἀγνοοῦσί τινες τὸ νήδυμος ὕπνος, ἀποδιδόντες τὸ ἡδύς.

When the word is preceded by a movable -ν there is no discussion ; cf. K 91, Ξ (242), μ 311.

Elsewhere in the *Iliad* there are notes (more or less abbreviated) calling attention to the fact that the letters of the text must be interpreted as νήδυμος ; cf. K 187, Ξ (253), 354, Π 454, Ψ 63, and arguing that therefore this spelling must be adopted ἐπὶ τῶν ἀμφιβόλων.

The interpolation was early enough to be known to Plato, *Rep.* iii. 388 c, who quotes :

---

[1] The distinction should be familiar to all who deal with textual criticism ; but cf. Shewan, *CP* 18 (1923). 347.

[2] It would be desperate to seek to avoid this by either (1) reading καὶ ἥδυμον or (2) καὶ (F)ήδυμον. Note in this interpolation δυσηχέος (442), ζών <ζωϝόν (445), and cf. *AJP* 33 (1912). 416 for the ' neglect ' of the digamma in the Sarpedon episode.

αἲ αἲ ἐγών, ὅτε μοι Σαρπηδόνα φίλτατον ἀνδρῶν
μοῖρ' ὑπὸ Πατρόκλοιο Μενοιτιάδαο δαμῆναι.

Wackernagel (SU 229 f.) has shown how abstemious Homer is in
the use of interjections. The one in Plato's quotation αἲ αἴ is
'unhomeric' and has disappeared from the later tradition. That
is, one piece at least of the evidence against this passage has been
suppressed—though no doubt with the most innocent intentions.
I have already discussed (p. 54 f.) the theory that Zenodotus had
a bowdlerized text, and need not repeat here the reasons for
finding it unsatisfactory. Looking at the problem from the other
angle, the motive for the interpolation is to be found in the pleasure
taken in the Olympian machinery. I should compare B 156–67,
an interpolation which accomplishes the same end by the same
cento technique.

After Patroclus has missed his cast:

466   Σαρπηδὼν δ' αὐτοῦ μὲν ἀπήμβροτε δουρὶ φαεινῷ
      δεύτερος ὁρμηθείς, ὁ δὲ Πήδασον οὔτασεν ἵππον
      ἔγχεϊ δεξιὸν ὦμον· ὁ δ' ἔβραχε θυμὸν ἀίσθων,
      κὰδ δ' ἔπεσ' ἐν κονίῃσι μακών, ἀπὸ δ' ἔπτατο θυμός.

In the T scholia a different text is ascribed to Aristarchus:
οὐτάσαι τὸ ἐκ χειρὸς τρῶσαι. ἐνταῦθα δὲ ἐπὶ τοῦ βαλεῖν τῷ ῥήματι
κέχρηται· λέγει γὰρ " Σαρπηδὼν δ' αὐτοῦ μὲν ἀπήμβροτεν ", ὅπερ
ἐπὶ τῶν ἀφιέντων τάσσεται· διὸ καὶ γράφει Ἀρίσταρχος·

      " ὁ δὲ Πήδασον ἀγλαὸν ἵππον,
τόν ῥά ποτ' Ἠετίωνος ἑλὼν πόλιν ἤγαγ' Ἀχιλλεύς, = Π 153
⟨ὃς⟩ καὶ θνητὸς ἐὼν ἔπεθ' ἵπποις ἀθανάτοισι,   = Π 154
τὸν βάλε δεξιὸν ὦμον."

Lehrs, Ludwich, and Roemer (cf. AJP 37 (1916). 25) have all
argued for reasons of their own that this was not the text of Aristarchus. Their conclusion is correct: had Aristarchus so read, the
lines would to-day stand in our MSS. But that is only the first
step towards a solution. Duentzer (Zenod. 160 f.) would read
γράφει Ζηνόδοτος, Wecklein (ZAV 75 f.) γράφει Ἀριστοφάνης.
Both are improbable, for the distinction of βαλεῖν and οὐτάσαι
seems to be the observation of Aristarchus himself. Wilamowitz

(*Ilias*, 137 n.), with his suggestion that this emendation was merely 'probeweise erfunden' is closer; and yet does not seem to me to hit the nail squarely upon the head.

There are two things to be noted: (1) the interpolation is an obviously desperate effort to save the distinction οὐτάσαι—βαλεῖν, so desperate indeed that we may think it meant to be such. One who really wished to emend the passage would certainly have hit on Πήδασον ἤλασεν ἵππον, which Didymus reports as the text of Philemon; (2) the source of our information is the T scholia, which are known to contain Pergamene material, and which in this neighbourhood exhibit antiaristarchean malice. Thus at line 467 οἱ ὑπομνηματισταὶ " δεύτερον " διὰ τοῦ v̄ and at line 21 Πηλέως οὕτω Πτολεμαῖος· οἱ δὲ ὑπομνηματισάμενοι Ἰακῶς ⟨Πηλῆος⟩. On the meaning of these suffixes cf. Debrunner, *Griech. Wortbildungslehre*, §§ 264, 273; I should interpret them as 'people who are always talking about the ὑπομνήματα, Aristarcholaters'.

Now in the note on our passage I think there is the same spirit of malice, and one quite equal to that which prompted Dionysius Thrax to compose his μή σ' ἀπογυμνωθέντα δάκῃ κορυθαίολος Ἕκτωρ. First comes a cold clear proof that the verbs are used alike—δοκεῖ συγκεχύσθαι (συγχεῖσθαι) is as much as Aristonicus and Didymus bring themselves to say—and then what is manifestly a *Verschlimmbesserung*. Between must have stood some taunting remark—διὰ τί οὖν οὐ γράφει Ἀρίσταρχος; διὸ καὶ ἔδει γράφειν Ἀρίσταρχον or the like—which the epitomator has spoilt.

Meriones slays Laogonos:

    τὸν βάλ' ὑπὸ γναθμοῖο καὶ οὔατος· ὦκα δὲ θυμὸς
607 ᾤχετ' ἀπὸ μελέων, στυγερὸς δ' ἄρα μιν σκότος εἷλεν.
    Αἰνείας δ' ἐπὶ Μηριόνῃ δόρυ χάλκεον ἧκεν·
    ἔλπετο γὰρ τεύξεσθαι ὑπασπίδια προβιβῶντος.

607ᵃ Μηριόνης δ' ἀνέπαλτο, φίλον δέ οἱ ἦτορ ἰάνθη.

The verse is introduced with the phrase ἔν τισιν ἐπεφέρετο in the V scholia. Ludwich (*HV* 26) suspects that it is in the T scholia also, and was overlooked by Maass.

No discussion (cf. Wecklein, *ZAV* 11) is needed.

In the battle over Sarpedon :

Αἰνείας δ' ἐπὶ Μηριόνῃ δόρυ χάλκεον ἧκεν·
ἔλπετο γὰρ τεύξεσθαι ὑπασπίδια προβιβῶντος.
ἀλλ' ὁ μὲν ἄντα ἰδὼν ἠλεύατο χάλκεον ἔγχος·   = P 526
πρόσσω γὰρ κατέκυψε, τὸ δ' ἐξόπιθεν δόρυ μακρὸν = P 527
612   οὔδει ἐνισκίμφθη, ἐπὶ δ' οὐρίαχος πελεμίχθη.   = P 528
616   Αἰνείας δ' ἄρα θυμὸν ἐχώσατο φώνησέν τε·

613   ἔγχεος· ἔνθα δ' ἔπειτ' ἀφίει μένος ὄβριμος Ἄρης. = P 529.
om. van. Leeuwen.   614–15 cf. supra p. 20.

The text followed is that of the first edition of Aristarchus and (presumably) of his predecessors. The plus verse was included in his second edition, but athetized. The evidence is given by Didymus (s A) : ἐν τῇ ἑτέρᾳ τῶν Ἀριστάρχου οὐκ ἐφέρετο καθάπαξ· ἐν δὲ τῇ δευτέρᾳ ὀβελὸς (Cobet, Lehrs : ἄλογος cod.) αὐτῷ παρέκειτο. An abbreviation of this note is misplaced in s T at line 612 : ἐν τῇ ἑτέρᾳ τῶν Ἀριστάρχου οὐκ ἐφέρετο.

We are thus shown the text growing, and the process continues after Aristarchus' time with the interpolation of two more lines. Compare also Wecklein, ZAV 35, ZuA 87.

After the armour is stripped from the shoulders of Sarpedon :

666   καὶ τότ' Ἀπόλλωνα προσέφη νεφεληγερέτα Ζεύς·
"εἰ δ' ἄγε νῦν, φίλε Φοῖβε, κελαινεφὲς αἷμα κάθηρον
ἐλθὼν ἐκ βελέων Σαρπηδόνα, καί μιν ἔπειτα
πολλὸν ἀπὸ πρὸ φέρων, λοῦσον ποταμοῖο ῥοῇσι
670   χρῖσόν τ' ἀμβροσίῃ, περὶ δ' ἄμβροτα εἵματα ἕσσον·
πέμπε δέ μιν πομποῖσιν ἅμα κραιπνοῖσι φέρεσθαι,
Ὕπνῳ καὶ Θανάτῳ διδυμάοσιν, οἵ ῥά μιν ὦκα,
θήσουσ' ἐν Λυκίης εὐρείης πίονι δήμῳ,
ἔνθα ἑ ταρχύσουσι κασίγνητοί τε ἔται τε
675   τύμβῳ τε στήλῃ τε· τὸ γὰρ γέρας ἐστὶ θανόντων."
676   ὡς ἔφατ', οὐδ' ἄρα πατρὸς ἀνηκούστησεν Ἀπόλλων.
                                              = O 236
678   αὐτίκα δ' ἐκ βελέων Σαρπηδόνα δῖον ἀείρας,
πολλὸν ἀπὸ πρὸ φέρων, λοῦσεν ποταμοῖο ῥοῇσι
680   χρῖσέν τ' ἀμβροσίῃ, κτλ.

677   βῆ δὲ κατ' Ἰδαίων ὀρέων ἐς φύλοπιν αἰνήν   ∽ O 237

The plus verse was not in the edition of Zenodotus according to Aristonicus (s A): ὅτι Ζηνόδοτος καὶ τοῦτον περιῄρηκε. Wecklein (*ZAV* 64) has misinterpreted this verb, and his treatment of the passage has suffered accordingly. The shorter version is complete and satisfactory. Wilamowitz, though he prints the line in his text, has given, *Ilias*, 140 n., the correct interpretation: ' wenn dieser Vater ruft, wird dieser Sohn immer und überall hören und gehorchen.' The vulgate has merely picked up a line from the fifteenth book.

The reading of Zenodotus in line 666—καὶ τότ' ἄρ' ἐξ ῎Ιδης προσέφη Ζεὺς ὃν φίλον υἱόν—has in reality nothing to do with this question. It is not so absurd as the Aristarcheans would have us believe, and simply stresses the presence of Zeus on Mount Ida. Variation in such formulas is not infrequent, and we are hardly justified in seeking for motives behind them.

Hector rushes at Automedon:

> τὸν δ' ἔκφερον ὠκέες ἵπποι
> 867 ἄμβροτοι, οὓς Πηλῆι θεοὶ δόσαν ἀγλαὰ δῶρα.

867ᵃ ἤματι τῷ, ὅτε γῆμε Θέτιν λιπαροκρήδεμνον cf. Σ 85

The verse is introduced with the phrase τινὲς ⟨προσ⟩γράφουσιν by the T scholiast, who proceeds to cite the parallel passage in support of the interpolation.

No discussion is needed; cf. Ludwich, *HV* 26; Wecklein, *ZAV* 11.

P

Compare on Λ 543 for the addition of P 99ᵃ by Barnes.

Hector is spoiling the body of Patroclus:

> Αἴας δ' ἐγγύθεν ἦλθε φέρων σάκος ἠύτε πύργον.
> ῞Εκτωρ δ' ἂψ ἐς ὅμιλον ἰὼν ἀνεχάζεθ' ἑταίρων,
> 130 ἐς δίφρον δ' ἀνόρουσε· δίδου δ' ὅ γε τεύχεα καλὰ
> Τρωσὶ φέρειν προτὶ ἄστυ, μέγα κλέος ἔμμεναι αὐτῷ.
> Αἴας δ' ἀμφὶ Μενοιτιάδῃ σάκος εὐρὺ καλύψας
> ἑστήκει ὥς τίς τε λέων περὶ οἷσι τέκεσσιν,
> ᾧ ῥά τε νήπι' ἄγοντι συναντήσωνται ἐν ὕλῃ
> 135 ἄνδρες ἐπακτῆρες· ὁ δέ τε σθένεϊ βλεμεαίνει·

πᾶν δέ τ' ἐπισκύνιον κάτω ἕλκεται ὅσσε καλύπτων·
ὣς Αἴας περὶ Πατρόκλῳ ἥρωι βεβήκει.
Ἀτρείδης δ' ἑτέρωθεν, ἀρηίφιλος Μενέλαος,
ἑστήκει, μέγα πένθος ἐνὶ στήθεσσιν ἀέξων.

A note of Didymus (5 A) referred by its lemma to line 133 reads παρὰ Ζηνοδότῳ καὶ ἐν τῇ Χίᾳ οὐκ ἦσαν οἱ γ´ στίχοι (133–5). If that is the truth—and it may well be the truth—it is a mechanical blunder, haplography starting from the similarity of ΑΙΑΣ and ΑΝΔΡΕΣ at the beginning of the lines. It will have happened in sources common to Zenodotus and the Chia, and need occasion no more surprise than the transposition of lines common to Zenodotus and PHibeh 19 discussed at Γ 328–39. If Zenodotus so read, it was not merely περιττὴ εὐλάβεια, but sheer heroism to let the text stand without any *Verschlimmbesserung* in spite of its obvious defectiveness.

The scholiast regards this, of course, as a deliberate excision, and proceeds to ascribe a motive to Zenodotus : ἴσως, φασὶν ἔνιοι, ὅτι οἱ ἄρσενες λέοντες οὐ σκυμναγωγοῦσιν, ἀλλὰ θήλειαι μόναι. That was set up to be overthrown, and it is overthrown easily by a reference to the fact that in Homer λέων is epicene. But a twist has been given to the subsequent study of the passage.

Modern scholars, beginning with Heyne and Dindorf, believing that Zenodotus must have had a perfect juncture, pushed the note down one line further, thus making 134–6 the missing lines. That also is well within the range of possibility. Only, as Heyne saw, γ´ must then be changed to δ´ since 134–7 are inseparable.

If I were convinced of the correctness of this I should argue as follows. The natural history—real or poetic—need not trouble us ; Fränkel (92 f.) has said all that is wanted. There is no question of the beauty of the lines ; 5 T with his ὑπερέβαλε δὲ ὁ λόγος καὶ τὴν γραφικήν is not too enthusiastic. But we have no right to assume that the *Iliad* had a monopoly of good similes, and therefore reject the conclusion to which the external evidence would point, that somebody had added to the text an excellent simile from another poem. It could be argued, too—though similes need not run on all fours—that the lion standing over its cubs in its lair is a better comparison for Aias over the dead Patroclus, than is the lion leading its whelps. That, however, would be a question of taste.

On reviewing the external evidence I should decide in favour of the first alternative. The double corruption in the scholium can be paralleled ; but for this corrupt note to strike by accident lines, the omission of which by haplography is easily intelligible, is already a very curious coincidence. That this should happen just when the interpolated lines are original poetry of the highest excellence (a thing rarely found in these interpolations) is too much for one to believe.

After a description of the battle over Patroclus :

400 τοῖον Ζεὺς ἐπὶ Πατρόκλῳ ἀνδρῶν τε καὶ ἵππων
ἤματι τῷ ἐτάνυσσε κακὸν πόνον. οὐδ᾽ ἄρα πώ τι
ᾔδεε Πάτροκλον τεθνηότα δῖος Ἀχιλλεύς·
403 πολλὸν γὰρ ἀπάνευθε νεῶν μάρναντο θοάων.
426 ἵπποι δ᾽ Αἰακίδαο μάχης ἀπάνευθεν ἐόντες
κλαῖον, ἐπεὶ δὴ πρῶτα πυθέσθην ἡνιόχοιο
ἐν κονίῃσι πεσόντος ὑφ᾽ Ἕκτορος ἀνδροφόνοιο.

4C4 τείχει ὕπο Τρώων· τό μιν οὔ ποτε ἔλπετο θυμῷ
405 τεθνάμεν, ἀλλὰ ζωόν, ἐνιχριμφθέντα πύλῃσιν,
ἂψ ἀπονοστήσειν, ἐπεὶ οὐδὲ τὸ ἔλπετο πάμπαν,
ἐκπέρσειν πτολίεθρον ἄνευ ἕθεν, οὐδὲ σὺν αὐτῷ·
πολλάκι γὰρ τό γε μητρὸς ἐπεύθετο νόσφιν ἀκούων,
ἥ οἱ ἀπαγγέλλεσκε Διὸς μεγάλοιο νόημα.
410 δὴ τότε γ᾽ οὔ οἱ ἔειπε κακὸν τόσον, ὅσσον ἐτύχθη,
μήτηρ, ὅττι ῥά οἱ πολὺ φίλτατος ὤλεθ᾽ ἑταῖρος.
οἱ δ᾽ αἰεὶ περὶ νεκρὸν ἀκαχμένα δούρατ᾽ ἔχοντες
νωλεμὲς ἐγχρίμπτοντο καὶ ἀλλήλους ἐνάριζον.
ὧδε δέ τις εἴπεσκεν Ἀχαιῶν χαλκοχιτώνων·
415 " ὦ φίλοι, οὐ μὰν ἧμιν ἐϋκλεὲς ἀπονέεσθαι
νῆας ἔπι γλαφυράς, ἀλλ᾽ αὐτοῦ γαῖα μέλαινα
πᾶσι χάνοι· τό κεν ἧμιν ἄφαρ πολὺ κέρδιον εἴη,
εἰ τοῦτον Τρώεσσι μεθήσομεν ἱπποδάμοισιν
ἄστυ πότι σφέτερον ἐρύσαι καὶ κῦδος ἀρέσθαι."
420 ὡς δέ τις αὖ Τρώων μεγαθύμων αὐδήσασκεν·
" ὦ φίλοι, εἰ καὶ μοῖρα παρ᾽ ἀνέρι τῷδε δαμῆναι
πάντας ὁμῶς, μή πώ τις ἐρωείτω πολέμοιο."
ὡς ἄρα τις εἴπεσκε, μένος δ᾽ ὄρσασκεν ἑκάστου.
ὡς οἱ μὲν μάρναντο, σιδήρειος δ᾽ ὀρυμαγδὸς
425 χάλκεον οὐρανὸν ἷκε δι᾽ αἰθέρος ἀτρυγέτοιο.
412–25 om. Bekker².

The text is that of Zenodotus according to Didymus (ṣ T) :

Ζηνόδοτος ἀπὸ τοῦ "τείχει ὑπὸ Τρώων" ἕως τοῦ "χάλκεον οὐρανόν" οὐ γράφει· Ἀρίσταρχος μόνον ἀθετεῖ "ὡς δέ τις αὖ Τρώων". The additional passage of the vulgate is well described by Leaf as containing 'nothing but a painfully conscientious endeavour to explain just so much of the situation as is already quite clear'; cf. also Wilamowitz, *Ilias*, 146 ; Wecklein, *ZAV* 44 f. The quality of the interpolation testifies to the merit of that recension which is free of it.

After the famous speech of Zeus to the horses of Achilles:

456   ὡς εἰπὼν ἵπποισιν ἐνέπνευσεν μένος ἠΰ·
τὼ δ' ἀπὸ χαιτάων κονίην οὖδας δὲ βαλόντε
ῥίμφ' ἔφερον θοὸν ἅρμα μετὰ Τρῶας καὶ Ἀχαιούς.

According to the TV scholia Zenodotus read for line 456:

ὡς εἰπὼν ἵπποισι μένος πολυθαρσὲς ἐνῆκεν,
αὐτὸς δ' Οὔλυμπον δὲ μετ' ἀθανάτοισι βεβήκει.

The worthlessness of the added line was seen by Duentzer (*Zenod.* 159), who noted also that the use of αὐτός and of ἀθανάτοισι, was faulty. To emend the latter with La Roche and Leaf to μετ' ἀθανάτους ἐβεβήκει may be simply destroying part of the evidence. The line is reminiscent of A 221–2, and would not surprise us in a Ptolemaic papyrus; but it is strange to find it in the edition of Zenodotus of Ephesos, even though Wecklein (*ZAV* 73) is content to note that he cannot be suspected of inventing it. Coming to us as the verse does, it is most probable that it was found in the text of Zenodotus of Mallos.

Erhardt (338 f.) understands the line correctly as meaning that Zeus returned from Ida to Olympus, where he seems (545–6) to be later in the book. These lines were probably not read by Zenodotus, and that is another reason for refusing to believe that this plus verse was contained in his text.

Wilamowitz (*Ilias*, 146 n.) infers from this line for Zenodotus an entirely different version of the story, in which some god (certainly not Zeus) descended to bring aid to the horses. The inference is without foundation, and most improbable.

After the *Aristeia* of Automedon:

ἂψ δ' ἐπὶ Πατρόκλῳ τέτατο κρατερὴ ὑσμίνη
544   ἀργαλέη, πολύδακρυς· ἔγειρε δὲ νεῖκος Ἀθήνη.

547 ἤΰτε πορφυρέην ἶριν θνητοῖσι τανύσσῃ
    Ζεὺς ἐξ οὐρανόθεν, τέρας ἔμμεναι ἢ πολέμοιο
    ἢ καὶ χειμῶνος δυσθαλπέος, ὅς ῥά τε ἔργων
550 ἀνθρώπους ἀνέπαυσεν ἐπὶ χθονί, μῆλα δὲ κήδει,
    ὣς ἡ πορφυρέη νεφέλη πυκάσασα ἓ αὐτὴν
    δύσετ' Ἀχαιῶν ἔθνος, ἔγειρε δὲ φῶτα ἕκαστον.

---

545 οὐρανόθεν καταβᾶσα· προῆκε γὰρ εὐρύοπα Ζεὺς
546 ὀρνύμεναι Δαναούς· δὴ γὰρ νόος ἐτράπετ' αὐτοῦ.
om. Bekker², van Leeuwen ; damn. Christ.

This text was read by certain ancient editors. Whether we can
name them depends on the correctness of the emendations proposed
for a corrupt scholium of TV : Ζηνόδοτος ἀθετεῖ· τινὲς οὐδὲ γράφουσιν. Following suggestions of Ludwich (AHT i. 425), Leaf, and
Wecklein (ZAV 58 n.), I should read : ⟨τοῦτον καὶ τὸν ἑξῆς⟩
Ἀρίσταρχος ἀθετεῖ· Ζηνόδοτος δὲ καὶ ⟨Ἀριστοφάνης⟩ οὐδὲ γράφουσιν.
The name, however, matters nothing to my argument.

The shorter version is complete and satisfactory, as is indicated
by the fact that the added lines have frequently been condemned,
from Heyne (vii. 369) to Finsler (Homer², ii. 184) and Wecklein.
The reminiscences, the improper use of αὐτοῦ, and the contradiction
with the sequel, all combine to show by contrast the merit of the
shorter text.

Σ

Achilles watching the Achaean retreat :

" ὤμοι ἐγώ, τί ταρ αὖτε καρηκομόωντες Ἀχαιοὶ
νηυσὶν ἔπι κλονέονται ἀτυζόμενοι πεδίοιο ;
μὴ δή μοι τελέσωσι θεοὶ κακὰ κήδεα θυμῷ,
9   ὣς ποτέ μοι μήτηρ διεπέφραδε καί μοι ἔειπε.
12 ἦ μάλα δὴ τέθνηκε Μενοιτίου ἄλκιμος υἱός,
σχέτλιος· ἦ τ' ἐκέλευον ἀπωσάμενον δήιον πῦρ
ἂψ ἐπὶ νῆας ἴμεν, μὴ δ' Ἕκτορι ἶφι μάχεσθαι."

---

10 Μυρμιδόνων τὸν ἄριστον ἔτι ζώοντος ἐμεῖο
11 χερσὶν ὕπο Τρώων λείψειν φάος ἠελίοιο.

The text is that of Rhianos and Aristophanes, possibly also that
of Zenodotus. The evidence is given by Didymus (ꜱ TV), ἐν τῇ
Ῥιανοῦ καὶ Ἀριστοφάνους οὐκ ἐφέροντο οἱ δύο, and with greater

abbreviation (ϛ A): ἐν τῇ 'Ριανοῦ οὐκ ἦσαν οἱ β'. That these editors had a predecessor in Zenodotus was a not unnatural assumption of Nauck and Duentzer (*Zenod.* 16 n. 61), though it is rejected by Ludwich (*AHT* i. 427) and Wecklein (*ZAV* 57). For my argument the assumption is not essential.

I am not troubled by the lack of pedantic preciseness in the phrase Μυρμιδόνων τὸν ἄριστον—to be obscure is the quintessence of the oracular style. Nor am I troubled by alleged contradictions with other passages, especially since P 408–11 have proved to be an interpolation. I can approve the Ameis-Hentze argument (*Anh.* vi. 118) against the omission of lines 9–11, noting that the omission of lines 10–11 is not thereby affected. But I do not see why the vagueness of line 9 is not perfectly satisfactory, and therefore cannot regard lines 10–11 as essential. This being so, I feel that we are constrained to follow the version that has so often proved superior.

Achilles laments the death of his comrade :

35   ἄκουσε δὲ πότνια μήτηρ
ἡμένη ἐν βένθεσσιν ἁλὸς παρὰ πατρὶ γέροντι,
κώκυσέν τ' ἄρ' ἔπειτα· θεαὶ δέ μιν ἀμφαγέροντο
38 πᾶσαι, ὅσαι κατὰ βένθος ἁλὸς Νηρηίδες ἦσαν.
50 τῶν δὲ καὶ ἀργύφεον πλῆτο σπέος· αἱ δ' ἅμα πᾶσαι
στήθεα πεπλήγοντο, Θέτις δ' ἐξῆρχε γόοιο·

     ἔνθ' ἄρ' ἔην Γλαύκη τε Θάλειά τε Κυμοδόκη τε,
40   Νησαίη Σπειώ τε Θόη θ' Ἁλίη τε βοῶπις,
     Κυμοθόη τε καὶ Ἀκταίη καὶ Λιμνώρεια
     καὶ Μελίτη καὶ Ἴαιρα καὶ Ἀμφιθόη καὶ Ἀγαυὴ
     Δωτώ τε Πρωτώ τε Φέρουσά τε Δυναμένη τε,
     Δεξαμένη τε καὶ Ἀμφινόμη καὶ Καλλιάνειρα,
45   Δωρὶς καὶ Πανόπη καὶ ἀγακλειτὴ Γαλάτεια,
     Νημερτής τε καὶ Ἀψευδὴς καὶ Καλλιάνασσα·
     ἔνθα δ' ἔην Κλυμένη Ἰάνειρά τε καὶ Ἰάνασσα,
     Μαῖρα καὶ Ὠρείθυια ἐυπλόκαμός τ' Ἀμάθυια
49   ἄλλαι θ', αἳ κατὰ βένθος ἁλὸς Νηρηίδες ἦσαν.

om. Bekker²; damn. Nauck, Christ, Ludwich.

The evidence for the shorter version is to be found in a long note of ϛ A, where the epitomator has probably (cf. Roemer, *AAH* 307) combined Aristonicus with Didymus. To the latter belongs the part of interest to us, which I think should be extracted and com-

pleted as follows: ὁ τῶν Νηρείδων χορὸς προηθέτηται· καὶ παρὰ Ζηνοδότῳ ⟨οὐδ' ἦσαν οἱ στίχοι⟩. ὁ δὲ Καλλίστρατος οὐδὲ ἐν τῇ Ἀργολικῇ φησιν αὐτοὺς φέρεσθαι. The emendation is again not essential to the argument; for even without it the absence of the lines from the *Argolike*, and their athetesis by Zenodotus, Aristophanes, and Aristarchus, is attested.

The intentional omission of the *Catalogue of the Ships* in some papyri and MSS. is not to be compared: in that case there was an appreciable saving of labour and material, while here there could be no such motive. But haplography due to the recurrence of κατὰ βένθος ἁλὸς Νηρηίδες ἦσαν is a possibility that must be considered. To assume it leads to difficulty: for either (1) this haplography imposed upon the Alexandrians, or (2) it coincided accidentally with their athetesis. Neither supposition is impossible, but I should regard either as most improbable.

The shorter version is perfectly satisfactory, and the case might rest simply on its better attestation. But Wilamowitz (*Ilias*, 165) has recently waxed enthusiastic over this interpolation. He praises the art with which the poet has known how to conceal the fact that he is uniting things incompatible; and as part of it ' die Aufzählung der Namen wohllautend wie das Plätschern des ruhigen Meeres, beruhigt unsere Aufregung, lenkt uns ab von der aufregenden Szene, macht uns empfänglich für die Stille des Gesprächs zwischen Mutter and Sohn, das so ganz anders gestimmt ist '.

That is a beautiful flight of the imagination, but leaves untouched the difficulties of the passages, which, for instance, forced the equally enthusiastic Lehrs (*Arist.*[3] 401 f.) to emend ἦσαν (49) to εἰσίν. Even that is a half-way measure. For the rest I may refer to Ameis-Hentze (*Anhang*, vi. 123, 144), to Leaf, and to Roemer's presentation (*AAH* 307 f.) of the Aristarchean view. Finsler (*Homer*[2], ii. 189) decides against the passage; and I think it right to claim that the shorter version is here intrinsically the superior.

Thetis speaking to Achilles:

95 " ὠκύμορος δή μοι, τέκος, ἔσσεαι, οἷ' ἀγορεύεις·
    αὐτίκα γάρ τοι ἔπειτα μεθ' Ἕκτορα πότμος ἑτοῖμος."
        τὴν δὲ μέγ' ὀχθήσας προσέφη πόδας ὠκὺς Ἀχιλλεύς·
    " αὐτίκα τεθναίην, ἐπεὶ οὐκ ἄρ' ἔμελλον ἑταίρῳ

κτεινομένῳ ἐπαμῦναι· ὁ μὲν μάλα τηλόθι πάτρης
100 ἔφθιτ', ἐμεῖο δὲ δῆσεν Ἄρεω ἀλκτῆρα γενέσθαι.

Aeschines (i. 150) quotes lines 95–9, the last ending ὅ μοι πολὺ φίλτατος ἔσκεν. La Roche (*HTk* 39) infers that line 100 was absent from Aeschines' text. Such a type of variation could not be paralleled easily, and I think it more probable that the orator's text contained a worthless plus verse:

τὴν δ' αὖτε προσέειπε ποδάρκης δῖος Ἀχιλλεύς·
" αὐτίκα τεθναίην, ἐπεὶ οὐκ ἄρ' ἔμελλον ἑταίρῳ
κτεινομένῳ ἐπαμῦναι, ὅ μοι πολὺ φίλτατος ἔσκεν
Μυρμιδόνων πάντων· καὶ ὁ μὲν μάλα τηλόθι πάτρης
100 ἔφθιτ', ἐμεῖο δὲ δῆσεν Ἄρεω ἀλκτῆρα γενέσθαι.

The retreat of the Achaeans :

οὐδέ κε Πάτροκλόν περ ἐυκνήμιδες Ἀχαιοὶ
ἐκ βελέων ἐρύσαντο νέκυν, θεράποντ' Ἀχιλῆος·
αὖτις γὰρ δὴ τόν γε κίχον λαός τε καὶ ἵπποι
Ἕκτωρ τε, Πριάμοιο πάις, συΐ εἴκελος ἀλκήν,
155 ὅς μιν τρὶς μετόπισθε ποδῶν λάβε καὶ μέγ' ἄυτει.
157 τρὶς δὲ δύ' Αἴαντες, θοῦριν ἐπιειμένοι ἀλκήν,
νεκροῦ ἀπεστυφέλιξαν· ὁ δ' ἔμπεδον, ἀλκὶ πεποιθώς,
ἄλλοτ' ἐπαΐξασκε κατὰ μόθον, ἄλλοτε δ' αὖτε
160 στάσκε μέγα ἰάχων· ὀπίσω δ' οὐ χάζετο πάμπαν.

---

154 Ἕκτωρ τε, Πριάμοιο πάις, φλογὶ εἴκελος ἀλκήν.
155 τρὶς μέν μιν μετόπισθε ποδῶν λάβε φαίδιμος Ἕκτωρ
156 ἑλκέμεναι μεμαώς, μέγα δὲ Τρώεσσιν ὁμόκλα·
post vm. 155 Zenodotus legit :
ἑλκέμεναι μεμαώς, κεφαλὴν δέ ἑ θυμὸς ἀνώγει
πῆξαι ἀνὰ σκολόπεσσι ταμόνθ' ἁπαλῆς ἀπὸ δειρῆς.

Iris describes this situation to Achilles :

οἱ δ' ἀλλήλους ὀλέκουσιν,
οἱ μὲν ἀμυνόμενοι νέκυος πέρι τεθνηῶτος,
οἱ δὲ ἐρύσσασθαι προτὶ Ἴλιον αἰπὺ θέλοντες
175 Τρῶες ἐπιθύουσι· μάλιστα δὲ φαίδιμος Ἕκτωρ.
178 ἀλλ' ἄνα, μηδ' ἔτι κεῖσο· σέβας δέ σε θυμὸν ἱκέσθω,
Πάτροκλον Τρῳῇσι κυσὶν μέλπηθρα γενέσθαι·
180 σοὶ λώβη, αἴ κέν τι νέκυς ᾐσχυμμένος ἔλθῃ."

174   προτὶ Ἴλιον ἠνεμόεσσαν
175 Τρῶες ἐπιθύουσι· μάλιστα δὲ φαίδιμος Ἕκτωρ
176 ἑλκέμεναι μέμονεν· κεφαλὴν δέ ἑ θυμὸς ἀνώγει
177 πῆξαι ἀνὰ σκολόπεσσι, ταμόνθ᾽ ἁπαλῆς ἀπὸ δειρῆς.

The text followed is in the main[1] that of Zenodotus. The evidence comes from Aristonicus (s A) at line 155: ὅτι Ζηνόδοτος γράφει οὕτως·

     " Ἕκτωρ τε Πριάμοιο πάϊς, συῒ ἴκελος ἀλκήν,
     ὅς μιν τρὶς μετόπισθε ποδῶν λάβε καὶ μέγ᾽ ἀΰτει,
     ἑλκέμεναι μεμαώς, κεφαλὴν δέ ἑ θυμὸς ἀνώγει
     πῆξαι ἀνὰ σκολόπεσσι ταμόνθ᾽ ἁπαλῆς ἀπὸ δειρῆς "

and at line 174: ὅτι Ζηνόδοτος γράφει " Ἴλιον αἰπὺ θέλοντες " καὶ τοὺς ἑξῆς ἀπὸ τοῦ " ἑλκέμεναι μέμονεν " ἕως τοῦ " πῆξαι ἀνὰ σκολόπεσσι " ἄνω μετατέθεικεν.

For Duentzer (*Zenod.* 155 f.) and Roemer (*Zenod.* 71) these are arbitrary changes; but Erhardt (374) and Wecklein (*ZAV* 39 ff.) have seen that Zenodotus could not possibly have started from the Aristarchean text. Wecklein's assumption, however, that the MSS. used by Zenodotus contained the plus verses in both positions, and that he dropped them at their second occurrence, is contrary to all our experience. The natural interpretation of the evidence is that we are dealing with *freifliegende Einschubverse*. That is fortunate, for otherwise we should have to encounter the suggestion that the lines had been expurgated.

The distich offers a serious verbal difficulty—the plural σκολόπεσσι. Leaf understands ' palisades along the top of the Trojan wall ', assuming their existence because the ' model town of Phaiakia is described (η 45) as having them '. But the σκόλοπες seem to have been stakes planted in a fosse, in η 45 as in other passages; and granting that Troy could have been conceived as having them, they do not seem a natural place for the display of such a trophy. Cutting off an enemy's head is not uncommon (cf. Murray, *RGE*[2] 147 f.) in the *Iliad*; but the fixing of it ' up on a post like an African king ' has no other parallel. Perhaps the (real or imagined) treatment of Leonidas' body after Thermopylae[2] suggested to some rhapsodist this added horror.

---

[1] The variant (160) μέγα ἀχέων shows merely the quality of the antigraphon used by the Aristarcheans; Ἴλιον αἰπύ (174) would lead into questions intentionally excluded from this book.

[2] Hdt. ix. 78 ἀποταμόντες τήν κεφαλὴν ἀνεσταύρωσαν. . . . ἀνασκολοπίσας.

The resulting text may seem not entirely satisfactory ; but if so
I should interpret it as an indication that the external evidence has
not revealed the whole of the interpolation.
Later than the intrusion of this distich is the expansion of line
155 into two lines. Had the vulgate been the original text, certainly
no one would ever have disturbed it. The change in the opposite
direction can be understood as the result of a wish to get in τρὶς
μὲν ... τρὶς δὲ ... a sequence of the usual (cf. *AJP* 34 (1913). 165 f.)
pattern. One consequence is that ῞Εκτωρ is repeated in an awkward
fashion.

Describing the work of Hephaistos :

> τρίποδας γὰρ ἐείκοσι πάντας ἔτευχεν
> ἑστάμεναι περὶ τοῖχον ἐυσταθέος μεγάροιο·
> 375 χρύσεα δέ σφ' ὑπὸ κύκλα ἑκάστῳ πυθμένι θῆκεν,
> ὄφρα οἱ αὐτόματοι θεῖον δυσαίατ' ἀγῶνα
> ἠδ' αὖτις πρὸς δῶμα νεοίατο, θαῦμα ἰδέσθαι.
> οἱ δ' ἤτοι τόσσον μὲν ἔχον τέλος, οὔατα δ' οὔ πω
> δαιδάλεα προσέκειτο· τά ῥ' ἤρτυε, κόπτε δὲ δεσμούς.

s T reads: δυσαίατ' ἀγῶνα] οὕτως· ἐν δὲ ταῖς εἰκαιοτέραις " θεῖον
κατὰ δῶμα νέοιντο". s A, immediately after explaining θεῖον ἀγῶνα,
continues: ἐν δὲ ταῖς εἰκαιοτέραις " θεῖον κατὰ δῶμα νέονται".

Ludwich (*AHT* i. 433) saw that if this statement is correct line
377 cannot have been read ἐν ταῖς εἰκαιοτέραις. Wecklein (*ZAV*
80 f.) also approves of the omission of this line, which he regards as
nothing but an expansion of the variant, or rather of its original
form δῖον πρὸς δῶμα νέοιντο.

Criticism is difficult, because it seems impossible to determine
exactly what the miracle was to be. Two points, however, seem
clear : the variant with νέοιντο (cf. Wackernagel, *SU* 96) cannot be
the original text ; the retention of θαῦμα ἰδέσθαι is highly desirable.
I think the trouble is in the scholia, where two notes have been
telescoped ; and would read : ἐν δὲ ταῖς εἰκαιοτέραις " θεῖον ⟨δύσον-
ται " καὶ⟩ " κατὰ δῶμα νέονται".

As the cattle approach the ambush :

> οἱ μὲν τὰ προϊδόντες ἐπέδραμον, ὦκα δ' ἔπειτα
> 528 τάμνοντ' ἀμφὶ βοῶν ἀγέλας καὶ πώεα καλὰ
> ἀργεννῶν οἴων, κτεῖνον δ' ἐπὶ μηλοβοτῆρας.

According to 5 A^t the reading of Zenodotus in line 528 was πῶυ μέγ᾽ οἰῶν.
Duentzer (*Zenod.* 175) inferred that Zenodotus must then have read ἀγέλην and omitted line 529. The motive for all this was supposed to be a desire to get rid of μηλοβοτῆρας "quum non solum μῆλα, verum etiam boves commemorarentur". Fick (508) accepted the idea that line 529 was not in Zenodotus, and regarded his as the earlier form of text. He was glad to be freed from the contracted ἀργεννῶν, and did not note that the contracted οἰῶν thus introduced was equally objectionable. Wecklein (*ZAV* 63) refuses to believe that the line was not read by Zenodotus.

I think that πῶυ μέγ᾽ οἰῶν is no more than a copyist's slip, a gliding into the phrase familiar from Δ 696, Ο 323, μ 299, and that we should not build further upon it.

Of Achilles' shield :

> ἐν δ᾽ ἐτίθει τέμενος βασιλήιον· ἔνθα δ᾽ ἔριθοι
> 551 ἤμων, ὀξείας δρεπάνας ἐν χερσὶν ἔχοντες.

551ᵃ   καρπὸν Ἐλευσινίης Δημήτερος ἀγλαοδώρου

A curious theory that the shield is an allegory of early Attic history is found in the scholia ; the A scholia (at 490) ascribe it to Agallias of Corcyra ὁ Ἀριστοφάνει γνώριμος, while the T scholia (at 483) give as its author Agallis of Corcyra. In the latter only is this line preserved : ἐν δέ τισιν ἐγράφετο μετὰ τὸν " ἤμων ὀξείας δρεπάνας " "καρπὸν ... ἀγλαοδώρου". Eustathius (Neumann, p. 303) knows of the line from some kindred source.

The only interest of the interpolation is its obvious Attic origin. Its purpose is to supply for ἤμων an object. Compare also Ludwich, *HV* 26 ; Wecklein, *ZAV* 11, 15 f.

The dance on the shield of Achilles :

> ἔνθα μὲν ἠίθεοι καὶ παρθένοι ἀλφεσίβοιαι
> ὠρχεῦντ᾽, ἀλλήλων ἐπὶ καρπῷ χεῖρας ἔχοντες.
> τῶν δ᾽ αἱ μὲν λεπτὰς ὀθόνας ἔχον, οἱ δὲ χιτῶνας
> 596 εἴατ᾽ ἐυννήτους, ἦκα στίλβοντας ἐλαίῳ.

597   καί ρ᾽ αἱ μὲν καλὰς στεφάνας ἔχον, οἱ δὲ μαχαίρας
598   εἴχον χρυσείας ἐξ ἀργυρέων τελαμώνων.

599 οἱ δ' ὁτὲ μὲν θρέξασκον ἐπισταμένοισι πόδεσσι
ρεῖα μάλ', ὡς ὅτε τις τροχὸν ἄρμενον ἐν παλάμῃσιν
ἑζόμενος κεραμεὺς πειρήσεται, αἴ κε θέῃσιν·
ἄλλοτε δ' αὖ θρέξασκον ἐπὶ στίχας ἀλλήλοισι.

The text is that of Aristophanes; the plus verses were read but obelized by Aristarchus. The evidence is in the A scholia: ἀθετοῦνται οἱ δύο (Aristonicus) and οὗτοι δὲ οὐδὲ παρ' Ἀριστοφάνει ἦσαν. The lines are found also in 1 a. PBerol. 9774, a papyrus which on account of its other plus verses is to be regarded as a belated survival of the Ptolemaic text.

The external evidence is to be somewhat discounted; since, on account of the similarity of lines 595 and 597,[1] the omission may be accidental. But the lines are needless, and Aristarchus brought against them two arguments: (1) μάχαιρα in the sense of sword; and (2) the impropriety of wearing swords at dances. Leaf values these objections too lightly. Elsewhere in Homer μάχαιρα designates a sacrificial knife, and there is no indication that such knives were carried ἐκ τελαμώνων. As for the other argument nothing else suggests that this dance is an 'acting of war-scenes', the sheathed swords suggesting indeed the contrary.

The Berlin papyrus which began at line 596 continues:

603   πολλὸς δ' ἱμερόεντα χορὸν περιίσταθ' ὅμιλος
604/5 τερπόμενοι· δοιὼ δὲ κυβιστητῆρε κατ' αὐτοὺς
606   μολπῆς ἐξάρχοντες ἐδίνευον κατὰ μέσσους.
*   ἐν δ' ἔσ[σαν σύ]ριγγε[ς, ἔσα]ν κίθαρίς τ[ε] καὶ [αὐλοί.
607   ἐν δ' ἐτίθει ποταμοῖο μέγα σθένος Ὠκεανοῖο
608   ἄντυγα πὰρ πυμάτην σάκεος πύκα ποιητοῖο.
*   ἐν δὲ λιμὴν ἐτέτυκ[το] ἐανοῦ κασσιτέρ[οιο
                          ∽ Hes. Asp. 207/8
*   κλυζ[ομ]ένῳ ἴκ[ε]λο]ς· δοιὼ δ' ἀναφυσιοῶ[ντες ∽ 209/11
*   ἀργύ[ρεοι] δελφῖνε[ς ἐ]φοίνεον ἔλλοπας [ἰχθῦς] ∽ 212
*   τοῦ δ' [ὕπ]ο χάλκε[ιοι τρέον ἰ]χθύες· α[ὐ]τὰ[ρ ἐπ' ἀκταῖς
                                ∽ 213

---

604 τερπόμενοι· μετὰ δέ σφιν ἐμέλπετο θεῖος ἀοιδὸς
605 φορμίζων· δοιὼ δὲ κυβιστητῆρε κατ' αὐτοὺς

[1] Note the weakly attested variant τῶν δ' αἱ μέν, probably due to the same cause.

The expansion of 604/5 into two lines, which Athenaeus declared to be the original text, has been discussed (p. 47 f.) above. The fuller form, though destitute of all other authority, was read by Wolf, Bekker, La Roche, Nauck, Christ, and Monro-Allen; while Leaf, Ludwich, and van Leeuwen have returned to the better-authenticated text.

That the longer text following line 608 is interpolated needs no argument. The thing of interest is that it gives us a clear example of these interpolators drawing upon Hesiod. It is a good parallel, for instance, to the *Catalogue of the Nereids*; only that is artistically better, and has had better luck.

Finally, it is a pleasure to note that the interpolation in Hesiod, *Asp.* 209–11, had already been detected by R. Peppmüller, *Phil.* 50 (1891). 655.

T

After Thetis' speech:

ὡς ἄρα φωνήσασα μένος πολυθαρσὲς ἐνῆκε,
Πατρόκλῳ δ' αὖτ' ἀμβροσίην καὶ νέκταρ ἐρυθρὸν
39 στάξε κατὰ ῥινῶν, ἵνα οἱ χρὼς ἔμπεδος εἴη.

39ᵃ ἡ μὲν ἄρ' ὡς ἔρξασ' ἀπέβη Θέτις ἀργυρόπεζα.

The T scholia contain a note μετὰ δὲ τὸ " ἔμπεδος εἴη " γράφεται which Ludwich completed by adding this verse that is found in a few MSS. It has consequently been discussed in Part I, and there is no doubt that it is an interpolation. The line is an adaptation of E 133, etc. under the influence of σ 197. The date of its interpolation will turn on the date of the scholium; its method of citing the last words of a line is unusual and probably late.

The Achaeans rejoice:

76 τοῖσι δ' ἀνιστάμενος μετέφη κρείων Ἀγαμέμνων·
78 " ὦ φίλοι, ἥρωες Δαναοί, θεράποντες Ἄρηος,
     ἑσταότος μὲν καλὸν ἀκούειν, οὐδὲ ἔοικεν

76 τοῖσι δὲ καὶ μετέειπεν ἄναξ ἀνδρῶν Ἀγαμέμνων
77 αὐτόθεν ἐξ ἕδρης, οὐδ' ἐν μέσσοισιν ἀναστάς·
vm. 77 om. Bekker; damn. Nauck.
76 τοῖσι δ' ἀνιστάμενος μετέφη κρείων Ἀγαμέμνων
  * μῆνιν ἀναστενάχων καὶ ἰφ' ἕλκεος ἄλγεα πάσχων·
sic Massiliotice et Chia.

80 ὑββάλλειν· χαλεπὸν γὰρ ἐπισταμένῳ περ' ἐόντι.
ἀνδρῶν δ' ἐν πολλῷ ὁμάδῳ πῶς κέν τις ἀκούσαι
ἢ εἴποι; βλάβεται δὲ λιγύς περ ἐὼν ἀγορητής.

The text is that of Zenodotus, which also underlies the interpolated
version offered by the Massaliotike and the Chia. The vulgate was
read and defended by Aristophanes and Aristarchus.

The evidence is a note of Didymus (s A): οὕτως καὶ παρ'
Ἀριστοφάνει· ἐν δὲ τῇ Μασσαλιωτικῇ καὶ Χίᾳ "τοῖσι ... πάσχων".
οὕτως ὁ Δίδυμος. The note is repeated in s T, with the omission of
καὶ Χίᾳ and οὕτως ὁ Δίδυμος, and with the addition to the quotation
of αὐτόθεν ἐξ ἕδρης. All of this I should regard as late corruption;
though if one wishes to believe that the Massaliotike contained both
plus verses, it is possible. Aristonicus also testifies (s A): ὅτι
Ζηνόδοτος τοῦτον μὲν (77) οὐκ ἔγραφε, τὸν δὲ πρὸ αὐτοῦ μόνον οὕτως
"τοῖσι ... Ἀγαμέμνων". Alexander of Kotyaïum (s A at 79), after
giving his interpretation, continues: τοῦτο ἀγνοήσας Ἀρίσταρχος καὶ
οἰηθεὶς παραίτησίν τινα ἐκ τοῦ Ἀγαμέμνονος γίνεσθαι, παρενέθηκε
τὸν "αὐτόθι ἐξ ἕδρης". Porphyry (Schrader, 233 ff.) in his long
discussion adds nothing to our knowledge of these ancient variants.

The intrinsic merits of the short version are clear. To appreciate
it one should read the varying attempts to interpret the proemium
of Agamemnon's speech when line 77 is 'retained'; cf., for instance,
Lendrum, CR 4 (1890). 47; Headlam, JPh 26 (1898). 92; Allen,
CR 20 (1906). 290 f.—the last even assuming a lacuna. Erhardt
(381 f.) recognizes the contradiction, but prefers to regard it as a
clue to the composition of this section rather than 'change' it.
Peppmüller (Phil. 50 (1891). 651 ff.) has given an excellent presentation of the case, except that he thought it was a question of 'rejecting' the line. Leaf also sees the merits of the Zenodotean text, but
is prevented from reaching the right conclusion by his belief that
line 77 is 'of respectable antiquity and older than Zenodotus'. The
verse is simply not in the oldest and best tradition, and we have no
right to import it; Wilamowitz (Ilias, 173 n.), Finsler (Homer², ii.
200), and Wecklein (ZAV 51) have all seen that.

Of the origin of the plus verses little need be said. Both are
efforts to recall that in Δ Agamemnon was wounded; the Ptolemaic
papyri have made us familiar enough with this type of interpolation,

and these lines must go back to some such source. That of the Massaliotike and Chia is tasteless and useless; that of the vulgate is, besides, in glaring contradiction to the story. The charge that Aristarchus inserted (παρενέθηκε) the line may be dismissed briefly. It is a counterpart to the charges made by Athenaeus and Plutarch that he removed (ἐξεῖλεν) certain lines, and need not be taken more seriously (cf. above, p. 47 f., and Ludwich, *AHT* i. 74 f.). In the present case we know that it was Aristophanes who did what was done, and have every reason to believe that he was guided by some MS. authority.

Between the two forms of line 76 I should follow that which is attested by Zenodotus, the Massaliotike, and the Chia. The other has weaker support, and is under suspicion of being adapted to the interpolation in connexion with which it occurs.

Compare on *I* 119ᵃ for the addition of *T* 137ᵃ by Barnes.

Lines 388–91 have been discussed already in connexion with *Π* 141–4.

Υ

Zeus speaking to the assembly of the gods :

ἀλλ' ἤτοι μὲν ἐγὼ μενέω πτυχὶ Οὐλύμποιο
ἥμενος, ἔνθ' ὁρόων φρένα τέρψομαι· οἱ δὲ δὴ ἄλλοι
ἔρχεσθ', ὄφρ' ἂν ἵκησθε μετὰ Τρῶας καὶ Ἀχαιούς,
25 ἀμφοτέροισι δ' ἀρήγεθ', ὅπη νόος ἐστὶν ἑκάστου.
εἰ γὰρ Ἀχιλλεὺς οἷος ἐπὶ Τρώεσσι μαχεῖται,
οὐδὲ μίνυνθ' ἕξουσι ποδώκεα Πηλείωνα.
καὶ δέ τί μιν καὶ πρόσθεν ὑποτρομέεσκον ὁρῶντες·
νῦν δ', ὅτε δὴ καὶ θυμὸν ἑταίρου χώεται αἰνῶς,
30 δείδω μὴ καὶ τεῖχος ὑπὲρ μόρον ἐξαλαπάξῃ."

The commentary of Ammonius (2 *p.* POxy. ii. 221 : xi. 20–30) at *Φ* 229–32 quotes *T* 25–7, and continues immediately with *T* 30 ; but the scribe breaks off when he has written ὑπέρ and erases and brackets the beginning of this line. This is in all probability no more than an accident, as Ammonius must be expected to use the Aristarchean vulgate.

According to the T scholia τινὲς γράφουσιν ἀντὶ τοῦ " δείδω μὴ καὶ τεῖχος "·

οὐ μέντοι μοῖρ' ἐστὶν ἔτι ζωοῦ Ἀχιλῆος   cf. ε 41, 114
'Ιλίου ἐκπέρσαι εὐναιόμενον πτολίεθρον·   Β 133
πέρσει δουράτεός ⟨θ'⟩ ἵππος καὶ μῆτις 'Επειοῦ.   cf. θ 492 f.

The superiority of the shorter version (cf. Ludwich, *HV* 26 ; Wecklein, *ZAV* 72) needs no discussion. Spitzner objected to the particles in the first line, and I find the genitive absolute ἔτι ζωοῦ Ἀχιλῆος strange without copula. It is modelled on ἔτι ζώοντος ἐμεῖο, Σ 10, which is itself interpolated.

Duentzer (*Zenod.* 161) did an injustice when he ascribed these lines to Zenodotus of Ephesus. The immediate source will be the Pergamene text from which the T scholia get their plus verses. Note the style of the comment in which they are defended : πῶς γὰρ ὁ εἰδὼς " μοῖράν τ' ἀμμορίην τε " νῦν διστάζει ; other examples of which are collected at Π 141–4. Ultimately they may go back to a cyclic epos through a Ptolemaic papyrus.

The *Etym. Mag.* 266. 40 quotes a hexameter :

δὴ τότε δηριόωντο Ποσειδάων καὶ Ἀπόλλων

which Barnes inserted after line 66 of this book. As Heyne (viii. 24) saw, it is impossible in this place.

Achilles feared the spear of Aeneas :

νήπιος· οὐδ' ἐνόησε κατὰ φρένα καὶ κατὰ θυμόν,
265   ὡς οὐ ῥηΐδι' ἐστὶ θεῶν ἐρικυδέα δῶρα
     ἀνδράσι γε θνητοῖσι δαμήμεναι οὐδ' ὑποείκειν.
     οὐδὲ τότ' Αἰνείαο δαΐφρονος ὄβριμον ἔγχος
268   ῥῆξε σάκος· χρυσὸς γὰρ ἐρύκακε, δῶρα θεοῖο.
273   δεύτερος αὖτ' Ἀχιλεὺς προΐει δολιχόσκιον ἔγχος,
     καὶ βάλεν Αἰνείαο κατ' ἀσπίδα κτλ.

---

269   ἀλλὰ δύω μὲν ἔλασσε διὰ πτύχας, αἱ δ' ἄρ' ἔτι τρεῖς
     ἦσαν, ἐπεὶ πέντε πτύχας ἤλασε κυλλοποδίων,
     τὰς δύο χαλκείας, δύο δ' ἔνδοθι κασσιτέροιο,
272   τὴν δὲ μίαν χρυσῆν· τῇ ῥ' ἔσχετο μείλινον ἔγχος.
om. van Leeuwen, damnat Christ.

The text is that of certain unnamed authorities ; the plus verses were read but athetized by Aristarchus and certain unnamed predecessors.

Aristonicus (ς A) furnishes part of the evidence ἀθετοῦνται στίχοι δ', which is supported by cross-references at Υ 266 (ς AT), Φ 165 (ς A), 594 (ς AT wrongly referred to Υ 365–8 by the editors). He also alleges that διεσκευασμένοι εἰσὶν ὑπό τινος τῶν βουλομένων πρόβλημα ποιεῖν—a not very probable bit of rationalizing. Didymus (ς TV) completes our information : οὗτοι καὶ προηθετοῦντο παρ' ἐνίοις τῶν σοφιστῶν, ἐν ἐνίοις δὲ οὐδὲ (om. T) ἐφέροντο. For σοφιστῶν I have nothing to suggest : Wecklein (ZAV 57) proposes to read πολιτικῶν, but that can hardly be right. We hear of no atheteses in the city editions, and should expect none.

The merit of the shorter version is evident ; cf. Leaf and Finsler (Homer², ii. 210). The interpolation makes the impression of a fairly early date on account of the freedom of its composition. That Aristotle may have known it is not impossible, though his quotation (Poet. xxv. 1461ᵃ 33) of τῇ ῥ' ἔσχετο χάλκεον ἔγχος could be otherwise explained. Robert's idea (Stud. 14) that this is the source of Σ 481 is to be rejected.

Φ

Achilles exulting over Asteropaeus :

ἀλλ' οὐκ ἔστι Διὶ Κρονίωνι μάχεσθαι,

194 τῷ οὐδὲ κρείων Ἀχελώϊος ἰσοφαρίζει,
196 ἐξ οὗ περ πάντες ποταμοὶ καὶ πᾶσα θάλασσα
καὶ πᾶσαι κρῆναι καὶ φρείατα μακρὰ νάουσιν·
ἀλλὰ καὶ ὃς δείδοικε Διὸς μεγάλοιο κεραυνὸν
δεινήν τε βροντήν, ὅτ' ἀπ' οὐρανόθεν σμαραγήσῃ."

194 τῷ οὔτε κρείων Ἀχελώϊος ἰσοφαρίζει
195 οὔτε βαθυρρείταο μέγα σθένος Ὠκεανοῖο,

The text is that of some unnamed poet, of Megaclides, and of Zenodotus ; the plus verse was read by Aristarchus and by Crates.

Part of the evidence is given by Aristonicus (ς A) : ὅτι Ζηνόδοτος αὐτὸν οὐκ ἔγραφε, and (ς G) Ἀριστόνικος ὅτι [δὲ] Ζηνόδοτος οὐ γράφει τὸν στίχον, and also (ς G) in a corrupt form (cf. above, p. 50) ὅτι Ζηνόδοτος τοῦτον ἠθέτηκεν ἄρας. The T scholia say more indefinitely τινὲς δὲ οὐ γράφουσι τὸν στίχον. The evidence for Megaclides is to be found in ς G and the Ammonius commentary, the latter of which supplies also the poetical quotation. The

ILIAD Φ 189

passages are cited above, p. 53, where I have discussed Schwartz' suggestion (*Advers.* 5) that the starting-point is an excision of the line by Megaclides. Crates is quoted in s G, and speaks of ἔνιοι ἐξαιροῦντες τὸν περὶ τοῦ Ὠκεανοῦ στίχον. The accusation is entitled to no more weight than is given to the similar ἐξεῖλεν accusations about I 458–61, Σ 604/5, against Aristarchus. It merely shows Crates' acquaintance with texts that did not contain the line, and the theory on which he accounted for their existence.

Our vulgate contains, of course, the Aristarchean line, but two traces of the earlier text still show through it. (1) The bulk of the MSS. read οὐδὲ ... οὐδὲ ..., not οὔτε ... οὔτε ... as did Aristarchus. (2) In line 198 the singular is found, not the plural ἀλλὰ καὶ οἱ δεδίασι, which would be the natural continuation of the Aristarchean text.

We have every reason (cf. Wecklein, *ZAV* 48) to accept this evidence. Oceanus as Father of Waters is of course commonplace in Homer, but the scholia show that the Achelous can also be regarded in the same light. This is the only mention of the Achelous in Homer, and the purpose of the interpolation is to reduce this oddity to a minimum.[1]

Leaf calls this verse ' one of the most majestic lines ever written '. So it is in sound, but it has been patched together from Hes. *Th.* 265 and Σ 607 in very humble fashion. It is dangerous to trust too much to our aesthetic impressions.

Poseidon and Athena come to Achilles:

χειρὶ δὲ χεῖρα λαβόντες ἐπιστώσαντ' ἐπέεσσι.
τοῖσι δὲ μύθων ἦρχε Ποσειδάων ἐνοσίχθων·
" Πηλείδη, μήτ' ἄρ τι λίην τρέε μήτε τι τάρβει·
289 τοίω γάρ τοι νῶι θεῶν ἐπιταρρόθω εἰμέν.

290 Ζηνὸς ἐπαινήσαντος, ἐγὼ καὶ Παλλὰς Ἀθήνη·
ὡς οὔ τοι ποταμῷ γε δαμήμεναι αἴσιμόν ἐστιν·
292 ἀλλ' ὅδε μὲν τάχα λωφήσει, σὺ δὲ εἴσεαι αὐτός.

[1] The reason for the existence of the oddity was discovered by Mülder (233 f. ; cf. Cauer, *GGA* 179 (1917). 242), in the imitation of a Herakles epos. As Finsler (*Homer²*, ii. 218) says, the reminiscence is obliterated at the end of Achilles' speech, but it is an interpolator who destroys it.

293   αὐτάρ τοι πυκινῶς ὑποθησόμεθ', αἴ κε πίθηαι·
       μὴ πρὶν παύειν χεῖρας ὁμοιίου πολέμοιο,
295   πρὶν κατὰ 'Ιλιόφι κλυτὰ τείχεα λαὸν ἐέλσαι
       Τρωικόν, ὅς κε φύγῃσι· σὺ δ' "Εκτορι θυμὸν ἀπούρας
       ἂψ ἐπὶ νῆας ἴμεν· δίδομεν δέ τοι εὖχος ἀρέσθαι."
       τὼ μὲν ἄρ' ὣς εἰπόντε μετ' ἀθανάτους ἀπεβήτην·
       αὐτὰρ ὁ βῆ, κτλ.

The text is that of the Kretike. The plus verses were read by
Aristarchus and Seleucus; the former athetizing the first line, the
latter all three.

Aristonicus (ˢ A) says of line 290 ἀθετεῖται, but fuller information
comes from the Ammonius commentary. In it, after Seleucus is
quoted as opposing ἐν τῷ γ' κατὰ τῶν Ἀριστάρχου σημείων the
athetesis of line 290, we are told ἐν δὲ τῷ ε' τῶν διορθωτικῶν ὁ αὐτὸς
ἀθετεῖ σὺν τοῖς ἑξῆς β' ὡς περισσούς· οὐκ εἶναι δὲ οὐδ' ἐν τῇ Κρητικῇ.

There is, at least, no difficulty in following the shorter and
better-attested version. Wecklein (ZAV 59 n.) has pointed out the
emptiness of σὺ δὲ εἴσεαι αὐτός (cf. β 40) and the unusual meaning
here given to λωφᾶν. I think that the origin of the interpolation is
clear. The poet told the story in the language of common-sense
(λαβόντες ἐπιστώσαντο—ὡς εἰπόντε ἀπεβήτην) with psychologic
directness that does not allow any dull logic to cool the quick cast
of his thought. Some prosaic individual objected to what he understood as two deities chanting in unison, and being fond of such
formulae interpolated line 287 :

       τοῖσι δὲ μύθων ἦρχε Ποσειδάων ἐνοσίχθων,

and then, having thus made Poseidon the spokesman, put confirma-
tory evidence into his speech.

The shorter version is again superior and line 287 must be
' excluded '.

In 3 a. PGerhard the first column closes with Φ 312 ; the next
column that is preserved begins with Φ 370 ; the editor, making the
lowest possible calculation, assumes that two columns with five plus
verses have been lost.

In col. iv (370–99) occurs :

       ὣς ἔφαθ'· "Ηφαιστος δὲ κατέσβεσε θεσπιδαὲς πῦρ,

382 ἄψορρον δ' ἄρα κῦμα κατέσχετο καλὰ ῥέεθρα
*   κὰρ ῥόον, ᾗ τὸ πάροιθεν ἵει καλλίρροον ὕδωρ. ᴕ M 33
The plus verse is obviously worthless.

In col. v (400–30) is found:

       ὣς εἰπὼν οὔτησε κατ' ἀσπίδα θυσανόεσσαν,
401 σμερδαλέην, ἣν οὐδὲ Διὸς δάμνησι κεραυνός.
403 ἡ δ' ἀναχασσαμένη λίθον εἵλετο χειρὶ παχείῃ.

<hr/>

402 τῇ μιν Ἄρης οὔτησε μιαιφόνος ἔγχεϊ μακρῷ.

The short version is, as Gerhard sees, perfectly satisfactory.
I think that it is entitled to all the more weight because it is found
this time in a text that tends to accept interpolations very freely.
Surely it was not removed intentionally, and there is nothing to
suggest that its omission was accidental. We must remember also
that the papyrus was worked upon by a corrector.

The same arguments apply also to:

       ἡ δ' ἀναχασσαμένη λίθον εἵλετο χειρὶ παχείῃ   ᴕ H 264
404 κείμενον ἐν πεδίῳ μέλανα, τρηχύν τε μέγαν τε·   = H 265
406 τῷ βάλε θοῦρον Ἄρηα κατ' αὐχένα, λῦσε δὲ γυῖα. ᴕ H 266

<hr/>

405 τόν ῥ' ἄνδρες πρότεροι θέσαν ἔμμεναι οὖρον ἀρούρης.

If there is a lacuna in the text of the papyrus, then in H too
there must be a lacuna ; if there is no lacuna, we have every reason
to regard the text of the vulgate as interpolated.

Considerations of space demand that two plus verses occur in
415–20 ; the editor suggests very probably that they were adapta-
tions of O 241–2 to follow Φ 417.

The next fragment (607–11) comes from the middle of a column,
and not until X 38 do we find a column end. The editor assumes
that five columns (vi–x) are missing, and that in them the papyrus
was shorter than the vulgate by two verses. The calculation does
not seem to me probable : for then cols. ii–x (= 279 lines) + 18 (19)
lines of col. xi = 297 (298) = Φ 313–611, or practically the same
length. Assuming another column the proportion is 328 : 299, and
though the increase is unequally distributed (cols. ii–v = 124 : 118,
and cols. vi–xi + 18 lines = 204 : 181), I think the result is more in
keeping with the calculations from other papyri ; cf. above, p. 45.

X

The preceding calculations have been made on the supposition
(cf. Gerhard, 66) that

10ᵃ 'Ιλίου ἐξαλαπάξαι εὐκτίμενον πτολίεθρον

is the only probable interpolation within X 1–26. If there were
more plus verses at this point the number in Φ 431–606 would be
diminished accordingly.

The line has been treated in Part I, since it occurs in the Syrian
palimpsest.

Achilles speaking to Apollo :

15   "ἔβλαψάς μ', ἑκάεργε, θεῶν ὀλοώτατε πάντων,
ἐνθάδε νῦν τρέψας ἀπὸ τείχεος· ἦ κ' ἔτι πολλοὶ
γαῖαν ὀδὰξ εἷλον, πρὶν "Ιλιον εἰσαφικέσθαι.
νῦν δ' ἐμὲ μὲν μέγα κῦδος ἀφείλεο, τοὺς δὲ σάωσας
ρηιδίως, ἐπεὶ οὔ τι τίσιν γ' ἔδδεισας ὀπίσσω.
20   ἦ σ' ἂν τεισαίμην, εἴ μοι δύναμίς γε παρείη."

Plato (*Rep.* iii. 391 a) quotes the first and last lines as if in succession. The curtness is effective, but it is also clear that this is as
much of the speech as Plato needed for his purposes. It is
impossible, therefore, to feel certain that the lines were not in his
text, though Murray (*RGE*² 311 n.) takes the omission seriously.

The corresponding portion of PGerhard is lost.

If column xvi begins with X 125 and 'line 104 is opposite line
137', then line 95 must be the head of column xv and the two
preceding columns contain six verses more than the corresponding
portion (39–94) of the vulgate. As Gerhard has shown, lines 52–5
being opposite lines 81–4, three excess lines must stand between
lines 38–77 and two between lines 55–81. But beyond that the
possibilities are too complicated. Gerhard considers an expansion
unlikely in the transition (78–80) from Priam to Hecuba's speech ;
but the repetition of line 92 as 78ᵃ would not have surprised me,
nor would an expansion (cf. Π 734, Σ 477) to describe the action of
Hecuba's other hand.

I may suggest that the writer of the papyrus first dropped lines
72–3 (haplography κείσονται, κεῖσθαι) and then wrote them after
line 76. The reading of the English editors, χαλκω]ι, φ[α]νειη,
χ]ερσιν, is confirmed on re-examination.

In column xv (95–124) there is then room for but one plus verse, if we assume that the papyrus contained the line which later was interpolated as X 121 in the vulgate. The plus verse stands after line 99, and is filled out by van Leeuwen:

λωβητός κεν ἰο[ιμι κακὸς ὥς· αὐτὰρ ἔπειτα.

The next point to be noted after the column-head X 125 is the close of a column with line 393—an interval of 269 vulgate lines. Gerhard (27) prefers to restore nine columns of 279 lines rather than ten columns with 310 lines. If this were all it might be conceded, although the latter proportion is not so high as that of the Θ papyrus, where 300 lines correspond to 251 lines of the vulgate. But fortunately there is a column beginning with line 259ᵇ that bisects this section. Gerhard is therefore forced to assume that four columns, 124 verses, corresponded to X 125–259, or 135 vulgate lines. Minus verses in anything like this quantity are not found in the Ptolemaic papyri, and I feel no hesitation in believing that there were five columns of 155 lines, or, on account of the attested omission of X 133–5, twenty-three plus verses.

The papyrus read:

126 οὐ μέν πως νῦν ἔστιν ἀπὸ δρυὸς οὐδ' ἀπὸ πέτρης
  * ὥς ἄμοτον πολέ]μοιο μεμαότα δακρυόεντος
127 τῷ ὀαριζέμεναι, ἅ τε παρθένον ἠίθεόν τε.
128 [παρθένος ἠίθεός τ' ὀαρίζετον ἀλλήλοιιν.]

The restoration of the plus verse is Gerhard's, and he recognizes that the line cannot be read here, though it might in his opinion be substituted for line 128. I do not like the restoration, because ὥς has no reference in the immediate context; contrast O 83, ν 389, the parallels adduced. The motive assumed contradicts also the usual chauvinism of the interpolators. I should prefer:

οὐκ ἄμοτον πολέμοιο μεμαότα δακρυόεντος

a metrical gloss on the preceding phrase.

In 127 the papyrus is corrected to παρθένος ἠίθεός τε, the vulgate reading. The reading of the first hand deserves the preference, and then line 128 must go. It too is a gloss. Gerhard approaches the correct solution in his note, but fails to reach it because like others he believed in a 'Neigung zu streichen'.

After Hector's soliloquy :

ὡς ὥρμαινε μένων· ὁ δέ οἱ σχεδὸν ἦλθεν Ἀχιλλεὺς
132 ἶσος Ἐνυαλίῳ, κορυθάϊκι πτολεμιστῇ.
136 Ἕκτορα δ', ὡς ἐνόησεν, ἕλε τρόμος· οὐδ' ἄρ' ἔτ' ἔτλη
αὖθι μένειν, ὀπίσω δὲ πύλας λίπε, βῆ δὲ φοβηθείς.

133 σείων Πηλιάδα μελίην κατὰ δεξιὸν ὦμον
δεινήν· ἀμφὶ δὲ χαλκὸς ἐλάμπετο εἴκελος αὐγῇ
135 ἢ πυρὸς αἰθομένου ἢ ἠελίου ἀνιόντος.

The text is that of the PGerhard, and should not be regarded as accidental, since after X 316 these lines (σεῖε δέ) are found in the papyrus. I think that we are compelled by the external evidence to regard them as *freifliegende Einschubverse,* that is, to insert them in neither place.

The papyrus version is entirely satisfactory, and very little can be said in criticism of the vulgate. Merely that elsewhere πυρὸς αἰθομένοιο or πυρὸς μένος αἰθομένοιο stands at the close of the line, except λ 220 πυρὸς κρατερὸν μένος αἰθομένοιο, and the still freer Ξ 396 οὔτε πυρὸς τόσσος γε πέλει βρόμος αἰθομένοιο. However, one may compare ἄστεος αἰθομένοιο (Φ 523) at the opening of a line.

But the cyclic poets had occasion to describe Achilles at many crises—battles with Cycnus, Penthesilea, Memnon, and that in which he met his death. The interpolators must have drawn on a famous passage of some such sort. It is probably not a mere coincidence that the Πηλιάδα μελίην figures in another interpolation : Π 141-4 = Τ 388-91.

After the description of the springs :

τῇ ῥα παραδραμέτην, φεύγων, ὁ δ' ὄπισθε διώκων·
158 πρόσθε μὲν ἐσθλὸς ἔφευγε, δίωκε δέ μιν μέγ' ἀμείνων
καρπαλίμως, ἐπεὶ οὐχ ἱερήϊον οὐδὲ βοείην
ἀρνύσθην, ἅ τε ποσσὶν ἀέθλια γίνεται ἀνδρῶν,
ἀλλὰ περὶ ψυχῆς θέον Ἕκτορος ἱπποδάμοιο.

158ᵃ φεῦγ' υἱὸς Πριάμοιο, δίωκε δὲ δῖος Ἀχιλλεύς.

The plus verse is attested by Didymus (5 A) ἐν ἐνίοις δὲ φέρεται στίχος ὑπὸ τοῦτον (158) εὐτελής· " φεῦγ' υἱὸς ... Ἀχιλλεύς ".
Of the addition of the line there can be no question (cf. Ludwich,

HV 25); but its presence raises another issue. It may well be meant as an alternative for line 158; and then as Didymus (s A) at *T* 327 well puts it: τεκμήριον δὲ τῆς διασκευῆς τὸ καὶ ἑτέρως φέρεσθαι τὸν στίχον.

Line 158 is omitted by Bekker[2], its genuineness is questioned by Nauck, and Erhardt (440) would gladly be rid of it; while Wilamowitz (*Ilias*, 99) feels it as highly pathetic. In this book I can only regret that PGerhard fails to give us further evidence for or against it.

PGerhard must have read in Hector's speech:

> οὐ γὰρ ἐγώ σ' ἔκπαγλον ἀεικιῶ, αἴ κεν ἐμοὶ Ζεὺς
> ⟨δώῃ καμμονίην, σὴν δὲ ψυχὴν ἀφέλωμαι·
> ἀλλ' ἐπεὶ ἄρ κέ σε συλήσω κλυτὰ τεύχε', Ἀχιλλεῦ,
> 259 νεκρὸν Ἀχαιοῖσιν δώσω πάλιν· ὡς δὲ σὺ ῥέζειν·
> * σῶμα δὲ οἴκαδ' ἐμὸν δόμεναι πάλιν, ὄφρα πυρός με⟩
>
>   = 342 = *H* 79
> * Τρῶες καὶ Τρώων ἄλοχοι λελάχωσι θανόντα."
>   = 343 = *H* 80
> 260 τὸν δ' ἄρ' ὑπόδρα ἰδὼν προσέφη κτλ.   = 344

The plus verses are simply an expansion of ὡς δὲ σὺ ῥέζειν that brings into concordance the close of the two similar speeches.

The verses in brackets are lost at the close of a column, but there can be no question of the correctness of Gerhard's restoration.

After line 262 follows a plus verse, Gerhard being clearly right in rejecting more radical explanations. Its ending is restored by van Leeuwen as ἐξ]οχο[ς ἄλλ]ος, but even that leads nowhere.[1] One, and only one, plus verse occurred between this point and line 291, which is opposite to line 262.

Between *X* 291 and *X* 316 must have stood not less than three nor more than ten plus verses. Gerhard suggests *T* 164–73 after *X* 311, or *T* 374–9 with slight modifications after *X* 313. In the latter case he would look to *T* 369–72 to furnish four plus verses after *X* 312, greater modifications being required. This last seems to me extremely doubtful, and I should rather carry the balance of four plus verses over to the space between *X* 343–92.

---

[1] The supplement is rather long for the space. It may be noted also that οχο stands under τα, the line being very long.

Between X 316 and 340 were exactly seven plus verses. Three after X 316 are extant and correspond to X 133–5 previously omitted. It is a brilliant suggestion of Gerhard's that the remaining four stood after X 320 and were the *freifliegende Einschubverse* which we have met as Π 141–4 = T 388–91. If all four of them were repeated here there was no room for the plus verse 330ᵃ (= O 48), on which cf. Part I ; Ludwich, HV 29 ; Wecklein, ZAV 14. The papyrus attests line 316 (for which cf. Wecklein, ZAV 32), a verse that was apparently (cf. Part I) originally foreign to the vulgate ; while for another verse of this class, X 363, its testimony is lacking.

For the beginning of Achilles' speech Zenodotus read, on the testimony of Aristonicus (s A) :

378   "Ἀτρείδη τε καὶ ἄλλοι ἀριστῆες Παναχαιῶν.

The vulgate wavers between :

"ὦ φίλοι, Ἀργείων ἡγήτορες ἠδὲ μέδοντες

and :

"ὦ φίλοι, ἥρωες Δαναοί, θεράποντες Ἄρηος.

The line seems to me suspect διὰ τὸ καὶ ἑτέρως φέρεσθαι, and because of the traces (cf. p. 9 n.) of the interpolation of such vocative lines as an easy sort of exegesis. The omission of any address would be in keeping with the tone of X, which ignores all Achaeans except Achilles. If the line be read we must, as Wilamowitz (*Ilias*, 104 n.) has seen, keep the Zenodotean form ; it is the form earliest attested, and the motive for the substitution of the others is obvious.

The papyrus had a plus verse after :

⟨νῦν δ' ἄγ' ἀείδοντες παιήονα, κοῦροι Ἀχαιῶν,
392   νηυσὶν ἐπὶ γλαφυρῇσι νεώμεθα, τόνδε δ' ἄγωμεν⟩
*   καὶ τεθνηότα περ· τόσα γὰρ κάκ' ἐμήσατ' Ἀχαιούς.

The line, as Gerhard notes, is compounded of Ω 20 + K 52, and the second half will recur in Ψ 183ᵃ.

For the remainder of the book columns xxv–xxvi (394–448), with an excess of seven lines, are definitely fixed. The next definitely determined datum is that Ψ 141 stood at the foot of a

column. The interval of 208 lines requires at least seven columns (nine plus verses), and that is Gerhard's calculation. I would not be so positive that eight columns (forty plus verses) are impossible. The increase would correspond well to the ratio (251 : 300) of the Θ papyrus; and besides, Gerhard has made a number of attractive suggestions : X 459ᵃ = λ 516, X 461ᵃ⁻ᵈ = Z 400–3, Ψ 18ᵃ⁻ᶠ = Σ 318–23 ; for all of which there is not room in the smaller number of columns. The matter is, however, too uncertain to warrant further discussion.

Ψ

Aeschines (i. 149) quotes :

οὐ γὰρ ἔτι ζωοί γε φίλων ἀπάνευθεν ἑταίρων
βουλὰς ἑζόμενοι βουλεύσομεν· ἀλλ' ἐμὲ μὲν κὴρ
ἀμφέχανε στυγερή, ἥπερ λάχε γεινόμενόν περ.
80 καὶ δὲ σοὶ αὐτῷ μοῖρα, θεοῖς ἐπιείκελ' Ἀχιλλεῦ,
τείχει ὕπο Τρώων εὐηγενέων ἀπολέσθαι
* μαρνάμενον δηΐοις Ἑλένης ἕνεκ' ἠυκόμοιο.
ἄλλο δέ τοι ἐρέω, σὺ δ' ἐνὶ φρεσὶ βάλλεο σῇσιν·
83 μὴ ἐμὰ σῶν ἀπάνευθε τιθήμεναι ὀστέ', Ἀχιλλεῦ,
* ἀλλ' ἵνα πέρ σε καὶ αὐτὸν ὁμοίη γαῖα κεκεύθῃ,
* χρυσέῳ ἐν ἀμφιφορεῖ, τόν τοι πόρε πότνια μήτηρ.

The worthlessness of these plus verses needs no discussion. PGerhard is unfortunately mutilated at this point, but there is every reason to believe that it too contained these verses. It and the text quoted by Aeschines are closely connected, as we shall now see.

Aeschines quotes also :

ἀλλ' ὁμοῦ, ὡς ἐτράφημεν ἐν ὑμετέροισι δόμοισιν,
85 εὖτέ με τυτθὸν ἐόντα Μενοίτιος ἐξ Ὀπόεντος
ἤγαγεν ὑμέτερον δ' ἀνδροκτασίης ὕπο λυγρῆς,
ἤματι τῷ, ὅτε παῖδα κατέκτανον Ἀμφιδάμαντος,
νήπιος, οὐκ ἐθέλων, ἀμφ' ἀστραγάλοισι χολωθείς·
ἔνθα με δεξάμενος ἐν δώμασιν ἱππότα Πηλεὺς
90 ἔτραφέ τ' ἐνδυκέως καὶ σὸν θεράποντ' ὀνόμηνεν·
ὡς δὲ καὶ ὀστέα νῶϊν ὁμὴ σορὸς ἀμφικαλύπτοι."

92 χρύσεος ἀμφιφορεύς, τόν τοι πόρε πότνια μήτηρ cf. ω 74
om. Bekker, Nauck, van Leeuwen ; damn. Christ, Ludwich. In 84 ὡς ὁμοῦ ἐτράφεμέν περ Aesch.

The text is that of Aeschines, certain unnamed editors, and PGerhard ; the plus verse was read but athetized by Aristarchus.

The evidence comes partly from Aristonicus (s A) ἀθετεῖται, and partly from Didymus (s TV) ἐν πάσαις δὲ οὐκ ἦν ὁ στίχος. The latter remark is misinterpreted by Gerhard (87) 'in allen Ausgaben gefehlt habe' ; that would have been as at δ 511 ἐν οὐδεμιᾷ ἐφέρετο, while this is not even as strong as οὐκ ἐφέροντο δὲ σχεδὸν ἐν πάσαις οἱ πέντε at δ 285-9.

That gives an unfortunate bias to his discussion of the passage. I look upon the two interpolations as independent. All knew the *Odyssey* passage; and some one interpolated one way, and some one the other.

According to Gerhard's final reconstruction (p. 89) column xxxii began with lines 83^{ab} and continued to line 112. The two additional plus verses that are needed can be located definitely, and have been supplied by Gerhard :

93   τὸν δ᾽ ἀπαμειβόμενος προσέφη πόδας ὠκὺς Ἀχιλλεύς,
*   ἡδὺ μάλα κνώσσων ἐ]ν ὀνειρείῃσι πύλῃσιν· ᴧ δ 809
94   "τίπτε μοι, ἠθείη κεφαλή, δεῦρ᾽ εἰλήλουθας
*   [αἰδοῖός τε φίλος τε; πάρος γε μὲν οὔ τι θαμίζεις.]= ε 88
95   καί μοι ταῦτα ἕκαστ᾽ ἐπιτέλλεαι; κτλ.

For the latter he suggests also a less probable alternative, ἐλθὼν ἐξ Ἀίδαο πυλάρταο κρατεροῖο, modelled on μ 17 and λ 277. The lines are evident interpolations, and no one is likely to demand their insertion.

In the following column, lines 113-41, van Leeuwen has restored :

128   αὐτὰρ Ἀχαιοῖς
129   κέκλετο [Πηλέος υἱὸς ἐπότρυνέν] τε μετελθών·

But the following lines 130-2 varied greatly from the vulgate, and it is impossible to see more than that there was one (130^{a}) plus verse.

Another plus verse is found :

136   ὄπιθεν δὲ κάρη ἔχε δῖος Ἀχιλλεὺς
*   ἀμφοτέρῃσι δὲ χερσὶ κόμην ἤσχυν]ε δαΐζων,
137   ἀχνύμενος· ἕταρον γὰρ ἀμύμονα πέμπ᾽ Ἄιδος δέ.

The verse is fabricated from Σ 23 and 27, and part is used as Θ 199^{a} in another Ptolemaic interpolation.

Between Ψ 142-52 the text was one line shorter than the vulgate; there are slight temptations to haplography, and I suspect that this, like Ψ 89, was an accidental omission. Gerhard suggests the omission of either line 148 or 149, but the material is too slight for further discussion.

Nor does it seem possible to say anything of the following fragmentary lines more definite than that there were after lines 157 and 158 plus verses. Gerhard, following Blass, restores

160   π[αρὰ δ' οἱ ταγοὶ ἄμμι μενόντων
*   ὅσσοι κηδ]εμόνες· σκέδ[ασον δ' ἀπὸ λαὸν ἅπαντα.

It is impossible to judge of this line while we are in ignorance of the text that preceded it; but it would be contrary to all our experience if the longer text of the papyrus were better than the vulgate.

The next plus verse:

162   αὐτίκα λαὸν μὲν σκέδασεν κατὰ νῆας ἐΐσας·
*   κάπνισσάν τε κατὰ κλισίας καὶ δεῖπνον ἕλοντο = B 399

is obviously interpolated.

In line 165 . . . .] παρααυτ.νεκρο[ν may describe the reading of the papyrus. To read πυρα is impossible, for the tail of the γ should appear. Further on υτη would suit the space and the slight marks of ink. I believe the scribe has blundered, and should have written:

165   ἐν δὲ πυρῇ ὑπάτῃ νεκρὸν θέσαν· αὐτὰρ ἔπειτα
*   μυρί' ὀνείατα χερσὶν ἀμησάμενοι κατέθηκαν

The new line adds a detail to be expected in the ritual; but only at the cost of introducing a harsh asyndeton. The lines may be from the funeral of Achilles himself in the *Little Iliad*.

Between lines 171-8 (perhaps between 171-4 may be said) were two plus verses; Gerhard suggests 171ᵃ ∽ K 306, 173ᵃ ∽ X 69, both very probable interpolations.

Interpolated also is the line after:

183   ἀλλὰ κύνεσσι
*   ὠμησ]ταῖς φαγέειν· τόσα γὰρ κάκ' ἐμήσατ' Ἀχαιούς.
Cf. X 392ᵃ for the close of the line.

To fill out the column Gerhard suggests Ψ 191^{ab} ∽ T 38–9, and there can be little doubt of the correctness of this suggestion.

The papyrus points to a text:

$$\text{ἔνθ' αὖτ' ἄλλ' ἐνόησε ποδάρκης δῖος Ἀχιλλεύς·}$$
$$\text{στὰς ἀπάνευθε πυρῆς δοιοῖς ἠρᾶτ' ἀνέμοισι,}$$
195 $\text{Βορέῃ καὶ Ζεφύρῳ, καὶ ὑπέσχετο ἱερὰ καλά,}$
* $\text{ἀρνῶν πρωτογόνων ῥέξειν κλειτὴν ἑκατόμβην.} = Δ$ 102
196 $\text{πολλὰ δ' ἀποσπένδων ἠρήσατο δῖος Ἀχιλλεὺς}$
ἐλθέμεν κτλ.

196 πολλὰ δὲ καὶ σπένδων χρυσέῳ δέπαϊ λιτάνευεν.

There can be no question of adding this plus verse, which is also repeated as Ψ 209^a; but Wecklein (*ZAV* 79 f.) uses it to support Duentzer's rejection of line 196, against which its double version might prove a stronger argument. The matter, however, is more doubtful than that which I wish to include in this book.

In the comparison:

$$\text{ὡς δὲ πατὴρ οὗ παιδὸς ὀδύρεται ὀστέα καίων}$$
223 $\text{νυμφίου, ὅς τε θανὼν δειλοὺς ἀκάχησε τοκῆας,}$
$\text{ὡς Ἀχιλεὺς ἑτάροιο ὀδύρετο ὀστέα καίων.}$

222 ὡς δ' ὃν παῖδα πατὴρ ὀλοφύρεται   v. l. PGerhard.
Post vm. 223 addunt:
χήρωσεν δ[ὲ γυναῖκα μυχῷ θαλάμοιο νέοιο ∽ P 36
ἀρη[τὸ]ν δὲ τ[οκεῦσι γόον καὶ πένθος ἔθηκεν ∽ P 37
PGerhard;
ἄρρητον δὲ τοκεῦσι γόον καὶ πένθος ἔθηκε ∽ P 37
μοῦνος τηλύγετος πολλοῖσιν ἐπὶ κτεάτεσσιν ∽ Ι 482
Plut. *Consol. ad Apoll.* 30. 117^c.

There can be no question of following either of these expanded versions. But as Gerhard has seen (cf. also Cauer, *Grundfr.*³ 43 f.), they are an important proof that 'wir mehrere der allgemeinen Tendenz nach verwandte, aber in der Einzelausführung verschiedene "erweiterte" Texte annehmen müssen'. Amoneit's view (p. 47) that Plutarch's citation is a slip of memory requires no discussion.

The second plus verse is not usually (but cf. van Leeuwen) treated as having been read at this point by Plutarch.

Of Achilles' horses PGerhard said:

277   ἀθάνατοί τε γάρ εἰσι, Ποσειδάων δὲ πόρ' αὐτοὺς
278   πατρὶ ἐμῷ Πηλῆι, ὁ δ' αὖτ' ἐμοὶ ἐγγυάλιξεν.
*   ὡς τώ γ' ἀθάνατοι κ[αὶ ἀγήραοι, οὐδὲ ἔοικε
*   θνητοὺς ἀθανάτοισι [δέμας καὶ εἶδος ἐρίζειν. ᴖ ε 213

The plus verses are again obviously worthless.

Nestor speaking to Antilochus:

σῆμα δέ τοι ἐρέω μάλ' ἀριφραδές, οὐδέ σε λήσει.
ἕστηκε ξύλον αὖον, ὅσον τ' ὄργυι', ὑπὲρ αἴης,
ἢ δρυὸς ἢ πεύκης· τὸ μὲν οὐ καταπύθεται ὄμβρῳ·
λᾶε δὲ τοῦ ἑκάτερθεν ἐρηρέδαται δύο λευκὼ
330   ἐν ξυνοχῇσιν ὁδοῦ, λεῖος δ' ἱππόδρομος ἀμφίς·
331   ἤ τευ σῆμα βροτοῖο πάλαι κατατεθνηῶτος,
*   ἠὲ σκῖρος ἔην· νῦν ἄνθετο τέρματ' Ἀχιλλεύς.
334   τῷ σὺ μάλ' ἐγχρίμψας ἐλάαν σχεδὸν ἅρμα καὶ ἵππους,
335   αὐτὸς δὲ κλινθῆναι κτλ.

---

332   ἢ τό γε νύσσα τέτυκτο ἐπὶ προτέρων ἀνθρώπων·
333   καὶ νῦν τέρματ' ἔθηκε ποδάρκης δῖος Ἀχιλλεύς.

The text is that of some scholar (Aristophanes?) whose name has been supplanted by that of Aristarchus.

The evidence is best given by Eustathius (Neumann, p. 328): ἐν δὲ τῷ " ἢ τό γε νύσσα τέτυκτο " καὶ ἑξῆς φασιν οἱ παλαιοὶ ὅτι Ἀρίσταρχος γράφει " ἢ τό γε σκῖρος ... Ἀχιλλεύς ". In 5 TV this is wrongly referred to line 331: Ἀρίσταρχος γράφει " ἠὲ σκῖρος ἔην· νῦν ἄνθετο τέρματ' Ἀχιλλεύς ". Ludwich, who has collected in his index other examples of the substitution of Aristarchus for less famous names, rightly refused (AHT i. 487) to believe that Aristarchus so read. Such a belief has become still more impossible with a better understanding of the relationship between our MSS. and the edition of Aristarchus.

The only difficulty with the text is the meaning of σκῖρος, for the assertion that it means 'root', 'stump', is as desperate as the etymology that supports it. Hesychius knows the word as a fragment of stone (λατύπη), and we may suspect that it was here

used in some specialized sense—'fetish', 'boundary-mark', which is what the context requires.

The vulgate looks like an attempt to evade this difficulty; note the emptiness of the close of each line—ἐπὶ προτέρων ἀνθρώπων being lifted from E 637, and ποδάρκης δῖος Ἀχιλλεύς being commonplace.

Achilles speaks:

"λοῖσθος ἀνὴρ ὤριστος ἐλαύνει μώνυχας ἵππους.
ἀλλ' ἄγε δή οἱ δῶμεν ἀέθλιον, ὡς ἐπιεικές,
538   δεύτερ'· ἀτὰρ τὰ πρῶτα φερέσθω Τυδέος υἱός."

538ᵃ   τὰ τρίτα δ' Ἀντίλοχος, τέτρατα ξανθὸς Μενέλαος,
538ᵇ   πέμπτα δὲ Μηριόνης θεράπων ἐὺς Ἰδομενῆος.

The verses are reported both in s A (Aristonicus) ὅτι ἔν τισιν ὑποτάσσονται τούτῳ "τὰ τρίτα . . . Ἰδομενῆος and in s T τινὰ δὲ τῶν ἀντιγράφων καὶ τούτους τοὺς εὐτελεῖς φέρει (φασὶ cod.) β΄ στίχους "τέτρατα . . . Ἰδομενῆος".

The verses are like the others found in the T scholia, and require no discussion; cf. Ludwich, HV 25; Wecklein, ZAV 71.

Ω

Hecuba speaking to Priam:

πῶς ἐθέλεις ἐπὶ νῆας Ἀχαιῶν ἐλθέμεν οἶος,
ἀνδρὸς ἐς ὀφθαλμούς, ὅς τοι πολέας τε καὶ ἐσθλοὺς
205   υἱέας ἐξενάριξε; σιδήρειόν νύ τοι ἦτορ.
εἰ γάρ σ' αἱρήσει καὶ ἐσόψεται ὀφθαλμοῖσιν
ὠμηστὴς καὶ ἄπιστος ἀνὴρ ὅ γε, οὔ σ' ἐλεήσει
οὐδέ τί σ' αἰδέσεται.

205ᵃ   ἀθάνατοι ποίησαν Ὀλύμπια δώματ' ἔχοντες
vel   οἱ οὐρανὸν εὐρὺν ἔχουσιν

The additional line is preserved by Aristonicus (s A): ὅτι ὑποτάσσουσι στίχον, ὡς ἐλλείποντος τοῦ λόγου, "ἀθάνατοι . . . ἔχοντες", or s TV τινὲς μετὰ τοῦτον γράφουσιν "ἀθάνατοι . . . ἔχουσιν".

There is no question (cf. Roemer, AAH 186; Cauer, Grundfr.³ 55) of the superiority of the shorter version. The motive of the

ILIAD Ω

203

interpolation is also plain and easy to parallel. Compare also Ludwich, *HV* 25; Wecklein, *ZAV* 13.

In the description of the assembling of Priam's car :

ἐκ μὲν ἄμαξαν ἄειραν εὔτροχον, ἡμιονείην,
καλήν, πρωτοπαγέα, πείρινθα δὲ δῆσαν ἐπ' αὐτῆς,
268 κὰδ δ' ἀπὸ πασσαλόφι ζυγὸν ᾑρεον ἡμιόνειον,
270 ἐκ δ' ἔφερον ζυγόδεσμον ἅμα ζυγῷ ἐννεάπηχυ.

269 πύξινον, ὀμφαλόεν, εὖ οἰήκεσσιν ἀρηρός·

The text is that of Zenodotus, on the testimony of Didymus (5 AT) : οὐκ ἦν παρὰ Ζηνοδότῳ οὗτος ὁ στίχος. The case must rest on the external evidence, for the line is neither necessary nor objectionable.

It is possible that the omission is, as Wecklein (*ZAV* 59) thinks, no more than an accident, be it in the sources of Zenodotus or in the antigrapha of his edition that reached the Aristarcheans. Still, there are several reasons that, when combined, tend to make this seem unlikely. (1) There is no temptation to haplography. (2) There is no other mention of boxwood in Homer. (3) There was a masculine variant (ὀμφαλόεντ' . . . ἀρηρότα) with elision (cf. Wackernagel, *SU* 161 ff.) at the end of the line. As the *lectio difficilior* this is presumably the original form of this verse, though it varies from the usage of our poems. So we are asked to believe that an accident of a rather infrequent type has happened to hit a line containing material and linguistic peculiarities. I find it easier to believe that the line was interpolated from a cyclic epos.

Plato, *Rep.* ii. 379 d, quotes :

κατακείαται ἐν Διὸς οὔδει
κηρῶν ἔμπλειοι, ὁ μὲν ἐσθλῶν, αὐτὰρ ὁ δειλῶν.

For the latter (Ω 528) the vulgate reads :

δώρων, οἷα δίδωσι, κακῶν, ἕτερος δὲ ἑάων.

The line is unneeded, and might διὰ τὸ καὶ ἑτέρως φέρεσθαι be regarded as an interpolation. Strongly in favour of this are the linguistic oddities in each form of the line (cf. Meister, *HK* 172) ; if so ἑάων

is first coined (θ 325) by the author of the song of Demodocus, and used afterwards only by interpolators.

As part of the *Cycle* the *Iliad* and the *Little Iliad* were (cf. Bethe, *Homer*, ii. 379) run together:

804   ὣς οἵ γ' ἀμφίεπον τάφον Ἕκτορος· ἦλθε δ' Ἀμάζων,

*   Ἄρηος θυγάτηρ μεγαλήτορος ἀνδροφόνοιο.

It is the T scholia (τινὲς γράφουσιν) that record the fact. To this the testimony of 1 *p*. PMus. Br. 1873 can now be added. It knew the second line, however, in a different form:

Ὀτρήρ[ης] θυγάτηρ, εὐειδὴς Πενθεσίλεια.

PART IV
THE INTERPOLATIONS OF THE ODYSSEY
I

IT has already been remarked that the *recensio* of the MSS. of the *Odyssey* seems to lead only to a text such as may have circulated A.D. *c.* 250 and not to the Aristarchean text itself. It seems to be next in order to see if we can detect any interpolations which, while foreign to Aristarchus and the original vulgate, may have become well established by the middle of the third century.

As the first example I may suggest the superfluous verse:

β 393   ἔνθ' αὖτ' ἄλλ' ἐνόησε θεὰ γλαυκῶπις Ἀθήνη.

It is attested by 2 *p*. POxy. 773, and is found in all our MSS. except the first hand of G and Allen's M². It should be followed by βῆ ῥ' ἴμεναι, as Ludwich reads on the authority of F alone; all other MSS. read βῆ δ' ἴμεναι, as they should do if line 393 were not present. There is nothing to suggest that the Alexandrians were acquainted with the line. Like other post-Aristarchean interpolations, its source is the *Odyssey*, where it is a common formula, β 382 being the nearest example. Blass has judged the situation well.

γ 308   Αἴγισθον δολόμητιν, ὅ οἱ πατέρα κλυτὸν ἔκτα.

The verse is a useless definition of πατροφονῆα at the close of line 307; as α 300, γ 198, it has previously followed that word, and is here thoughtlessly repeated. Of Ludwich's MSS. the first hand of G and U are free of the interpolation, and the same is said by Allen of his k family. The scholia show no acquaintance with the line, which is condemned by Kirchhoff (184), Ludwich, Blass, and Wecklein (*ZAV* 21).

After Nestor has given various directions he ends quite tamely:

γ 427   οἱ δ' ἄλλοι μένετ' αὐτοῦ ἀολλέες, εἴπατε δ' εἴσω
δμῳῆσιν κατὰ δώματ' ἀγακλυτὰ δαῖτα πένεσθαι,
ἕδρας τε ξύλα τ' ἀμφὶ καὶ ἀγλαὸν οἰσέμεν ὕδωρ.

Duentzer rejected the lines because the execution of these commands is not told in the sequel. The external evidence against the passage is Ludwich's supplement (*Homerica*, vi. 5) of a scholium in PMus. Br. 271 ὅτι Τ(ίμαρχος?) οὐκ ⟨ἔγραφεν⟩, for the omission of line 429 by the first hand of H will best be considered an accident. But the lines are not στίχοι διφορούμενοι, and there is a scholium (HQ) to attest Aristophanes' acquaintance with one of them. I should conclude therefore that Ludwich's restoration of the papyrus, though ingenious, has not hit the mark.

A more than doubtful example is found in δ 37 f.:

$$\text{ὣς φάθ᾽, ὁ δὲ μεγάροιο διέσσυτο, κέκλετο δ᾽ ἄλλους}$$
$$\text{ὀτρηροὺς θεράποντας ἅμα σπέσθαι ἑοῖ αὐτῷ.}$$

Wecklein (*ZAV* 21) objects to the second of these lines because it is not written by the first hand of U, and because σπέσθαι ἑοῖ αὐτῷ is to be found only in N 495, which he regards as late. The discussion of the latter argument would lead too far from the work in hand; but the interpolation, if interpolation it be, evidently does not belong in this class. The scholium on χ 324 that quotes it shows at least that it passed current among grammarians of a fairly early date. The line is not a στίχος διφορούμενος, and its borrowings are from the *Iliad*. The omission by U[1] will therefore best be classed as an accident.

δ 511 ὣς ὁ μὲν ἔνθ᾽ ἀπόλωλεν, ἐπεὶ πίεν ἁλμυρὸν ὕδωρ.

---

om. Bekker, van Leeuwen; damn. La Roche, Nauck, Ludwich, Merry, Blass.

A scholium on this line (confirmed also by Eustathius, 1506. 40) says: ἐν οὐδεμιᾷ ἐφέρετο. καὶ λίαν γάρ ἐστιν εὐτελής. θαυμάσαιμεν δ᾽ ἂν πῶς παρέλαθε τὸν Ἀρίσταρχον ὀβελίσαι αὐτόν (H P). According to Dindorf the two last words are added to line 515; Ludwich (*AHT* i. 546) misapplied the remark to the whole scholium, and Blass follows him. The scholium is treated as Didymean by Blass, but it seems to me that Ludwich has good reason to doubt this: the question asked is too naïve, after we have just been told that the line was not in Aristarchus' edition. Ludwich, Blass, and Wecklein (*ZAV* 19) all have the right solution.

The line is made up of ξ 137 ὡς ὁ μὲν ἔνθ' ἀπόλωλε, and λ 98 ἐπεὶ πίεν αἷμα κελαινόν, with the substitution of one stock phrase ἁλμυρὸν ὕδωρ for another. As Blass notes, the borrowing has caused a misuse of the perfect tense.

δ 569 οὕνεκ' ἔχεις Ἑλένην καί σφιν γαμβρὸς Διός ἐσσι.

damn. Nauck, Ludwich.

Of this line a scholium (HPQ) declares: ἐν ἐνίοις δὲ οὐ φέρεται ὁ στίχος. I think it probable that a scholiast is speaking of the ἀντίγραφα of his own time. I would suggest further that the interpolator meant his veres to follow line 564, and that it got into our tradition at the wrong place; to that extent Kirchhoff (190) was on the right track.

The line is rejected by Wecklein (*ZAV* 19) and defended in a half-hearted fashion by Blass.

For its source I may begin by recalling the old reading of Servius, *Comm. ad Aen.* v. 735: ' insulae fortunatae ... quarum descriptionem Pius commentator dicit esse sublatam.' To be sure *Porphyrius* is now read by Thilo and Hagen, with some MS. authority but with doubtful right; Pius is the less familiar name, *commentator* describes him as well, and it is from him that such a statement would be expected. For the allegation must be that our vulgate has been thus curtailed by Aristarchus—an allegation like the more familiar ones by Plutarch and Athenaeus already discussed. In each case there is in the background the same thing—an interpolated text such as a Ptolemaic papyrus would present. In the *Iliad* we have already found vulgate interpolations originating in such a source, and I would assume for δ 569 a similar origin. Ultimately the line may go back to the *Nostoi*, which may well have closed with a prophecy of Menelaos' happiness—another instance of the contrast between the fates of the two brothers which dominated (cf. Bethe, *Homer*, ii. 258–79) the whole poem. Compare also O. Kern, *Neue Jahrbb.* 51 (1923). 64.

The deceptive appearance of evidence for such an interpolation is to be found within ε 47–9 = Ω 343–5:

εἵλετο δὲ ῥάβδον, τῇ τ' ἀνδρῶν ὄμματα θέλγει
ὧν ἐθέλει, τοὺς δ' αὖτε καὶ ὑπνώοντας ἐγείρει·
τὴν μετὰ χερσὶν ἔχων πέτετο κρατὺς ἀργειφόντης.

The second verse is omitted by the first hand of F, and Wecklein (*ZAV* 21) very properly mentions in connexion with this fact the omission of Ω 344 in 2 *p*. PMus. Br. 114. The latter is clearly a mechanical error : the line was read by Aristarchus, it is found in 1 *a*. PMus. Br. 128, and in all MSS. The cause is haplography (θέλγει, ἐγείρει), and in the tradition of the *Odyssey* at a much later time the same cause produced the same effect.

Nausicaa is asleep, and we are told of Athena :

ζ 20   ἡ δ᾽ ἀνέμου ὡς πνοιὴ ἐπέσσυτο δέμνια κούρης,
22   εἰδομένη κούρῃ ναυσικλείτοιο Δύμαντος,
ἥ οἱ ὁμηλικίη μὲν ἔην, κεχάριστο δὲ θυμῷ.
τῇ μιν ἐεισαμένη προσέφη γλαυκῶπις Ἀθήνη·

21   στῆ δ᾽ ἄρ᾽ ὑπὲρ κεφαλῆς καί μιν πρὸς μῦθον ἔειπεν.

The line I have marked as interpolated is not to be found in G, and is a needless repetition of δ 803, ν 32, ψ 4 ; the scholia give it no attestation.

That, however, amounts to no more than the suggestion of one possibility; and only the discovery of early papyri will permit a positive decision. The internal evidence seems to me to point with even greater probability to a different conclusion : that line 21 is genuine and the following superfluous speech formula interpolated. This particular formula is not used elsewhere in the *Odyssey*, but is frequent in the *Iliad*.

Laodamas has suggested that the stranger be invited to participate in the contests :

θ 140   τὸν δ᾽ αὖτ᾽ Εὐρύαλος ἀπαμείβετο φώνησέν τε·
141   " Λαοδάμα, μάλα τοῦτο ἔπος κατὰ μοῖραν ἔειπες."
143   αὐτὰρ ἐπεὶ τό γ᾽ ἄκουσ᾽ ἀγαθὸς παῖς Ἀλκινόοιο,
στῆ ῥ᾽ ἐς μέσσον ἰὼν καὶ Ὀδυσσῆα προσέειπε·

142   αὐτὸς νῦν προκάλεσσαι ἰὼν καὶ πέφραδε μῦθον."
om. Bekker ; damn. Ludwich, Blass.

The line is found in all MSS.—there are no papyri—but the scholia (H) testify : οὔτε Ἀρίσταρχος οὔτε Ἀριστοφάνης οὔτε Ζηνόδοτος ἐπίστανται τοῦτον τὸν στίχον, and: οὗτος ὁ στίχος ἐν ταῖς Ἀρισταρχείαις οὐ φέρεται.

Blass found no intrinsic objection to the line, but Ameis-Hentze *Anhang*, ii. 27) note that the formula of verse 141 is elsewhere followed up in a different fashion.

In the H scholia we are told at θ 333 ἐν ἐνίοις ἀντιγράφοις οἱ δέκα στίχοι οὐ φέρονται. Applying this to our vulgate it means that θ 333–42 were not read in certain ἀντίγραφα. Wecklein (*ZAV* 19) approves the resulting text, but Blass (270 f.) has shown that line 343 must then be emended (ὡς φάσαν), and that even then the text would not be entirely satisfactory.

The difficulty can be met as follows: verses 333–43 were the missing lines, one of them having been interpolated after the time of this scholium. For the absence of a formula to summarize the speech σ 400–4 can be compared. The interpolated line would probably be verse 335—a needless vocative; it is omitted by G, though this may well be nothing more than haplography.

This is a possibility I consider it proper to mention, although I believe that I can offer below a more acceptable explanation.

In κ Odysseus has told how he slew a stag, and of the feast that followed:

> ἦμος δ' ἠριγένεια φάνη ῥοδοδάκτυλος Ἠώς,
> 188 καὶ τότ' ἐγὼν ἀγορὴν θέμενος μετὰ πᾶσιν ἔειπον·
> 190 " ὦ φίλοι, οὐ γάρ τ' ἴδμεν ὅπη ζόφος οὐδ' ὅπη ἠώς,
> οὐδ' ὅπη ἠέλιος φαεσίμβροτος εἶσ' ὑπὸ γαῖαν
> οὐδ' ὅπη ἀννεῖται· κτλ.

---

189 κέκλυτέ μευ μύθων, κακά περ πάσχοντες ἑταῖροι.
om. Bekker, Nauck, van Leeuwen; damn. La Roche, Ludwich, Merry, Blass.

The plus verse was read neither by Aristophanes nor Aristarchus; its intrusion began early enough to come under the notice of Callistratus. The evidence is that the scholiast on Euripides, *Phoen.* 886—whom Cobet conjectures to be Aristophanes—and Aristonicus (s A) at P 221, both cite κ 190 to illustrate Homer's way of beginning a speech with a γάρ-clause. The scholia (H) further state: Καλλίστρατός φησιν ὡς ὑπό τινος ὁ στίχος προτέτακται ἀγνοοῦντος τὸ Ὁμηρικὸν ἔθος, ὡς θέλει ἄρχεσθαι ἀπὸ τοῦ γάρ.

Lentz (29), Blass, and Wecklein (*ZAV* 67) all approve the absence of the verse. Ameis-Hentze (*Anhang*, ii. 87) clinch the

argument : 'weil Homer in Anreden nie einen doppelten Eingang so gebraucht, dass erst bei der zweiten Anrede eine Begründung derselben mit γάρ hinzugefügt würde.' The verse is a repetition of μ 271, 340 ; we have already seen it interpolated as μ 153ᵃ at a later time.

Apollonius (*pron.* 84. 13) omits κ 211 in his quotation. The line could be spared, but is wanted to serve as a source for κ 253 which is clearly interpolated. Quite likely then we are confronted with nothing but an inaccurate quotation.

After the transformation :

241   ὡς οἱ μὲν κλαίοντες ἐέρχατο· τοῖσι δὲ Κίρκη
242   πάρ ῥ' ἄκυλον βάλανόν τε βάλεν καρπόν τε κρανείης.

243   ἔδμεναι, οἷα σύες χαμαιευνάδες αἰὲν ἔδουσιν.
vel   παντοίης ὕλης ἐτίθει μελιηδέα καρπόν.

A note going back to Didymus : Ἀρίσταρχος οὐκ οἶδε τὸν στίχον. ὁ δὲ Καλλίστρατος ἀντ' αὐτοῦ γράφει "παντοίης ... καρπόν" is preserved in HQV, but in connexion with line 242. That something is wrong is obvious, and my solution seems simpler and more satisfactory than those given by Dindorf and by Ludwich (*AHT* i. 581 f.).

In either form the plus verse is a needless gloss.

The discovery of a fragment—3 *p.* POxy. 412—of the eighteenth book of Julius Africanus' Κεστοί is of double interest.

(1) The author quotes some thirty lines which were either withheld by the poet or excised by the Pisistratidae—he cannot decide which. This longer version is so obviously hocus pocus, that the mere mention of its existence is sufficient.

(2) Africanus quotes λ 34–50, but without λ 44–7 = κ 531–4 :

δὴ τότ' ἔπειθ' ἑτάροισιν ἐποτρύνας ἐκέλευσα
μῆλα, τὰ δὴ κατέκειτ' ἐσφαγμένα νηλέι χαλκῷ,
δείραντας κατακῆαι, ἐπεύξασθαι δὲ θεοῖσιν,
ἰφθίμῳ τ' Ἀίδῃ καὶ ἐπαινῇ Περσεφονείῃ.

There is no reason to assume that the lines were purposely omitted (cf. Blass, 120 n., against Ludwich), on the contrary they would have been grist for this mill. Besides, the assumption must en-

counter an embarrassing dilemma : either Africanus was working as
a higher critic, or for reasons of his own he has happened to get rid
of some στίχοι διφορούμενοι. The short text as Africanus gives it
must be the text he knew. As he wrote c. 250 his testimony is
equivalent to that of a papyrus c. 150–250.

There is nothing to connect these lines with the Alexandrian
critics—certainly the trivial scholia on lines 44 (V) and 46 (H)
cannot be so employed. On the contrary, we can prove from their
atheteses that Zenodotus, Aristophanes, and Aristarchus had λ 38–
43 in their texts ; and that our evidence breaks off just at this point
may well be significant.

The pictorial tradition as presented by Müller (110–18) seems to
me to be consistent with the view here advocated. The Esquiline
landscape shows two of Odysseus' comrades busied with the
slaughtered ram, and Müller is possibly right in connecting this fact
with our passage ; but if so it merely gives a *terminus ante quem*
for the interpolation. The Berlin gems are inconsistent with these
lines, while the Louvre relief is neutral. If all descend from the
ἀειζώουσα Νέκυια we have no right (to say the least) to ascribe to
Nicias an acquaintance with this interpolation. Polygnotus also
gives no evidence that he knew the lines—cf. Robert *ap.* Müller,
110 n. Of the crater from Pisticci we can speak more positively :
the victims stay lying by the trench and bleed into it ; that is the
concept of the uninterpolated text.

It is a curious result of the way the evidence has reached us that
Bekker, Ludwich, and Merry should all condemn λ 38–43, while
leaving the later interpolation untouched. Blass rejected lines 38–
47, and saw that κ 531–4 must also be interpolated.

Odysseus speaking of the deeds of Neoptolemus :

λ   αὐτὰρ ὅτ' εἰς ἵππον κατεβαίνομεν, ὃν κάμ' Ἐπειός,
524   Ἀργείων οἱ ἄριστοι, ἐμοὶ δ' ἐπὶ πάντ' ἐτέταλτο,
526   ἔνθ' ἄλλοι Δαναῶν ἡγήτορες ἠδὲ μέδοντες
        δάκρυά τ' ὠμόργνυντο, τρέμον θ' ὑπὸ γυῖα ἑκάστου·

525 ἠμὲν ἀνακλῖναι πυκινὸν λόχον ἠδ' ἐπιθεῖναι ∽ E 751, Θ 395
om. Bekker, van Leeuwen ; damn. Nauck, Ludwich, Merry, Blass.

The line was not read by Aristarchus but mentioned in his com-

mentaries, according to Didymus (ѕ H): Ἀρίσταρχος οὐκ οἶδε τὸν στίχον, ἔνια δὲ τῶν ὑπομνημάτων. Aristonicus (ѕ H) therefore demands (cf. above, p. 49) not that we athetize but that we *cancel* the line: περιγραπτέον ὡς ἀπρεπῆ. With its early start the line has made its way into 2/3 *p*. POxy. 780 and all our MSS. On the worthlessness of the line cf. Wecklein, *ZAV* 67; Blass, 130; Ameis-Hentze, *Anhang*, ii. 121, where further literature is cited.

λ 604   παῖδα Διὸς μεγάλοιο καὶ Ἥρης χρυσοπεδίλου
= Hes. *Th*. 952

In Part I this line has already been designated as an interpolation because 1/2 *p*. PFayum 310 and PH omit it. Diod. Sic. iv. 39. 3 quotes lines 602–3 alone; though the addition of 604 would be natural, had he known it.

The scholia are in great confusion, but seem to indicate that Aristarchus did not read line 604, which is what the evidence just adduced would lead us to expect. According to the fragment of Aristonicus prefixed in Cod. Venetus A (Dindorf, p. 2), λ 603 was athetized by Aristarchus—an impossibility if line 604 followed. Some one preferred to athetize λ 602–3, and he too could not have known our plus verse; nor could the author of the TV scholium who agrees with him: τοὺς δὲ δύο στίχους καὶ ἡμεῖς ἀθετοῦμεν " εἴδωλον " καὶ " τέρπεται ἐν θαλίης ". Nor could those of whom the H² scholia say: ἔνιοι δὲ οὐ τὴν οἰνοχόον Ἥβην, ἀλλὰ τὴν ἑαυτοῦ ἀνδρείαν (i. e. ἥβην).

The evidence for the line is later. The second hand of H adds the line (misplacing it after line 606) and a scholium: τοῦτον ὑπὸ Ὀνομακρίτου πεποιῆσθαί φασιν. ἠθέτηται δέ. Kirchhoff (232) emended to the plural; very probably correctly, only the reference must be to 602–3 if the note is early, which Ludwich denies. In J obels are placed before lines 602–4, and in Y² it is said of the same lines ἀθετοῦνται καὶ λέγονται Ὀνομακρίτου εἶναι. That is, in these late authorities what was said of lines 602–3 has been extended to verse 604 after its interpolation. Wecklein (*ZAV* 23) should not have followed in their footsteps.

The verse:

ἀνδρῶν μνηστήρων, οἵ τοι βίοτον κατέδουσιν

is thrice (ν 396, 428, ο 32) repeated. In ν 396 it is omitted by PRyl. 53 and one of Allen's M̲SS., and in Part i I have accepted this evidence as conclusive. In the second passage the external evidence is not so strong, for while H and Eustathius omit the line the papyrus attests it; but Blass (150) and Wecklein (*ZAV* 23) point out the impossibility ˙of reading this line there. I would assign the interpolation to the period here under discussion, and regard the papyrus as furnishing merely a *terminus ante quem* for the interpolation. On neither of these lines are there scholia, while the third passage (ο 32), which the MSS. support without wavering, can be traced back to Dionysius (of Sidon), a pupil of Aristarchus.

ξ 451 νόσφιν δεσποίνης καὶ Λαέρταο γέροντος = ξ 9

The line is omitted by Vind. 5, Ven. Marc. 456, but attested by PRyl. 53; and could well be spared, as Kirchhoff (501 f.) has shown. It might have been judged like the preceding examples were it not for the fact that haplography (ἄνακτος, γέροντος) suffices to explain the slight disturbance in the MS. tradition.

Another line that may be placed here is:

π 50 ὀπταλέων, ἅ ῥα τῇ προτέρῃ ὑπέλειπον ἔδοντες.

There is a considerable disturbance in the MSS.: according to Allen *om.* d q P¹ R⁴, to which must be added, on the testimony of La Roche and Ludwich, the first hand of Vind. 133 of the thirteenth century. Plutarch, *Quaest. conv.* vii. 704ᵃ, is the earliest evidence for the line, there being neither scholia nor papyri. Athenaeus (vi. 228 c) attests π 49—but no more—for Aristophanes: 'Ομήρου γὰρ εἰπόντος ἐν 'Οδυσσείᾳ " τοῖσιν δ' αὖ πίνακας κρειῶν παρέθηκε συβώτης " (π 49) 'Αριστοφάνης ὁ Βυζάντιος νεώτερόν φησιν εἶναι τὸ ἐπὶ πινάκων παρατιθέναι τὰ ὄψα ἀγνοῶν ὅτι κἂν ἄλλοις εἴρηκεν ὁ ποιητὴς " δαιτρὸς δὲ κρειῶν πίνακας παρέθηκεν ἀείρας ".—In passing I may note that either Athenaeus already knew δ 57 = α 141 or his ἐν ἄλλοις is an exaggeration.

All of this can be best understood by supposing that the line was not read by Aristarchus, but was interpolated in the vulgate at an early time; coming from a text of the Ptolemaic type by way of scholia. My reason for hesitating is that the line is not a στίχος διφορούμενος.

The witticism—

π 224 οὐ μὲν γάρ τί σε πεζὸν ὀίομαι ἐνθάδ᾽ ἱκέσθαι

is found also α 173, ξ 190, π 59. Here it is omitted by two (GU) important MSS., which, however, are assigned to the same family (k) by Allen. Blass (168) and Wecklein (*ZAV* 24) accept their testimony, and I do likewise. Wecklein rejects also π 226, which is omitted by U alone. This looks to me rather like haplography (τόν, τοί), and the interpolation (should it be such) will be of pre-Aristarchean date.

There is much confusion in the scholia on ρ 147 ff. At line 147 is a note (H) ἀθετοῦνται ιϛ´ στίχοι, another (Q) at line 150 ἀθετοῦνται ιβ´ στίχοι, and finally at line 160 (Q Vind. 133) ἐν τοῖς χαριεστέροις οὗτοι μόνοι οἱ β´ (ιβ´ codd.) ἀθετοῦνται, ἐπεὶ καὶ πρὶν εἰσελθεῖν ἐν τῇ νηὶ τὸν οἰωνὸν εἶδε, καὶ ἐγεγώνευν [οὐκ] ἀκαίρως ἐστίν. ἐν δὲ τοῖς κοινοτέροις (εἰκαιοτέροις) ἀπὸ τοῦ "ὡς ἔφατο" (147), ἕως τοῦ "ἐξ ἐμεῦ" (165).

Usually this is rendered intelligible by the following changes. (1) Read with H ιϛ´ στίχοι, but place the note with Q at line 150. (2) Emend to ἀπὸ τοῦ "ὡς φάτο" (150). I should hold to the first and last note (the second has absorbed an evident corruption from the third, and seems to have been shifted in consequence of this) and understand: sixteen lines 147–65 are athetized. Then three lines have been added to the passage since Aristarchus; they are probably lines 152 and 155–6.

τ 62 καὶ δέπα, ἔνθεν ἄρ᾽ ἄνδρες ὑπερμενέοντες ἔπινον

is omitted by Allen's d1 families (by DZ Ludwich), but there is a scholium going back to Herodian. The line is not a στίχος διφορούμενος, and haplography (αἱ δ᾽ ἀπό, καὶ δέπα) may best account for the behaviour of the MSS.

τ 110 ἀνδράσιν ἐν πολλοῖσι καὶ ἰφθίμοισιν ἀνάσσων ℧ ω 26

damn. Blass.

The line is omitted in quotations by Plato (*Rep*. ii. 363 b), Philodemus of Gadara (Ludwich, *HZAD* 15), Plutarch (*ad Princ. inerud*. 780 f), Themistius (xv. 189 a). It is objectionable (cf. Blass, 187 f.) because of ἔν τισιν ἀνάσσειν, at variance with Homeric usage.

The only question is the date of the interpolation, and as there are no scholia, I should place it shortly after Aristarchus.

ODYSSEY   215

τ 122 φῆ δὲ δακρυπλώειν βεβαρηότα με φρένας οἴνῳ.
The line is omitted by the first hands of GU, or according to
Allen by the k family. There are scholia BHQV, which do not,
however, seem to be very old. Aristotle (*Probl.* xxx. 1. 953ᵇ 12)
quotes καί μέ φησι δακρυπλώειν βεβαρημένον οἴνῳ.
The external evidence seems pretty well balanced. Wecklein
(*ZAV* 25) calls attention to a number of linguistic oddities φῆ
δακρυπλώειν, and the scansion δάκρυ.

Later we shall see that τ 130-61 are interpolated, and these are
said (H) to be thirty (λ′) lines. Porson suggested that thirty-two
(λβ′) be read ; but Blass, noting the external evidence (cf. Part I)
against line 153, proposed to read λα′, and Wecklein (*ZAV* 20)
follows him. I am inclined to suspect that either line 135 or line
131 is another interpolation of this sort ; so that after all λ′ defines
the omission correctly according to the Aristarchean text.

With regard to τ 250-1, 275-7, there is a certain amount of
fluctuation in the MSS. It cannot be pressed, however, because
haplography (γόοιο, γόοιο and πόντῳ, πόντῳ) is in each case the
probable cause. Ludwich rejects the former passage, and Wecklein
(*ZAV* 25) seems inclined to agree. The latter passage is suspected
by Bethe, *Homer*, ii. 101 n. In each case the decision must be
reached on internal evidence.

The omission of ν 298 (= ρ 402, etc.) by Eustathius is probably
significant, though the line is found in PRyl. 53 as well as in our
MSS. But the omission by Gregory of Corinth (*Rhet. gr.* vii. 2 :
1281. 13) of line 340, which is similarly attested, is probably
accidental. Note the temptation to haplography (οὐ, ὅς) and the
fact that it is not a στίχος διφορούμενος. Blass (200) approves the
omission of the first of these lines.

In φ the omission of lines 122-3 by Allen's C and of line 189 by
his L⁵ will probably be an accident, while that of line 381 by FPU¹Z
is best ascribed to haplography (Εὐρύκλειαν, Εὐρύκλεια). PRyl. 53
contains all these lines.

Many MSS. write χ 37 after χ 38, thus showing that at one time
it must have stood in the margin. It may, however, have been

dropped accidentally as there is a slight temptation (δήμου, δμῳῆσιν) to haplography. This is all the more probable because there is no obvious source for the line, which was read perhaps by Philodemus of Gadara (Ludwich, *HZAD* 16), and is found in PRyl. 53, POxy. 448.

Without temptation to haplography there are slight disturbances in the MSS. at ω 53 (= β 160, etc.), 113 (ᴧ λ 403), and 238 (= δ 119). All are found in PRyl. 53, but the omission of two of them would accord well with the stichometry of PTebt. 432 of the second century. The first is a superfluous speech formula ; the last was suspected by Nauck, tolerated by Blass, omitted by van Leeuwen, and condemned by Wecklein (*ZAV* 26).

II

α

WE now approach the problem of the pre-Aristarchean interpolations in the *Odyssey*, beginning with the lines that follow the last speech of Athene in the council of the gods:

96   ὣς εἰποῦσ' ὑπὸ ποσσὶν ἐδήσατο καλὰ πέδιλα,
102   βῆ δὲ κατ' Οὐλύμποιο καρήνων ἀίξασα,
     στῆ δ' Ἰθάκης ἐνὶ δήμῳ ἐπὶ προθύροις Ὀδυσῆος,
     οὐδοῦ ἐπ' αὐλείου, παλάμῃ δ' ἔχε χάλκεον ἔγχος,
     εἰδομένη ξείνῳ, Ταφίων ἡγήτορι, Μέντῃ.

97   ἀμβρόσια, χρύσεια, τά μιν φέρον ἠμὲν ἐφ' ὑγρὴν = ε 45, Ω 341
     ἠδ' ἐπ' ἀπείρονα γαῖαν ἅμα πνοιῆς ἀνέμοιο.   = ε 46, Ω 342
     εἵλετο δ' ἄλκιμον ἔγχος, ἀκαχμένον ὀξέι χαλκῷ,   = ο 551, Κ 135, etc.
     βριθύ, μέγα, στιβαρόν, τῷ δάμνησι στίχας ἀνδρῶν = Ε 746, Θ 390
101   ἡρώων, τοῖσίν τε κοτέσσεται ὀβριμοπάτρη.   = Ε 747, Θ 391

om. Bekker², van Leeuwen; damn. Hayman, Ludwich, Cauer.   vss. 99–101 om. Bekker¹, damn. Merry.

The text is that of the Massaliotike; the plus verses were read but athetized by Aristarchus and (probably) Aristophanes.

The best evidence is a note (MT) going back to Didymus: προηθετοῦντο κατ' ἔνια τῶν ἀντιγράφων οἱ στίχοι, κατὰ δὲ τὴν Μασσαλιωτικὴν οὐδ' ἦσαν. The note stands at line 97, and is referred by the following discussion to the whole group of lines. Aristonicus divided his treatment into three parts according to the sources of the interpolated lines. Only the last part has reached us standing in s MV at line 99, one verse too early: ἀθετοῦνται μετὰ ἀστερίσκων ὅτι ἐν τῇ ε΄ τῆς Ἰλιάδος καλῶς. This is confirmed by his note (s A) on Ε 746–7: ὅτι ἐντεῦθεν εἰς τὴν Ὀδύσσειαν μετάκεινται. Similarly his notes at Ω 341–2: ὅτι ἐνταῦθα ὀρθῶς κεῖνται καὶ ἐπὶ τοῦ πρὸς Καλυψὼ διαπεραιουμένου Ἑρμοῦ· ἐν δὲ τῇ α΄ ῥαψῳδίᾳ τῆς Ὀδυσσείας οὐκέτι, and at ε 43 (HPQ), give us the substance of the first part of his treatment. There is no reason why the two authorities should not overlap, but unfortunately Ludwich, apparently to prevent this, has restricted the note of Didymus to lines 97–8, and Wecklein (*ZAV* 18, 45) has followed him.

For objections to the long version cf. Lentz (16) and Blass (30); but the superiority of the short text is in reality so evident that no discussion is required.

The *Vita Herodotea* (p. 15 Wilam.) reads :

153 κῆρυξ δ' ἐν χερσὶν κίθαριν περικαλλέ' ἔθηκεν
154 Φημίῳ, ὅς τε πολλὸν ἐκαίνυτο πάντας ἀείδων.

This is probably no more than a variant to the vulgate :

154 Φημίῳ, ὅς ῥ' ἤειδε παρὰ μνηστῆρσιν ἀνάγκῃ.

but Barnes is said to have taken it for a plus verse (153ᵃ) and so printed it. Wolf (*Proll.* 259 n. 45) easily showed that such a text was not known to Aristarchus and his followers. Line 154 is then suspect διὰ τὸ καὶ ἑτέρως φέρεσθαι.

Telemachus to Athene (Mentes) :

   ἀλλ' ἄγε μοι τόδε εἰπὲ καὶ ἀτρεκέως κατάλεξον·
170 τίς, πόθεν εἰς ἀνδρῶν; πόθι τοι πόλις ἠδὲ τοκῆες;
174 καί μοι τοῦτ' ἀγόρευσον ἐτήτυμον, ὄφρ' ἐὺ εἰδῶ,
   ἠὲ νέον μεθέπεις, ἦ καὶ πατρώιός ἐσσι
   ξεῖνος, ἐπεὶ πολλοὶ ἴσαν ἀνέρες ἡμέτερον δῶ
   ἄλλοι, ἐπεὶ καὶ κεῖνος ἐπίστροφος ἦν ἀνθρώπων.

---

171 ὁπποίης τ' ἐπὶ νηὸς ἀφίκεο· πῶς δέ σε ναῦται
   ἤγαγον εἰς Ἰθάκην; τίνες ἔμμεναι εὐχετόωντο;
173 οὐ μὲν γάρ τί σε πεζὸν ὀίομαι ἐνθάδ' ἱκέσθαι.

The text is that of certain unnamed authorities. The plus verses which recur as ξ 188–90, π 57–9 were read but athetized by Aristarchus. The latter fact is implied by the scholia (HQ) at ξ 188: ἀστερίσκος πρόσκειται ἄχρι στίχων γ', ὅτι νῦν ὡς πρὸς ῥάκεσιν ἠμφιεσμένον ὀρθῶς λέγονται· ὡς δὲ πρὸς τὴν Ἀθηνᾶν ὁμοιωθεῖσαν Μέντῃ καὶ βασιλικὴν ἔχουσαν στολὴν οὐ πάνυ. The omission is here attested (HM): οἰκειότερον ταῦτα ὑπὸ Εὐμαίου ἂν λέγοιντο. διὸ ἔν τισιν οὐκ ἐφέροντο.

Hug (*ap.* Ameis-Hentze, *Anhang*, i. 24 f.) claimed that Athene's reply implied the presence of the plus verses, but I think the claim will not hold even on a careful reading of the vulgate, in which lines 185-6 have, however, been interpolated. Lentz (9), Blass (32 f.), and Wecklein (*ZAV* 18) all recognize the inappropriateness of the lines in this passage, and there can be no question of foisting them upon the text.

Athene's reply begins :

"τοὶ γὰρ ἐγώ τοι ταῦτα μάλ' ἀτρεκέως ἀγορεύσω.
180 Μέντης Ἀγχιάλοιο δαΐφρονος εὔχομαι εἶναι
        υἱός, ἀτὰρ Ταφίοισι φιληρέτμοισιν ἀνάσσω.
        νῦν δ' ὧδε ξὺν νηὶ κατήλυθον ἠδ' ἑτάροισι,
        πλέων ἐπὶ οἴνοπα πόντον ἐπ' ἀλλοθρόους ἀνθρώπους,
184 ἐς Τεμέσην μετὰ χαλκόν, ἄγω δ' αἴθωνα σίδηρον.
187 ξεῖνοι δ' ἀλλήλων πατρώιοι εὐχόμεθ' εἶναι
        ἐξ ἀρχῆς, κτλ.

185 νηῦς δέ μοι ἥδ' ἕστηκεν ἐπ' ἀγροῦ νόσφι πόληος,
186 ἐν λιμένι Ῥείθρῳ, ὑπὸ Νηΐῳ ὑλήεντι.

The text is again that of nameless editors. The plus verses (185 = ω 308) were read but athetized by Aristophanes and Aristarchus. The evidence is in the scholia (HMQR): προηθετοῦντο δὲ ὑπὸ Ἀριστοφάνους· κατ' ἔνια δὲ τῶν ἀντιγράφων οὐδ' ἐφέροντο. The quotation (Aristotle, *Poet.* xxi : 1457ᵇ 9) of νηῦς ... ἕστηκεν must be referred to ω 308.

The geography of the second line is peculiar, 'Ῥεῖθρον not being mentioned elsewhere, while Νηΐῳ seems abstracted from ὑπονήιος (γ 81). In α, but not in ω, ἥδε and νόσφι πόληος are in contradiction. For these reasons Blass (33) regards the lines as interpolated ; while Wecklein (*ZAV* 18) and Cauer (in the revision of Ameis-Hentze) reach the same conclusion.

The short version is superior, and if it be argued that the longer text is not too bad for the author of α the answer is simple : we must leave it to the external evidence to determine what he actually wrote.

In Athene's advice to Telemachus :

        μνηστῆρας μὲν ἐπὶ σφέτερα σκίδνασθαι ἄνωχθι,
        μητέρα δ', εἴ οἱ θυμὸς ἐφορμᾶται γαμέεσθαι,
        ἂψ ἴτω ἐς μέγαρον πατρὸς μέγα δυναμένοιο·
277 οἱ δὲ γάμον τεύξουσι καὶ ἀρτυνέουσιν ἔεδνα. = β 196
279 σοὶ δ' αὐτῷ πυκινῶς ὑποθήσομαι, αἴ κε πίθηαι·
        νῆ' ἄρσας, κτλ.

278 πολλὰ μάλ', ὅσσα ἔοικε φίλης ἐπὶ παιδὸς ἕπεσθαι. = β 197
om. van Leeuwen, damn. Ludwich ; vss. 277–8 damn. Cauer.

The text is that of Rhianus, if a scholium (H²M) οὗτος δὲ ὁ στίχος ἐν τῇ κατὰ 'Ριανὸν οὐκ ἦν attached to line 279 should be moved to this place. The omission of line 279 could be nothing but an accident, and the transposition of the note is made by Kirchhoff (246 n.), Blass (37), and Wecklein (*ZAV* 18), following a suggestion of Bekker.

There is no need to insert the line, and we must stand on the external evidence. On the ἔεδνα problem compare most recently Cauer, *Grundfr.*³ 333 ff.; I believe its solution would prove simpler had we even as much information about the text of the *Odyssey* as we have about that of the *Iliad*.

Certain unnamed editors read for Telemachus' speech to his mother simply lines 346–55—a perfectly satisfactory text. The edition of Aristarchus contained also (though obelized) :

356 ἀλλ' εἰς οἶκον ἰοῦσα τὰ σ' αὐτῆς ἔργα κόμιζε,
     ἱστόν τ' ἠλακάτην τε, καὶ ἀμφιπόλοισι κέλευε
     ἔργον ἐποίχεσθαι. μῦθος δ' ἄνδρεσσι μελήσει
359 πᾶσι, μάλιστα δ' ἐμοί· τοῦ γὰρ κράτος ἔστ' ἐνὶ οἴκῳ.
om. Bekker ; damn. Ludwich, Merry ; vss. 355–9 damn. Cauer.

The evidence is given (H) : τινὲς οὖν ἀθετοῦσιν. ἐν δὲ ταῖς χαριεστέραις γραφαῖς οὐδ' (Dindorf, οὐκ cod.) ἦσαν, and still more freely for Aristarchus: ἀθετοῦνται ἐνταῦθα ...(HM), also Ἀρίσταρχος δὲ ἀθετεῖ ... (HMQR). Compare also on the parallel passage Z 490–3, Aristonicus (ϛ A): τέσσαρσι στίχοις ἐξῆς ἀστερίσκοι παράκεινται, ὅτι νῦν μὲν ὀρθῶς κεῖνται καὶ πρὸ τῆς μνηστηροφονίας, ἐν δὲ τῇ α΄ ῥαψῳδίᾳ τῆς Ὀδυσσείας οὐκέτι.

The plus verses (= φ 350–3) have been intruded because the following lines 360–4 are taken from φ 354–8. Like most of the earlier scholars (cf. Ameis-Hentze, *Anhang*, 42 f.), Lentz (20), Blass (42), and Wecklein (*ZAV* 18 f., 78), approve the shorter text, which is clearly superior. Kirchhoff (175) and Wilamowitz (*HU* 8) retain the lines because nothing is too bad for the author of this section. We must, however, permit the external evidence to indicate just how bad he was.

The suitors amuse themselves :

423 τοῖσι δὲ τερπομένοισι μέλας ἐπὶ ἕσπερος ἦλθε·
     δὴ τότε κακκείοντες ἔβαν οἶκον δὲ ἕκαστος.

The scholia say : ἔνιοι·

δὴ τότε κοιμήσαντο καὶ ὕπνου δῶρον ἕλοντο
μεταποιηθῆναι δέ φασιν ὑπὸ Ἀριστοφάνους τὸν στίχον. ἐν δὲ τῇ
Ἀργολικῇ προστέθειται.

My interpretation differs from that of Ludwich (AHT i. 518),
followed by Wecklein (TSO 9 f.; ZAV 13) : some give as the
original text δὴ τότε κοιμήσαντο κτλ., and assert that it was changed
into the vulgate reading by Aristophanes; the Argolike has the
vulgate, and the variant added to it. That is a perfectly credible
story; the Argolic text having an exact parallel, for instance, in
PMel. Nic. 222, where Σ 617 is repeated in variant form. Ludwich's
very attractive emendation then becomes unnecessary. It may
suffice to point out that the longer text—lines corresponding to
I 712–13 taking the place of α 424—which he finds in or behind the
Argolike would be no whit better than the vulgate ; and so it would
have to be regarded as interpolated.

On my interpretation the attested readings admit of simpler
explanation : the vulgate has preserved the original version, but as
α 423 and τ 426 both end ἐπὶ ἕσπερος (κνέφας) ἦλθε some scribes
thoughtlessly wrote τ 427 in this place ; both the true text and the
corruption were to be found in the Argolic edition.

β

Telemachus speaking before the assembly :

50   μητέρι μοι μνηστῆρες ἐπέχραον οὐκ ἐθελούσῃ,
     τῶν ἀνδρῶν φίλοι υἶες οἳ ἐνθάδε γ' εἰσὶν ἄριστοι,
     οἳ πατρὸς μὲν ἐς οἶκον ἀπερρίγασι νέεσθαι
     Ἰκαρίου, ὥς κ' αὐτὸς ἐεδνώσαιτο θύγατρα,
     δοίη δ' ᾧ κ' ἐθέλῃ καί οἱ κεχαρισμένος ἔλθῃ.

51ᵃ ἄλλοι θ' οἳ νήσοισιν ἐπικρατέουσιν ἄριστοι,
51ᵇ Δουλιχίῳ τε Σάμῃ τε καὶ ὑλήεντι Ζακύνθῳ.

These plus verses (∽ α 245–6) were to be found in the edition of
Aristophanes according to the scholia (HM) : Ἀριστοφάνης προστί-
θησιν " ἄλλοι . . . Ζακύνθῳ ".

The lines are so obviously interpolated that it is a work of
supererogation to point out that they were not known to Heraclides

Ponticus (*ap.* Porph. 26. 5 ff. Schr.). They look like a λύσις for the problem there discussed. It is surprising that they should have made their way into the edition of Aristophanes.

γ

After Nestor has suggested that Telemachus may prevail against the suitors:

> τὸν δ' αὖ Τηλέμαχος πεπνυμένος ἀντίον ηὔδα·
> "ὦ γέρον, οὔ πως τοῦτο ἔπος τελέεσθαι ὀίω·
> λίην γὰρ μέγα εἶπες· ἄγη μ' ἔχει. οὐκ ἂν ἔμοιγε
> ἐλπομένῳ τὰ γένοιτ', εἰ μὴ θεοὶ ὣς ἐθέλοιεν."
> 229   τὸν δ' αὖτε προσέειπε θεὰ γλαυκῶπις Ἀθήνη·
> 232   "βουλοίμην δ' ἂν ἔγωγε καὶ ἄλγεα πολλὰ μογήσας
> οἴκαδέ τ' ἐλθέμεναι καὶ νόστιμον ἦμαρ ἰδέσθαι,
> ἢ ἐλθὼν ἀπολέσθαι ἐφέστιος, ὡς Ἀγαμέμνων
> ὤλεθ' ὑπ' Αἰγίσθοιο δόλῳ καὶ ἧς ἀλόχοιο—κτλ.

> 230 "Τηλέμαχε, ποῖόν σε ἔπος φύγεν ἕρκος ὀδόντων;
> 231 ῥεῖα θεός γ' ἐθέλων καὶ τηλόθεν ἄνδρα σαώσαι
> addidit Aristarchus.
> 230 "Τηλέμαχ' ὑψαγόρη, μέγα νήπιε, ποῖον ἔειπες;
> addidit Zenodotus.

The text is that of Zenodotus (in line 228 the vulgate reads οὐδ' εἰ θεοὶ ὣς ἐθέλοιεν), except that διὰ τὸ καὶ ἑτέρως φέρεσθαι I have dropped the vocative line. The evidence (rationalized) is to be found in the scholia (HM): οὗτος ὁ στίχος (230) λαγαρός ἐστι· διὸ Ζηνόδοτος ἴσως μετέγραφε " Τηλέμαχ' ... ἔειπες". τὸν δὲ δεύτερον (231) περιῄρει τελέως διὰ τὸ μαχόμενον αὐτῷ " εἰ μὴ θεοὶ ὣς ἐθέλοιεν".

With this must be connected also Zenodotus' reading:

> 216 τίς δ' οἶδ' εἴ κέ ποτέ σφι βίας ἀποτίσεαι ἐλθών,
> 217 ἢ σύ γε μοῦνος ἐὼν ἢ καὶ σύμπαντες Ἀχαιοί;

which makes Nestor's speech a speculation on one subject alone—the possibility that Telemachus may one day settle his account with the suitors. Wecklein (*ZAV* 60) has noted that Zenodotus' reading is required because of the following εἰ γάρ σ' ὣς ἐθέλοι κτλ.; and Blass (59 f.) has argued to the same result. I may add that the composition of this section points to the same conclusion.

Telemachus has exclaimed (208-9): 'But the gods have spun no such blessed lot πατρί τ' ἐμῷ καὶ ἐμοί.' Nestor answers the ἐμοί— that blessing may still be in store for you; Athene answers the πατρί—your father is more blessed than Agamemnon. The conversation is thus brought round to the desired goal. One corollary may be drawn : it will be impossible to follow Aristarchus in athetizing lines 232-8. We may notice also the order of Nestor's and Athena's replies, ὕστερον πρότερον—on which compare Bassett, *Harvard Studies*, 31 (1920). 39-62.

In Telemachus' reply to Nestor both Blass and Wecklein condemn the Zenodotean reading εἰ μὴ θεοὶ ὣς ἐθέλοιεν, which seems to me better adapted to the situation and character of the speaker. Nestor's suggestion appeals to the youthful hero so strongly that it dazzles him, and his reactions oscillate rapidly. The task is too great. He is filled with admiration and awe at the idea. He cannot hope for its achievement—unless God so wills. Thus at the very instant he renounces his hope it rises again undaunted, and piously phrased as it should be. I see no reason to interfere with that ; and as the text of Zenodotus has been proving a safe guide immediately before we shall do well to continue to follow it here also.

Athene's speech is a reply, as I have already indicated, not to Telemachus' last remark, but to the despairing close (208-9) of his former speech. The composition is on a small scale, but the same in principle as the larger scenes dealing with contemporary actions which Zielinski has explained. Three-cornered conversation is difficult for the author's technique. The young man may deserve some rebuke, but Zenodotus' ὑψαγόρη, μέγα νήπιε is obviously illsuited. Against the vulgate there is nothing to urge except the improbability that after proving inferior to the Zenodotean text in 216, 217, and 228, it should here in 230 preserve the formula actually used. It is a matter of personal opinion whether that should outweigh the certain amount of abruptness in the text as I have constituted it.

Be that as it may, I do not see how it can be claimed that line 231 is necessary—and that is for me the point of real importance. Its meaning is uncertain. The current interpretation runs : ' easily can God, if he wills, bring a man safely home, though from a distant land.' I will not dispute the possibility of so translating

it ; but in Homer—with certain restrictions for *B* 849, 857, 877—
τηλόθεν shows that the subject acts from afar, and I should see in
the line an assertion that ' God's power to save can be exerted even
at a distance ', implying that it is subject to no limitation but his
will. Aristarchus must have taken the words in this fashion, since
he found lines 236–8 in contradiction to this verse. If so, the line
must be a *sententia* borrowed from some gnomic poet ; for the
thought goes beyond the limits usual to the Homeric poems, where
such powers (cf. Nägelsbach, 23 ff.) are ascribed to Zeus alone. It
is the intrusion of this line that has caused the change to οὐδ' εἰ
θεοὶ ὣς ἐθέλοιεν, which is impious, and intended to be so.

For other recent treatments of this passage cf. Belzner, ii. 37 f. ;
Mülder, *BJ* 182 (1920). 122 f. ; Bethe, *Homer*, ii. 25. Compare also
Porphyry's λύσις (35. 4 ff. Schr.) for the problem, which does not
exist when the short version is followed.

Menelaus was gathering wealth in Egypt :

303   τόφρα δὲ ταῦτ' Αἴγισθος ἐμήσατο οἴκοθι λυγρά,
305   ἑπτάετες δ' ἤνασσε πολυχρύσοιο Μυκήνης,
304   κτείνας Ἀτρείδην, δέδμητο δὲ λαὸς ὑπ' αὐτῷ·
306   τῷ δέ οἱ ὀγδοάτῳ κακὸν ἤλυθε δῖος Ὀρέστης
307   ἂψ ἀπ' Ἀθηνάων, κατὰ δ' ἔκτανε πατροφονῆα,
311   αὐτῆμαρ δέ οἱ ἦλθε βοὴν ἀγαθὸς Μενέλαος,
         πολλὰ κτήματ' ἄγων, ὅσα οἱ νέες ἄχθος ἄειραν.

309   ἤτοι ὁ τὸν κτείνας δαίνυ τάφον Ἀργείοισι
310   , μητρός τε στυγερῆς καὶ ἀνάλκιδος Αἰγίσθοιο.
vm. 310 damn. Ludwich.

I have already given my reasons for believing that line 308 was
not contained in the edition of Aristarchus, but interpolated in the
vulgate shortly after his day. The order of verses 305, 304 is
attested by the scholium to Sophocles, *El.* 267, which is believed
(cf. Ameis-Hentze, *Anhang*, i. 84) to go back to Didymus. Bergk
advocated this reading, which, since La Roche, has been generally
adopted. The necessary corollary is a common archetype later
than Aristarchus for all MSS. showing the transposition. Allen
alone cites MSS. as containing the verses in the order given by

Didymus; and of such only two, and both as late as the fifteenth
century; but for Ven. Marc. 456 the statement is not confirmed by
La Roche, and Allen's note seems greatly confused.

The HMQRT scholia say ἔν τισι τῶν ἐκδόσεων οὐκ ἦσαν—a
statement referred in MT to lines 309-10, but placed at line 303 in
the other MSS. The latter was regarded as a blunder and
corrected by Dindorf, and there is no reason to doubt the correctness of his solution. The scholia furthermore attest lines 309-10
as Aristarchean.

Bethe (*Homer*, ii. 263 f.) argues against the ' rejection' of the
lines—but that is not the problem. The lines were not in the
oldest editions of which we know, and the question is, must they be
inserted? I can see no reason why Menelaus should not have
arrived on the day of Aigisthos' death, immediately after the event.
Hennings (83 f.), Blass (63) are of the same opinion. The idea is
not contradicted by lines 256 ff., where Nestor tells what Menelaus
would have done had he himself punished Aigisthos. As the condition was not fulfilled the control of the situation rested not with
Menelaus but with Orestes. Nor is the prophecy of Proteus σὺ δέ
κεν τάφου ἀντιβολήσαις (δ 547) unfulfilled. Only it does not mean
' you will not arrive until the funeral is actually under way '. The
interpolator, however, took it in some such fashion, and has tried to
make the fulfilment fit the prophecy as he understood it. At the
same time he wished to bring in some allusion to the fate of
Clytaemestra—which the poet had left unmentioned. Why the
poet so chose need not be discussed here ; but were I to attempt
an explanation I should start not from Finsler (*Homer*, ii. 278),
but from Bethe's exposition of the sources of the *Telemachy*.

Wilamowitz' rejection of line 310 and his defence of 309 (*HU*
154 f.) need little further discussion. They are a half-way measure,
a putting asunder of what the external evidence has bound
together.

Henning's criticism of the sentence structure seems to me also to
be well taken. He has appreciated the force of the external
evidence, and so has Wecklein (*ZAV* 20) ; while Blass, though
seeing it, tries to avoid the necessary conclusion by assuming that
the text has been bowdlerized.

In Nestor's palace :

αὐτὰρ ἐπεὶ σπεῖσάν τε πίον θ' ὅσον ἤθελε θυμός,
οἱ μὲν κακκείοντες ἔβαν οἶκον δὲ ἕκαστος,
τὸν δ' αὐτοῦ κοίμησε Γερήνιος ἱππότα Νέστωρ,
Τηλέμαχον, φίλον υἱὸν Ὀδυσσῆος θείοιο,
399 τρητοῖς ἐν λεχέεσσιν, ὑπ' αἰθούσῃ ἐριδούπῳ.
402 αὐτὸς δ' αὖτε καθεῦδε μυχῷ δόμου ὑψηλοῖο,
τῷ δ' ἄλοχος δέσποινα λέχος πόρσυνε καὶ εὐνήν.

400 πὰρ δ' ἄρ' ἐυμμελίην Πεισίστρατον, ὄρχαμον ἀνδρῶν,
401 ὃς οἱ ἔτ' ἠίθεος παίδων ἦν ἐν μεγάροισιν.

The text is that of Zenodotus; the plus verses were read and defended by Aristarchus. The evidence is given by the scholia (HMQR) : οἱ ἄλλοι γυναῖκας εἶχον. διόπερ οὐ συνιδὼν ὁ Ζηνόδοτος τὸ φιλότεχνον (φιλότεκνον H) τοῦ ποιητοῦ τοὺς δύο στίχους περιέγραψεν. The use of περιγράφειν (cf. p. 48 f.) points to Aristonicus at the source of this note, a conclusion reached on other grounds by Roemer, *Zenod.* 7 n.

The lines are superfluous, so that the shorter text can be followed without difficulty. The plus verses contain the only instance of ἐυμμελίης in the *Odyssey*, and the epithet is for Pisistratus inappropriate. Whether he is unmarried or not is left unclear in the poem —certainly γ 415 is no evidence, though Blass (64) claims it as such. Apparently some one wished to settle the question and interpolated these lines. On the other hand there is no reason why any one should have excised the lines, had they been original ; Aristonicus could make no better guess than Zenodotean stupidity. The case must rest on the external evidence. Misinterpreting it has led Wecklein (*ZAV* 64) astray.

δ

The fourth book opens :

οἱ δ' ἷξον κοίλην Λακεδαίμονα κητώεσσαν,
πρὸς δ' ἄρα δώματ' ἔλων Μενελάου κυδαλίμοιο.
τὸν δ' εὗρον δαίνυντα γάμον πολλοῖσιν ἔτῃσιν
υἱέος ἠδὲ θυγατρὸς ἀμύμονος ᾧ ἐνὶ οἴκῳ.
5 τὴν μὲν Ἀχιλλῆος ῥηξήνορος υἱέι πέμπεν·
ἐν Τροίῃ γὰρ πρῶτον ὑπέσχετο καὶ κατένευσε

δωσέμεναι, τοῖσιν δὲ θεοὶ γάμον ἐξετέλειον.
τὴν ἄρ' ὅ γ' ἔνθ' ἵπποισι καί ἅρμασι πέμπε νέεσθαι
Μυρμιδόνων προτὶ ἄστυ περικλυτόν, οἷσιν ἄνασσεν.
10   υἱέι δὲ Σπάρτηθεν Ἀλέκτορος ἤγετο κούρην,
ὅς οἱ τηλύγετος γένετο κρατερὸς Μεγαπένθης
ἐκ δούλης· Ἑλένῃ δὲ θεοὶ γόνον οὐκέτ' ἔφαινον,
ἐπεὶ δὴ τὸ πρῶτον ἐγείνατο παῖδ' ἐρατεινήν,
14   Ἑρμιόνην, ἣ εἶδος ἔχε χρυσῆς Ἀφροδίτης.
20   τὼ δ' αὖτ' ἐν προθύροισι δόμων αὐτώ τε καὶ ἵππω,
Τηλέμαχός θ' ἥρως καὶ Νέστορος ἀγλαὸς υἱός,
στῆσαν.

15   ὡς οἱ μὲν δαίνυντο καθ' ὑψερεφὲς μέγα δῶμα
γείτονες ἠδὲ ἔται Μενελάου κυδαλίμοιο,
τερπόμενοι· μετὰ δέ σφιν ἐμέλπετο θεῖος ἀοιδὸς
φορμίζων· δοιὼ δὲ κυβιστητῆρε κατ' αὐτούς,
19   μολπῆς ἐξάρχοντες, ἐδίνευον κατὰ μέσσους.

om. Bekker ; damn. Hayman, Ludwich ; vss. 16–19 damn. Cauer.

Athenaeus (v. 180 e) makes the assertion: Διόδωρος δ' ὁ Ἀριστο-
φάνειος ὅλον τὸν γάμον (δ 3–19) περιέγραψε, τοπάζων πρώτας
ἡμέρας εἶναι, καὶ τὸ λῆγον αὐτῶν ἔτι δὲ καὶ τὸ ἔωλον τῆς συμ-
ποσίας οὐκ ἐπιλογιζόμενος. ἔπειτα κελεύει γράφειν " δοιὼ δὲ κυβιστητῆρε καθ' αὐτούς" ἐν τῷ δασεῖ γράμματι σολοικίζειν ἀναγκάζων.
Unfortunately Athenaeus is capable (cf. ii. 39d) of using περιγράφειν
as a synonym of ἀθετεῖν, and there are reasons which tend to make
this probable in our passage.   For Athenaeus himself quotes
line 18 as read by Diodorus, so that lines 3–19 could not have been
lacking in his text.   To suppose that Athenaeus is commenting on
Diodorus' reading of Σ 605 would meet this argument, but only at
the cost of assuming that Athenaeus' presentation of the case was
terribly confused.   Besides, it is extremely unlikely that the texts
read by Diodorus and Aristarchus should differ so greatly ; while
it is perfectly natural that they should hold varying opinions about
the desirability of an athetesis.   There is, then, no evidence for the
existence of texts in which the whole of this section was lacking.
I consider that favourable to my main argument ; for in spite of
Bethe's view (Homer, ii. 374)—'δ 3–19 sind interpolirt, wenn es
überhaupt Interpolationen gibt'—I cannot share the conviction.

Hennings (86 f.), on whom Bethe relies, must concede the necessity of changing the beginning of line 20, if the 'interpolation' be removed; while the arguments of Kirchhoff (185 ff.), Wilamowitz (*HU* 92), and Blass (65 ff.) as to the need of some such background seem valid.

On the other hand we have testimony for the existence of texts in which either δ 17–19 or 15–19 were lacking : Athenaeus, v. 180 c : οἱ περὶ Ἀρίσταρχον . . . προσσυνῆψαν τοιούτους τινὰς στίχους "ὡς οἱ μὲν . . . κατὰ μέσσους" (15–19) μετενεγκόντες ἐκ τῆς Ὁπλοποιΐα σὺν αὐτῷ γε τῷ περὶ τὴν λέξιν ἁμαρτήματι. οὐ γὰρ "ἐξάρχοντες" οἱ κυβιστητῆρες, ἀλλ' "ἐξάρχοντος" τοῦ ᾠδοῦ πάντως ὠρχοῦντο. τὸ γὰρ ἐξάρχειν τῆς φόρμιγγος ἴδιον. From this is derived ultimately the scholium (MT) : φασὶ τοὺς γ' στίχους τούτους (17–19) μὴ εἶναι τοῦ Ὁμήρου ἀλλὰ τοῦ Ἀριστάρχου. Athenaeus means, of course, that the interpolation was made from what he regards as the genuine Ὁπλοποιΐα, not from the Aristarchean text.

From this statement and Athenaeus' discussion (v. 181 c) of the passage in Σ we must infer : (1) that Athenaeus believed the text of Aristarchus contained both in Σ and in δ exactly the lines found in our MSS. ; (2) that he knew directly or indirectly of texts longer in Σ and shorter in δ ; (3) that he generalized this into a belief that the same was true of all pre-Aristarchean texts. Of these we have every reason to believe that the first is true, no reason to doubt the second, and good grounds for pronouncing the third a rash generalization.

Now Athenaeus declares that the interpolated lines come from the *Hoplopoiïa*, and only δ 17–19 have that source. It is possible that Athenaeus has been careless in his statement, naming only the source of the greater part of the interpolation ; but it is also possible that he wrote out part of the genuine context to show where the interpolation came in. The scholium with its τοὺς γ' στίχους seems to support the latter alternative ; but the tradition is so poor that γ' may well be no more than a mistake for ε' (so Dindorf), not to mention the possibility of an effort to correct Athenaeus. Ludwich (*HV* 117 f.) attempts to show from Aristophanes (*Pax*, 1280 ff.) that the comic poet found δ 15 ff. in his text of the *Odyssey*. But an acquaintance with δ 15 is the most that could thus be proved ; while E. Meyer (*Hermes*, 27 (1892).

377 ff.) seems to me to have shown that Aristophanes is parodying the *Certamen*, and so gives no testimony for the text of the *Odyssey*. The possibilities balance so evenly that it seems necessary to conclude that the external evidence is plain only against lines 17–19. The superiority of the text free from them is obvious. Not only are the bard and tumblers not mentioned later, but their presence is actually incompatible with the narrative; Kirchhoff (187), Wilamowitz (*HU* 92 n.), Blass (65 f.), Finsler (*Homer²*, ii. 281), and Wecklein (*ZAV* 46) all see that we have no right to import such a difficulty into our text. The charge that Aristarchus was the interpolator is absurd. We should expect this sort of thing in a Ptolemaic papyrus, and must accept Aristarchus' text as proof that he knew MSS. which contained the interpolated lines. Athenaeus had a better text of δ but a worse one of Σ, and in his eagerness to show that the great critic was doubly wrong he himself drew erroneous conclusions.

Blass well argues that after the exclusion of δ 17–19, Μενελάου κυδαλίμοιο (in lines 16 and 23) is repeated at an improbably short interval. Consequently line 16 is an interpolation. If that is so the probability is that δ 15–19 were lacking in Athenaeus' text, and there is no reason why we should not follow its authority.

Menelaos is telling of his adventures:

90 εἷος ἐγὼ περὶ κεῖνα πολὺν βίοτον ξυναγείρων
    ἠλώμην, τείως μοι ἀδελφεὸν ἄλλος ἔπεφνε
    λάθρῃ, ἀνωιστί, δόλῳ οὐλομένης ἀλόχοιο·
    ὡς οὔ τοι χαίρων τοῖσδε κτεάτεσσιν ἀνάσσω.

On the last line is a scholium (HMQ): ἔν τισιν ὑπὸ τοῦτον φέρεται στίχος·

    οὐδέ τι βουλόμενος, ἀλλὰ κρατερῆς ὑπ' ἀνάγκης.

This note is not misplaced, for it continues: γελοίως· οὐδεὶς γὰρ μετὰ ἀνάγκης ἀνάσσει χρημάτων.

Still, the verse must have been meant to follow line 90. In other words the interpolation entered the text in so mechanical a fashion that it became fixed in the wrong place, and yet it is seriously discussed in the scholia. Γ 333 ff., Δ 123, have already given us good parallels. Ludwich thinks that the scholium goes back to

Aristonicus, whom we have seen hawking at small game. Then his antigraphon of Zenodotus must have contained the line—nothing else would have called forth such criticism.

Peisistratos speaking to Menelaos :

"Ἀτρείδη Μενέλαε διοτρεφές, ὄρχαμε λαῶν,
157 κείνου μέν τοι ὅδ' υἱὸς ἐτήτυμον, ὡς ἀγορεύεις·
161 αὐτὰρ ἐμὲ προέηκε Γερήνιος ἱππότα Νέστωρ
τῷ ἅμα πομπὸν ἕπεσθαι· ἐέλδετο γάρ σε ἰδέσθαι,
ὄφρα οἱ ἤ τι ἔπος ὑποθήσεαι ἠέ τι ἔργον.
πολλὰ γὰρ ἄλγε' ἔχει πατρὸς παῖς οἰχομένοιο
165 ἐν μεγάροις, ᾧ μὴ ἄλλοι ἀοσσητῆρες ἔωσιν,
ὡς νῦν Τηλεμάχῳ ὁ μὲν οἴχεται, οὐδέ οἱ ἄλλοι
εἴσ', οἵ κεν κατὰ δῆμον ἀλάλκοιεν κακότητα."

158 ἀλλὰ σαόφρων ἐστί, νεμεσσᾶται δ' ἐνὶ θυμῷ
ὧδ' ἐλθὼν τὸ πρῶτον ἐπεσβολίας ἀναφαίνειν
160 ἄντα σέθεν, τοῦ νῶι θεοῦ ὡς τερπόμεθ' αὐδῇ.

The text is that of Rhianus ; the plus verses were read but athetized by Aristarchus, who obelized also lines 163-7. At least such is the most natural interpretation of the scholia, but the attempts to make them tell a different story need examination. There are four items of evidence :

(1) at line 158 : οὐκ ἐφέροντο ἐν τῇ Ῥιανοῦ οἱ τρεῖς στίχοι (H).

(2) ἀλλὰ σαόφρων] παρὰ τὰ πάτρια καὶ οὐχ ἁρμόττοντα τῷ Πεισιστράτου προσώπῳ. καὶ τὸ νεμεσσᾶται ἀντὶ τοῦ αἰδεῖται οὐχ Ὁμηρικῶς. καὶ αἱ ἐπεσβολίαι δὲ γέλοιαι. ὅθεν Ζηνόδοτος μεταποιεῖ "ἐπιστομίας ἀναφαίνειν".

(3) in immediate succession : ἀθετοῦνται δὲ στίχοι ε' (γ' H) ὡς περιττοὶ καὶ ὑπὸ νέου παντάπασι λέγεσθαι ἀπρεπεῖς. ἄλλως τε οὐδὲ συμβουλευσόμενος τῷ Μενελάῳ πάρεστιν, ἀλλ' "εἴ τινά οἱ κληηδόνα πατρὸς ἐνίσποι" (HMQR).

(4) at line 163 after a long explanation : τὸ δὲ ἦθος οὐ συνιέντες τινὲς ἠθέτησαν τὰ ἔπη (HMQR).

The third of these notes must be misplaced, as it refers clearly to lines 163-7 ; the fourth is a refutation of it. To this debate Blass (70) would refer also the first sentence of the second note. With

Roemer (*AAH* 419 f.) I can see no valid reason for the change ; and then Blass' suggestion that lines 165-7 (the only ones to which he objects) are the ones not read by Rhianos loses all plausibility. The scholia must consequently retain the meaning that they bear upon the surface.

Rhianos' text is perfectly satisfactory, and the insertion of lines 158-60 cannot be seriously advocated, even though Rothe (*Odyssee*, 43), Finsler (*Homer*², ii. 283), and Stürmer (iii. 76 n.) have not seen the necessity for 'ejecting' them. Wecklein (*ZAV* 19) and Bethe (*Homer*, ii. 25 f.) recognize the interpolation—the latter citing an inaccessible work by Duentzer. The language also seems objectionable. Gilbert Murray (*RGE*² 103 ff.) puts well the distinction : ' Aidos is what you feel about an act of your own : Nemesis is what you feel for the act of another.' As the scholia observe, the distinction is here violated ; and it seems to be the only instance of such a violation in Homer. Certainly the passages cited by Blass and Hennings (*Odyssee*, 90) do not invalidate the distinction. The scholia also call ἐπεσβολίαι ridiculous,[1] finding in its meaning, no doubt, an element of abuse or scurrility. Notice in the Palatine Anthology, 7. 70 ; 9. 185 (cf. 4. 3), the connexion with Archilochus ; and how Apollonius Rhodius (iv. 1727) traces to the γλυκερὴ . . . κερτομίη, νεῖκος ἐπεσβόλον of the Argonauts and Medea's hand-maidens the χλευασμός of the festival held in honour of Apollo on the island Anaphe. We are in no position to controvert that opinion since B 275, λωβητῆρα ἐπεσβόλον, supports it, without excluding the possibility that the word may mean no more than ' prating', 'chattering'. Still, to translate in our passage ' start his prating', or ' his chit-chat ' ought to be cold comfort for the defenders of these lines.

Lines 163-7 have no evidence against them of the sort that is considered in this book. If Bethe is right in ascribing them to the author of our *Odyssey*, they are an interpolation in a different sense, and there should be no evidence of that sort against them.

---

[1] The variant attributed to Zenodotus ἐπιστομίας is obviously corrupt. I may suggest ἐπιστοβίας—though the noun seems unquotable. Apollonius Rhodius (iv. 1725) uses ἐπιστοβέεσκον, and ἐπεσβόλον in iv. 1727, and I would infer that he knew both the Zenodotean and the vulgate reading.

Menelaos tells of how Helen came to see the wooden horse:

τρὶς δὲ περίστειξας κοῖλον λόχον ἀμφαφόωσα,
ἐκ δ' ὀνομακλήδην Δαναῶν ὀνόμαζες ἀρίστους,
πάντων Ἀργείων φωνὴν ἴσκουσ' ἀλόχοισιν.
280 αὐτὰρ ἐγὼ καὶ Τυδείδης καὶ δῖος Ὀδυσσεὺς
ἥμενοι ἐν μέσσοισιν ἀκούσαμεν ὡς ἐβόησας.
νῶι μὲν ἀμφοτέρω μενεήναμεν ὁρμηθέντε
ἢ ἐξελθέμεναι ἢ ἔνδοθεν αἶψ' ὑπακοῦσαι·
284 ἀλλ' Ὀδυσεὺς κατέρυκε καὶ ἔσχεθεν ἱεμένω περ."

285 ἔνθ' ἄλλοι μὲν πάντες ἀκὴν ἔσαν υἷες Ἀχαιῶν,
Ἄντικλος δὲ σέ γ' οἶος ἀμείψασθαι ἐπέεσσιν
ἤθελεν· ἀλλ' Ὀδυσεὺς ἐπὶ μάστακα χερσὶ πίεζε
νωλεμέως κρατερῇσι, σάωσε δὲ πάντας Ἀχαιούς,
289 τόφρα δ' ἔχ' ὄφρα σε νόσφιν ἀπήγαγε Παλλὰς Ἀθήνη.
om. Bekker; damn. Hayman, Nauck, Ludwich, Merry, Cauer.

The plus verses read but athetized by Aristarchus had according to the scholia almost no support in the tradition: Ἀρίσταρχος τοὺς ε' (Porson: δύο codd.) ἀθετεῖ (HQ). οὐκ ἐφέροντο δὲ σχεδὸν ἐν πάσαις οἱ πέντε (H).

Evidently lines 280–4, 285–9 are doublets; Ameis-Hentze (Anhang, i. 107) and Blass (72 f.) have shown the impossibility of making the two stories fit. The result is accepted by Roemer, AAH 410 f. (= Rh. M. 61 (1906). 342 f.); Rothe, Odyssee, 44 n.; Allen, Catalogue, 158; Wecklein, ZAV 19; and Bethe, Homer, ii. 256 n. Kirchhoff (189), stating frankly that he did not know what importance should attach to the external evidence, found the Antiklos episode a desirable climax; Stürmer (iii. 78 n.) comes to the same conclusion, adding that the poet's intention is to prepare us for the way Odysseus seizes Eurykleia in the Niptra.

The origin of the doublets is clear. Lines 285–9 are a fragment of the Little Iliad—ὁ Ἄντικλος ἐκ τοῦ κύκλου (H); lines 280–4 are the reworking of this story by the author of the Telemachy. The interpolation seems very mechanical—the absorption of a parallel passage written in the margin. It was indeed περιττὴ εὐλάβεια for Aristarchus to take the lines into his text, but we must be grateful to him for so doing.

Menelaos telling of his adventures:

Αἰγύπτῳ μ' ἔτι δεῦρο θεοὶ μεμαῶτα νέεσθαι
352 ἔσχον, ἐπεὶ οὔ σφιν ἔρεξα τεληέσσας ἑκατόμβας.
354 νῆσος ἔπειτά τίς ἐστι πολυκλύστῳ ἐνὶ πόντῳ
Αἰγύπτου προπάροιθε, Φάρον δέ ἑ κικλήσκουσι κτλ.

353 οἱ δ' αἰεὶ βούλοντο θεοὶ μεμνῆσθαι ἐφετμέων.
om. Bekker ; damn. Nauck, Ludwich, Merry, Cauer.

The verse is undoubtedly (cf. Ameis-Hentze, i. 109; Blass, 75) an interpolation, but does not come strictly within the scope of my book.

Herodotus (ii. 116) or his interpolator fails to quote it after quoting the two preceding lines. The scholia say that the line was athetized by Zenodotus: βούλεται μὲν λέγειν θυσιῶν. ἀσαφέστερον δὲ εἴρηται. διὸ Ζηνόδοτος ἠθέτει. ποῖαι γάρ, φησίν, ἐγένοντο ἐντολαί;

The style of this passage (cf. above on Π 141 ff.) points towards Pergamum ; and I may suggest that it was Zenodotus of Mallos who read and athetized the line. It is quite possible that the Alexandrians knew nothing of it.

Proteus speaking to Menelaos:

ἀρχοὶ δ' αὖ δύο μοῦνοι Ἀχαιῶν χαλκοχιτώνων
ἐν νόστῳ ἀπόλοντο· μάχῃ δέ τε καὶ σὺ παρῆσθα.
498 εἷς δ' ἔτι που ζωὸς κατερύκεται εὐρέι πόντῳ.

On the last line is a corrupt scholium: Ζηνόδοτος τοῦτον ὃς γράφει (H), which has been emended either to τοῦτον περιγράφει or to τοῦτον οὐ γράφει. Wecklein (ZAV 64) prefers the former; understanding that Zenodotus read the line, but doubted its genuineness. I regard the phrases as synonymous, and prefer the latter emendation as easier palaeographically.

The line (cf. Blass, 75) is clearly genuine, and Aristonicus proceeds to point it out: ἀναγκαῖον δὲ καὶ αὐτὸν εἶναι διὰ τὸ λέγειν ὕστερον (551) Μενέλαον "σὺ δὲ τρίτον ἄνδρ' ὀνόμαζε". We have then a mechanical blunder, be it in Zenodotus' sources or in the antigraphon of his text used by the Aristarcheans; and we notice that there is at least a slight temptation (ΕΝ, ΕΙC) to haplography.

The speech of Proteus ended :

σοὶ δ' οὐ θέσφατόν ἐστι, διοτρεφὲς ὦ Μενέλαε,
Ἄργει ἐν ἱπποβότῳ θανέειν καὶ πότμον ἐπισπεῖν,
ἀλλά σ' ἐς Ἠλύσιον πεδίον καὶ πείρατα γαίης
ἀθάνατοι πέμψουσιν, ὅθι ξανθὸς Ῥαδάμανθυς,
τῇ περ ῥηίστη βιοτὴ πέλει ἀνθρώποισιν·
566 οὐ νιφετός, οὔτ' ἀρ χειμὼν πολὺς οὔτε ποτ' ὄμβρος,
* ἀλλ' αἰεὶ Ζεφύροιο διαπνείουσιν ἀῆται "
570 ὣς εἰπὼν ὑπὸ πόντον ἐδύσετο κυμαίνοντα.

567 ἀλλ' αἰεὶ Ζεφύροιο λιγὺ πνείοντος ἀήτας
568 Ὠκεανὸς ἀνίησιν ἀναψύχειν ἀνθρώπους.
569 cf. supr. p. 207.

The text is that of Aristotle, *Probl.* xxvi. 31 : 943ᵇ 21—the earliest and simplest form of the text known to us. I see no reason to depart from it. To be sure, the post-Homeric (cf. Finsler, *Homer²*, i. 78) character of Zephyrus is more strongly marked in this version than in the vulgate ; but that is no objection in a passage dealing with the Elysian fields. The longer text looks like an artificial effort to keep Zephyrus a cool, if not a cold wind—the λύσις of some lost ἀπορία.

Strabo (i. 59) omits from his quotation δ 845 ; but the temptation to haplography (πετρήεσσα, παιπαλοέσσης) is too great to permit us to attach any significance to the fact.

ε

Odysseus is at the mercy of wind and wave :

τὸν δὲ ἴδεν Κάδμου θυγάτηρ, καλλίσφυρος Ἰνώ.
Λευκοθέη, ἣ πρὶν μὲν ἔην βροτὸς αὐδήεσσα,
νῦν δ' ἁλὸς ἐν πελάγεσσι θεῶν ἐξέμμορε τιμῆς.
336 ἥ ῥ' Ὀδυσῆ' ἐλέησεν ἀλώμενον, ἄλγε' ἔχοντα·
338 ἷζε δ' ἐπὶ σχεδίης καί μιν πρὸς μῦθον ἔειπε·

337 αἰθυίῃ δ' εἰκυῖα ποτῇ ἀνεδύσετο λίμνης ω ε 352 f.
om. Bekker, Nauck, van Leeuwen ; damn. Hayman, Ludwich, Merry, Cauer.

The scholia (HPQ) say : οὐκ ἐφέρετο ἐν τοῖς πλείοσι. Ἀρίσταρχος δὲ περὶ μὲν τῆς ἀθετήσεως διστάζει, γράφει δὲ διὰ τοῦ ῡ ὑπεδύσετο. ἐν δέ τισιν ἀνεδύσατο. ἔοικε δὲ ὁ στίχος ἐκ τῶν ὕστερον εἰρημένων

ὑπό τινος παρεμβεβλῆσθαι. The term διστάζει seems to occur in the scholia of the *Odyssey* (ε 337, ζ 244, η 311, μ 439) alone; and its use probably signifies that the scholiast had more detailed information than he could conveniently carry. One might conjecture that Didymus reported that the line was not contained in Aristarchus' first edition, but read and athetized in the second.

The shorter text is unquestionably superior. Aristonicus has designated the source of the interpolation; Cauer, *Grundfr.*[3] 353 (cf. Wecklein, *ZAV* 19) has explained its motive—a patent misunderstanding of the parallel passage; Buttmann *ap.* Dindorf and Ameis-Hentze (*Anhang*, i. 138) have discussed the difficulties of the language. Blass (87) can give the line short shrift, and Finsler (*Homer*[2], ii. 296) can ignore it. If it fits into Stürmer's (iii. 138) scheme of symmetry, that is so much the worse for his theory.

ζ

Nausicaa speaking to her handmaids:

ἀλλ' ὅδε τις δύστηνος ἀλώμενος ἐνθάδ' ἱκάνει,
τὸν νῦν χρὴ κομέειν· πρὸς γὰρ Διός εἰσιν ἅπαντες
ξεῖνοί τε πτωχοί τε, δόσις δ' ὀλίγη τε φίλη τε.
209 ἀλλὰ δότ', ἀμφίπολοι, ξείνῳ βρῶσίν τε πόσιν τε,
λούσατέ τ' ἐν ποταμῷ, ὅθ' ἐπὶ σκέπας ἔστ' ἀνέμοιο."

209ᵃ ἀλλ' ἄγε οἱ δότε φᾶρος ἐυπλυνὲς ἠδὲ χιτῶνα

The plus verse is found only in Ven. 456, a MS. of the fifteenth century; and being meant as a variant to line 209 does not come strictly within the scope of this book. But Kirchhoff (203) argued that line 209 (= ζ 246) is itself an intruder, and that if 209ᵃ is not the genuine text its author has struck upon the substance of the genuine verse which line 209 had displaced. This idea has commended itself to Ameis-Hentze (*Anhang*, i. 152), Blass (91), and Cauer (Ameis-Hentze revision); but still I must dissent.

The process assumed is without parallel in the tradition of the poems. The nature of these lines that crop out in single late MSS. is too plain to allow us to take line 209ᵃ for anything but a late conjecture for which θ 392 supplied the pattern. Unfortunately we have not as yet papyrus evidence against it; for 1*p*. PFayum 7 breaks off immediately after attesting line 209.

The conjecture is also a bad one. After deciding (207) to provide for the comfort of the stranger, Nausicaa gives merely general directions, naming the last act and the first. In describing the execution of her commands there is more detail, and naturally the clothing is mentioned. The process is interrupted by the description of the beauty of Odysseus and its effect upon Nausicaa. The princess then repeats (246) the command for what still remains to be done. That should occasion no difficulty.

η

The royal lineage begins :

54 Ἀρήτη δ' ὄνομ' ἐστὶν ἐπώνυμον, ἐκ δὲ τοκήων
τῶν αὐτῶν οἵ περ τέκον Ἀλκίνοον βασιλῆα.

as if king and queen were brother and sister, but the detailed account that follows makes them merely uncle and niece.

The obvious explanation is that a more primitive story has been glossed over to suit the tastes of a more refined period. This is confirmed by the statement of the scholia (BPQTVind.) : Ἡσίοδος δὲ ἀδελφὴν Ἀλκινόου τὴν Ἀρήτην ὑπέλαβεν. There is no occasion to resort to artificial interpretations of τοκήων = προγόνων with the scholia and Rothe (Odysee, 59 n.); nor to assume with Blass (95) that Hesiod read carelessly. The more primitive story still shows through our text; and that story, we are told, was known to Hesiod. The fact is to be accepted.

The earlier version, however, cannot be recovered by a clean-cut excision—as Kirchhoff's attempt shows. The inference to be drawn is that the passage stood thus in our tradition from its beginning. In other words, we are not dealing with an 'interpolation' in the strict sense, but with a reworking of the story between the times of Hesiod and of Pisistratus. Bethe (Homer, ii. 124) is essentially of the same opinion.

The garden of Alkinoos :

ἔνθα δὲ δένδρεα μακρὰ πεφύκασι τηλεθόωντα,
115 ὄγχναι καὶ ῥοιαὶ καὶ μηλέαι ἀγλαόκαρποι
συκέαι τε γλυκεραὶ καὶ ἐλαῖαι τηλεθόωσαι.
τάων οὔ ποτε καρπὸς ἀπόλλυται οὐδ' ἀπολείπει
χείματος οὐδὲ θέρευς, ἐπετήσιος· ἀλλὰ μάλ' αἰεὶ

Ζεφυρίη πνείουσα τὰ μὲν φύει, ἄλλα δὲ πέσσει.
120/1 ὄγχνη ἐπ' ὄγχνῃ γηράσκει, σῦκον δ' ἐπὶ σύκῳ.

120 ὄγχνη ἐπ' ὄγχνῃ γηράσκει, μῆλον δ' ἐπὶ μήλῳ,
121 αὐτὰρ ἐπὶ σταφυλῇ σταφυλή, σῦκον δ' ἐπὶ σύκῳ.

The text is that of Aristotle, frgm. 667, from which (cf. Ludwich, *HV* 121) are derived Aelian, *VH* iii. 36, Diog. La. v. 9 ; and also Antigonos of Karystos, *FHG* iv. 359, used by Athenaeus i. 25 a.

Anton (*RhM* 18 (1863). 417 f.), followed by Blass (97), objected to the vulgate as anticipating the description of the vineyard. The objection was well taken, but the proposed cure—to excise line 121 —is shown by the external evidence to be wrong.

In the absence of scholia and papyri it is impossible to be sure of Aristarchus' text, but on account of the testimony of Diodorus Siculus (ii. 56. 7) and our MSS. it is most probable that it included the interpolation.

θ

In Alkinoos' hall they feasted :

αὐτὰρ ἐπεὶ πόσιος καὶ ἐδητύος ἐξ ἔρον ἕντο,
Μοῦσ' ἄρ' ἀοιδὸν ἀνῆκεν ἀειδέμεναι κλέα ἀνδρῶν,
οἴμης τῆς τότ' ἄρα κλέος οὐρανὸν εὐρὺν ἵκανε,
75 νεῖκος 'Οδυσσῆος καὶ Πηλείδεω Ἀχιλῆος,
ὥς ποτε δηρίσαντο θεῶν ἐν δαιτὶ θαλείῃ
ἐκπάγλοις ἐπέεσσιν, ἄναξ δ' ἀνδρῶν Ἀγαμέμνων
78 χαῖρε νόῳ, ὅ τ' ἄριστοι Ἀχαιῶν δηριόωντο.
83   ταῦτ' ἄρ' ἀοιδὸς ἄειδε περικλυτός· κτλ.

79 ὡς γάρ οἱ χρείων μυθήσατο Φοῖβος Ἀπόλλων
Πυθοῖ ἐν ἠγαθέῃ, ὅθ' ὑπέρβη λάινον οὐδὸν
χρησόμενος· τότε γάρ ῥα κυλίνδετο πήματος ἀρχή
82 Τρωσί τε καὶ Δαναοῖσι Διὸς μεγάλου διὰ βουλάς.

A note in the H scholia ἐν ἐνίαις τῶν ἐκδόσεων οὐκ ἐφέροντο· διὸ ἀθετοῦνται stands after short and empty scholia on line 80, and has consequently been referred to the last two only of the lines I have not taken into the text. But as Blass (103) has shown, the four verses hang together, and it is most probable that the notes on line 80 were added in the wrong place. Confusion of οἱ δ' στίχοι and οἱ δύο στίχοι may have helped.

The passage is the only instance in Homer of the consultation of the Delphic oracle. That may be, as Finsler (*Homer²*, i. 57) claims, no sufficient reason for 'excising' the lines; but in combination with the fact that they fail to accomplish their purpose—to explain the riddle of lines 77 f.—it is ample ground for preferring the version in which they are not contained. Seeck (289) gave the explanation of their origin—an interpolated λύσις.

Alkinoos in reply to Odysseus' challenge:

> ἀλλ' ἄγε νῦν ἐμέθεν ξυνίει ἔπος, ὄφρα καὶ ἄλλῳ
> εἴπῃς ἡρώων, ὅτε κεν σοῖς ἐν μεγάροισι
> δαινύῃ παρὰ σῇ τ' ἀλόχῳ καὶ σοῖσι τέκεσσιν,
> ἡμετέρης ἀρετῆς μεμνημένος, οἷα καὶ ἡμῖν
> 245 Ζεὺς ἐπὶ ἔργα τίθησι διαμπερὲς ἐξ ἔτι πατρῶν.
> οὐ γὰρ πυγμάχοι εἰμὲν ἀμύμονες οὐδὲ παλαισταί,
> ἀλλὰ ποσὶ κραιπνῶς θέομεν καὶ νηυσὶν ἄριστοι,
> 248 αἰεὶ δ' ἥμιν δαίς τε φίλη κίθαρίς τε χοροί τε.
> 250 ἀλλ' ἄγε, Φαιήκων βητάρμονες ὅσσοι ἄριστοι,
> παίσατε, ὥς χ' ὁ ξεῖνος ἐνίσπῃ οἷσι φίλοισιν κτλ.

---

249 εἵματά τ' ἐξημοιβὰ λοετρά τε θερμὰ καὶ εὐναί.
om. van Leeuwen ; damn. Ludwich.

The text is that known to Heraclides Ponticus and to Megaclides, both of whom quote line 248 alone, where the addition of line 249 would have been decidedly to their purpose. Porphyry in the scholia at ν 119 (Schr. 115 ff.), ι 5 (Schr. 81), and Athenaeus (xii. 513 b) have preserved the evidence.

The irrelevance of the interpolation has long been recognized—cf. most recently Blass (107), Wecklein (*ZAV* 21); and so the short version is again the superior.

The gods gather in the house of Hephaistos:

> ἄσβεστος δ' ἄρ' ἐνῶρτο γέλως μακάρεσσι θεοῖσι
> τέχνας εἰσορόωσι πολύφρονος Ἡφαίστοιο.
> ὧδε δέ τις εἴπεσκεν ἰδὼν ἐς πλησίον ἄλλον·
> " οὐκ ἀρετᾷ κακὰ ἔργα· κιχάνει τοι βραδὺς ὠκύν,
> 330 ὡς καὶ νῦν Ἥφαιστος ἐὼν βραδὺς εἷλεν Ἄρηα,
> ὠκύτατόν περ ἐόντα θεῶν οἳ Ὄλυμπον ἔχουσι,

χωλὸς ἐών, τέχνῃσι· τὸ καὶ μοιχάγρι᾽ ὀφέλλει."
333   ὡς οἱ μὲν τοιαῦτα πρὸς ἀλλήλους ἀγόρευον·
344   οὐ δὲ Ποσειδάωνα γέλως ἔχε, λίσσετο δ᾽ αἰεὶ
"Ηφαιστον κλυτοεργόν, ὅπως λύσειεν Ἄρηα·
καί μιν φωνήσας ἔπεα πτερόεντα προσηύδα·

334   Ἑρμῆν δὲ προσέειπεν ἄναξ, Διὸς υἱός, Ἀπόλλων·
      "'Ἑρμεία, Διὸς υἱέ, διάκτορε, δῶτορ ἐάων,
      ἦ ῥά κεν ἐν δεσμοῖς ἐθέλοις κρατεροῖσι πιεσθεὶς
      εὕδειν ἐν λέκτροισι παρὰ χρυσῇ Ἀφροδίτῃ;"
      τὸν δ᾽ ἠμείβετ᾽ ἔπειτα διάκτορος ἀργειφόντης·
      " αἲ γὰρ τοῦτο γένοιτο, ἄναξ ἑκατηβόλ᾽ Ἄπολλον
340   δεσμοὶ μὲν τρὶς τόσσοι ἀπείρονες ἀμφὶς ἔχοιεν,
      ὑμεῖς δ᾽ εἰσορόῳτε θεοὶ πᾶσαί τε θέαιναι,
      αὐτὰρ ἐγὼν εὕδοιμι παρὰ χρυσῇ Ἀφροδίτῃ."
343   ὡς ἔφατ᾽, ἐν δὲ γέλως ὦρτ᾽ ἀθανάτοισι θεοῖσιν.

vss. 333–43 damn. Hayman.

In the H scholia attached without lemma to line 333 is a note :
ἐν ἐνίοις ἀντιγράφοις οἱ δέκα στίχοι οὐ φέρονται διὰ τὸ ἀπρέπειαν
ἐμφαίνειν. νεωτερικὸν γὰρ τὸ φρόνημα. This means the existence
of texts without lines 333–42, and Wecklein (ZAV 19) approves
the result ; but Blass (270 f.) has shown that view to be unsatisfactory. In his wish to show that the whole section θ 266–369 is
interpolated he has failed, however, to consider the possibility of
other less radical remedies.

One such been discussed above, p. 209 ; but it seems to me
still more satisfactory to push the scholium down one line (not even
transposition of notes is necessary) and make lines 334–43 the
verses in question.

The suspicion of bowdlerizing (cf. Cobet, *Misc. Crit.* 231,
Wackernagel, *SU* 227 n.) lies near at hand, but an expurgator
would certainly have cut deeper. We have no right to assume that
interpolators were always clean-minded people. Why should not
some Athenian wit have sought to render the scandal still more
spicy? His verses are, however, by no means a cento, and that
points to a relatively early date. It is not surprising therefore that
Zoilus (fr. 38 Friedl.) should have known them ; but Plato could
hardly have failed (*Rep.* iii. 390 c) to allude directly to this part of
the episode had it stood in his text.

The shorter text seems open to no criticism except that the formula of line 333 is not used (cf. Hayman at θ 268) after a τις εἴπεσκε speech elsewhere. But as other plural formulas are used that fact cannot weigh heavily. On the other hand, line 343 after line 326 is very awkward; and I think the shorter must be regarded as the better text.

λ

Tyro fell in love with the river Enipeus:

τῷ δ' ἄρα εἰσάμενος γαιήοχος ἐννοσίγαιος
ἐν προχοῇς ποταμοῦ παρελέξατο δινήεντος·
πορφύρεον δ' ἄρα κῦμα περιστάθη, οὔρεϊ ἶσον,
244 κυρτωθέν, κρύψεν δὲ θεὸν θνητήν τε γυναῖκα.
246 αὐτὰρ ἐπεί ῥ' ἐτέλεσσε θεὸς φιλοτήσια ἔργα,
ἔν τ' ἄρα οἱ φῦ χειρὶ ἔπος τ' ἔφατ' ἔκ τ' ὀνόμαζε·

245 λῦσε δὲ παρθενίην ζώνην, κατὰ δ' ὕπνον ἔχευεν.
om. Bekker, van Leeuwen ; damn. Hayman, Nauck, Ludwich, Merry, Cauer.

The text is that of Zenodotus, on the testimony of Didymus (ƽ H): Ζηνόδοτος δὲ ἀγνοεῖ τὸν στίχον. According to Aristonicus (ibid.) the plus verse was read but athetized by Aristarchus.

The intrinsic superiority of the shorter text is here so evident, that Blass (124) and Wecklein (ZAV 53) can give the extra line short shrift. It begins with an unhomeric phrase (cf. Ameis-Hentze, Anhang, ii. 110), λύειν ζώνην, suggested by Hom. Hymn, v. 164, in which context it is appropriate. The close is obtained from σ 188, but is here, as the scholia argue, utterly purposeless. The line violates also the Homeric practice (cf. Wackernagel, SU 224-9) of leaving such details unmentioned.

Another section in the Catalogue of Heroines:

Φαίδρην τε Πρόκριν τε ἴδον καλήν τ' Ἀριάδνην,
322 κούρην Μίνωος ὀλοόφρονος, ἥν ποτε Θησεὺς
324 γήμας οὐδ' ἀπόνητο· πάρος δέ μιν Ἄρτεμις ἔκτα
Δίῃ ἐν ἀμφιρύτῃ Διονύσου μαρτυρίῃσι.

323 ἐκ Κρήτης ἐς γουνὸν Ἀθηνάων ἱεράων
324 ἦγε μέν, οὐ δ' ἀπόνητο· πάρος δέ μιν Ἄρτεμις ἔκτα

The text is that of the scholiast to Apollonius Rhodius, iii. 997, to which there is also a variant γῆμεν | Θησεὺς οὐδ' ἀπόνητο. There can be no question of an accidental omission, since the quotation is made to show that Theseus did not bring Ariadne to Athens. 'Interpolations' in the interest of Athens are usually supposed to date from the sixth century; but A 265, B 558 have already proved to be much later interpolations, and there is no reason why λ 323 should not be in line with them.

The shorter version offers a verbal difficulty, though a comparison of ω 93 might be made in its defence. I am inclined to look upon the trouble as secondary: the original text, γῆμε μέν, οὐδ' ἀπόνητο, was changed by haplography to γῆμεν οὐδ' ἀπόνητο, and the metrical defect 'remedied' in two ways.

The interpolated line contains the only instance of γουνός, except in the phrase γουνὸς ἀλωῆς, and its application to the Acropolis does not seem very likely. It must be noted also that line 325 with its Διονύσου is quite probably evidence for the activity of an interpolator in this section.

Agamemnon, in telling the story of his death :

> ἡ δὲ κυνῶπις
> νοσφίσατ', οὐδέ μοι ἔτλη ἰόντι περ εἰς Ἀίδαο
> χερσὶ κατ' ὀφθαλμοὺς ἑλέειν σύν τε στόμ' ἐρεῖσαι.
> 427 ὡς οὐκ αἰνότερον καὶ κύντερον ἄλλο γυναικός.
> 429 οἷον δὴ καὶ κείνη ἐμήσατο ἔργον ἀεικές,
> κουριδίῳ τεύξασα πόσει φόνον. κτλ.

---

428 ἤ τις δὴ τοιαῦτα μετὰ φρεσὶν ἔργα βάληται.
om. Bekker; damn. Hayman, Nauck, Ludwich, Merry, Cauer.

The H scholia say : ἐν πολλοῖς οὐ φέρεται, ὡς ἐκλύων τὸν θυμόν κτλ. The reasons given are to support an athetesis; and we must infer (cf. Ludwich, AHT i. 591) that the line was read but athetized by Aristarchus, and was not to be found in 'many' earlier texts.

Most will feel that the limitation made by the plus verse, while logical and fair, is entirely unsuited to the passionate mood of the speaker. The short version is then (cf. also Blass, 126 f. ; Wecklein, ZAV 19 f.) intrinsically superior.

The verses printed by Barnes after λ 439 call for no discussion; they were taken from the scholia on Euripides, *Orest.* 249, though there cited as Hesiod (= fr. 117, 5–7 Rz.).

Agamemnon speaking:

ἀλλ' οὐ σοί γ', 'Οδυσεῦ, φόνος ἔσσεται ἔκ γε γυναικός·
445   λίην γὰρ πινυτή τε καὶ εὖ φρεσὶ μήδεα οἶδε
κούρη 'Ικαρίοιο, περίφρων Πηνελόπεια.
ἦ μέν μιν νύμφην γε νέην κατελείπομεν ἡμεῖς
ἐρχόμενοι πόλεμον δέ· πάις δέ οἱ ἦν ἐπὶ μαζῷ
νήπιος, ὅς που νῦν γε μετ' ἀνδρῶν ἵζει ἀριθμῷ,
450   ὄλβιος· ἦ γὰρ τόν γε πατὴρ φίλος ὄψεται ἐλθών,
καὶ κεῖνος πατέρα προσπτύξεται, ἢ θέμις ἐστίν.
ἡ δ' ἐμὴ οὐδέ περ υἷος ἐνιπλησθῆναι ἄκοιτις
453   ὀφθαλμοῖσιν ἔασε· πάρος δέ με πέφνε καὶ αὐτόν.
457   ἀλλ' ἄγε μοι τόδε εἰπὲ καὶ ἀτρεκέως κατάλεξον,
εἴ που ἔτι ζώοντος ἀκούετε παιδὸς ἐμοῖο,
ἤ που ἐν 'Ορχομενῷ ἢ ἐν Πύλῳ ἠμαθόεντι,
460   ἤ που πὰρ Μενελάῳ ἐνὶ Σπάρτῃ εὐρείῃ·
οὐ γάρ πω τέθνηκεν ἐπὶ χθονὶ δῖος 'Ορέστης."

---

454   ἄλλο δέ τοι ἐρέω, σὺ δ' ἐνὶ φρεσὶ βάλλεο σῇσι·
        κρύβδην μηδ' ἀναφανδὰ φίλην ἐς πατρίδα γαῖαν
456   νῆα κατισχέμεναι, ἐπεὶ οὐκέτι πιστὰ γυναιξίν.

om. Bekker, van Leeuwen; damn. Hayman, Ludwich, Merry, Cauer.

At line 452 (or 451) is a scholium in H: οὐδὲ οὗτοι ἐφέροντο ἐν τοῖς πλείστοις ὡς μαχόμενοι τοῖς προκειμένοις. We may infer again that the lines meant were read but athetized by Aristarchus, and found in few (if any) other editions. The only lines of which this could be true are lines 454–6, and Dindorf suggested the necessary transposition of the scholium which is generally accepted. The short version (cf. Blass, 128; Wecklein, *ZAV* 20) is obviously superior.

Odysseus reaches the end of the νέκυια:

καί νύ κ' ἔτι προτέρους ἴδον ἀνέρας, οὓς ἔθελόν περ,
631   Θησέα Πειρίθοόν τε, θεῶν ἐρικυδέα τέκνα·
ἀλλὰ πρὶν ἐπὶ ἔθνε' ἀγείρετο μυρία νεκρῶν κτλ.

---

vm. 631 om. Bekker, Nauck; damn. Hayman, Ludwich, Merry.

According to Plutarch, *Theseus* 20: Πεισίστρατον . . . φησὶν
'Ηρέας ὁ Μεγαρεὺς . . . . ἐμβαλεῖν εἰς τὴν 'Ομήρου νεκυίαν τὸ
" Θησέα Πειρίθοόν τε, θεῶν ἀριδείκετα τέκνα" χαριζόμενον Ἀθηναίοις.
There is no direct evidence for the existence of texts without this
line, which can be traced (cf. F. Müller, 112) back to Polygnotus.
The question, therefore, of its interpolation falls outside the scope
of this book. If it be argued that Hereas' idea was suggested by
the fluctuation of MSS. known to him, we must conclude that he
antedated the interpolation. If his opinion was based—as is likely
—upon internal evidence, it is substantially correct.

μ

The description of Elpenor's funeral ends :
   αὐτὰρ ἐπεὶ νεκρός τε κάη καὶ τεύχεα νεκροῦ,
   τύμβον χεύαντες καὶ ἐπὶ στήλην ἐρύσαντες
15 πήξαμεν ἀκροτάτῳ τύμβῳ εὐῆρες ἐρετμόν.
According to the H scholia : Ζηνόδοτος γράφει·
            ἀκροτάτῳ τύμβῳ ⟨εὐῆρες ἐρετμόν,
   τῷ καὶ ζωὸς ἔρεσσεν ἐών,⟩ ἵνα σῆμα πέλοιτο.
the lines corresponding to λ 77–8, and the supplement being due to
Wecklein (*TSO* 10, *ZAV* 73).

The only question is as to just who has been corrected. If the
fault lies in the transmission of the scholium, the text is probably
that of Zenodotus of Mallos. If the scholium is reported correctly,
then Aristonicus is criticizing an obvious blemish of the Zenodotean
text, whether it was taken over by Zenodotus from his sources (so
Wecklein) or was a mechanical blunder of the antigraphon used by
Aristonicus.

The short version is at all events entirely satisfactory, and there
is no need to demand the insertion of the plus verse.

Cobet's interpretation of s A on B 489, which would lead, on a
correct understanding of περιγράφειν, to the belief that μ 77–8 (or
μ 78) were not in the text of Zenodotus, needs no discussion ; cf.
Ludwich, *AHT* i. 220.

The omission by the first hand of G of :
105 τρὶς μὲν γάρ τ' ἀνίησιν ἐπ' ἤματι, τρὶς δ' ἀναροιβδεῖ

must be classed as an accident. The line was known to Callistratus, Macrobius, Polybius, Crates, and Virgil ; and must therefore have been found in Aristarchus and the vulgate. In this book I have no occasion to deal with the internal evidence which has led Blass (135) and Wecklein (*ZAV* 20) to follow Callistratus and question the genuineness of the line.

o

Menelaos is speaking :

68   " Τηλέμαχ', οὔ τί σ' ἔγωγε πολὺν χρόνον ἐνθάδ' ἐρύξω·

*   καὶ δ' ἄλλῳ νεμεσῶ, ὅς κ' ἔξοχα μὲν φιλέῃσιν

71 ἔξοχα δ' ἐχθαίρῃσιν· ἀμείνω δ' αἴσιμα πάντα.

ἴσόν τοι κακόν ἐσθ', ὅς τ' οὐκ ἐθέλοντα νέεσθαι

73 ξεῖνον ἐποτρύνει καὶ ὃς ἐσσύμενον κατερύκει.

75 ἀλλὰ μέν' εἰς ὅ κε δῶρα φέρων ἐπιδίφρια θείω

καλά, σὺ δ' ὀφθαλμοῖσιν ἴδῃς, κτλ.

---

69 ἱέμενον νόστοιο· νεμεσσῶμαι δὲ καὶ ἄλλῳ
70 ἀνδρὶ ξεινοδόκῳ, ὅς κ' ἔξοχα μὲν φιλέῃσιν
74 χρὴ ξεῖνον παρεόντα φιλεῖν, ἐθέλοντα δὲ πέμπειν.
vm. 74 om. Bekker[1], van Leeuwen ; damn. Nauck, Ludwich, Monro, Merry.
vss. 72–4 om. Bekker[2].

The text in lines 68–71 is that of [Plutarch] *Vita Hom.* ii. 151 and is perfectly clear. That is more (cf. Blass, 160) than can be said for the longer version of the vulgate.

The scholia (HQVind. 133) say of line 74 : ἐν πολλοῖς οὐκ ἐφέρετο. καὶ ἔστιν Ἡσιόδειος τῆς φράσεως ὁ χαρακτήρ. εἰ δὲ δεχοίμεθα αὐτόν, πρὸ τῶν πρὸ ἑαυτοῦ δύο στίχων ὀφείλει γράφεσθαι. There can be no question of inserting the line (cf. Blass, 160 ; Wecklein, *ZAV* 20).

The return voyage of Telemachus :

τοῖσιν δ' ἴκμενον οὖρον ἵει γλαυκῶπις Ἀθήνη,

λάβρον ἐπαιγίζοντα δι' αἰθέρος, ὄφρα τάχιστα

294 νηῦς ἀνύσειε θέουσα θαλάσσης ἁλμυρὸν ὕδωρ.

296 δύσετό τ' ἠέλιος σκιόωντό τε πᾶσαι ἀγυιαί·

---

295 βὰν δὲ παρὰ Κρουνοὺς καὶ Χαλκίδα καλλιρέεθρον

297 ἡ δὲ Φεὰς ἐπέβαλλεν ἐπειγομένη Διὸς οὔρῳ,
299 ἔνθεν δ' αὖ νήσοισιν ἐπιπροέηκε θοῇσιν,
     ὁρμαίνων ἤ κεν θάνατον φύγοι ἦ κεν ἀλώῃ.

298 ἠδὲ παρ' Ἤλιδα δῖαν, ὅθι κρατέουσιν Ἐπειοί.
vm. 295 om. Bekker, Nauck, Ludwich, van Leeuwen ; damn. Hayman, Merry, Cauer.

The two plus verses correspond to *Hom. Hymn,* iii. 425–6, and after the discovery of PVitelli a text contaminated with one of the hymns is for Ptolemaic times nothing surprising. Such a text is quoted by Strabo (viii. 350) in a passage derived, according to Bidder (43), from Demetrius of Scepsis. Strabo (x. 447) quotes also line 295 separately with a variant Χαλκίδα πετρήεσσαν.

Now this longest text is clearly interpolated : unless 298 follows 295 immediately παρ' Ἤλιδα is without construction. In other words, a parallel passage written in the margin has been absorbed in a most mechanical fashion, so that the resulting text is in reality unreadable.

Our vulgate too has been corrupted, but in a different fashion ; for it has absorbed only one (298) of these plus verses. Line 295 is found in no MS., and was brought in from Strabo by Barnes. In the absence of scholia and papyri the time at which line 298 was absorbed cannot be determined ; if one should suppose that it happened after Aristarchus, there would be no evidence to disprove the supposition. Without line 295, line 298 is impossible, and Blass (165) and Wecklein (*ZAV* 80) have seen the necessity of ' rejecting ' both lines.

The conservatism of the tradition is shown by the way in which these blunders when once made have been allowed to stand without correction.

ρ

Reference to Ludwich (*HV* 129) may suffice for the various attempts to extract from Aristotle, *Polit.* viii. 3 : 1338ᵃ 21 ff., some information about the text of ρ 382–5 known to him. As Wecklein (*ZAV* 14) sees, they have led to naught.

I may suggest that Aristotle is quoting not the *Odyssey* but a παίγνιον that has drawn on the *Odyssey*. It began :

ἀλλ' οἷον μὲν ἔστι καλεῖν ἐπὶ δαῖτα θαλείην

and after discussing the advantages and disadvantages of various guests, concluded that the wisest hosts are those :

οἵ καλέουσιν ἀοιδόν, ὅ κεν τέρπῃσιν ἅπαντας.

The Suitors in rebuking Antinoos :

καί τε θεοὶ ξείνοισιν ἐοικότες ἀλλοδαποῖσι,
486 παντοῖοι τελέθοντες, ἐπιστρωφῶσι πόληας,
ἀνθρώπων ὕβριν τε καὶ εὐνομίην ἐφορῶντες.

That this is the text of Aristarchus and the vulgate cannot be doubted : the MSS. are unanimous, and Ludwich cites the testimonia of five authors.

However, Chariton of Aphrodisias (ii. 3. 7) quotes the passage, omitting line 486 and reading ἐφορῶσι. His text is satisfactory, but it seems more probable that he has quoted inexactly than that he was using a pre-Aristarchean text—especially as the omitted line can be traced as far back as Plato, *Rep.* ii. 381 d.

σ

The Suitors to Odysseus after his victory over Iros :

" Ζεύς τοι δοίη, ξεῖνε, καὶ ἀθάνατοι θεοὶ ἄλλοι
ὅττι μάλιστ᾽ ἐθέλεις καί τοι φίλον ἔπλετο θυμῷ,
114 ὃς τοῦτον τὸν ἄναλτον ἀλητεύειν ἀπέπαυσας."
117 ὣς ἄρ᾽ ἔφαν, χαῖρεν δὲ κλεηδόνι δῖος Ὀδυσσεύς.

---

115 ἐν δήμῳ· τάχα γάρ μιν ἀνάξομεν ἤπειρον δὲ
116 εἰς Ἔχετον βασιλῆα, βροτῶν δηλήμονα πάντων."
om. Bekker², Nauck ; damn. Ludwich.

The plus verses correspond to σ 84–5, and of them the H scholiast (as emended by Kirchhoff and Roemer, *AAH* 234 f.) says : οὗτοι οἱ β΄ ἐκ τῶν ἄνωθεν μετηνέχθησαν· ἐκεῖ μὲν γὰρ προτρέπων φοβεῖ, ἐνταῦθα δὲ ἀπάνθρωπον τελέως τῷ ἡμιθνῆτι ἀπειλεῖν· διὸ περιγράφονται. Ludwich (*AHT* i. 623) ascribes this note to Aristonicus, and I believe that the use of περιγράφονται confirms his ascription. As Aristonicus uses this verb only of Zenodotus we must infer that the lines were not read by Zenodotus, but were read and athetized by Aristarchus.

Lentz 21 ' defends ' the lines as not too brutal for the heroic age ; while Roemer (*l. c.*) and Finsler (*Homer*², ii. 385) recognize that they

are interpolated. Blass (180) claims that they are needed because ἀλητεύειν ἀπέπαυσας by itself is not true: 'denn tot ist Iros nicht, und wenn er sich erholt hat, was soll er dann tun als wieder betteln? Nicht in diesem Haus, vielleicht gar in Ithaka nicht; aber davon wird, wenn man athetiert, nichts mehr gesagt.' All of this is taking the problem of Iros' future too seriously; for the present his begging is stopped, and that is sufficient grounds for congratulating the other beggar. Nobody is really concerned about a further settlement of the case. There is no occasion therefore to insert the lines.

τ.

Penelope's speech to Odysseus:

"ξεῖν', ἤτοι μὲν ἐμὴν ἀρετὴν εἶδός τε δέμας τε
125 ὤλεσαν ἀθάνατοι, ὅτε Ἴλιον εἰσανέβαινον
Ἀργεῖοι, μετὰ τοῖσι δ' ἐμὸς πόσις ἦεν Ὀδυσσεύς.
εἰ κεῖνός γ' ἐλθὼν τὸν ἐμὸν βίον ἀμφιπολεύοι,
μεῖζόν κε κλέος εἴη ἐμὸν καὶ κάλλιον οὕτω.
129 νῦν δ' ἄχομαι· τόσα γάρ μοι ἐπέσσευεν κακὰ δαίμων.
162 ἀλλὰ καὶ ὥς μοι εἰπὲ τεὸν γένος, ὁππόθεν ἐσσί·
οὐ γὰρ ἀπὸ δρυός ἐσσι παλαιφάτου οὐδ' ἀπὸ πέτρης."

_____

130 ὅσσοι γὰρ νήσοισιν ἐπικρατέουσιν ἄριστοι,
Δουλιχίῳ τε Σάμῃ τε καὶ ὑλήεντι Ζακύνθῳ,
οἵ τ' αὐτὴν Ἰθάκην εὐδείελον ἀμφινέμονται,
οἵ μ' ἀεκαζομένην μνῶνται, τρύχουσι δὲ οἶκον.
τῷ οὔτε ξείνων ἐμπάζομαι οὔθ' ἱκετάων
135 οὔτε τι κηρύκων, οἳ δημιοεργοὶ ἔασιν·
ἀλλ' Ὀδυσῆ ποθέουσα φίλον κατατήκομαι ἦτορ.
οἱ δὲ γάμον σπεύδουσιν· ἐγὼ δὲ δόλους τολυπεύω.
φᾶρος μέν μοι πρῶτον ἐνέπνευσε φρεσὶ δαίμων
στησαμένη μέγαν ἱστὸν ἐνὶ μεγάροισιν ὑφαίνειν,
140 λεπτὸν καὶ περίμετρον· ἄφαρ δ' αὐτοῖς μετέειπον·
'κοῦροι, ἐμοὶ μνηστῆρες, ἐπεὶ θάνε δῖος Ὀδυσσεύς,
μίμνετ' ἐπειγόμενοι τὸν ἐμὸν γάμον, εἰς ὅ κε φᾶρος
ἐκτελέσω — μή μοι μεταμώνια νήματ' ὄληται —
Λαέρτῃ ἥρωι ταφήιον, εἰς ὅτε κέν μιν
145 μοῖρ' ὀλοὴ καθέλῃσι τανηλεγέος θανάτοιο·
μή τίς μοι κατὰ δῆμον Ἀχαιιάδων νεμεσήσῃ,
αἴ κεν ἄτερ σπείρου κεῖται πολλὰ κτεατίσσας.'
ὣς ἐφάμην, τοῖσιν δ' ἐπεπείθετο θυμὸς ἀγήνωρ.

ἔνθα καὶ ἠματίη μὲν ὑφαίνεσκον μέγαν ἱστόν,
150 νύκτας δ᾽ ἀλλύεσκον, ἐπὴν δαΐδας παραθείμην.
ὡς τρίετες μὲν ἔληθον ἐγὼ καὶ ἔπειθον Ἀχαιούς·
152 ἀλλ᾽ ὅτε τέτρατον ἦλθεν ἔτος καὶ ἐπήλυθον ὧραι,
154 καὶ τότε δή με διὰ δμῳάς, κύνας οὐκ ἀλεγούσας,
155 εἷλον ἐπελθόντες καὶ ὁμόκλησαν ἐπέεσσιν.
ὡς τὸ μὲν ἐξετέλεσσα, καὶ οὐκ ἐθέλουσ᾽, ὑπ᾽ ἀνάγκης·
νῦν δ᾽ οὔτ᾽ ἐκφυγέειν δύναμαι γάμον οὔτε τιν᾽ ἄλλην
μῆτιν ἔθ᾽ εὑρίσκω. μάλα δ᾽ ὀτρύνουσι τοκῆες
γήμασθ᾽, ἀσχαλάᾳ δὲ πάις βίοτον κατεδόντων,
160 γινώσκων· ἤδη γὰρ ἀνὴρ οἷός τε μάλιστα
οἴκου κήδεσθαι, τῷ τε Ζεὺς κῦδος ὀπάζει.
vss. 130-3 om. Bekker, Nauck ; damn. Hayman, Ludwich, Monro, Merry.

At line 130 is a scholium (H): ἠθέτηνται λ΄· ἐν δὲ τοῖς πλείστοις οὐδὲ ἐφέροντο. Porson saw the ✔difficulty, and two solutions, of which he unfortunately chose the worse : correcting λ΄ to δ΄ and understanding that lines 130–3 were the ones commented upon. The other alternative was to extend the athetesis, so that it should end with line 161, thus including thirty-two (λβ΄) lines of our printed text. La Roche is said to have advocated (in an inaccessible article in *Oester. Zeitschr. f. Gymn.* 1863, 199) the rejection of 136–61, thus approximating the correct solution, which was given by Roemer, *Hom. Stud.* 415 f. Blass (190), noting the external evidence against line 153, saw that the athetesis included only 31 (λα΄) lines in Aristarchus' text. Wecklein (*ZAV* 20) has followed him, and I would merely suggest that there may be another line (131 ?, 135 ?) of this sort.

The short version is entirely satisfactory, while the plus verses are largely a cento (cf. α 245–8, β 94–110, α 249–50), comprising many oddities and infelicities, for which reference to Blass (188–90) and Bethe (*Homer,* ii. 98–100) may be made. Bethe includes lines 134–6 in the original text, and assigns the interpolation to the 'letzte Bearbeiter der Odyssee'; I think we may say that the external evidence demands on each of these points a different decision.

Odysseus in his feigned adventures :

Κρήτη τις γαῖ᾽ ἔστι, μέσῳ ἐνὶ οἴνοπι πόντῳ,
καλὴ καὶ πίειρα, περίρρυτος· ἐν δ᾽ ἄνθρωποι

174 πολλοί, ἀπειρέσιοι, καὶ ἐννήκοντα πόληες.
178 τῇσι δ' ἐνὶ Κνωσός, μεγάλη πόλις, ἔνθα τε Μίνως
ἐννέωρος βασίλευε Διὸς μεγάλου ὀαριστής—κτλ.

175 ἄλλη δ' ἄλλων γλῶσσα μεμιγμένη· ἐν μὲν 'Αχαιοί,
176 ἐν δ' 'Ετεόκρητες μεγαλήτορες, ἐν δὲ Κύδωνες
177 Δωριέες τε τριχάικες δῖοί τε Πελασγοί.

The text is that attested by [Plato] *Minos* 319 b, and is entirely satisfactory. Of course it is possible that the quoter has discarded lines not needed for his purposes; but it would be rather curious that in doing so he should hit upon lines that modern scholars have found objectionable for other reasons. Hoffman (i. 75) objected to the lines because containing the only mention of the Dorians, and because their interpolator could be held responsible for καὶ ἐννήκοντα in line 174 instead of ἐν δ' ἐννήκοντα. Following Beloch, Sir Arthur Evans (i. 12) has also argued that the lines are interpolated. There would certainly be no reason to insert the lines were the existence of texts without them established securely. The latter, it must be admitted, is not the case; and to that extent the question must remain *sub iudice*.

The question whether Aristotle (cf. *Poet*. viii. 5: 1451ᵃ 24 ff.) had τ 394–466 in his text of the *Odyssey* is still debatable; Blass (238) maintaining the affirmative, and Finsler (*Homer*², ii. 400) the negative. Blass is right in declaring that the philosopher knew the substance of the story (πληγῆναι μὲν ἐν τῷ Παρνασσῷ), but that does not yet prove that he knew it from the *Odyssey*. Finsler is right in suggesting that Aristotle may have read the story in another poem; but he goes too far when he claims that this must be so because it is mentioned in the same breath with Odysseus' feigning of madness which does come from a different source. If the philosopher wished to arrange in chronological order various pre-war experiences of Odysseus, he had the right to take his material wherever he found it.

This seems to bring us to a deadlock; but there are, I think, further considerations that make Blass' view probable. (1) We can designate the source of the madness episode—the *Cypria*; while for the *Hunt on Mt. Parnassus* we must invent a poem *ad hoc*, it being clearly not a part of the *Cycle*. (2) This poem was known to Sophocles (fr. 408) and to Plato (*Rep*. i. 334 a)—the latter citing it

as 'Homer'. Finsler argues that in Plato's time any epic poem could be called Homer. But such is not Plato's own usage; for us at least he is a leader in the 'critical process'—to borrow a phrase from Fitch's excellent discussion, *CP* 19 (1924). 57-65—that resulted in making Homer the author of two poems only. Bethe's index shows but one citation of the *Cycle*, namely Euthyphro, 12 a–c, where the Cypria is quoted anonymously; it is only the spurious Alcibiades (ii. 149 d) that quotes verses from a Cyclic epos as found παρ' Ὁμήρῳ. (3) It might still be argued that Plato (and presumably Sophocles) had interpolated texts of the *Odyssey*, while Aristotle used an uninterpolated text. But my index will show that, on the contrary, Plato's text is as a rule conservative, while Aristotle is more inclined to texts of a 'wild' type. (4) The interpolation would be unusually long and independent.

The discovery of the scar:

τὴν γρηῢς χείρεσσι καταπρηνέσσι λαβοῦσα
γνῶ ῥ' ἐπιμασσαμένη, πόδα δὲ προέηκε φέρεσθαι·
469 ἐν δὲ λέβητι πέσε κνήμη, κανάχησε δὲ χαλκός,
ἂψ δ' ἑτέρωσ' ἐκλίθη· τὸ δ' ἐπὶ χθονὸς ἐξέχυθ' ὕδωρ.

[Plutarch] *vita Hom.* ii. 217 omits verse 469 from his quotation. This cannot be anything but an accident, as his discussion shows.

υ

The text of 3 a. PHibeh 23 seems to have run somewhat as follows:

αὐτὰρ ἐγὼ θεός εἰ]μι, διαμπερὲς ἤ σε φυλάσσω
48 13 letters]πων. ἐρέω δέ σοι ἐξαναφανδόν·
εἴ περ πεντήκον]τα λόχοι μερόπων ἀνθρώπων
νῶι περισταῖεν, κ]τεῖναι μεμαῶτες Ἄρηι,
51 καί κεν τῶν ἐλάσ]αιο βόας, κα[ὶ τέ]κν[α καὶ αὐτούς
* δουλώσας κτείν]ειας ἀπ[ούρας κτήματα πάντα.
52 ἀλλ' ἐλέτω σε καὶ ὕ]πνος ἐ[πὴ]ν ἐπὶ κ[νέφας ἔλθῃ"

48 ἐν πάντεσσι πόνοις codd.
51 καί κεν τῶν ἐλάσαιο βόας καὶ ἴφια μῆλα.
ἀλλ' ἐλέτω σε καὶ ὕπνος· ἀνίη καὶ τὸ φυλάσσειν

54　ὣς φάτο, καί ῥά οἱ ὕ]πνον ἐπὶ βλεφάρο[ισιν ἔχευεν
55　αὐτὴ δ' ἄψ ἐς Ὄλυμ]πον ἀφίκετο δῖα [θεάων
*　δώματ' ἐς αἰγιόχοιο πατ]ρὸς με[τὰ δαίμονας ἄλλους.

53　πάννυχον ἐγρήσσοντα, κακῶν δ' ὑποδύσεαι ἤδη.

Of the restorations I have offered 55 a ꭒ A 222 is obvious ; the only question being whether πατρός is a corruption of Διός, or whether the unhomeric phraseology is an indication of the late date of the interpolation. The others are doubtful and presented with hesitation. Only a re-examination of the papyrus can determine whether the last two doubtful letters visible in line 51 can be read as κν or not. In line 52 ἐπήν will be a modernism for ἐπεί κεν, as in PGerhard at X 125, on which compare the editor's note. The meaning of the phrase seems, however, curiously twisted—after the house gets dark (and quiet), at the end of the revelry. As a variant to ἀνίη καὶ τὸ φυλάσσειν it is distinctly inferior. But that phrase by itself is sufficient, and we may on the testimony of the papyrus regard line 53 as an intruder.

The plus verse following line 58 may have begun ἀμφίπολοι δ' ὡς πρό]σθεν ἀκὴν ἔχον, but if the following traces (οι.) cannot be reconciled with οὐδέ τι εἶπον I do not see how the line can be completed. At all events the unhomeric phrase ἀκὴν ἔχον may assure us—if assurance be needed—that we have lost nothing more interesting than an interpolation.

The prophecy of Theoklymenos :

"ἆ δειλοί, τί κακὸν τόδε πάσχετε ; νυκτὶ μὲν ὑμέων
εἰλύαται κεφαλαί τε πρόσωπά τε νέρθε τε γοῦνα.
353　οἰμωγὴ δὲ δέδηε, δεδάκρυνται δὲ παρειαί,
354　αἵματι δ' ἐρράδαται τοῖχοι καλαί τε μεσόδμαι·
εἰδώλων δὲ πλέον πρόθυρον, πλείη δὲ καὶ αὐλή,
ἱεμένων Ἔρεβος δὲ ὑπὸ ζόφον· ἠέλιος δὲ
οὐρανοῦ ἐξαπόλωλε, κακὴ δ' ἐπιδέδρομεν ἀχλύς."

Porphyry (Quaest. Il. 271. 22 ff. Schr.) quotes υ 351-2, 355-6, but as the quotations are separated by καὶ ἐπάγει the break is probably intentional. [Plutarch], vita Hom. ii. 108, likewise omits

lines 353–4 in his quotation. Finally, Plato (*Ion*, 539 a) quotes the speech with the omission of line 354, which may, however, be due merely to haplography.

I cannot feel that texts without 353–4 are sufficiently well attested to warrant our regarding the lines as interpolated.

296   ἀσπάσιοι λέκτροιο παλαιοῦ θεσμὸν ἵκοντο.

I cannot find evidence sufficient to make reasonable the belief that any text of the *Odyssey* stopped at this point. Had the edition of Aristarchus ended here our MSS. would do the same. The famous scholium (MV Vind. 133) Ἀριστοφάνης δὲ καὶ Ἀρίσταρχος πέρας τῆς Ὀδυσσείας τοῦτο ποιοῦνται, or in another form (HMQ) τοῦτο τέλος τῆς Ὀδυσσείας φησὶν Ἀρίσταρχος καὶ Ἀριστοφάνης, proves no more than that these critics believed the genuine poem to end here. Nor need more be inferred from the ending of the Argonautika:

ἀσπασίως ἀκτὰς Παγασηίδας εἰσαπέβητε

than that Apollonius already held that opinion. Of course they may all have been guided by MS. evidence; but if so no indication of the fact has reached us.

On the surface it appears that the recapitulation (ψ 310–41) of Odysseus' adventures filled sixty verses in the text used by Aristotle; cf. *Rhet.* iii. 16 : 1417ᵃ 13 παράδειγμα ὁ Ἀλκίνου ἀπόλογος, ὅτι πρὸς τὴν Πηνελόπην ἐν ἑξήκοντα ἔπεσιν πεποίηται. It is easy to emend (τριάκοντα) or to assume a slip of memory. In the light of our past experiences we must believe that, if we have lost anything, we have lost an interpolation.

PART V
CONCLUSION

In its application the hypothesis seems to me to have enabled us to take the facts of this type in the Homeric tradition as far as known to us and weave them into a more complete and consistent picture than could otherwise be obtained. That, however, is a question which may best be left to the judgement of others without further argument. Instead I may indicate briefly the line that may be taken in future investigations.

Our texts are reconstructions of an Alexandrian text. Behind them lies the problem of reconstructing some earlier form of the poems—that which they had, I should say, at the beginning of our written tradition. So far that problem has baffled and still baffles us. I would suggest that we approach it in the spirit of one who prefers half a loaf to no bread ; that we attempt to reconstruct this text, if not in its words, at least in its lines. The task will consist of the removal of accretions. The first and clearest cases will be those I have discussed, the lines that we know were not to be found in all versions of the text. The burden of proof must lie upon him who wishes to include such lines in the reconstruction.

However, our sources of information are so fragmentary that we cannot believe that we know all the lines of this class, and it becomes necessary to continue the search for others. Sometimes (cf. for instance Π 140, Φ 287) the detection of one interpolation will lead directly to the detection of another. Others must lurk among the lines athetized by the Alexandrians. In their circle interest in internal evidence overgrew and overshadowed the arguments from external evidence, which, however, they possessed more fully than we can hope to have it. A re-examination of their ἀθετήσεις may enable us to designate some cases in which we can infer with reasonable probability the existence of such evidence. Finally, some interpolations—especially in parts of the poems (for instance, ικνξπφχ) for which the scholia are conspicuously deficient—may be recognized from their kinship with other interpolations. The difficulty there

will be that these interpolators have in reality no style, no individuality—nothing but a sort of family resemblance. The oldest
of them are not far separated from the men responsible for the
Pisistratean texts of the two poems, and in the absence of external
evidence the distinguishing of their work will not be easy.

Much remains to be done, more perhaps than ever can be done,
and meanwhile the Pisistratean text must remain like a vase that is
only partly cleansed. But the work that may be bestowed upon its
recovery will not be labour lost; for it is, as Bethe has shown, the
one real object for our study. It must therefore be our effort to
recover it as perfectly as the resources at our command permit.

ADDENDA

Pp. 8–30. I can now add to the papyri previously cited (p. 16 n.) the following:

A 152–66: 2 *p*. PBodl. g 16 (unpubl.) | A 215–52, 276–312, 337–41, 345–6, 348, 360–5: 2 *p*. PSI vii. 745 | A 298–333: 2 *p*. PBodl. e 58 (unpubl.) | A 468–73: wooden tablet, *JHS* 29 (1909). 39 | A 608–11: 2 *p*. PMus. Br. 1862 A (unpubl.) | B 251–4, 267–84, 296–309, 331–45, 364–95, 398–430, 435–62, 466–94, 498–526, 529–57, 562–92, 597–625, 630–60, 663–91, 696–726, 730–60, 803–30, 838–75: 1 *p*. PMus. Br. 1873 (unpubl.) | B 459–535: 1/2 *p*. PBodl. d 41 (unpubl.) | B 494–519, 528–76, 594–614, 631–41, 667–78: 6 *p*. PCairo Byz. ii. 67172–4. | B 625–85: 3/4 *p*. PSI vii. 746. | B 638–743: 2/3 *p*. PRoss.-Georg. i. 2. | B 781–94: 2 *p*. PRoss.-Georg. i. 3. | Γ 273–85: wooden tablet, *JHS* 29 (1909). 39. | Δ 33–65: 2 *p*. PSI vii. 747. | E 724–35, 744–55: 4 *p*. PSI vii. 748 | E 855–79: 2 *p*. PBodl. f 42. (unpubl.) | Z 99–102, 119–22: 4 *p*. PSI vii. 749. | H 118–22, 143–7, 167–74: *p*. PBodl. b 10. (unpubl.) | H 329–48, 353–74: 4/5 *p*. PSI vii. 750 | Θ 198–213: 2/3 *p*. PBodl. f. 24. (unpubl.) | Θ 332–6, 362–9: 2/1 *a*. PFay. 4 | I 75–92: 1 *p*. PBerol. Nr. 40 | I 103–23, 155–78: 3/4 *p*. PMus. Br. 2037ᶜ (unpubl.) | I 300–17: 2 *p*. PMus. Br. 1862ᶠ (unpubl.) | N 590–606, 610–13, 621–4, 627–9, 633–9: 2 *p*. PBodl. d. 45 (unpubl.) | O 575–94, 623–40: 1 *p*. PSI vii. 751 | P 50–2, 86–99, 106–12, 136–71, 182–221, 236–67, 277–307, 323–51, 363–94, 406–35, 439–58, 461–78, 483–520, 523–761: 3 *p*. PRoss.-Georg. i. 4 | P 335–46, 368–81: 4/5 *p*. PSI vii. 752 | Σ 439–617: 2/3 *p*. PMichigan (TAPA 53 [1922] 128–617) | Φ 511–27: 3 *p*. PSI vii. 753 |

β 34–370 (scraps too small for use): 1 *p*. PMus. Br. 127 D (unpubl.) | β 127–40 152–66: 2/3 *p*. PGenav.—(Berard, *Odyssée*, I. i. 65) | δ 166–76: 2/3 *p*. PSI vii. 754 | δ 840–7: 2 *p*. PRoss.-Georg. i. 5 | ε 1–7: ostrakon BGU vi. 1470 | θ 537–54: 3 *p*. PSI vii. 755 | κ 291–9: 3 *p*. PRoss.-Georg. i. 6 | μ 250–2, 281–304: 1 *a*. PNash, PSBA 24 (1902). 290–2 | σ 103–12, 128–39: 4 *p*. PRoss.-Georg. i. 7 |

These papyri have again (cf. *AJP* 259) tested and confirmed my predictions. I shall not set forth in detail the lines accidentally omitted by them ; their significant omissions are as follows. B 558 is not in the text of the Cairo papyrus, late (6 *p*.) as it is ; the line is added in the top margin, 'perhaps by a different hand'. In 1 *p*. PMus. Br. 1873 only slight traces can be read of the line following B 557 ; they are probably T]ϵΙ[PYNΘA of line 559, though the possibility of AΘ]ϵΙ[NAIωN of line 558 cannot be denied. B 642ᵃ is not found either in 2/3 *p*. PRoss.-Georg. i. 2, nor in 3/4 *p*. PSI vii. 746. Of H 368–9 only the first half has made its way into

4/5 *p*. PSI vii. 750, so the interpolation is seen in its incipience.   O 578 is not in 1 *p*. PSI vii. 751.   From 3 *p*. PRoss.-Georg. i. 4 are absent P 145ª, 219, 326, 455, 585, 683ª ; it must be noted also that no one of these lines has been added by the corrector who has so often supplied verses accidentally omitted.   Σ 441 604/5 are not to be found in the Michigan papyrus.   Finally σ 111ª (the editors miscall it 112) and σ 131 are not contained in 4 *p*. PRoss.-Georg. i. 7.   All of these lines have been included [1] in my *Conspectus of Vulgate Interpolations*, and there is no other line in that list for which the testimony of these papyri is available.

[1] For Σ 604/5 cf. pp. 3, 12, and 16.

INDICES TO PARTS III AND IV

References to Part IV. i are marked with an asterisk.

I

II